## Praise for *Gaudí*

"This book is written with not only immense sympathy and understanding for Gaudí himself and his work but also for the cultural and political background. In its scope and ambition, its clarity and its feeling for the period and personality, it is the most definitive book on Gaudí which has yet been produced."
—Colm Toibin, author of *Homage to Barcelona*

"Gaudí was the best loved, most hated, and least understood architect in the history of the world. Lack of sources defeats most would-be biographers, but Gijs van Hensbergen sympathizes with his subject so well that he succeeds in overleaping the gaps. His book is an excellent preparation for confronting the challenge of Gaudí—the originality of the artist, the self-sorrow of the sinner, the greatness of the saint—while admitting how little is really intelligible and how much just has to be felt."
—Felipe Fernández-Armesto, author of *Civilizations*

"It is rare for the biography of an architect to be so human and so humorous. Gijs van Hensbergen has managed to re-create in his book that same combination of playfulness and seriousness that characterizes Gaudí and Barcelona. His infectious enthusiasm is conveyed through vibrant and witty prose. Altogether a delight." —Paul Preston, author of *Franco*

"Vivid and engaging." —*Booklist*

"At last, the story of the eccentric Catalan genius who engendered the Sagrada Família. I found it enthralling." —Ian Gibson, author of *Federico García Lorca: A Life* and *The Shameful Life of Salvador Dalí*

"Elegantly written, handsomely illustrated, *Gaudí* . . . [is] a memorable account of an original life." —*Camden Courier-Post*

"A well-researched study of the mad and wonderful Spanish architect Antoni Gaudí." —*Seattle Times*

"This first significant biography of [the] Catalan architect in English makes an informed and highly readable argument for Gaudí's greatness, placing him in the social and political context of his times and clarifying his indelible impact on modern architecture." —*Austin American-Statesman*

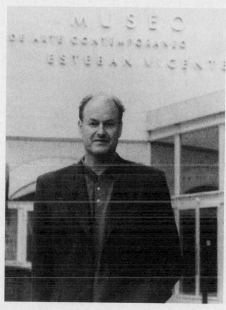

Fernando Penalosa

## *About the Author*

Gijs van Hensbergen lectures in architecture and is the author of *Art Deco* and the highly acclaimed travel book *A Taste of Castile*. He lives in Dorset, England.

# GAUDÍ

Also by Gijs van Hensbergen

*Art Deco*
*A Taste of Castile*

# GAUDÍ

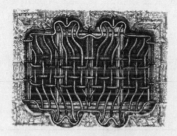

A Biography

*Gijs van Hensbergen*

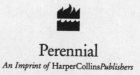

Perennial
*An Imprint of* HarperCollins*Publishers*

Title page and chapter ornaments (based on Gaudí's window at Bellesguard, Drac de
Pedralbes [Dragon's Gate] at Finca Güell, and balcony at Casa Milà)
by Jane Conway

First published in Great Britain in 2001 by HarperCollins Publishers.

A hardcover edition of this book was published in 2001 by HarperCollins Publishers.

HarperCollins books may be purchased for educational, business, or sales promotional use.
For information please write: Special Markets
Department, HarperCollins Publishers Inc., 10 East 53rd Street,
New York, NY 10022.

First Perennial edition published 2003.

*Maps by Leslie Robinson*

The Library of Congress has catalogued the hardcover edition as follows:
Van Hensbergen, Gijs.
Gaudí / Gijs Van Hensbergen.
p.  cm.
Includes bibliographical references and index.
ISBN 0-06-621065-8
1. Gaudí, Antoni, 1852–1926. 2. Architects—Spain—Catalonia—Biography.
I. Title.
NA1313.G3  V36  2001  2001024820
720'.92—dc21
[B]

ISBN 0-06-093563-4 (pbk.)

03 04 05 06 07 ❖/RRD 10 9 8 7 6 5 4 3 2 1

For my children
Hendrikus, Rosa and Hester

The reasonable man adapts himself to the world; the unreasonable one persists in trying to adapt the world to himself. Therefore all progress depends on the unreasonable man.

GEORGE BERNARD SHAW, *Man and Superman*

# CONTENTS

# ILLUSTRATIONS

COLOUR PLATE SECTION

Plan of Poblet (Real Cátedra Gaudí)
El Capricho (Institut Amatller d'Art Hispànic)
Corner detail of the gatekeeper's house at the Finca Güell (Gijs
  van Hensbergen)
Shards of tile at the Finca Güell pavilions (Gijs van Hensbergen)
Exterior of the Casa Vicens 1883–85 (Gijs van Hensbergen)
Interior of the Casa Calvet (Francesc Català-Roca)
The *trencadís* technique on a chimney from the Palau Güell (Gijs
  van Hensbergen)
The Apostles' Towers at the Sagrada Família (Francesc
  Català-Roca)
Bellesguard (Francesc Català-Roca)
Windows over entrance to Bellesguard (Gijs van Hensbergen)
Decorated benches at Bellesguard (Gijs van Hensbergen)
The marketplace, Park Güell (Gijs van Hensbergen)
An inscription to the Virgin on the serpentine bench of the Park
  Güell (Gijs van Hensbergen)
Detail of the *trencadís* tile decoration of the bench (Gijs van
  Hensbergen)
Casa Batlló (Gijs van Hensbergen)
A network of arches in the crypt in the Colònia Güell (Francesc
  Català-Roca)
Rooftop figure on the Casa Milà (Gijs van Hensbergen;
  reproduced by kind permission of the Fundación Caixa
  Catalunya. The Casa Milà, *la Pedrera*, is the head office of the
  Centro Cultural Caixa Catalunya)
Postcard of the Casa Milà (author's collection)
Roofscape of the Casa Milà (Klaus Lahnstein/Tony Stone Images)

Shells grouped to approximate a Gaudí building (Robert
  Descharnes/© Descharnes & Descharnes)
Study of Alpine peaks by John Ruskin (Birmingham Museums &
  Art Gallery; photo: Courtauld Institute of Art)

The perimeter walls of the Park Güell (Arxiu Històric de la Ciutat de Barcelona)

Lluis Domènech i Muntaner (Arxiu Històric de la Ciutat de Barcelona)

Claudio Lopez, the second Marquès of Comillas (Real Cátedra Gaudí)

Jacint Verdaguer (Arxiu Històric de la Ciutat de Barcelona)

Don Eusebi Güell (Arxiu Històric de la Ciutat de Barcelona)

The Güell Tertulía (Institut Amatller d'Art Hispànic)

Bishop Grau (Real Cátedra Gaudí)

Bishop Torras i Bages (Institut Amatller d'Art Hispànic)

Francesc Berenguer (Real Cátedra Gaudí)

Josep M Jujol (Arxiu Històric de la Ciutat de Barcelona)

Joan Maragall (Arxiu Històric de la Ciutat de Barcelona)

Joan Rubió I Bellver (Real Cátedra Gaudí)

Colónia Güell drawing (Real Cátedra Gaudí)

Colónia Güell workers prepare to offer skin grafts (Institut Amatller d'Art Hispànic)

A funicular model for the Colónia Güell crypt (Real Cátedra Gaudí)

The model for the crypt ready for further work (Real Cátedra Gaudí)

The covered porch area of the crypt at the Colónia Güell (Francesc Català-Roca)

Entrance to the Casa Batlló (Gijs van Hensbergen)

Casa Batlló in strong contrast to Casa Amattler (Gijs van Hensbergen)

The Garraf wine bodegas (author's collection)


The Sagrada Família (Institut Amatller d'Art Hispànic)

The Sagrada Família: Nativity façade (Francesc Català-Roca)

Lorenzo Matamala

Joan Matamala (Real Cátedra Gaudí)

Dancing skeletons

A crucified model poses in Gaudí's elaborate system of mirrors

Gaudí's studio in the Sagrada Família

*Illustrations*

The six-toed centurion slaughters the innocents: Nativity façade, Sagrada Família (Gijs van Hensbergen)

The Holy Family on the nativity façade, Sagrada Família (Gijs van Hensbergen)

The ceiling of the Casa Milà (Gijs van Hensbergen: reproduced by kind permission of the Fundación Caixa Catalunya)

Casa Milà exterior (Gijs van Hensbergen)

Window at the Casa Milà (Gijs Van Hensbergen: reproduced by kind permission of the Fundación Caixa Catalunya)

Window grille to Casa Milà basement (Gijs van Hensbergen)

Political postcard (Author's collection)

Postcard celebrating the victory of the Catalan Solidaritat party in the local elections (Author's collection)

Disinterred nuns (Institut Amatller d'Art Hispànic)

View across Barcelona (Arxiu Històric de la Ciutat de Barcelona)

Antoni Gaudí for the 1910 Paris exhibition (Arxiu Històric de la Ciutat de Barcelona)

Gaudí explaining the Sagrada Familia to Cardinal Ragonesi (Arxiu Històric de la Ciutat de Barcelona)

Gaudí in Corpus Christi procession (Real Cátedra Gaudí)

Gaudí's death mask (Gijs van Hensbergen)

Gaudí's funeral procession (Real Cátedra Gaudí)

# ACKNOWLEDGEMENTS

Any book written on Gaudí has to begin with a dedication to earlier Gaudí scholars. First and foremost, recognition must be given to Juan Bassegoda i Nonell, who, at the Catedra Gaudí has inspired and aided scholars over generations. Without his openness, kindness, good humour and profound knowledge distilled into the pages of his masterwork *El Gran Gaudí*, the study of this remarkable architect would still be somewhere in the dark ages.

My researches in Catalonia, however, also led me to other libraries and institutions whose unique character often brought me closer to Gaudí's life and the Modernista world. The Biblioteca de Catalunya, based in the old Hospital de Santa Cruz where Gaudí died, must be thanked for its efficient response to any and every request. So too the Maragall archive, the art library at the Tapiés foundation, the library at the Collegi de Arquitectes de Catalunya and the atmospheric clubhouse library at the Excurcionistas in the carrer Paradis. Many in Barcelona opened their doors to me: the Diputació de Barcelona, the Fundació Caixa Catalunya at La Pedrera, Lourdes Figueras i Borrull at Canet de Mar, the sculptor Subirachs at the Sagrada Familia, the owners of the Casa Lleo Morera, the nuns at the Teresianas, Maria Serrat at the Casa Batlló, the Palau Moja, the owners of Gaudí's Bellesguard, the staff of the Palau Güell, the Asador de Aranda 'Frare Blanca', the Hotel España, the restaurant at the Casa Calvet, the staff at the Modern Art Museum of MNAC, the cultural department of the Generalitat, David Miró at the Catalan Tourist Board in London, Maria Luisa Albacar at Turisme de Barcelona, Blanca Cros at Turisme de Catalunya, the late Javier Amat de Marti and Maria Angeles Tomas and Anna Llanes i Tuset at the Museu Cau Ferrat. Numerous private houses in Barcelona allowed an inquisitive stranger in for a privileged view of late nineteenth-century life.

In the villages of Riudoms and Reus I was treated with kindness, and sometimes curiosity that a foreigner might take an interest in their most famous son. The Centro de Lectura in Reus opened relevant files and documents and the museum was equally generous. At Casa Navas, the Gasull olive-oil plant, the psychiatric clinic of Pere Mata, the holy shrine of Montserrat, the olive-oil cooperative at Espluga de Francoli and the monastery of Poblet I was given permission to tread where others rarely go: Sebastia, the owner of the Mas de la Calderera showed me into the garden and house; the priest at Riudoms gave me a guided tour of his church.

Many people also opened their hearts to me. In childhood, the Bargallo family from Montroig more than anyone else inspired my love of Catalonia and provided my passport to Spain. I will never forget Toni Pujol's kindness and hospitality in Vic. In Barcelona I thank Nicholas Law and Mercedes Darbra for everything, and also Montsé Albàs, Aurea Marquez, Jaume Grau, Carles Caparros, Ferran Juste, Sergi Hernandez, Rogier Dedeu and Jordi Daroca.

This book has also benefitted from research in other Spanish cities. In Madrid, Peter Wessel and Marga Lucas have always provided a home from home. Alex and Romana Canneti also came to the rescue; as did Bob and Clare's house in Comillas. I thank the staff of the library at the Museo Nacional Centro de Arte Reina Sofia.

In Sergovia the architect Juan José Condé and Lara Carrasco-Munoz have always provided hospitality and friendship. So too with special affection, and in recognition of a debt long overdue, I thank Teresa Sanz, Angel Yagüe, Joy and Carlos Angulo, Carmen Lois, Julio Michel, Pilar Soria, Vicki Armentia, Luis Marfagon, Nieves Moran, Cruz Ciria, Fernando Esteban, Matilde Losano, Diego and Juan Peñalosa, Ana Lopez, Regina, Asun, Gema Sanz, Loli and the Peter Poguntke family, who have all fuelled my love of the Iberian peninsula. I have also learnt a great deal from sharing life, warmth, fiestas and friendship with the special neighbours and friends of Arevalillo de Cega.

In London I thank the staff of the British Library, the Institute of Historical Research and the Instituto Cervantes, Exeter University Library and the trustees of the London Library for facilitating research. At the Arts Institute at Bournemouth I was aided particularly by Jim Hunter, Keith Bartlett, Emma Hunt and Paul Briglin in the library. A big thank-you to Tom Titherington and Rebecca Howson

*Acknowledgements*

for always providing a haven in London. And to Martin Randall and Fiona Urquhart – comrades in arms. Closer to home a big thank you to my extended family: Sonia Martinez, Sandra Bovier, Vanessa Gil Fernandez, Loles Cabel, Marta Torrijo Sanjuan and Mireia Ferrer. On Spanish matters and liturgy José Leal Fernandez and Father Patrick O'Leary came to the rescue. Thank you also to the Hispanists Michael Jacobs and Joan Bolton, as well as Daphne Mundy. Condor Ferries were kind enough to assist with various journeys.

At my literary agency, Curtis Brown, I would like to thank Euan Thorneycroft for his continued help and support and Jane Bradish-Ellames, of course, whose energy, extraordinary enthusiasm and belief sustain far more than she knows.

At HarperCollins I would especially like to thank Caroline Hotblack who discovered photos however obscure, Vera Brice the designer and the editorial staff of Mike Fishwick, Arabella Pike and Georgina Laycock who through their valuable attention and judicious advice transformed a manuscript into a book. I am extremely grateful.

Throughout the writing of this book I have always been helped by two special women and two special friends. At home, my wife, Alexandra Coulter, has kept the home fires burning and the children at bay while waiting patiently for this book to appear. In Barcelona, Debbie Chambers has been the most remarkably generous hostess, never even flinching when my whole family arrived at her door.

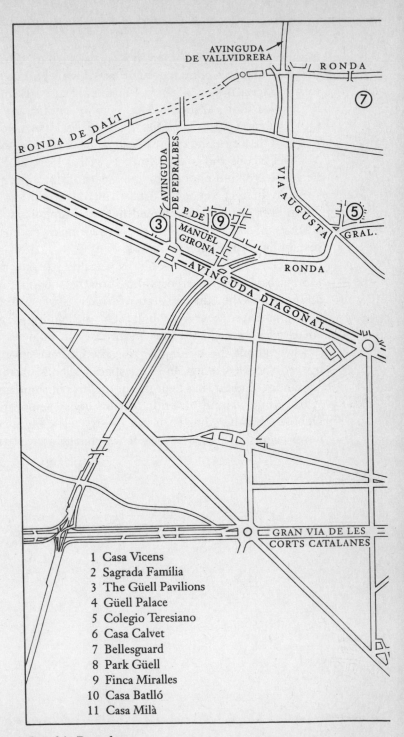

1 Casa Vicens
2 Sagrada Família
3 The Güell Pavilions
4 Güell Palace
5 Colegio Teresiano
6 Casa Calvet
7 Bellesguard
8 Park Güell
9 Finca Miralles
10 Casa Batlló
11 Casa Milà

*Gaudí's Barcelona*

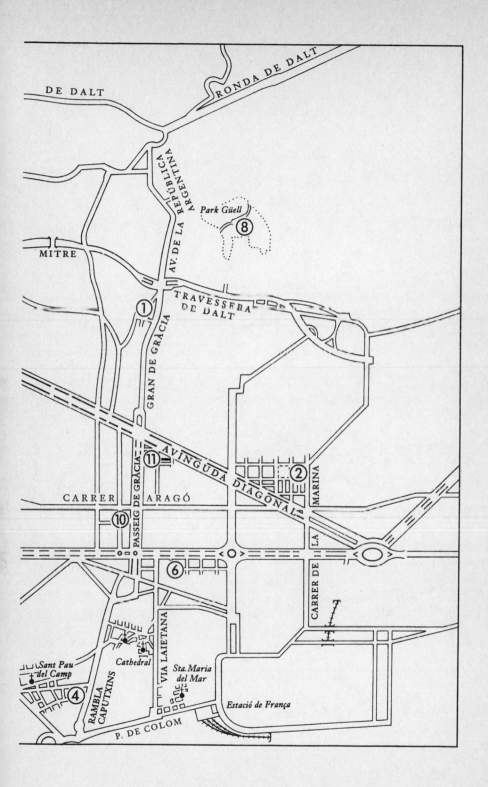

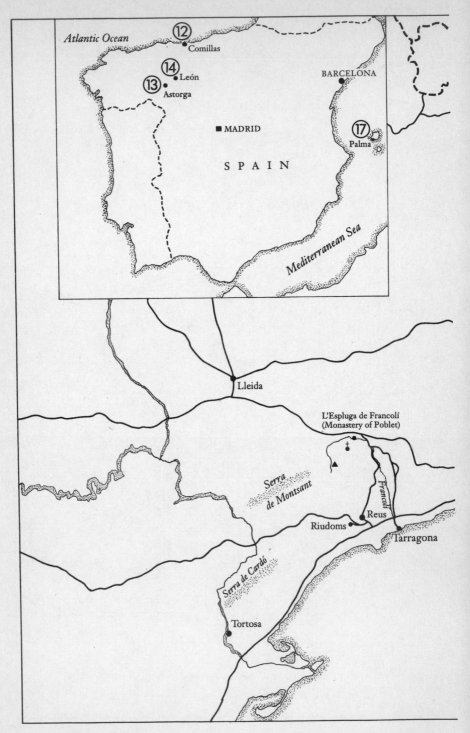

*Gaudí's Catalonia*

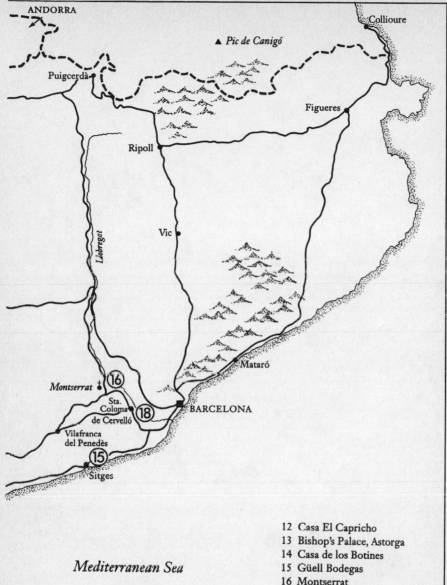

ANDORRA

▲ *Pic de Canigó*

Collioure

Puigcerdà

Figueres

Ripoll

*Llobregat*

Vic

Mataró

Montserrat

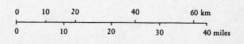

Sta.
Coloma
de Cervelló

BARCELONA

Vilafranca
del Penedès

Sitges

12  Casa El Capricho
13  Bishop's Palace, Astorga
14  Casa de los Botines
15  Güell Bodegas
16  Montserrat
17  Palma Cathedral
18  Güell Colony Crypt

*Mediterranean Sea*

| 0 | 10 | 20 | | 40 | | 60 km |

| 0 | 10 | 20 | 30 | 40 miles |

# PREFACE

Few artists have shaped our perceptions of a city as completely as Gaudí. And few architects have proved so emblematic of their culture. Gaudí, Barcelona and Catalonia were, and still are, eternally intertwined.

Slowly Gaudí's reputation has spread and he is arguably the world's most famous architect. Throughout Japan and Korea, Germany and Latin America, Gaudí's architectural legacy is celebrated. One Japanese admirer describes his wonder that, while his work would be in museums in Japan, in Barcelona it is still integral to the fabric of the city. Perhaps Gaudí's real appeal lies in his sheer accessibility. Some of his work has a Disney-fied vulgarity, but at best it is both sensual and profoundly simple. Art for everyman, it is both generous and humane. His architecture is once again in vogue.

Gaudí is a very contemporary figure—holistic, spiritual and astonishingly original. He was an ecologist: recycling broken tiles, crockery, children's toys, old needles from textile mills, metal bands for baling cotton cloth, bedsprings and the burnt-out linings of industrial ovens to create his buildings.

Like a twentieth-century Leonardo, Gaudí is the apotheosis of the artist as inventor. Fantastically fertile, his imagination burnt holes through the musty pattern books. His gift was an amazing capacity to imagine a building and then transform it into reality. In so doing he created an entirely new typology.

Some find Gaudí's work hard to understand, and avoid acknowledging his style's generosity. For them his towers display

*xxvii*

the signs of imminent disintegration, but Gaudí will always appeal to a variety of different audiences. His keen eye for detail is very Japanese, his profound religiosity strongly Catholic – yet the structural brilliance of his white attic rooms is Calvinist in its purity.

And Gaudí is still building – from beyond the grave. God was his main patron and, according to Gaudí, in no real hurry. He had waited hundreds of years for the completion of Chartres and Seville. Against those standards, another hundred and fifty years for the Sagrada Família would not be long.

All that is set to change. The Sagrada Família is predicted to reach completion around 2030; assuming that the steady flow of donations does not dry up.

While Gaudí's architecture is an open book, his personality, as Barcelona's solitary 'priest of beauty', has always been far less accessible. He remains an enigma, the last great modern artist to escape the biographer's gaze.

Many previous studies of Gaudí have either avoided putting him into cultural context, preferring the lonely figure stalking across the Catalan stage; or concentrating rather on his elaborate architectural forms. But many key events in Gaudí's life that proved touchstones and touch paper for the architect, his work and immediate circle have been overlooked. For instance, Spain's loss of her empire in 1898 and the Tragic Week of 1909 in which convents and churches were burnt down, both had strong effects on Gaudí, his friends and patrons, completely changing his working patterns.

The political situation in Catalonia was a complex, potentially explosive one. Catalonia's uneasy alliance with Spain (Castile) was one of immense tension. For this reason, whenever possible I have allowed Spanish and Catalan writers to speak in their own words.

Before the Civil War, some Spanish intellectuals and politicians recognised the dangers, but tragically they didn't have the power to halt the momentum of the approaching crisis. Few generations have ever been so savagely self-analytical as Gaudí's. Few have put themselves through such painful self-discovery. Harsh at the time, much of their criticism still draws blood today. These social and political tensions between reform and reaction provide the subtext and hidden structures of Gaudí's work.

A biography that deals with such a myth is fraught with complications. But there are problems beyond methodology. All Gaudí's personal and working archives were destroyed at the beginning of the Spanish Civil War. On 20 July 1936 the Sagrada Família crypt was broken into and over the next two days Gaudí's drawings, records and models were burnt or smashed up. In the same month, Gaudí's friend, the Sagrada Família parish priest Gil Parés, was assassinated in the quarry nearby. And yet, for the last fifteen years of his life we know what he was doing almost every minute of the day. Gaudí was a creature of habit. You could set your watch by him: mass, morning prayers, the Angelus and his evening stroll to confession. We know when he picked up his evening paper and which kiosk he bought it from. But the workings of his spirit are lost for ever, in the silence of the confessional.

After years of lobbying, the Asociació por beatificació d'Antoni Gaudí – labouring to speed on his beatification by selling booklets and devotional cards – is finally getting close to its goal. In summer 1998, the Archbishop of Barcelona, Ricard Maria Carles, started the process by declaring Gaudí patron saint of his profession. The Vatican has yet to ratify this. He was an artist-architect who produced (according to the archbishop) a mystical body of work only equalled by the towering *Cántico Espiritual* of St John of the Cross. As Ruskin wrote of Fra Angelico, he was far more than an artist he was, in fact, 'an inspired saint'.

# INTRODUCTION

The most successful products of the Spanish genius
have been created as a result of the constant effort
to give life and perfection to individual qualities
sprung from traditional roots, but ripened at a late season.
Such fruits are esteemed for their rarity:
being no longer found in other countries they introduce
elements whose efficacy has been missed.

*Menéndez Pidal*, 'Material and Moral Austerity'[1]

Both revered and reviled, Antoni Gaudí looms over the twentieth
century like Goya's brooding giant. As with most myths the real
Gaudí lies obscured by layers (and decades) of neglect and facile
criticism.

For over forty years Franco's regime stifled the Catalan
cultural identity, concealing the meaning of Gaudí's work.
There were those who still proclaimed him the 'Dante of
Architecture', passionate supporters of the unfinished Sagrada
Família, a single towering edifice that had come to represent
the 'theology of the Catalan people'. But more often than not
he was dismissed as a stylistic dinosaur trapped in the Middle
Ages.

However, the 1960s saw a resurgence of interest. On the steps
of the Sagrada Família and along the multicoloured serpentine
bench of the Park Güell, rebellious Catalan counterculture
encountered hordes of free-loving European youth. By the
seventies Gaudí's buildings provided the ideal backdrop for

movies such as Antonioni's *The Passenger*, which starred Jack Nicholson and Maria Schneider.

We are still no closer to understanding who Gaudí was. There are no English biographies. And only hagiographies in Castilian and Catalan: the best research still focused safely on architectural appreciation. The intricacies of his hyperbolic and catenary curves are argued over and his empiricism wondered at. But, of Gaudí the man, all we have is still only about a dozen photographs. He was notoriously private.

Gaudí told a reporter working for the Montevideo newspaper *La Razón* in 1913:

> Men may be divided into two types: men of words and men of action. The first speak; the latter act. I am of the second group. I lack the means to express myself adequately. I would not be able to explain to anyone my artistic concepts. I have not yet concretised them. I have never had time to reflect on them. My hours have been spent in my work.

His words are specious. Gaudí delighted in using original forms and colour combinations. But his buildings also contain clearly decipherable meanings; much as Romanesque fresco cycles or Gothic cathedrals do. Gaudí's autobiography was written in stone; in broken tiles, tortoiseshell, twisted metal, stained glass and burnished gold; in cement and mortar. To build up an image of the man, we have to look more closely at the buildings he built, those he lived in, the objects he venerated and the sources of his imagination: what he himself described as 'the Great Book of Nature'.

Gaudí appreciation has, in general, been founded on ignorance. The dismissive English viewpoint was summed up by Sir Nikolaus Pevsner's leaving him out of his *Pioneers of Modern Design*.[2] Evelyn Waugh couldn't even muster up the energy to get out of the cab to review Gaudí's work. Catalan writer Carles

Soldevila produced a wonderful skit in this vein. In his essay 'The Art of Showing Barcelona', written just after Gaudí's death, Soldevila explains his tactics for dealing with Gaudí enthusiasts.

> Don't approve of their judgement, but don't contradict it openly either. Let them slide on their own down the slopes of architectural expressionism.[3]

George Orwell was even more inflammatory. In *Homage to Catalonia* he wrote:

> I went to look at the cathedral [*sic*], a modern cathedral, and one of the most hideous buildings in the world. It has four crenellated spires exactly the shape of hock bottles. Unlike most of the churches in Barcelona it was not damaged during the Revolution – it was spared because of its 'Artistic value', people said. I think the anarchists showed bad taste in not blowing it up when they had the chance . . .[4]

Gaudí fared better at the hands of German and American commentators. Walter Gropius admired Gaudí's work, 'Some of the Sagrada Família walls are a marvel of technical perfection.'[5] Louis Sullivan, Frank Lloyd Wright's teacher, was even more enthusiastic. 'The greatest piece of creative architecture in the last twenty-five years. It is spirit symbolised in stone!'[6]

But the artist/architect Hermann Finsterlin displayed the most extreme reaction:

> The Sagrada Família is for me one of the building-wonders of the world . . . Like the Taj Mahal, the Sagrada Familia was no house of God, but a house of the Goddess, of his Goddess, his heavenly and therefore unhappy love. For such cathedrals are only built by a heart in monstrous despair or one in Dionysian ecstasy, and only a superman is capable of such creative despair.[7]

Within his lifetime Gaudí was already recognised as an oddity. His architecture dated rapidly and his difficult personality, steeped in religiosity, ran counter to the spirit of the age. Meyer Schapiro untangled the paradox:

> Hegel said very unjustly that in an age of piety one does not have to be religious in order to create a truly religious work of art, whereas today the most deeply pious artist is incapable of producing it.[8]

Gaudí was a symbol of what Mario Praz described as 'untamed Spain'. He stank of incense and original sin.

Back in Barcelona, on his home territory, Gaudí was also out of fashion. The young Picasso warned against him, and the critic Eugeni d'Ors tried to finish him off. By the time of the Primo de Rivera dictatorship in 1923, Gaudí's style was old news. A cooler Mediterranean classicism that many saw as representing the true Catalan spirit had replaced Gaudí's 'hot' humour.

Paradoxically, what proved Gaudí's real undoing was the praise heaped on his work by Salvador Dalí in the December 1933 issue of the Surrealists' magazine, *Minotaure*. In '*De la beauté terrifiante et comestible de l'architecture modern style*', Dalí deconstructed, chopped up and melted his oeuvre. In a single article, Dalí managed to brand Gaudí's architecture for a generation as 'tapas' art.

Gaudí's reputation has suffered further still from other detractors: the Basque philosopher Miguel de Unamuno described his architecture as 'drunken art'; Oliver Sacks used Gaudí's buildings to diagnose Tourette's syndrome; and Pevsner, in *The Anti-Rationalists* (1973), placed Gaudí alongside architectural freaks like the French postman Ferdinand Cheval, who filled his postbag on his way home to build, over thirty-three years, his shell-encrusted Palais Ideal. This sidelining was all to do with fashion and taste. What his detractors disliked more than anything was the wayward vulgarity of his buildings, what T. G. Jackson in

1904 dismissed as his 'conscious striving after novelty and eccentricity, which is the basest of all motives in art'. They saw him as the prime example of an architect 'infatuated by the charm of the picturesque to the point of absurdity'.[9]

Gaudí was 'a monster, one of those overwhelming personalities like Francesco Borromini', a neo-Baroque in pursuit of fading dreams.[10] His fantastical architecture, many argued, amounted to nothing more than architectural heresy, a false trail.

Throughout the twentieth century Gaudí has been isolated, but so have the other great Spanish geniuses. Ortega y Gasset suggested this was the fate of the Spanish character:

> Once in a while a genius appears, but his work, abrupt and isolated as it is, fails to raise the mediocre level of national production. Between him, a single individual, and the masses, there are no intermediaries and, by the same token, no communication. And this, in spite of the fact that even these rare Spanish geniuses have always half belonged to the people, and that their work has never completely freed itself from the plebeian and popular touch.[11]

It has suited most apologists and critics to focus on Gaudí, the isolated genius: a misunderstood, slightly mad, eccentric, the last of the Romantics.

Oversimplification, however, has led to an unbalanced picture. In Catalan folklore Gaudí has been reduced to a clearly recognisable type – the ascetic hermit of architecture. Apparently, architecture was his monastic order. The most common myth has Gaudí living and working his last twenty years in the basement cave of the Sagrada Família – whereas he actually only slept there for his last six months.

Outside Catalonia the myth has served Gaudí's memory well but at home his reputation is both celebrated and desecrated. There is no halfway house. He is seen as a false prophet – yet a very active group is also vigorously lobbying the Vatican for his beatification. Like St Joseph, Gaudí is held up as the symbol of the working man, Ruskinian in his belief in manual creativity.

Gaudí's character as reported by close collaborators and contemporaries comprised a catalogue of opposites: noble yet mean; a dandy and tramp; wise yet senile, witty yet dull. All these observations were made by those who knew, or felt they knew Gaudí well; and all are at odds. Perhaps all or none of these, but his architectural triumphs and religiosity provoked impassioned responses.

Ortega y Gasset imagined he understood this phenomenon well.

> Pride is an anti-social force . . . a great people cannot be made with it, and it leads inevitably to degeneration of the human type, which is what has happened in the Spanish race.[12]

Gaudí belonged to a spectacularly gifted generation of writers, poets, artists and architects, every one an exception to Ortega's rule. He was no loner. He was, in fact, part of a vital group of architects, patrons, politicians and high churchmen, among the most innovative minds of their time.[13]

It is commonly thought that Gaudí completed, or failed to complete, just nine buildings within Barcelona and its suburbs, and three elsewhere in Spain. Like so many turn-of-the-century architects whose style fell out of favour, Gaudí fell victim to the city developer. During his working life Gaudí (and his studio) were responsible for seventy-five commissions. Although some never got beyond the drawing board, Gaudí was far more prolific than previously imagined. His work included plans for a

Franciscan mission in Tangiers, a luxury Manhattan hotel, numerous exhibition and trade-fair stands, an early cinema interior, private chapels, a flower kiosk, a stylish café interior, a pharmacy shop, endless religious commissions and a list of previously unknown private houses.[14]

Any discussion of Gaudí's contribution to the history of architecture is already contentious. His work neatly breaks up into three periods: early eclecticism, maturity and decadence. Some historians see him as the misfit of the European Art Nouveau movement, others as leader of the Catalan *modernistes*. What is unusual, and this is almost impossible for a non-Spanish public to understand, is how deeply politicised Gaudí's work has become.

Where you stand on Catalan independence is roughly mirrored by where you stand on Gaudí. This also extends to Gaudí's relationship to Castile. Gaudí appreciation, within Spain, has become a confusing but effective sociopolitical barometer.

The acknowledged expert on Gaudí's work, Professor Bassegoda, looks at the larger view – of Gaudí as an integral member of the international architectural community with a strong regional expression. But he warns against colourful discussions of Gaudí as a Freemason, as an obsessive dabbler in the occult, an ultra right-wing Catholic and Fascist, and as a misanthrope. One book, produced by the Delft University Gaudí research project, even begins bluntly with, '*Was Gaudí een fantast? Was hij een religieus fanaticus? Was Gaudí een rationalist? Een pedofiel?*'[15] When I interviewed him Bassegoda looked at me mischievously. 'I'm thinking of publishing a biographical study of Gaudí. "Gaudí, the bullfighter." For the amount of truth there is to find in many of the cheap Gaudí biographies I may as well.'

Gaudí's appearance is easy to describe; from the dandyism of his youth to the dishevelled neglect of his later years. But his conversation is more difficult to reproduce. He didn't write much, and whatever correspondence remained was destroyed. Despite his self-proclaimed reticence, many friends and assistants remembered him as a great talker. Many of Gaudí's best-known sayings, however, don't have the authentic timbre of real conversation but instead seem to have been edited down into enigmatic, pungent aphorisms for posterity.

To find the real Antoni Gaudí we have to allow his central character traits to emerge from out of the shadows of myth. For Catalans, the source of Gaudí's genius is very simple to trace – an unwavering loyalty to his origins. Gaudí's ability to stick to this guiding principle nourished him throughout his life.

It is true that, in Catalonia, imagination and meaning has always exploded from the 'significant detail' out. Nature, particularly Catalan nature, relinquishes its mystery slowly. With an almost Proustian intensity, connections arise from fascinated concentration on a particular object: a wind-weathered stone pitted like a honeycomb, or an ancient olive tree.

Gaudí's homeland, the *Baix Camp* – the low country that surrounds Reus and Tarragona, an hour's drive south of Barcelona – is caught in a cultivated plain between a mountain range and the Mediterranean. The landscape is punctuated only by the occasional *masia* – the evocative Catalan farmhouse – strung out between villages, which are just clusters of houses marked out by their proud honey-coloured bell towers. Every few miles, the landscape is striped from mountain to sea by flash-flood rivercourses, cutting a swathe through the fields of maize and the olive and almond groves.

As a seven-year-old I played in the dried-out bed of the riera de Maspujols. In daylight my brothers and I looked for lizards and ran from scorpions. And, at night, under the railway bridge of the main Barcelona–Valencia line, we netted and chloroformed bats for one of the world's leading bat experts. Little did

I know then that three kilometres away, almost exactly a century earlier, the seven-year-old Gaudí had traipsed up and down the same riverbed, lovingly describing it later as 'the most beautiful place in the world'. Without knowing it I had caught the aesthetic of the *Baix Camp*.

# GAUDÍ

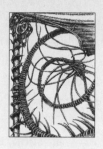

# 'People of Space and Circumstance'[1]

As water, drop by drop, wears away the stone, so the
landscape models its men, custom by custom.
A people is, in the last analysis, a repertory of customs.
Momentary bursts of genius serve to mark only its profile.[2]

José Ortega y Gasset

ANTONI GAUDÍ I CORNET was born as he died, untidily – the
subject of controversy.

On 25 June 1852 a son was born to Francesc Gaudí and his
wife, Antonia Cornet, residents of Reus. His baptism was unusually hasty. Although he was Antonia's fifth child, she had previously lost five-year-old Maria and two-year-old Francesc, within
three months. Antonia's pregnancy had been a difficult one. The
birth was traumatic and to save the baby's soul he was rushed
to the church of Sant Pere Apostol in the first hour of his life.

Antoni Gaudí's baptismal papers leave little room for doubt
as to where and when he was born. However, later in life, Gaudí
mischievously left his options open by implying that he might
in fact have been born at his father's workshop, just over the
municipal boundaries in Riudoms.

I

But neither Riudoms nor Reus has done much with their legacies. Unsignposted buildings remain abandoned and drawings and documents are locked behind imposing museum doors. It is hardly a legacy to fight over. But the stakes have always been higher: local pride, fame, part-ownership in a future Catholic saint.

Francesc Gaudí's country workshop, the Mas de la Calderera, lies two hours' walk southwest of Reus. From the city boundary the road towards Riudoms leads almost directly west towards the mountains of the Serra de Montsant. Trapped between mountain and sea, the ever-changing weather creates drama across this narrow plain. On some days the stratocirrus clouds are teased out like wispy cotton threads across the deep blue sky. But the weather can change rapidly as blue turns to purple and thunder rolls off the high sierra bringing torrential rain.

From the main road the dried-out riera de Maspujols leads directly to the sea. On either side, farm tracks have been flattened in the soft red earth. The banks of the river are littered with brittle spindle brush and pieces of driftwood brought down from the villages above. To walk down the riverbed is to travel through time. Almost nothing here has changed in the last hundred years. Across the fields the spire of Riudoms church is clearly visible. But there is no sign of Francesc Gaudí's workshop. Clumps of umbrella pine surround the occasional farmhouse. High walls of cactus obscure the view. And it is utterly silent.

Almost a kilometre down, protected by a high mound, lies the Mas de la Calderera. A commemorative plaque claims it is Gaudí's birthplace.[3] It is a simple brick and plaster construction, one room deep and about five metres wide. Two giant plantains keep the front courtyard almost permanently in the shade. With its back placed square to the hills behind and its small Dutch gable, the house has an air of formality. Around the windows and doors, a simple Greek key pattern is cut into the plaster and above the front door a small balcony faces the sea. The railings are brushed by the plantain leaves. Under the gable a Catalan flag is carved proudly in plaster central to the overall design. It is a house trying to stretch out. On one side facing the riverbed there is a lean-to that must have been Gaudí's father's workshop and stable. The dishevelled feel is accentuated by the jerry-built kennels under the trees. There is no museum and certainly no shrine.

Sebastià, the present owner, runs the spit-roast chicken shop in Riudoms. The farmhouse is used as store and shade for a small but thriving agricultural business. Just ten metres away in polytunnels, cucumbers, peppers and aubergines are grown for the Reus market.

Through the open main door a small central hall remains almost permanently in the dark. Doors lead off either side. Past the collapsed sofa, on the back wall a dog-eared Xerox portrait of Gaudí, pinned up with a thumbtack, is the only reminder of the building's previous owners.

Gaudí was born, most accounts have it, in the carrer Sant Joan, just off the Plaça Prim in Reus. An anonymous office block now stands there. Youngest of three surviving children, Gaudí took pride in his mother's recollection that, throughout his difficult birth, he battled to live. The theme of having being chosen for some higher purpose runs throughout his life.

Antoni was named after his mother, Antonia. His brother Francisco was thirteen months older; the eldest son named in the Catalan custom after his father. The two brothers, divided by their parents' names, were also rivals for their love. They were Antonia's replacements for the children she had recently lost.

Antoni Gaudí inherited, from both the Gaudí and Cornet

lines, a long craft tradition.[4] For eight generations, dating back to the early seventeenth century, they had been merchants, miners, farmers, weavers, boilermakers and coppersmiths. Gaudí was proud of his heritage:

> I have that quality of spatial apprehension because I am the son, grandson, and the great-grandson of copper-smiths. My father was a smith; my grandfather also. On my mother's side of the family there were also smiths; her grandfather was a cooper; my maternal grandfather was a sailor, who also are people of space and circumstance. All these generations of people give a preparation.[5]

Significantly, the genealogical tree had its roots further afield than the *Baix Camp*. In 1634, Antoni Gaudí, of Saint Quentin-sur-Sioule, in the department of Clermont-Ferrand, witnessed the marriage of their son Joan to Maria Escura in Riudoms. Pre-industrial life was predominantly static. Gaudí's bloodline was thus an unusually cosmopolitan one; demonstrating that Catalonia was already part of a trans-Pyrenean culture in the seventeenth century, its very language demonstrated a closer affinity to Provençal, the tongue of the Languedoc, than to Castilian. In Scotland, France and Prussia, other Gaudís have been found. Bassegoda (tongue in cheek) even refers to the eighteenth-century Prussian General Gaudí, who published a book on fortifications and campaign tent construction in 1806.[6]

Gaudí's tribal inheritance came primarily from Reus and Riudoms. It provided the young Gaudí with a catalogue of images and ideas and a lifelong sense of belonging. For Gaudí, even later in life, for someone to have come from the *Baix Camp* was more than sufficient. His childhood friendships lasted. One only has to look at how many of Gaudí's collaborators came from Reus and Tarragona to understand the strength of his roots.[7]

Gaudí was a weak baby. After a lung infection he developed rheumatoid arthritis. It was a long road to recovery. When in

remission he could go to school normally but sometimes he was
so crippled that he could only be transported by donkey. One of
Gaudí's first memories was overhearing the doctor discussing his
health. An early death was predicted unless he was given plenty of
rest. An indication of Gaudí's willpower is that on hearing of
his own imminent demise he concentrated singlemindedly on
confounding the doctor.[8] But the disease took its toll. Toda, his
closest childhood friend, remembered Gaudí as old before his
time – as the most ancient friend that ever walked the earth.

Riudoms and the riverbed were his playground. And, without
playmates, he quickly discovered an imaginary world to match
the beauty and variety found in nature.

In the early Middle Ages, Riudoms had been a walled settlement
with a castle. The fashionable romanticism of the late nineteenth
century made a cult out of architectural decomposition. Riudoms
lay between the mountain monastery of Escornalbou and Castell
Vilafortuny.[9] Two supposed Roman villas nearby fuelled dreams
of rediscovering the wealth of the past.[10]

But even more intriguing were the rumours that very near by
lay the ancient drowned Iron Age village of Llaberia. The *Baix
Camp* had a rich and sophisticated heritage.

Life in Riudoms was marked out by its feast and saints' days:
Three Kings, Carnival, Palm Sunday, Easter week, Corpus
Christi, Sant Joan and Sant Pere, the village saint's day, All
Saints' Day and Christmas.

The mountains promised other things. From a young age,
Antonio visited the churches of Sant Pere and Sant Jaume and
would have been told the legends of Montserrat. Montroig too
had its black Madonna but a visit to the local shrine of Nostra
Senyora de la Roca was a mere shadow of the real thing. Nothing
in Catalan religious life was as important as Montserrat. The
ambition of every pious Catholic boy was to go on the ultimate
Catalan pilgrimage.

Looking up the riera de Maspujols, the young Gaudí was

5

surrounded by church spires and mountains. The light there has an extraordinary clarity that telescopes distances and flattens the view into a cubist landscape.

The effect of light on stone is magical throughout Spain but in Catalonia it is almost mystical. It became a leitmotif of Gaudí's work. This appreciation was first and foremost a visceral reaction. In the *Baix Camp* the Moors' brief occupation had brought an aesthetic of light that manipulated surface decoration with repeated relief motifs. For Gaudí, however, it would always be personal experience as much as a grounding in the history of architecture that characterised his genius.

From the top of the serra one can look south down the coast-line towards Tortosa and the marshlands of the Ebre delta. To the north, the horizon is marked by the snowcapped Pyrenees and the mountain chain running down to the coast to meet the Mediterranean at Port Bou. Nearby lies Valls, and beyond in the distance Santa Coloma de Queralt and Vilafranca del Pen-edès, both ancestral towns on Gaudí's mother's side. And there, hovering in the distance, is Montserrat. The young Gaudí would look up at the mountains and be told that from there one day he would go and see it himself.

While at the workshop, most visits were made to Riudoms. The village was closer. There were cousins to visit, and church to attend. The Baroque church, Sant Jaume, faced onto the main square. Its main entrance, an imposing one flanked by empty niches, is capped by two overfed cherubs unrolling a scroll with a hazelnut tree on it. Pragmatically sometimes the agricultural calendar took precedence over that of the church. St Bonaventura, a seventeenth-century moderniser of the Franciscan order, the village's patron saint, had his birthday midway through the hazel-nut harvest. It was more practical, if unorthodox, to celebrate his death – when the crops were safely in. But religious life was of enormous importance to the village. St Bonaventura (canonised in 1911), had from 1662 lain in state in a gold and glass catafalque, transforming Riudoms into a place of pilgrimage. The church of Sant Jaume, even today, feels far too large for the village.

Gaudí went to school in Reus. However, there was plenty of excitement to be found in his father's workshop.

Introduced to the family craft tradition, Gaudí was transfixed by his father's ability to beat flat copper sheets into gleaming vessels. It was in the workshop that he first learnt to understand space and feel and imagine in three dimensions. For him it would prove revelatory. As a mature architect, Gaudí would always acknowledge the importance of his father's creativity.[11]

Antonia and Francesc's marriage was a practical one. It brought together two dynasties of coppersmiths, and enabled Antonia's father, Anton Cornet, to retire, leaving his business in the capable hands of his son-in-law, and it was an indication of the closeness of a social circle centred primarily around craftsmen of a similar social standing. Reus was a small city, with a population hovering around 27,000: in short, provincial. This provinciality encouraged a strong sense of tradition manifested in the continuance of the medieval guilds and fervent Catholicism, while also allowing greater liberalism which was reinforced by the cooperative movement. Francesc Gaudí was a prime example of the marriage of these seemingly irreconcilable worlds. But he was keen that neither son should continue in his trade.

Perhaps he recognised that industry would eventually sideline all craft trades. But education and its possibilities also offered social mobility. Francesc Gaudí was an ambitious and well-respected craftsman. He served as Reus council's *'mostassà'* – responsible for weights and measures – which in Catalonia's second industrial city suggests that he was respected for his integrity.[12] Francisco pushed, cajoled and encouraged his children in their schooling and only Reus offered what was required.

There are few records of Gaudí's primary education and what information we do have comes almost exclusively from the recollections of his earliest biographer Ràfols and lifelong friend Eduardo Toda Güell.[13] He went initially to the primary school of Rafael Palau, moving quickly to a small school founded by Francisco Berenguer (father of Gaudí's future collaborator) in an attic on the carrer Monterols. It was here that the young Gaudí first met Toda, who recalled a telling incident while at school.

During a natural history class on birds in which their use of wings was discussed, the young Gaudí blurted out, 'At our country-house our chickens have wings but they only use them to run faster.' Forced inactivity had taught him to look hard and listen.

In the academic year 1863–64, Antonio Gaudí appears for the first time on the official registers of the Instituto Colegio de las Escuelas Pías de Reus. By 1865 the Gaudí family had moved to a fourth-floor flat on carrer San Vicenç five minutes away from the workshop. Christian doctrine, religion, morals and religious history formed an essential part of Gaudí's secondary education, alongside Greek, Latin, geometry, history, rhetoric and poetry.

Apart from the few exceptional 'free' schools based in Madrid and Barcelona, state education meant a Catholic one. And, at the Instituto, housed in an old Franciscan convent, Gaudí was taught the liturgy. On Saturday afternoons attendance was obligatory at the prayers to the Virgin. For the Gaudí-Cornet family, remaining at the Instituto till sixteen already represented a major step forward – state secondary education had only been introduced in 1845. If class and economic well-being was measured through secondary education, it was also there that the division between the sexes was made plain. Even as late as the 1930s only one in eight students at the Institutos was a girl. For Antoni Gaudí, the female world was that of the hearth and home; once outside he entered a predominantly male domain.

At school Gaudí was not precocious. The only subject in which he excelled was geometry. All his other marks ranged from notable to failure. By contrast Eduardo Toda and José Ribera, his inseparable friends, scored highly throughout. Hampered by sporadic illness Gaudí also hated, according to Toda, learning by rote. Nothing bored him so much as the endless repetition of singing *la cantinela*.[14] It was a poor substitute for his father's forge, the archaeological discoveries waiting to be made around the Mas de la Calderera or outings with his friends.

Reus was full of distractions. Since the early Middle Ages, Reus had been the central market town of the *Baix Camp* and cosmopolitan enough to support a small Jewish community. Ravaged by the plague during the fifteenth century, the city slowly restored its fortune under the religious jurisdiction of neighbouring Tarragona. Reus retained its singular and cosmopolitan identity throughout.

Reus' famous Monday market controlled virtually all of the Spanish hazelnut market, half of the peninsula's almonds and the sale of produce from the flourishing textile and alcohol industries. In 1862 the Banc de Reus was founded to help finance economic expansion and profit from the growth. Reus, through the nearby ports of Salou and Tarragona, was in direct contact with the rest of Europe and the Americas.[15] Indeed, even before the peak of nineteenth-century trade there were twelve European consulates and an American one in Reus.

The Spanish rail network, which had grown without any clear strategy, served Reus well. In 1856 the Tarragona line opened to the public, the route inland to Montblanc in 1863, finally reaching Lleida in 1879. It was significant that Gaudí's first fifteen years marked the broadening of horizons for all but the most provincial Reuseño.

Reus' wealth is reflected in its architecture. The medieval ruins of the Castell de Cambrer, a place attached to the Gothic prioral church of Sant Pere, evoke the town's splendour in the Middle

Ages. The prioral, a short but impressive essay on the simplicity and restrained grandeur of Catalan Gothic, also shows off later Renaissance and Baroque additions. Its tower has an imposing stone nautilus staircase that Gaudí reinterpreted later in the towers of the Sagrada Família. There are the neoclassical chapels of the Santuari del Roser and the Santuari de la Misericòrdia and the equally impressive, highly decorated eighteenth-century vestry of the Mercè. Even on walks to school Gaudí could admire and absorb the language of neoclassical architecture, as the eighteenth-century Palau de Bofarrull was just behind his flat. Its interior, following the Counter-Reformation model, was built in a highly ornate Baroque style decorated with a vivid fresco cycle. This level of visual complexity, the abundance of gold-burnished imagery and a bold palette, became not the exception but the norm, setting him standards of good and bad taste.

Despite Reus' wealth and architectural heritage, it remained provincial. However, during Gaudí's schooldays Reus became famous for producing two of nineteenth-century Spain's most illustrious men: General Joan Prim and the painter Mariano Fortuny. Prim's political career had direct repercussions on Gaudí's education when in September 1868, with General Serrano and Admiral Topete, he wrested power from the ineffectual Moderates and Queen Isabel, in a proclamation ambitiously entitled 'Spain with Honour'. Turmoil followed inevitably, with the brief incumbency of Amadeo of Savoy as king, the subsequent First Republic and the assassination of General Prim. During the First Republic, Spain had four prime ministers in eleven months. For Gaudí's generation, in their late teens, political education was built on mutual distrust. It was an exciting time of change nevertheless, one for trying out new ideologies.[16]

Mariano Fortuny was a much more practical influence. Gaudí had already started to display artistic skills, painting props and backdrops for school plays. Toda remembered his ambitious set designs for Zorrilla's *Don Juan Tenorio* in which the Sevillian sybarite is only saved by the prayers of the virtuous Doña Inés – a morality play undoubtedly used by the priests to warn their impressionable pupils of the dangers of sexual depravity.

It may seem strange that the irascibly eccentric Gaudí of myth might express any interest in an artist as fashionable as Fortuny. His most famous painting *The Battle of Tetuan* depicted General Prim completely routing the Moroccan troops. Fortuny's dandy-ism, and the commercial success that permitted him to live in Rome, was reported almost weekly in the *Diario de Reus* and was the subject of local gossip.[17] He must have provided a role model for a young man anxious to spread his wings beyond Reus. But the lessons in polish and poise learnt from Fortuny were perhaps less important than the skills Gaudí picked up copying his bravura.[18]

Life in Reus provided plenty of diversion for a fourteen-year-old boy. It was a microcosm of the greater world outside. What Gaudí remembered most fondly were his adventures outside the city boundaries. His fellow adventurers Eduardo Toda and José Ribera Sans, provided him with a companionship that quickly replaced his earlier isolation. While at school, the three even published a dozen issues of their in-house magazine *El Arlequin*, of which Gaudí was artistic editor and chief illustrator. Their friendship was strictly bound by the romantic conventions of the late nineteenth century; tokens of friendship exchanged, plans for their future careers elaborated, everlasting friendship pledged. Just across the border into Provence, in a similar vein, Paul Cézanne and Émile Zola sat together under umbrella pines forging their long, rocky artistic friendship.

For the Toda–Gaudí–Ribera trio there were plenty of Cata-lan heroes. They imagined boarding Jaume el Conqueridor's thirteenth-century flagship, setting out to conquer Mallorca and secure the sea lanes for Catalonia, or far out at sea witnessing Columbus' return. The boys composed poetry and discussed chivalry, romantic love, Catalan history, and the restoration of national monuments.

Visiting the Roman kilns, they attempted to track down the rumoured Lower Paleolithic remains at Burgar. They looked for a Bronze Age burial site at Boella and, heading out to the walled town of Montblanc, stopped off at Alcover's Romanesque church of La Sang.[19] Once Gaudí led them up into the Priorato mountains to see his family landholdings at Masroig.

In a short story, *Calaverada*, the poet Joan Maragall described a group of men obviously based on the three friends.[20] Each of them takes it in turn to relate an intimate episode. The painter's story was quaintly innocent and the poet's full of hilarity. The third member, the architect with the ginger beard, based on Gaudí, remained silent. His uneasiness and mournful eyes reminded them of a child stuck amongst adults. They move forward to listen to him as he sinks deeper into the sofa stroking his beard and smiling enigmatically. Finally, he speaks:

> It was the first trip I had taken on my own. I was going to visit cathedrals and everyone in my family knew exactly where I should go. My father had put together a detailed itinerary in which he had actually written down the time I should spend at each stop – not just to the hour but he had actually calculated it down to the last minute. From every place I visited I had to write home with my descriptions of the buildings and the other sites and detail to my worried mother the exact state of my precarious health.

Maragall had obviously exercised a great deal of poetic licence but the general mood was accurate. The caring mother and interfering father who come close to suffocating their son's pleasure in his first adventure are vividly portrayed.

The most exciting visit for the three boys was to Tarragona, full of Roman remains. It was served by a large amphitheatre, a covered marketplace, thermal baths, a circus, numerous temples and the only forum in Catalonia.

Tarragona was in itself a potted history of Spanish architecture complete with a paleochristian necropolis, simple Visigothic and Romanesque structures, crowned finally by the Gothic cathedral of Santa Maria. Whilst studying Tarragona's architectural ensemble it must have struck Gaudí that church building was both a symbolic and very real expression of the communal spirit; that stone and mortar could cement together local and religious identity. Casanelles wrote:

> The people of Tarragona, like the landscape, are noble, serene and impetuous. Unlike the individualistic Catalans they may most easily be defined as community spirited ... In this context we can understand the spirit that conceives collectively vast and human undertakings because they are in the common interest.[21]

Tarragona's Santa Maria is built on high, above a steep wall of steps. Its imposing, fortified simplicity hides a Romanesque cloister, with its groupings of triple arches carved from porous golden sandstone. Facing onto its garden it provides a space for contemplation. But stepping into the body of the church the viewer is suddenly overwhelmed by huge expanses of masonry, carved from a cold grey stone. The nave dwarfs the viewer, transforming him into insignificance. Swept away by this vertiginous drama it feels like being trapped in the spider's web of one of Piranesi's *Carceri d'Invenzione* etchings.

Tarragona taught Gaudí that architecture could be emotionally potent. Stepping aside for a moment from his compatriots to contemplate Santa Maria, Gaudí understood that 'architecture reigns also in utter silence'. Savouring the moment he instinctively understood that architecture could both intimidate and elevate.

This conjunction of architecture and amateur archaeology developed Gaudí's particular feeling for material, discerning the aesthetic value of pottery shards and rock while responding enthusiastically to the power of the antique and time-worn details. Gaudí would later say, epigrammatically, 'Elegance is the sister of poverty but you must never muddle poverty with misery.'[22] Or as Picasso told a friend: 'I love poverty but the problem is it's so damn expensive.' Joan Miró also had that special gift for discovering arcane and hidden beauty in everyday objects. An admirer once said, 'When I pick up a stone it's a stone. When Miró picks up a stone it's a Miró.' Although very different, all three artists shared a special Catalan sensibility, distilled from nature. Picasso learnt it at Horta, Miró at Mont-Roig and del Camp Gaudí at Riudoms.

For Gaudí, this aesthetic of the humble and 'incomplete', delighting in adobe, baked brick and clay, took almost fifty years to emerge. But when it did, married with all his other skills, he produced one of the greatest masterpieces in the history of architecture.

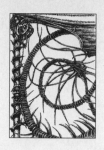

# Voices in the Desert

Oh you coward who profanes art.
If this is liberty! Then liberty stinks.

*Eduardo Toda*

THE THREE BOYS were inseparable, always exploring the surrounding countryside, searching for new archaeological sites. But
according to Ribera, nowhere that they explored around Reus
could compete with the ruins of the Cistercian monastery of
Poblet. It was both burial ground and palace of the Catalan
kings, Pere the Ceremonious, Alfons the Magnanimous, Alfons
the Chaste and Martí the Humane. Various dates have been
proposed for the boys' visit to Poblet between 1865 and 1870.
But it is most likely to have been in the summer of 1867.

Poblet was absolutely essential to the fortunes of Catalan Catholicism during the period of the *reconquista*. The monastery was
founded in 1153 from a gift of land by the Count King of
Catalonia, Ramón Berenguer IV to the abbot Fontfreda of
Languedoc. Sited in the border province of what was then known
as New Catalonia, it was protected from the rear by the foothills

of the Serra de Prades. The laying of its foundation stone was a clear statement of Christian ambition in this wilderness. Even nearby Tarragona had only been reintroduced into Christendom in 1129, just twenty years previously, and it remained for the next four hundred years on the outer edges of the Moorish kingdom of Tolosa.

Choosing the asceticism of St Anthony the Great, the third-century Egyptian hermit, the Cistercians hoped to return monastic life to purity, rejecting wealth for obedience, poverty and chastity. In doing so they produced an architecture of splendid severity. At the height of Cistercian influence it was estimated that 11,000 'white monks' inhabited 300 monasteries. And Poblet was the perfect model of the measured Cistercian style.

Austerity, however, didn't rule out construction on a gigantic scale. By 1185, through legacies and donations, the patrimony of Poblet had grown to include an impressive library, and a hospital for the poor and needy. By 1400 the monastery owned sixty villages and controlled ten neighbouring towns through the right to appoint their mayors. Poblet was effectively a small principality, controlled by its vigilant abbot. At the high point of Poblet's fortunes – at the end of the fourteenth century – King Martí the Humane built his palace adjoining the monastery walls.

In 1833, Spain sank into the civil war known as the Carlist Wars. Outbursts of anticlerical rioting resulted in the sacking of monasteries across Catalonia. Poblet's 'white monks' pre-empted their tormentors and packed up and left. In the summer of 1835 vandals entered the monastery grounds and set about smashing up the building, looting anything of value and burning the rest. Two years later, in 1837, these acts were lent a certain legitimacy when the prime minister, Juan Alvarez Mendizábal, managed to pass a law legitimising the confiscation of church property. The democratically minded hoped this might result in a sharing out of wealth and agricultural lands. But the wealthy quickly bought up estates on the cheap, adding to their substantial fortunes. There were, and still are, many who saw Mendizábal's daring *Desamortización* as nothing better than an act of state-sponsored vandalism.

Over the next thirty years Poblet was regularly looted; graves opened in search of treasure, useful building materials and stone stolen. What scavengers failed to reach the elements destroyed. Once one of the richest architectural treasures in Christendom, it was now an abandoned ruin.

But it was on its rubble that Gaudí and Toda founded their long and distinguished careers. From the mist-covered slopes of Poblet these 'voices in the desert' called to Catalonia to look again at its glorious past.[1]

Remarkably, a few documents – drawings, essays, a library catalogue, a poetic eulogy by Toda and a groundplan – still exist. Written mostly on the reverse of a manifesto, dated 25 September 1869, calling for self-restraint in these difficult times, these 'Poblet' documents are invaluable, showing, as they do, the formation of the sensibilities of the three boys.

Gaudí and Toda were still only seventeen and fifteen respectively. Toda's 1871 eulogy *A Poblet* strikes a portentous note:

> Oh Poblet! – King without compare . . .
> You are the fecund breast, lactating peace and love
> The consolatory sad and saintly heart
> The brilliant star of science and truth.

Appropriating all the contemporary romantic conventions, Toda's lugubrious litany continues even more passionately:

> Infamous assassins . . .
> All of this to the cries of liberty and peace! . . .
> Destroying the glories of our culture,
> And violating the tombs of our heroes.
> Sowing terror everywhere and the fear of death . . .
> Oh you coward who profanes art
> If this is liberty! Then liberty stinks.

Unlike Toda, Gaudí had no literary ambitions.[2] His excitement derived directly from the broken stone: 'architecture reigns also in utter silence'.

Their intervention didn't simply amount to a folder of drawings and notes. They set about the seemingly hopeless task of the restoration itself. Overriding optimism and bravado disguised their lack of technical skill. But for Gaudí, it provided his first architectural laboratory, offering the chance to unpick 'little portions' of the buildings to see how they worked. What percentage of rubble to facing stone was used in a flying buttress? How heavy was a keystone? Gaudí was fascinated by the structural hints revealed, that the 'nudity of the beggar is seen through his rags'.[3] Poblet was like an anatomical model, its tendons and musculature open to view. As Martinell suggested, 'He imagined himself confronted with a dying person who called out for help.'[4]

After swearing to dedicate their every moment to reviving Poblet, they set to work. Gaudí was in charge of rebuilding the walls, securing the vaults, the entire reroofing and stopping up the holes opened by treasure hunters. Ribera would research the history of Poblet and its illustrious inhabitants. Toda was to catalogue the library and its archives. In between these duties, Eduardo would rush through a monograph on Poblet, and its profits would pay for all the initial phases. With a little cash the monastery would soon return to self-sufficiency. In their five-year plan the boys had even allowed for an employee, a woman who would travel daily to Montblanc to sell the fresh vegetables.

But that was just the beginning. Alongside the standard farm animals, there would also be a hundred cattle, beehives, and a centre for breeding horses. And when the visitors were taking their siesta the boys could shoot wild rabbits and hares. Somewhere near the entrance to the monastery they envisaged a gift shop which would sell reproduction coins, books on Poblet written by Toda and Ribera, homemade soap, honey, dried and fresh herbs, vinegar and a selection of stuffed birds.

Ever resourceful, Gaudí and Toda also recognised the limitations and financial implications of asceticism as a business principle. They planned more recreational pastimes like billiards at a local café which sold tobacco and the monastery's own muscatel. The café would also play a part in the sentimental education of Poblet. For, after all, it was there that the inhabitants would learn their '*hábitos de amor*'.

The excellent local spring water and the dairy would necessitate setting up an efficient supply network around the neighbouring villages. And, naturally, the young entrepreneurs recognised that there would have to be serious capital investment; so they allowed for a flour mill, an industrial olive-oil press, and a still, presumably fashioned by Gaudí's own father.

From these beginnings they hoped to expand quickly into other businesses: a sawmill, pharmacy, and a carriage to meet the train at L'Espluga de Francolí. Success was dependent on a reliable local bank. So they would set one up as well.

Stuck in the middle of their list, almost as an afterthought, was the radical suggestion of approaching the government for an annual grant.

They had catered for most eventualities, including an allowance for the inevitable seasonal fluctuations in income. In the winter, to cover the shortfall, they would harvest wood, burning it for charcoal while in the summer they would sell snow, which would be carefully stored underground.

But the biggest money spinner was going to be the 'Hospedería Poblet', and its self-catering flats. Everything had been fairly priced with reductions calculated for long-term guests. The guests would have no choice but to buy the Poblet produce. At a modest guess 50 per cent of the workers' daily wages would come back across the counter. As far as the labour force was concerned, they felt that they could start with fifteen, comprising twelve labourers, a shepherd, a cook, and a general dogsbody.

Not once, throughout numerous visits, did it occur to them

that they were actually playing with government property. But Poblet was totally abandoned. The invention of the heritage industry and the strategic restoration of national monuments was over a generation away.

The boys were full of energy and enthusiasm. Toda had catalogued more than 160 books and 70 boxes of documents. Most of the books appeared to belong to an antiquarian bookseller from Barcelona, La Antiquària, who had left them there in store. Toda borrowed a few volumes on accounting and natural history, while Gaudí opted for religious volumes, *El Camino Real de la Cruz* and a biography of Dr Francisco de Queralt by Father Miguel Conill, perhaps hoping it might throw light on his Queralt ancestry (on his mother's side).

Their plans didn't stop there. What the boys really envisaged was a model community based on contemporary cooperative principles, never contemplating a return to the monastery's original purpose. They hoped that local builders employed at Poblet would bring their families across and settle. Attracted by its beauty, artists would use the upper floors, with their north-facing lights, as studios and exhibition spaces, and as a museum of natural sciences.

Remarkably much of this came to pass. Toda wrote his book and in the 1930s, freed at last from his diplomatic duties, he headed up the Poblet restoration foundation as honorary president.

Gaudí, on the other hand, drew profounder lessons. He returned to Poblet occasionally though it never again absorbed all his attention. However, Poblet was invaluable for Gaudí. His thinking through all the implications of this utopian model proved a catalyst for the architect in the making. Henceforth, dreams of creating a whole society based on honest labour and art informed his work.

The dreams, however, also unwittingly pinpointed his weaknesses – his overriding ambition, lack of modesty and problems with finding an appropriate scale for his work. Their work on Poblet was fantasy run riot; they agreed in the *Manuscrito* that one Poblet director would commandeer a ship and sail to Asia in search of a cargo of ebony and other precious materials.

Gaudí and Toda were plagued by nightmare visions of nocturnal birds of prey escaping from tombstones and peeping out from the eye sockets of a mouldering corpse. Perhaps they had been thinking of Goya's etching *The Sleep of Reason Produces Monsters*, in which Goya himself, head in hand and slumped over a desk, is surrounded by threatening demons and creatures of the night. Later Gaudí returned to the idea when discussing the quality of Mediterranean light: 'the people of the South, because of the excess of light, neglect reason and produce monsters'.[5]

Gaudí's ideas had a habit of recurring. Considering his reputation as revolutionary and innovator, his thoughts were surprisingly circular and self-contained. His every public utterance about architecture and art was thoroughly considered. He had claimed in his 1913 interview that his ideas had 'not yet concretised' but that was patently untrue.[6] Many of his youthful ideas passed through the dust and noise of the builders' yard essentially unscathed.

Behind all the enthusiasm and the high seriousness lay another element of Gaudí's character. In a real sense, he was playing the adult, self-dramatising himself, and deliberately constructing a persona. Later he would become the dandy. And, later still, a Cistercian monk and an artist-priest.

But Poblet had performed its magic. Ribera had not disappointed his other two friends. And with dramatic finality the *Manuscrito de Poblet* announced, unequivocally, their final intentions:

> Poblet is going to be restored, so that it will never fall back in the clutches of those black vultures that once gorged themselves on the conscience of the Spanish people. Restored, it will choke off the dreadful memory of those terrible acts.[7]

In September the young men were split up. Toda went to
Madrid, Ribera went south to Andalucia, but Gaudí, now deter-
mined to be an architect, had to wait. His older brother's medical
studies had swallowed up enough of the family funds.

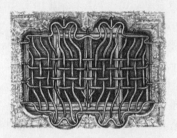

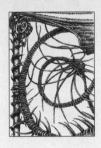

# City of Marvels

Without Barcelona, the Catalans would have lacked
a crucible in which to blend their hopes . . .
They would never have had the hammer and the anvil,
the forge – in short – of a renascent nation.

*Jaume Vicèns Vivès*[1]

THE YEAR 1867–68 WAS GAUDI'S final one in Reus and,
separated from Toda and Ribera, it must have seemed endless.
But in his isolation he held on to the dream of Poblet, not so
much for its architectural importance but as a lifeline.

He spent much more time in his father's workshop, although,
sadly, nothing he made there survives. From Francesc he learnt
all the rudimentary skills: working with fire, hammering copper
and bending iron. Although most of the work was technical and
not artistic, it was how he learnt the grammar of his craft. At
the peak of his career, Gaudí was still refining the skills passed
down to him from his father sixty years before.

That year, Gaudí completed just three of the five required
courses. Two were left for the following year. He studied mathematics, Christian doctrine and history in Reus, leaving natural

history and elementary physics for the Instituto Jaume Balmes in Barcelona. However, he scored highly in just one subject – mathematics.

Later Gaudí made a great deal of having been a bad student. Did his cavalier attitude disguise arrogant disdain or was he below average? His results tell us all we need to know. Gaudí was average but improved gradually. This slow but marked improvement highlighted a key element in his personality – tenacity.[2] Later he was able to cope with astonishing workloads.

The history of late-nineteenth-century art is the first moment where struggle becomes a virtue. Artlessness and going back to basics becomes the means of escape from academic art. Artists like Cézanne and Van Gogh are finally victorious because of, rather than despite, their apparent ineptitude. They are true to themselves. Repetition and abstractions were anathema to the young Gaudí and he had already learnt to look for solutions through the direct and practical manipulation of surfaces and shapes.

Gaudí's departure for Barcelona in the autumn of 1868 must have been bittersweet. The poignancy of the farewell at Reus railway station was magnified by the mutual understanding that the cost of his adventure had involved considerable sacrifice – Francesc had sold his lands in Riudoms.

The longer Gaudí stayed away, the more homesick he was. This chimed perfectly with the major contemporary intellectual movement, the *Renaixença*. This was the rebirth of a Catalan identity, spearheading the move towards modernity by digging through Catalonia's medieval past.

When Gaudí arrived in Barcelona in autumn 1868 he entered a seething, dynamic metropolis. Steeped in history, with the largest medieval quarter in Europe, Barcelona also embraced the indus-

trial revolution with open arms. Even today, Barcelona – despite
a deep conservatism – is a city that has learnt to cohabit with
recurrent change.

Barcelona's unsanitary conditions were legendary, and the
cramped housing conditions intolerable. Four years after Gaudí
got off the train, the English traveller Augustus Hare, described
a city at play, celebrating a fiesta:

> The life and animation of Barcelona are charming. As
> we drove into the town after leaving the solitudes of
> Montserrat, it seemed as if the whole of the gay, pleasure-
> loving population must be in the streets . . .

From there, climbing up onto the fortress hill of Montjüic, with
its breathtaking views, he surveyed the city

> across a foreground of wild aloes, which are here fre-
> quently formed into hedges, the whole white town is seen
> like a map, lying in its brown burnt-up plain, surrounded
> by mountains, the flat tops of the houses giving it a
> peculiarly eastern appearance.[3]

But this was at odds with the view of young cellist Pau Casals
in 1883. Nothing in the interim had dramatically changed,
although in many ways things had got better. Transport was more
efficient and the railway industry was flooded with speculative
capital. There was an explosion in the building trade, money was
pouring in from exports to Cuba; banks proliferated; the stock
market was bullish; and a host of limited liability companies were
rapidly formed. The boom in the textile industry along with an
unprecedented growth in shipping and steel production had filled
the city coffers with remarkable speed. But Casals wrote:

> How much evil! How much pain and travail! I would ask
> myself: Was man created to live in such squalor and
> degradation? . . . I walked the streets of Barcelona feeling
> sick and full of apprehension.[4]

There are no diaries or records of this formative period in Gaudí's life, apart from his course examination results at the Instituto, so it is impossible to tell which Barcelona he found – the filthy gutter or the relaxed, sociable, exotic paradise.

Gaudí, like Casals, was sensitive. What the *Manuscrito de Poblet* revealed was the tendency towards mawkish romanticism in Gaudí's upbringing. The young Gaudí was an idealist, a patriot but not yet a Catalan Nationalist. He had started to think about working conditions and puzzled over the structure of an ideal society.

Gaudí first moved into the Born, the predominantly labouring-class area. His first lodgings above a butcher's shop at no 12, plaça de Montcada, were probably shared with his brother Francisco.[5] The Born was at the heart of the Ribera quarter; and as the old Catalan saying had it, '*Roda el món i torna al Born*' – 'Go round the world and come back to the Born.'

By Gaudí's arrival, however, it was degenerating. Twice, in the previous 150 years, this section of the Ribera had been completely destroyed. First, in 1715 as punishment for Barcelona's support of the Hapsburgs during the War of Succession. Secondly, in the autumn of 1868 when the much-hated Ciutadella fort, serving as Barcelona's prison, was finally pulled down.

By the 1870s, despite its new cast-iron covered marketplace, the backstreets of the Born were slowly disintegrating.[6] Just one street from the sea, the Born was washed up with all sorts of human flotsam. In Eduardo Mendoza's historical novel *The City of Marvels*, Onofre Bouvila gravitates quickly to the edge of the Born.

> The sea peopled the back alleys with twisted characters
> speaking foreign tongues and producing knives, pistols,
> or clubs at the drop of a hat; the sea covered the tracks
> of evildoers who fled to the open waters, leaving behind
> bloodcurdling cries in the night and crimes unpunished.

The Born's proliferation of slums was just one of the many changes taking place in the city. On the southern side of the Rambles – Barcelona's main thoroughfare – most of the monastic foundations that lined the street had been burnt and looted in 1835. At the city's western edges, facing towards the Colserolla hills, the recently authorised project for urban expansion – the *eixample* – was also the scene of frenetic building and the marking out in the dust of its grid-pattern streets. The city's stone heart expanded in waves outwards from the Gothic quarter, each of which recorded the relative wealth of its inhabitants in their employment of ever cheaper materials: first marble and stone, then baked brick, followed by adobe, cheap whitewashed plaster, salvaged wood, and finally all the other detritus of the expanding industrial city.

Newly arrived in the metropolis, Gaudí walked wide-eyed through the Born and the Gothic quarter, to the Instituto de Jaume Balmes to study his two remaining courses – elementary physics and natural history. The light workload must have left plenty of time for the student to develop his growing interest in the city's architectural heritage. But, once again, the older Gaudí distorts and colours our view of the younger man. Looking back to his childhood, Gaudí remembered himself at sixteen as already an opinionated autodidact. His exam records show, however, that while at the Instituto, Gaudí fulfilled all requirements.

Gaudí's immediate surroundings provided him with inspiration. The narrow streets, thrown dramatically into the shade by six-storey tenement blocks, opened into sunny intimate squares. The smell, the washing lines, the brawling, lovemaking and the noise were a permanent feature of everyday life crammed into the narrow alleys of brick and flaking plaster. Maragall wrote evocatively of his childhood in the Ribera:

> When I was a boy
> I lived timidly
> in a dark street
> The walls were damp
> but the sun was joy.

The changes of temperature and mood from sun to shade were echoed by the abrupt fractures from one structure to the other in the Ribera's narrow streets. One style was absorbed or taken over, creating an almost theatrical dissonance. Visually jarring, it was also very picturesque. Behind plain façades lay a wealth of architectural detail. Each age had built on top of the last. Weathered wooden doors held together by ornamental iron hinges disguised surprisingly ornate interiors. Wrought-iron gates opened out onto modest patios. The massive granite blocks of the Roman wall became the foundations for Gothic churches. Romanesque columns were taken over to support neoclassical balconies. Everywhere you looked there was a ragbag of styles. Small doorways in otherwise plainly plastered façades opened up to reveal half-abandoned medieval merchants' palaces with elegant staircases gracefully sweeping up into the *piano nobile*. Discovery lay around each corner. A shop exterior might disguise the entrance to a twelfth-century Templar church; the tranquillity and solitude of a Romanesque cloister one minute away from the busiest thoroughfare.

Within a stone's throw of their lodgings stood Santa Maria del Mar, one of the greatest achievements in Gothic architecture and Gaudí's local parish church, known affectionately as the 'Cathedral of the Ribera'. Tarragona cathedral had impressed Gaudí with its scale, its complexity, the variety of architectural and spatial effects and its accumulation of different styles. But Santa Maria del Mar was a Gothic masterpiece.

Santa Maria del Mar was just one of many Gothic churches

to go up during the frenetic building boom of the 1320s and '30s. Unlike the Royal Chapel of Santa Àgata, across in the heart of the Gothic quarter, and the muddle of the Cathedral, both of which were built at the same time, Santa Maria del Mar was rushed up apace. The speed of its execution led to its unified power. Originally, the beach had come up to the basilica's walls. So that, facing the sands sideways on, Santa Maria del Mar took on the aspect of a marooned hulk. As with so many of Barcelona's most exciting buildings, however, it is the interior that holds the viewer spellbound. Looking down the church from the main south door the nave is supported on both sides by widely spaced columns, setting up a visual rhythm quickening in tempo as it reaches around the semicircular transparent ambulatory. Bounced back up along the opposite aisle, the eye is invited to start all over again. From there, the viewer's attention is led sweeping skywards as it follows the explosive energy and dynamic potential of the ribbed vaults that rest squarely on top of the hexagonal column caps. There is something elastic about Santa Maria's highly charged space. But there is also something contradictory. It agitates as it soothes and it remains static as the eye moves on. The solidity of the stone breathes the illusion of space. And all of these effects are produced in a building that wears its engineering openly.

How it had been built during the fourteenth century provided Gaudí with a model for a possible future union between building and belief.

Santa Maria del Mar had been built by the community. Funded by the Ribera merchants, it was assisted by skills and donations from dozens of guilds: the chandlers, tanners and codmongers. Even the unskilled stevedores hefting giant lumps of stone from the quarries at nearby Montjüic were made part of the gigantic project. Slave labourers, they bought their freedom by offering their services for this backbreaking work. Santa Maria del Mar integrated its outsiders and brought them safely into the fold. It was an exemplary study in the creation of a Christian family. It would later underpin Gaudí's architectural philosophy for the Sagrada Família.

Crossing the Born, in the lemon light of early evening, Gaudí would have often passed under its plane trees as he approached the docks and sea. Just across the Born square stood the neoclassical merchant palace, the Porxos d'en Xifré.

Named after its characteristic colonnade, the Porxos was one of the new type of large-scale luxury property developments on the recently opened section of the old sea wall. Built for Josep Xifré i Cases, the Porxos was one of the few buildings of any architectural worth built immediately after the 1835 anticlerical uprisings.

Xifré, Barcelona's richest property owner, was one of the wealthiest representatives of a new urban elite, the *indianos*, who had amassed fortunes in the colonies dealing in sugar, rum, cotton and slaves. Xifré built his trade-house palace on an exaggerated scale. The strictly symmetrical façade was given a decorative fillip through concentration on its surface embellishment.

Xifré's need to honour the memory of his father who had lost his fleet in the war against the British was paramount in his 'stylish' oversized dockside development. But this propaganda generates only the briefest interest, the enormous building is blunted by its clumsiness.

The Porxos displays the uncomplicated relationship to wealth that lies at the heart of *indiano* culture: slaves and cherubs load produce among swags of tropical fruits, while above Saturn and Uranus watch over them with their instruments of navigation – set square, compass and hourglass. Sculpted medallions of famous Catalan wayfarers intermingle with stereotypical images of natives from the Americas. In some of its decorative detail, the Porxos provided a puzzling language of symbols that was enigmatic and deliberately esoteric.[7] The industry and commerce of its day, the Porxos suggested, was as epic and heroic as the Argonauts' pursuit of the Golden Fleece. Studying in the school of architecture opposite the Porxos, Gaudí had plenty of opportunity to familiarise himself with the building's decorative ensemble and slowly dissect its possible meanings. The vivid contrast between Santa Maria del Mar and the Porxos bound his immediate surroundings – on the one hand, the extraordinarily beautiful Gothic church built by communal effort, on the other, a palace dedicated to industry based on colonial exploitation – and defined the extremes at which he might later be expected to work (one a flagship of Catalan identity, the other an attempt to rewrite the successes and failures of history).

In October 1868, Gaudí enrolled in the Instituto as an *alumno libre* – a free pupil whose attendance was only required for certain subjects – a special status that gave him more freedom than most. But it was really only a stopgap while waiting to enter the University proper the following year. After a summer back in Reus, in which his time was divided between the city, the Mas de la Calderera and his plans for Poblet, he returned late to Barcelona to enter the University's Science Faculty. At the Science Faculty he hoped to study a five-year programme of specialist subjects that included: integral and differential calculus, mechanics, geometry, chemistry, geography, physics, natural history, algebra and trigonometry. As a preparation for architecture it represented the standard education of the time.

There were good reasons for his delay. Following Prim's coup of the previous year there had been further disturbances. On 11 October 1869 he made a request in writing to the University authorities for delayed registration, citing 'political' reasons.

Gaudí and Francisco frequently changed lodgings. It was usual then, as it still is today, to leave the city for the home village during the summer. From the Plaça de Montcada in 1869 they moved nearby to carrer Espaseria 10, and in 1872 to the carrer

Montjüic de Sant Pere 16, on the fourth floor. Prior to the invention of lifts, top-floor flats were considerably more economical; attics often housed the servants as they were hotter in the summer and colder in the winter.

Gaudí enjoyed his early years in the city and proved a capable, if erratic, student. Again results delayed his final entrance into the School of Architecture by a year but his parents remained supportive – especially so, considering that his studies would in the end take ten years to complete. This was not unusual for an architect but it nevertheless represented a radical break from the craft training of his forebears where it was expected that a young man might earn a wage by sixteen. While in class Gaudí already expressed his preference for art over abstract analysis. Martinell testified:

> Abstractions bored him; he could not bear them. For Gaudí, Analytical Geometry which converted the geometric plasticity of forms into algebraic formulae – 'abstractions of abstractions' he called them – was pure torture. He himself confessed that when the professors would expound theoretical 'doctrine' he was bored, but when they stuck to concrete practical material he would listen with enthusiasm.[8]

The impression of precocious arrogance is countered by his very real enthusiasm when fired up by an inspiring teacher. Rovira Rabassa's classes in warped surfaces and perspectival study were a favourite, later underpinning Gaudí's late architectural style in the crypt at the Colonia Güell and the Sagrada Família.

Before entering the school Gaudí had to pass exams in line and life drawing and French. He was also proficient in German: in later years he was able to quote whole sections of Goethe's poems. He was only really handicapped by his lack of English. However, the most influential English writers (like Ruskin and Morris) were translated quickly into Catalan and French.

He was an avid reader. A fellow student remembered that he

would tear his books into blocks of pages which he would carry folded up in his trousers, ready to be devoured in any free minute. At times this approach got him into trouble. He borrowed a copy of *Dictionnaire raisonné de l'architecture française* by Viollet-le-Duc – the bible of the neo-medievalists – from his friend Emilio Cabanyes Rabassa. When he finally returned it, the book was covered in scribbled notes and underlinings.[9]

Gaudí was a member of the student society Niu Guerrer – the New Warriors – who decorated carnival floats and played out political and historical skits on the lives of renowned Catalan figures.[10] Life outside the university also offered a wide choice of cultural entertainment; there were debates in the Ateneu, Barcelona's preeminent cultural club; and cheap seats in the gods of the Liceu Opera House nurtured a growing love for opera and theatre.[11]

Adjusting to the pace and subtleties of social life in the city was difficult. In Barcelona too, particularly during the second half of the nineteenth century, a rigid class system (based in admiration on the English model) developed.[12] With spare income from part-time work, Gaudí quickly developed the reputation of a dandy, fastidious and perfectly manicured, satisfied only by the very best. Kid gloves came from Esteban Comella's shop on carrer Avinyó. A special wooden hat mould was held at Arnau's on the calle Conde de Asalto* for made-to-measure trilbys, summer straw boaters and Gaudí's preferred black silk top hats. Rumour has it that Gaudí was so effete that he required his brother Francesc to wear in his shoes in order to avoid bunions, blisters and corns. But this clashes with the Gaudí who was fond of cross-city strolls, prepared to walk hour after hour across rocky terrain in pursuit of architectural or archaeological quarry. One likely explanation is that this Proustian pose covered up the Gaudí brothers' necessity to share clothes and for the younger to have to make do with the older's castoffs.

* Calle Conde de Asalto is now named carrer Nou de la Rambla.

Another puzzle that sits right at the heart of Gaudí's personality is whether he was anticlerical in his youth. Sources suggest that he was a key member of a riotous *tertulia* – an informal debating group that entertained itself by insulting priests and mocking religious processions – based at the infamous Café Pelayo. It seems that most of the stories relating to Gaudí's involvement with the Pelayo set come back to the same source – that 'bilious, and infuriating scandal-monger', his teacher and onetime colleague – Domènech i Muntaner.[13] High spirits and student rebellion is a common enough experience, as is the centuries-old licence to satirise and mock the clergy during carnival. If, however, his anticlericalism was more deep-seated it was hardly new. In Goya's savagely satirical *Caprichos*, image after image cuts through the clerical fat to reveal the vainglorious church fathers as hypocritical, cruel, parasitic and overwhelmingly greedy.

In the *Manuscrito de Poblet*, Toda and Gaudí spoke out against the 'ominous power of the black vultures'. But this suggests anticlerical leanings only if we accept the 'black vultures' to be priests – they could just as easily be read as the desecrators of the tombs and monasteries.[14] Nevertheless, a contemporary couplet, in common use, read

> We have torn down the throne, now on to the priests
> Who devour the nation like the strangest of beasts.

Anticlerical views were a well-worn nineteenth-century path in which initial rejection of the Catholic faith presaged the sudden spiritual and religious volte-face. Casanelles described Gaudí at this time as

> both sanguine and epicurean, a lover of good food, frequenter of drawing rooms ... anticlerical, indifferent towards religion and if not an out-and-out atheist, at least tinged with atheism.[15]

On 24 October 1874, aged twenty-two, having successfully completed the foundation exams, Gaudí finally enrolled officially at the architectural school. Its success is borne out by the large number of Barcelona-trained architects whose names have come down to posterity.[16] As it was a new school, teaching practice had yet to calcify into boring routine. Studies were shared between teacher and pupil and often spilt over into actual commissions. This stimulating atmosphere was boosted further by the closeness in age between student and professor – Domènech was just two years older than many of his students.

Gaudí's passage through was slowed by his unwillingness to flatter or slavishly copy his teachers' style. With characteristic scorn, he later dismissed teaching as nothing more than discipline.[17] Passing on his experience later to his young assistant Rubió i Bellver, he cynically suggested that he would do well to imitate his teacher's favoured neoclassical forms for his final exams. Rubió then sailed easily through.

Gaudí arrived at architectural school at a fortuitous moment when photography had made it possible, for the first time, to have easy access to the world's architectural heritage. And Gaudí was an obsessive habitué of the University's architectural library.

He found it impossible to exercise his 'capacity for self-control'.[18] In the library he wondered over the classical canon illustrated in Luigi Canina's *L'Architettura Romana: Descrizione Dei Monumenti*, Rome 1842.[19] But more importantly he could also browse through dangerously decadent architectural aberrations from far away. In Pascal Cost's *Architecture Arabe ou Monuments de Kaire*, Paris 1839, or Prisse d'Avennes' *L'Art Arabe d'après les Monuments de Kaire*, Paris 1877, he could admire the exotic and decorative qualities of Islamic architecture.[20] French publishers had pioneered exotic architectural photography. The effect of the explosion of architectural publications in the 1870s and 1880s on European taste, at the height of colonial adventure, was powerful.

The architectural school had also acquired a set of original photographs of Indian and Egyptian monuments which Gaudí found an enchanting 'spiritual feast'. There were also the latest daguerreotype reproductions of Mayan ruins; Assyrian and Persian architectural masterpieces like Darius and Xerxes' Hall of a Hundred Columns at Persepolis; Indian stupas and Cambodian temples, Chinese and Japanese monuments. But what Gaudí found increasingly interesting were the more modest everyday structures. He pored over photos and drawings of the makeshift architecture of clay dwellings from the Upper Nile; those curious clay pigeon lofts, drawn up to a point like inverted ice cream cones. Brought up on tales of the Crusades and the Spanish *reconquista*, he was fascinated by the fort construction used in Melilla, part of Spanish Morocco, which used a curiously elongated egg-shaped arch that he developed into his hallmark catenary arch. He also admired the sculptural quality of Moroccan mud huts, the fortified villages of the higher Atlas mountains and the strange dwellings carved into the rocks in eastern Turkey at Cappadocia and in Petra.

The trade exhibitions that mushroomed across Europe after the 1851 Great Exhibition at Crystal Palace led to a demand for increasingly exotic architecture.[21] But the theatrical settings, photographs and prints all shared a lack of context. A two-dimensional photograph cannot portray a sense of geographical reality, or comprehend how a Saharan clay dwelling, for example, had been blended into its setting by its use of local material. Freed from the need to consider geographical 'appropriateness', visual information could be easily cannibalised.

No previous generation had been able to gorge itself on such a feast of various styles. Cast adrift amongst this ocean of images, Gaudí needed something solid. His teachers provided him with a practical and intellectual structure. He studied the resistance of materials, stress analysis, perspective drawing, mechanics, topography and sketching. But it was not enough. Gaudí sought answers elsewhere in the University's other faculties by attending

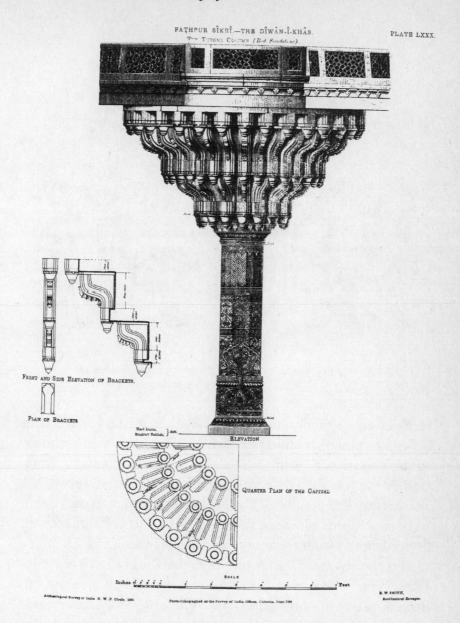

FATHPUR SÎKRÎ.—THE DÎWÂN-Î-KHÂS.
The Throne Column (*Red Sandstone*).

PLATE LXXX.

Front and Side Elevation of Brackets.

Plan of Brackets

Elevation

Quarter Plan of the Capital

Scale

Inches        Feet

Archæological Survey of India N. W. P. Circle, 1892.

Photo-lithographed at the Survey of India Offices, Calcutta, June 1894.

E. W. SMITH,
*Architectural Surveyor.*

An eccentric column from Fathpur Sîkrî, India.
Illustrations like this fuelled the late-nineteenth-century
European orgy of exotic and eclectic styles.

37

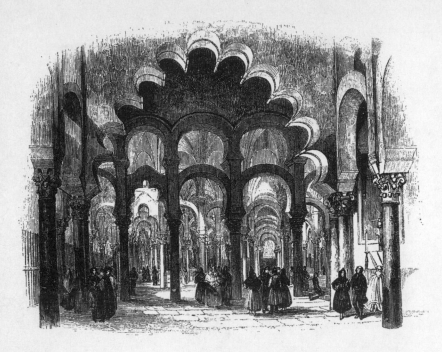

A romantic nineteenth-century print of the interior of
Cordoba's Great Mosque.

lectures on aesthetics and philosophy.[22] Spain was awash with
different cultural traditions, which still lived on in its architecture: Phoenician, Roman, Greek, Visigothic, Celtic, Arab,
Berber and Jewish. These had become completely absorbed into
the culture. For a Catalan, Castilian or Andalusian, the adoption
of Islamic motifs and decorative designs was no mere affectation.

But before Gaudí could indulge himself in new Spanish architecture, he absorbed the lessons of Pugin, Ruskin and Viollet-le-
Duc. What these three gave him was the critical apparatus to
make sense of all this information. Viollet-le-Duc (the restorer
of Notre Dame), perhaps even more than Ruskin and Pugin,
had the capacity for a radical architectural analysis that Gaudí
found particularly stimulating.

Viollet-le-Duc had been reviled at first. Attempting to inspire

the unappreciative audience at the École des Beaux Arts, he had
been heckled. His argument spoke strongly to Gaudí:

> Are not all possible forms of expression worn out, and
> all compositions already used? No, gentlemen, the
> human soul is still the same, and still capable of finding
> new expression for its thoughts and feelings. But to pos-
> sess this creative power, there must be an inner awareness
> of it, of its location, and of the efforts required to bring
> it to life. We must find this creativity through an accurate
> knowledge of the works of our ancestors. Not that such
> knowledge must lead us to imitate them slavishly, but
> rather it will reveal and make available all the secret skills
> of our predecessors. No doubt the very multiplicity of
> these skills makes their use today difficult. But when you
> discover these secrets lying behind the finest works in
> the bosom of the highest and most beautiful civilisations,
> you quickly recognise that all these secrets can be reduced
> to just a few principles, and that as a result of the sort
> of fermentation initiated when they are combined, new
> can and must appear unceasingly.[23]

Viollet insisted that all masterpieces of the past must be analysed
and reduced to an argument. And then the building should be
measured against its ability to confront its particular problems.
A good example was Gothic architecture's use of the flying buttress as a support. Were the buttresses necessary? Or were the
masons limited by a lack of understanding of stresses? This was
a revelatory approach for dealing with the sheer weight of the
history of architecture. A building was an object under scrutiny
in a laboratory. Gaudí's later genius lay in his analysis of the
strengths and weaknesses not just of masterpieces but of the
everyday structures of the factory, stable block and home. Thus
released from stylistic snobbery, Gaudí remained effectively
unhampered by hierarchies of traditional taste.

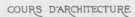

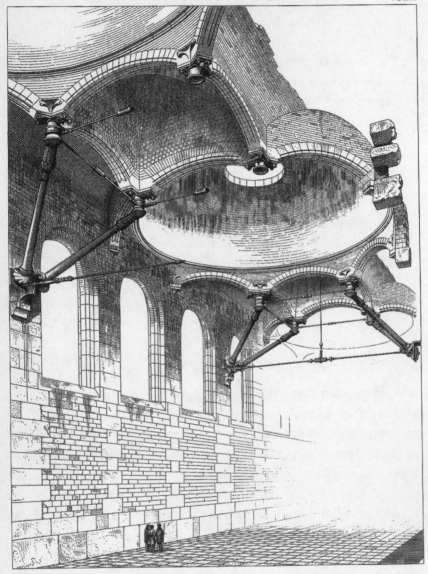

Viollet-le-Duc's illustration in *Cours d'Architecture* showing his novel approach to structural analysis.

It was not just Viollet's practical philosophy that proved inspirational, it was also the way that he guided the attentive student through the architectural labyrinth. Though an architect of merit, Viollet's real genius lay in deconstruction. This brought the older forms of architecture back to life, so that they could be used in new contexts, throwing light on old problems.[24]

In France and England the contemporary architectural debate raged over the appropriateness of national styles, eclecticism and the clear superiority of certain classical models. Viollet's teacher, Le Grand Durand, promoted an open attitude. And by the 1860s France's adoption of Renaissance models and 'rationalist' approach to city planning had put France at the artistic and architectural forefront.

In England, until the 1860s, there was no such self-confidence, but rather a deep-seated feeling of inferiority to French design. But growing debate over the use of Renaissance or Gothic forms forced a new approach. Ruskin's *The Seven Lamps of Architecture* (1849) and *The Stones of Venice* (1851–53) acted as catalysts. The eventual victory of the Gothic revivalists divided the debate between the 'softs' and the 'hards'. The 'softs' were interested in outward appearance and style, while the 'hards' expended their energy on structural analysis, engineering and experimentation – the mechanics of building. Gaudí was both.[25]

Spain was not peripheral to the late-nineteenth-century architectural debate. And with its unique Gothic architecture, Catalonia could just as well see itself as a southern territory of France as a northern outpost of Moorish Spain.[26]

The writings of Viollet, Ruskin and Morris had already prepared the ground. Gaudí built on their solid foundations. He had perhaps, as Sir Kenneth Clarke said of Ruskin, a tendency to 'rely on holy writ to save him further thought'. But even as a student Gaudí was developing a ruthless selectivity about the way he worked, jettisoning everything extraneous.

It is striking just how much Gaudí and Viollet had in common.

Flaubert's *Dictionnaire des idées reçues* (1881) had dismissed architects:

> Architects: all idiots. Always forgetting the staircase.

But Viollet had made architecture a noble profession: championing the medieval guild while legitimising Islamic art. Viollet and Gaudí shared the same uncompromising character. Viollet was deeply anti-establishment, passionate and anticlerical, but profoundly analytical and rigorous. He preferred to be thought of, like Gaudí, as a doer not a thinker. He was happiest when in his own company or 'at ease only with his pupils', and his loyal craftsmen. Gaudí later talked affectionately of Berenguer as his irreplaceable right arm and highly praised his sculptor Matamala.

Gaudí's architectural training was rounded out by site visits and study trips. The director of the architectural school, Elías Rogent, took his keenest students to look at monuments and practise what Viollet had preached.[27] One such visit was to see Viollet's restoration of medieval Carcassonne. This trip was just a day visit but (according to Ràfols) Gaudí was so serious that local villagers thought they were dealing with Viollet himself and wished to honour him.[28] Here, so often, Gaudí's personality had proved a fertile ground for myths. Here, the mistake takes on symbolic resonance, a Freudian slip. However, according to one witness, 'he found the restoration work of the brilliant French architect too scenographic, in spite of the rigorous archaeological criteria employed'.[29]

Another myth about Gaudí's Carcassonne trip involves his first love. As Maragall's thinly disguised protagonist slumps into his sofa he relates his sad tale.

> Three years ago I was in love with a young girl who had spent a fortnight lodging with some family friends. It was a short visit as she was a foreigner. But, I fell madly in love with her and visited her every moment I could.

I think she knew my true feelings for her because she was so kind to me in all of our conversations. I was swept away by her but I soon found out that in her home country she was already promised to another. Finally, the day of her departure arrived but I didn't have the heart to say goodbye and stayed at home in a state of abject despair. I never heard anymore about her except that she had married in her home town as expected. But, even though three years have passed I still see her every waking moment – there in front of my eyes.[30]

The story as told by Maragall in *Calaverada* is a mawkish one.[31] His images are derived from the language of courtly love, of the hidden garden – the *hortus conclusus* – a perfect sanctuary to protect the purity of the unattainable maiden dressed all in shimmering white. However, the romantic clichés, trotted out one after the other, do give some indication as to the mores and the boundaries of social intercourse set between the sexes during Gaudí's day.

Many have accepted the charge, put about by the architect himself later in life, that he was never more than a mediocre draftsman. But this was false modesty. Gaudí insisted on the value of working from models or improvising on the building site itself: but he was much more accomplished than has been believed. By relegating drawing to a secondary status, he cleverly turned his early misfortune to advantage. For drawing is painful for the arthritic.

One of the finest examples of Gaudí's student work is an elaborate student project for a cemetery gate. The drawing had a strange genesis. It concluded the final major project of the academic year 1874–75, but in June 1875, according to Joan Bergós Massó, Gaudí was requested to leave the exam hall for failing to complete it in the required manner. For Gaudí had insisted on starting his drawing with the sketch of a funeral cortège, an avenue of cypresses and weeping mourners – all set under a brooding sky. It was a fine piece of theatre and a way for Gaudí slowly to set the scene. He was incapable of imagining any other way to begin and it pinpoints a paradox that would become a constant in his creative process – never were flights of fancy so painstakingly prepared.[32]

Conforming to the examination committee's strictures, Gaudí produced a piece of work deemed outstanding. As Arleen Pabon-Charneco presciently said,

> Gaudí had started to conceive architecture not as an object isolated in the ground, but as *parlante*, capable of mystic and spiritual interaction with the beholder, through its forms and grandiose scale. This last door of life conveys all the majesty of a triumphal arch and the solemnity of death.[33]

Perhaps Gaudí's tentative beginnings and struggle to create atmosphere were a subterfuge. But his search for emotional reality and symbolic meaning in his drawing was genuine enough. Using the current neomedieval style he had fleshed out the basic structure with ornamental additions. Ruskin had already lectured on the use of appropriate ornament, and how to obey its 'natural' hierarchy:

> Imitated flowers are nobler than imitated stones, imitated animals than flowers; imitated human form of all animal forms the noblest.

But Gaudí had reached beyond Ruskin to define architectural and sociohistorical function. At just twenty-three, Gaudí had created a monument of deep symbolic weight. And Gaudí had gone to the book of Revelation to seek out the drama for his first-year student piece.[34] An almost literal reinterpretation of biblical texts and Catholic liturgy would remain forever central to his working method.

> Behold, a door was opened in heaven: and the first voice which I heard was as it were of a trumpet talking with me; which said, Come up hither, and I will shew thee things which must be hereafter.

Gaudí's cemetery gate was the exit of all exits, the Final Judgment which promised a new beginning. At the apex of the gate's shallow pitched roof sat God enthroned in majesty. Below him stood the praying figure of Christ surrounded by the four apocalyptic beasts. Below were the 'four and twenty elders sitting clothed in white raiment; and they had on their heads crowns of gold'. These symbolised the summation of the twelve Old Testament patriarchs and the twelve apostles of the New. Beneath them were those 'which came out of great tribulation, and have washed their robes, and made them white in the blood of the Lamb'. The hinge stones were decorated with the first and last letters of the Greek alphabet:

> I am Alpha and Omega, the beginning and the end, the first and the last. Blessed are they that do his commandments, that they may have right to the tree of life, and may enter in through the gates into the city. For without are dogs, and sorcerers, and whoremongers, and murderers, and idolators, and whosoever loveth and maketh a lie.

Gaudí had chosen the most militant book in the Bible. It was a curious choice for a twenty-three-year-old architectural student to make, but Revelation's language and images were to recur throughout Gaudí's work.

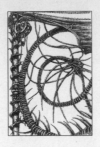

# The Architectural Apprentice

'Must work hard to overcome the difficulties'
*Antoni Gaudí, Diary entry, 25 November 1876*

FROM ALMOST HIS FIRST DAY at the architectural school, Gaudí was an apprentice. For him it was imperative. He had no protectors and family friends. Gaudí was dependent purely on his talent and growing reputation.

Students were required from the very start of their course to submit detailed, finished projects. In 1874 he completed drawings for an ornamental candelabrum, a water tower, and the cemetery gate. This dry theory was balanced by fieldwork: Gaudí was permitted to join a team given a brief of a topographical survey of the riera de Malla, the proposed site for a major school building.

For students who failed to pass specific exams in June there was always an opportunity to retake in September. In June 1875, Gaudí made his first such request. But this was due to being served his military conscription papers and his acceptance into the infantry reserves in February 1975. This was a difficult time for Spain – and a potentially dangerous time to join the army.

General Pavia's coup and the continuing third Carlist War had made the country's situation very unstable. This was finally resolved in July 1876 with the pretender Carlos VII's exile to France, and the Restoration was firmly in place. For his small part in the victory, as an active serviceman, Gaudí was awarded the honour *Benemérito de Patria*, but there are no records of action, or indeed any letters to family and friends surviving. And frustratingly, it had disrupted his academic year, forcing him to stall his art theory exams, 'due to being completely tied up in the military service'.[1]

The academic year of 1876–77 was to prove even more taxing. The year's two major projects were designing a patio for the local government offices and a Spanish pavilion for the Philadelphia Centennial exhibition. Drawn in a style described as 'Gustave Moreau-[meets]-Viollet-le-Duc', the neo-Grecian detailing, ornamentation and arabesques across the surface reflected Gaudí's desire to satisfy his teachers – by mimicking their style. This relaxed neoclassicism, concentrating on surface texture, was standard for its day. An elaborate and painstakingly executed ornamental frieze for the Diputación's dome also showed little individuality. Gaudí had realised from bitter experience that innovation was rarely rewarded by teachers, so he bided his time.

In other coursework, however, Gaudí was more able to show off his peculiar gifts. Josep Fontserè i Mestre had recently been put in charge of designing the new Cuitadella Park, General Prim's gift to the Barcelonese. Gaudí, his part-time assistant, was requested to work out the complex hydrological calculations for the reservoir needed to feed the giant ornamental fountain and its boating lake. His work was so accurate that when the school's professor of resistance of materials, Joan Torras Guardiola, double-checked his calculations he immediately passed him for the relevant course, despite the fact that Gaudí had never attended a single class. Gaudí was described as gregarious, popular and hard-working. His friends included Cristóbal

Cascante i Colom, Emilio Cabanyes Rabassa and two years their senior, Camil Oliveras i Gensana.

The year 1876 brought tragedy – the death of Gaudí's brother Francesc. At only twenty-five he had not even started his promising medical career. Just two months later, on 6 September, Francesc was followed to the grave by his grieving mother. These bereavements could only be assimilated slowly and in Gaudí's own particular way. Later he would talk of this period with an all-enveloping depression. But with their deaths fresh in his mind Gaudí immersed himself in work. He was now the only son and responsible for the family fortunes.

Significantly, just two months later Gaudí started a diary. This is the only brief day-to-day record we have of Gaudí's life. Started on 21 November 1876 its final entry was just two months later. It totalled little more than a thousand words. 'Must work hard to overcome the difficulties', he wrote on 25 November, having worked three and a half hours for Villar on a shrine for the Virgin of Montserrat, and a further two and a half hours on a holiday chalet for the architect-teacher Leandro Serrallach. The invocation probably referred specifically to the architectural problems at hand. But it could also stand for his general frame of mind. Although the diary was unsentimental, it gives the impression of someone running hard to stay ahead of his emotions.

On 19 October Gaudí added to his substantial workload, entering a competition for which he designed a castellated lakeside pavilion with a landing jetty. By chance these drawings survived the 1936 fire, having been lent with much of his other schoolwork for an exhibition at the school. Finely detailed and coloured with a delicate watercolour wash they had clearly taken a long time. By the end of November, Gaudí was working most days for sometimes as many as three or four different architectural practices, simultaneously studying folios of photos of Spain's best-known monuments and designing for the industrial machinery firm of Padrós y Borrás. Juggling his studies with his architectural work he occasionally fell sick. Entries read: Villar 2 hours. Villar 1 hour. Fontserè 3 hours. Serrallach 1 hour, etc. etc. Only on rest days, Christmas Day and Boxing Day, did he fail to work, and it was perhaps with a mixture of frustration and relief that on two other days he pointedly scribbled,

> Absolutely Nothing . . .
> Nothing, did nothing all day!

Mourning his family, he wrote a brief meditation on the '*Casa Pairal*' – an idealised study of the Catalan family home.

> The house is the small nation of the family. One's own home is his native country: a rented home is the country of emigration; thus to own his own home is every man's dream. One cannot imagine his own home without family; only a rented house can be imagined in that manner. The family home has been given the name *casa pairal*. On hearing this name, who does not recall some beautiful place in the country or in the city?

However, his new family soon emerged – in the companionship of the workshop.

On 15 March 1878, Gaudí officially qualified as an architect, which enabled him to join the Col.legi de Arquitectes de Cataluña – the official body that regulated architectural practice, offered legal advice, established a pricing policy, registered projects and provided a library and club.

Gaudí's graduation, however, had not passed by without incident. His attendance at the school had been sporadic. His approach to assignments had often bent the rules. On his Hospital's project, for instance, he researched other buildings so closely – the Boston Free in Massachusetts, the Lariboisière in Paris and Blackburn Hospital – that he ran out of time. The night before the deadline he took his project home, drawing the

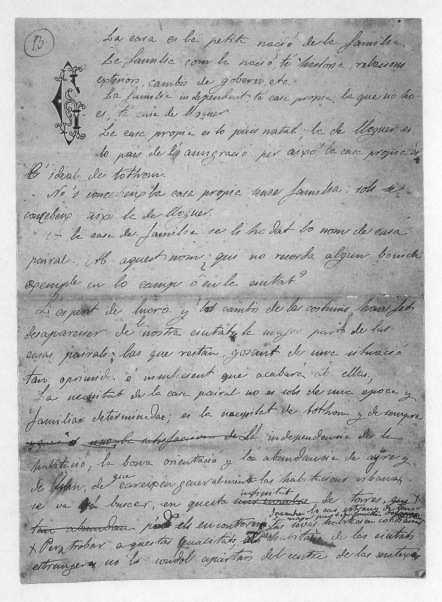

Page from Gaudí's 1878 Reus manuscript in which he describes his ideal image of the *Casa Pairal*.

missing façade in one rushed sitting. Rogent, the school director, then invited all his classmates to his home, informing them they had passed – excepting, of course, Gaudí. Agreeing finally to a compromise, Gaudí was permitted to submit a design for a monumental fountain instead.

Rogent and his fellow professors had noted Gaudí's talent throughout the course. But his sometimes belligerent manner had not always won him friends. On his graduating (passing by a majority vote rather than unanimously), Rogent pronounced finally, 'Gentlemen, we are here today either in the presence of a genius or a madman!' Gaudí responded sardonically, 'So now it appears I'm an architect.'

But who had voted against him? Villar, Serrallach, Fontseré, Vilaseca, Font, Domènech i Muntaner or Rogent? All had worked with him. The most likely was Domènech, who was already beginning to see Gaudí as a potential rival.

If 1878 was a key year in Gaudí's burgeoning career it was equally significant for Domènech. Shadowing each other's careers, and often crossing paths, Domènech was a civic-minded Renaissance architect who rapidly transformed himself into an institution. An extraordinary polymath and organisational genius, Domènech was not just an architect but publisher, book designer, author, lecturer, distinguished politician and finally director of the Barcelona School of Architecture.[2]

It was Domènech's groundbreaking essay of 1878, 'In Search of a National Architecture', that put him at the centre of the Catalan architectural debate.[3] Like Viollet-le-Duc and Gottfried Semper before him Domènech argued for a stripping away of stale academic conventions, replacing them with a more functional, rational approach. 'Let us subject decorative forms to the principles of structure, as the classic periods did,' he argued forcefully.

In just eleven pages, Domènech systematically analysed several architectural styles, subsequently throwing each out as inappropriate for Catalonia. Spain's architectural treasury came from the Islamic south and the Romanesque and Gothic north. All else was extraneous, but Domènech's clever twist was stressing a building's structural rationale above all, thus freeing the national style from the provincial. This proved vitally important for the development of the *modernista* style. Domènech managed to integrate architecture into the whole Catalan cultural debate known as the *Renaixença*. Paradoxically, it would fall to Gaudí, more than any other architect, to illustrate Domènech's thesis through his buildings and unique Catalan style.

The *Renaixença* put forward a specific Catalan response to Romanticism, central to much of Gaudí's thinking. The role of religion and Catalan nationalism was very important but its driving purpose was the complete re-establishment of the Catalan language. The birth of this linguistic nationalism dates back to the publication of Aribau's poem *La Pàtria* in 1833, in which he declaims fervently:

> Death to the ingrate, who hears upon his lip
> In foreign land, his native tongue, yet does not weep,
> Or, when he thinks of home, unmoved by deep desire,
> Does not pluck from the wall his ancestor's own lyre.

And others quickly rose to his challenge. In 1841, Joaquim Rubió i Ors published his *Lo Gayter de Llobregat* (The Bagpiper of Llobregat) in which he demanded that Catalan be unshackled from the dominant Castilian tongue and eternally protected from mongrelisation.

The *Renaixença* was not merely a linguistic phenomenon. It also found its outlet in a growing political movement that argued for a separate Catalan identity and protectionist tariffs to nurture Catalonia's rapidly expanding industrial base. It was here that the frustrations harboured against Madrid were most forcefully aired.

Joan Güell i Ferrer, a leading Catalan businessman and father of Gaudí's future patron Eusebi Güell, was a leading voice in the Catalan protectionist movement. His tone was unforgiving:

People who rely on hard work, intelligently managed, and on thrift, create capital and increase with wealth. Indolent, lazy people, who put their faith only in what others' work produces, or in liquid wealth or in the gold of other nations, such people get their just deserts in the form of poverty, decline and ruin.[4]

What the *Renaixença* had achieved, beyond a magnificent flowering of the arts, was a deliberate cataloguing of the specific attributes of the authentic Catalan character: namely, thrift, honesty, hard work, loyalty, love of family, landscape and home. But the *Renaixença* also had a deeply religious strain. Laymen like Barcelona University's professor of literature Manuel Milà i Fontanals lectured to a whole generation about true Catalan identity. 'The Literary Whale', as he was known, pontificated on the value above everything else of tradition. Gaudí, with many hundred others, sat at his feet to hear him talk of Schiller, the Romantics, the Nazarenes and Rome and quote from half-forgotten Catalan folk songs.

Within the Catalan Church, Bishop Morgades promoted a traditionalist approach. Leading an energetic revival, Morgades secured backing for hugely symbolic renovation works such as those at Santa Maria de Ripoll, which like Poblet was ransacked in 1935. For Morgades and his followers Josep Torras i Bages and Jaume Collell the real Catalan identity was found in peasant piety. This was, of course, a piety that recognised old privileges and feudal laws favouring the Church and the status quo. It was this piety that Gaudí himself would later come to represent.

The most symbolically powerful manifestation of the *Renaixença*, however, and one that Gaudí took an immense interest in, was the reinstatement of the ancient national poetry contest, the *Jocs Florals*. Catalan poets read out hymns, odes and epics that celebrated the beauty of their language and land in Catalan. The prizes awarded were: first, a rose for a poem on any subject;

second, the *eglantina d'or* – a rose made of gold awarded for a
poem on Catalan customs and its history; and, third, a gold and
silver violet for a religious or morally uplifting piece. The natural
rose was apt because nothing fashioned by man could aspire to
the beauty of Catalan nature and God's handiwork. The ultimate
goal was to win all three prizes and become a Catalan legend,
the *Mester de Gay Saber*. One of the few to win this was Jacint
Verdaguer in 1877, during Gaudí's last year at the School of
Architecture, with his monumental *L'Atlàntida*.

Between 1878 and 1880, under the shadow of the *Renaixença*,
Gaudí laid the foundations for his subsequent career. Early successes in business were, however, once again marred by personal
tragedy with the death of his elder sister Rosa in 1879, leaving
him the only child.

Some of Gaudí's first designs, as an official architect, were for
himself. A simple design for a professional visiting card and a
working desk, they were of great symbolic importance. For like
the medieval journeyman Gaudí fashioned the tools of his trade.
Stylistically too, his designs were of their moment. The flourish
and flowery tail applied to the whiplash lettering on his buff-
coloured card was Art Nouveau. His desk had the feel of William
Morris. Elaborately decorated, it was also designed to be practical.

Gaudí had spent hours puzzling over the place of ornament in both architecture and design. In an unpublished essay,
'Ornamentation', he wrote:

> has been, is, and will be polychrome. Nature does not
> present us with any object in monochrome, totally uni-
> form with respect to colour – not in vegetation, not in
> geology, not in topography, not in the animal kingdom.

Always the contrast of colour is more or less lively, and for this reason we must colour wholly or in part every architectural element.

The desk was ideal to test out his evolving theories on. Its heavy coffin form resting on four tapered legs, joined by a kicking plate, presented a cleverly wrought balance between the desk's function and form. Its rounded book ends were smooth. Set against the wood, the young architect applied metal decoration which gathered together a 'topographic kingdom'. Snakes, birds of prey, a squirrel and a lizard, a praying mantis, a cockerel, butterflies and bees swarmed through the trailing ivy and sprigs of bay. This was Gaudí's 'Great Book of Nature' – but domesticated and brought safely indoors.

The desk was important for other reasons too. It was constructed at Eudaldo Puntí's workshop on the carrer Cendra. And while visiting the workshop one day Gaudí was introduced to the fantastically wealthy Don Eusebi Güell. The two men immediately became friends. This quickly developed into one of the most extraordinary relationships ever between artist and patron. At their first meeting, Gaudí had completed only four projects: his desk; a cast-iron flower stall for Enrique Girossi designed for mass production but never completed due to Girossi's bankruptcy; a glass display case for the 1878 Paris Exposition for the Barcelona glove manufacturers Comella; drawings for a set of cast-iron lampposts.

The monumental lampposts, which are still in the Plaça Reial today, constitute the beginning of any serious tour of Gaudí's work because they were his first official commission. But he was the second choice: only being offered the job after the death of Jaume Serra y Gilbert, through, according to Bassegoda, Martorell's active intervention.[5] After four months Gaudí submitted illustrations drawn up to a 1:10 scale. The model mock-up for the lampposts was also entrusted to Puntí.

The six-armed candelabrum, placed on a marble support and crowned with Mercury's helmet, symbol of Barcelona's booming commerce, was reminiscent of the Porxos d'en Xifré, perhaps deliberately so, as it was planned to install some of the lampposts in front of it. For less imposing spaces Gaudí provided a pared down triple-armed version. Both were received with both critical and public approval.

Gaudí's payment, however, became a long drawn-out battle. He was offered a mere 336 pesetas. By splitting the bill into constituent parts he had asked for 2,300 pesetas, almost seven times that amount. The following March, the city's chief municipal architect, Rovira y Trías, scaled it down to 850 pesetas. In April, an unsatisfied Gaudí accepted the lower amount. But it proved an expensive 514 pesetas as Gaudí never received another municipal commission in Barcelona.

Having learnt from this experience, Gaudí was offered his next commission by Martorell – designing furniture for the wealthy Marquès de Comillas. Comillas was intent upon creating a whole new architectural language to represent his astonishing success. Ignoring precedent, he planned to transform his birthplace, the village of Comillas, into a showcase for Barcelona's *modernista* architects. Comillas asked Martinell to build the Palacio Sobrellano, with a Pantheon-chapel alongside and a Jesuit seminary on the facing hill. Martinell's design team included Cascante and Oliveras. And Gaudí was invited, at Eusebi Güell's suggestion, to design some furniture for the chapel. Gaudí's desk at Puntí's could have convinced Güell of Gaudí's aptitude for the job. Like all High Victorian religious furniture, Gaudí's prayer stool, benches and throne are both decorous and overrefined. Extra carving is squeezed in everywhere. Classical columns abound but fiddly detailing wins the day: the overmastering impression is of the Marquès' wealth.

Gaudí worked for the Comillas branch of the family twice more. In the summer of 1881, he designed a gazebo in the shape of a turban as a setting for amateur theatricals based on the *Thousand and One Nights* for a royal visit.[6] Covered in mosaics and a constellation of metal spikes and mobiles that supported bells and chimes, the gazebo repaid all his studies in Orientalism. In its centre Gaudí placed a glass table on a fine-weave Turkish rug. The day before Alfonso XII's visit a workman tripped on the rug and his head smashed through the glass table surface. While Gaudí was happy that no one had been seriously hurt, Matamala suggested that he immediately rush back to Barcelona to get a replacement. The king's visit was a no-expense-spared success. Two hundred train carriages had wound slowly across Spain loaded with luxurious items to ensure his comfort.

Gaudí's next commission for a worker's cooperative in Mataró was a complete contrast. Gaudí worked hard for his success. There were many failures along the way. A small theatre in Sant Gervasi de Cassoles, long since disappeared, made no impact at all on the architectural scene. In 1880 he entered a competition for the Casino in San Sebastian but failed. A project for providing lighting for Barcelona's sea wall floundered. So too had a retable altarpiece for San Fèlix de Alella. A planned country estate, the Can Rosell de la Llena in Gelida, never got off the drawing board. His famous drawing of a new façade for Barcelona's Gothic cathedral, a competition sponsored by the multi-millionaire Manuel Girona, on which Gaudí, Domènech and Martorell collaborated, got no further than the presentation drawing.

These are only a few of the failed projects that have come to light. There may have been many more. Timoteo Padrós, a friend of Gaudí's, once asked him to come up with some ideas for a textile factory in Madrid. Gaudí responded tetchily, 'As you know very well, I live by my work and cannot dedicate myself to projects that are vague and exploratory, and I am sure that you yourself would not want me to give up the certain for the uncertain.'

Gaudí met Salvador Pagès i Anglada, the director of the Sociedad Cooperativa Obrera Mataronesa, at the chess tables of the Ateneu whilst still a student.[7] The poet Joacquim Bartrina, Gaudí's old classmate, was also a friend, supporter and spokesman of Pagès. One of the first cooperatives in Spain, the Mataronesa, just fifteen kilometres north of Barcelona, had taken a pioneering approach that could have seriously threatened the oligarchy of Barcelona's leading textile families. In the optimistic late 1870s, an industrial utopia still seemed achievable. Intent on expansion, Pagès had asked Gaudí and his friend Emilio Cabañes for plans for workers' housing, an industrial bleaching hall and a company logo. Gaudí and Cabañes' experiments in creating a corporate identity were revolutionary enough. Every aspect of the Cooperativa's image from stationery to workers' housing was clearly thought out.[8] Few of the buildings planned were completed. The most interesting building, however, was the industrial shed, a perfect demonstration of mechanical thrusts. A dozen parabolic arches, formed from a triple laminate of thin planks bolted together, swept across the space leaving the central hall airy and free. The parabolic arch evenly distributes its load along its full length. It was a simple, cheap solution. Both utilitarian and egalitarian it was the perfect spatial metaphor for the Sociedad's cooperative working philosophy.

Pagès' industrial utopia has a disarming innocence. The company logo depicted the hive of industry; bees working away harmoniously at the spinning textile looms.

Gaudí's slogans, spelling out the company philosophy, were painted on the walls. 'Do you wish to be an intelligent man? Be kind!' read one. 'Comrade, be sound, practise kindness!' another, and 'Nothing is greater than fraternity', another. Not all Gaudí's mottos were couched in the language of brotherhood and love, however. A dynamic business sometimes needs to release ruder energies. One motto warned the workforce against fake civility. 'Too much courtesy is proof of a false education.' This one

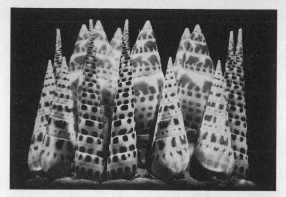

ABOVE A collection of
Mediterranean shells grouped
to approximate a Gaudí
building – 'The Great Book of
Nature'.

RIGHT Study of Alpine peaks
by John Ruskin, drawing,
1846.

BELOW The holy shrine of
Montserrat.

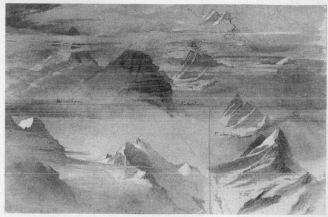

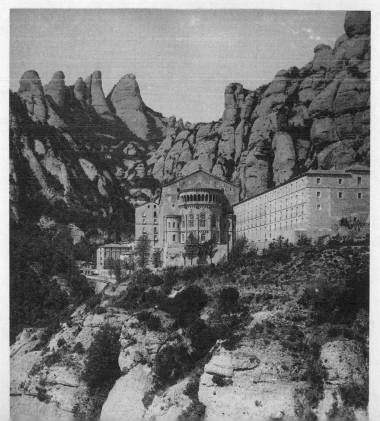

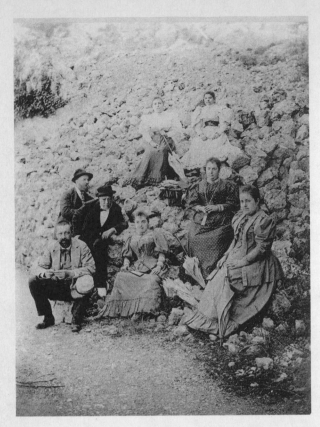

LEFT The Gaudí and Santaló families on an excursion to Montserrat in 1904: Gaudí to the left, Rosa seated in centre.

BELOW The Mas de la Calderera – the Gaudí family's house in Riudoms.

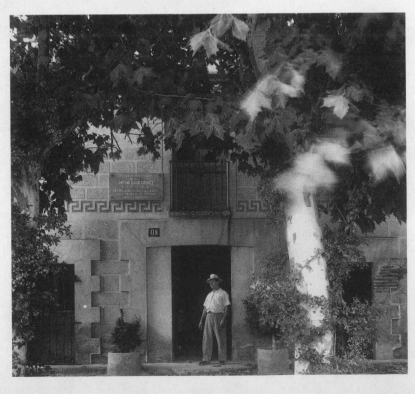

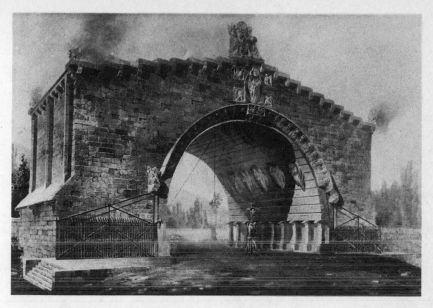

A cemetery gate drawing by Gaudí (1875): one of his projects at architectural school.

Entrance pass for exhibitors to the 1888 Exposition. Gaudí was responsible for the Compañía Trasatlántica stand.

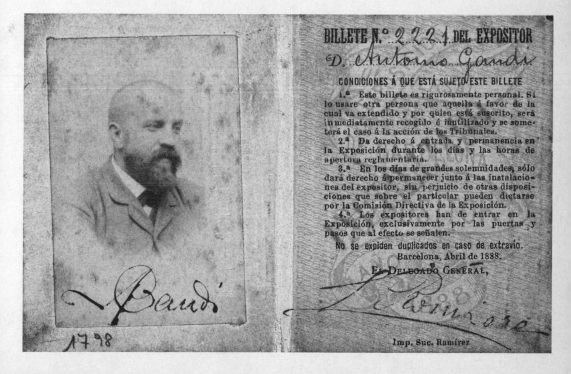

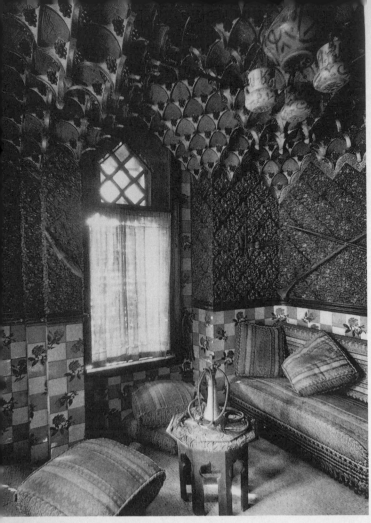

LEFT The Arab smoking room at the Casa Vicens.

BELOW The famous palmetto leaf fence at the Casa Vicens.

OPPOSITE
ABOVE The Bishop's Palace, Astorga 1887-93.

BELOW The 'Drac de Pedralbes' – the Dragon's Gate at the Finca Güell. The building below the ornamental tower today houses the Catedra Gaudí.

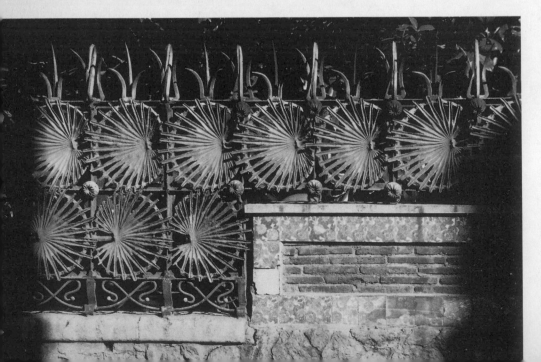

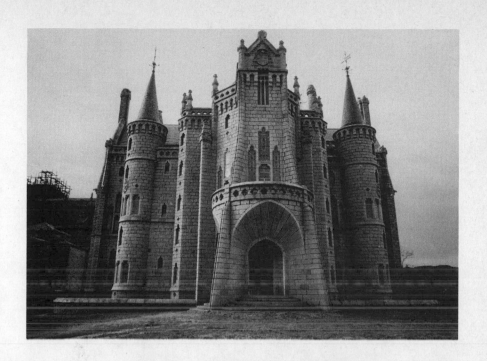

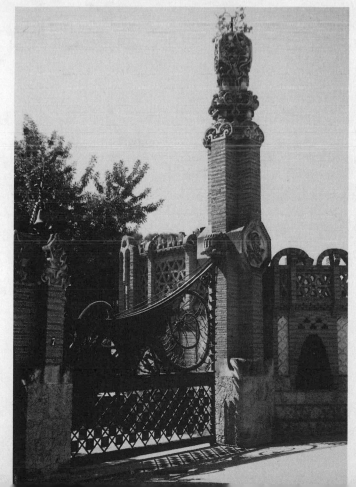

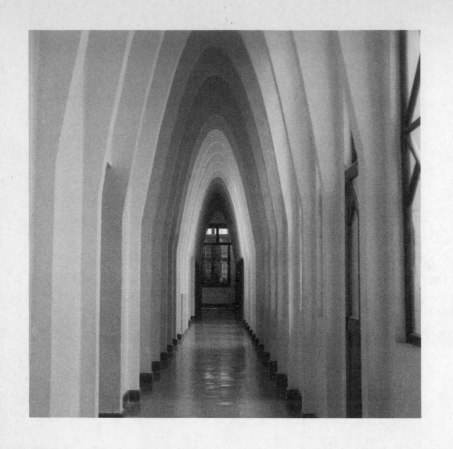

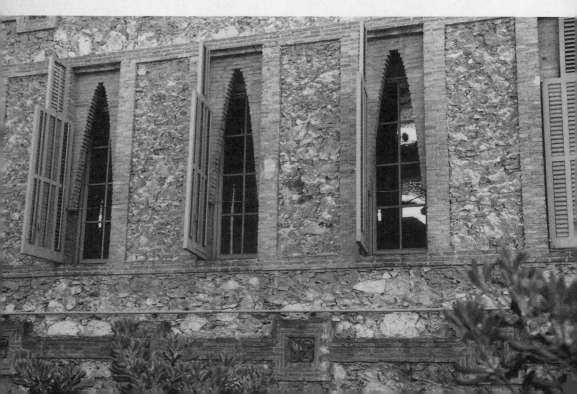

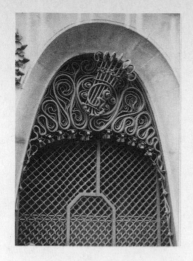

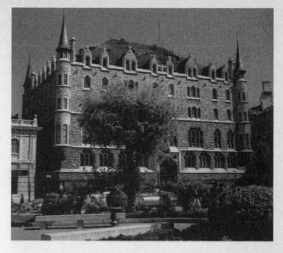

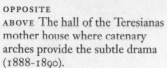

OPPOSITE

ABOVE The hall of the Teresianas
mother house where catenary
arches provide the subtle drama
(1888-1890).

BELOW The elegant rhythm of
catenary arch windows at the
Teresianas echo the spartan corridor
inside.

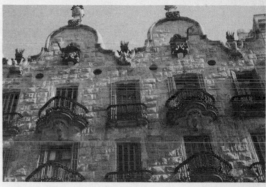

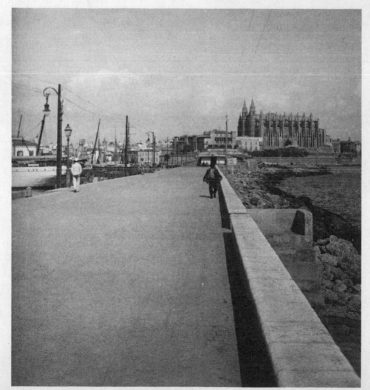

TOP LEFT One of
two entrance gates
to the Palau Güell
with its typical
catenary arch
c.1888.

TOP Casa de Los
Botines, Leon
1891-2.

CENTRE Façade of
the prize-winning
Casa Calvet
(1898-1900).

LEFT The
Cathedral of
Palma de
Mallorca.

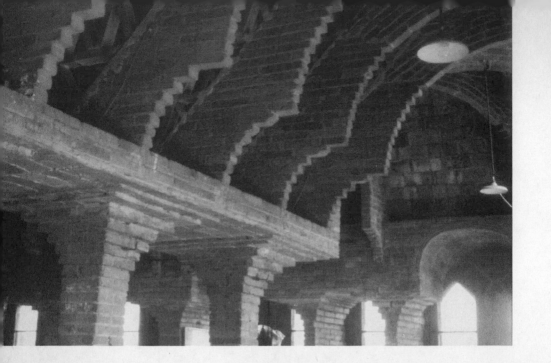

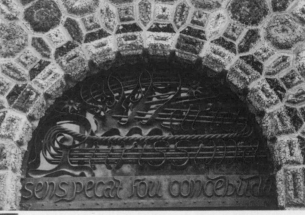

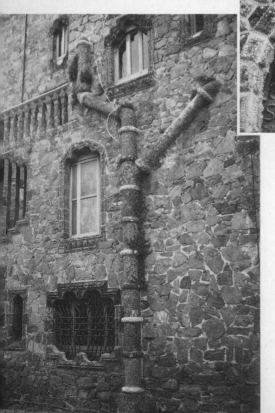

TOP Slender brick arches span the roofspace at Bellesguard.

LEFT Rubble and cladding bring a certain unity to the eccentric fenestration of the side façade at Bellesguard.

ABOVE A wrought iron invocation to the Virgin welcomes the visitor to Bellesguard.

obviously came from the heart: Gaudí became famous in later life for his abrupt and cutting manner.

Gaudí's contradictions were noticed by others. Martinell analysed them thus:

> He admired the select and refined worker whom he found in his friend Salvador Pagès, the manager of the Mataró cooperative, and the industrious aristocrat whom he had seen in Eusebi Güell, and he hoped for a fraternal integration of the two living side by side ... In later years he retracted his liberal ways, but he never abandoned his labourist ideals, though he did cease to flaunt them. What he did was to substitute Christian charity for secular philanthropy.[9]

The Mataró commission came at a crucial juncture in his architectural career. On Gaudí's frequent visits to Mataró, he became friendly with two sisters, Josefa, nicknamed 'Pepeta', and Agustina Moreu, who were teachers in the Cooperativa school. They lived close to him in Barcelona on the calle Diputació and he frequently visited them. Gaudí found Pepeta the most sympathetic. Beautiful and dynamic, she was a republican sympathiser and freethinker. Divorcing her first husband, she was, for her time, completely unconventional. Bowled over by her beauty and energy, Gaudí's reserve and inexperience meant he found it very hard to make his feelings clear.

Finally, with much awkwardness, he asked her to marry him, but Pepeta announced that she was engaged to the successful wood-merchant Ignasi Caballol.[10] Gaudí had lost his chance. He fell in love with only one other woman – a young American – and they lost contact when she returned to the United States. Resigned to celibacy Gaudí treated his arid love life with fatalism. He later chose, as had so many of Spain's Golden Age mystics, 'The Living Flame of Love', the spiritual pilgrimage that led towards God and favoured denial of the self and the abnegation of the flesh.[11] He turned his back forever on female companion-ship, becoming (according to Lluís Permanyer) a misogynist who chastised his assistants if they visited cafés of ill repute or were seen out walking with women.[12]

Gaudí entered the 1880s with a reputation for being both radical and innovatory. Known only to a small circle that included Martorell, Fontserè, Vilaseca and Rogent, he still only had (temporary) exhibition stands, kiosks and shop interiors to his name. By the end of the 1880s, just seven years later, he had become along with Domènech one of the most revered and famous architects in Catalonia, if not Spain. His dramatic change in fortune was due to a few key commissions and his transforma-tion into a key figure in the Catalan cultural renaissance.

Gaudí's entrance into Barcelona's cultural life was eased by his joining some of the many societies that had exploded onto the scene during the optimism of the post Civil-War period.

On 29 April 1879, Gaudí joined the Associació Catalanista d'Excursions Científicas, formed to promote sport, mountaineer-ing, sketching, topography, the natural sciences, an interest in the Catalan countryside and architectural heritage.[13] Only three years old, the Associació had quickly become an institution.[14] It continues today in its original clubhouse, behind the cathedral, on the narrow carrer Paradís.

The all-male *Excurcionista* societies were formed so that Catalans could rediscover their splendid past. The seemingly innocuous pastimes of strolling through mountain meadows took on a distinctly politicised, nationalistic agenda.[15] The beginnings of the *Excurcionista* movement coincided almost exactly with a resurgence in political Catalanism.[16]

All across Europe, mountaineering societies had flourished. Both Ruskin and Viollet had promoted the mountain-peak aes-thetic but its pedigree went back much further. Its roots were in romanticism and a new pantheistic regard for nature – especially mountains. In Finland, the nationalist philosophy of Karelianism had rapidly snowballed into a wholesale and wholesome 'back to nature' movement. Thousands of Finns explored their spiritual roots while digging up mushrooms to spice up their winter stews. However, in France, mountaineering and physical exercise took on an increasingly millennial flavour. Déroulède wrote about fears that sedentary modern life would produce racial degeneration.

In contrast, the Catalan *Excurcionista* movement, though sometimes dismissed as mere cultural navel-gazing, was almost entirely benevolent. It could almost be described as the purely physical manifestation of the *Renaixença*. On the Associació's first anniversary, in December 1887, Antoni Masso wrote a report, '*Conveniencia del Estudi de las Montanyes*', in which he delighted in their shared 'love of the motherland' that evoked 'amongst the ruins shades of their illustrious past'. Naive and patriotic, it was heady stuff.

At the clubhouse in the carrer Paradís, members met, as they still do today, for lectures, to use the library, pore over maps, buy mountaineering equipment and for informal discussion. There were lectures on literature, music, architecture, archaeology and the Catalan economy. This was very much the age of the amateur. Gaudí's frequent participation in club events was made considerably easier, in the early years of his involvement, by his move to his first architectural studio and flat at carrer Call 11. It was a two-minute walk away. It placed Gaudí at the heart of the city – he had finally arrived.

The club magazine kept its readership up to date with its many members, on the roving diplomat Toda's many trips to Egypt, Nubia and China; Domènech and Vilaseca were congratulated in 1878 for winning the competition for the school's building on the Ronda de Sant Pere. Even Gaudí's lampposts were mentioned.

But it wasn't all educational. The club had an annual party for St George's Day, when members including Gaudí decorated the clubhouse. Its Roman column tops were draped with flower garlands and wrapped with ivy. Busts and portraits of Catalan cultural heroes ranging from Ramon Llull to Clavé were crowned with laurels and placed in a decorative ensemble surrounded by the words 'Past' and 'Future' in Catalan, flanking the emblazoned central motto '*Patria*'.

As their name suggests, it was on the organised trips and excursions that the Associació came into its own. These often explored the architecture of medieval Catalonia. In the society's first year, outings were organised to Poblet, San Cugat de Vallès, Ripoll, Montserrat, Santes Creus, the castle at Montjüich, Tibidabo and to Tarragona to view a recently excavated Roman mosaic. These trips covered more than just sightseeing. Local mayors and priests were tirelessly badgered if their restoration efforts were found wanting or deemed overzealous. So, for instance, the mayor of San Cugat de Vallès received a stern letter recommending he restore the famous Romanesque cloister containing Arnau Cadell's twelfth-century self-portrait, one of the earliest in Western art.

Gaudí's involvement was low-key at first. On 23 May 1879 he joined a group of fifty-two at Barcelona Cathedral, the most successful excursion yet organised, hardly surprising considering that the clubhouse was just twenty metres away. Six months later Gaudí joined a visit to the Gothic church of San Esteban in Granollers where, as the only architect present, his opinion was sought on the building's restoration and the removal of an unsightly fortification rushed up during one of the Carlist Wars.[17] The next month he was voted unanimously onto the Junta and named the official keeper of the Associació's Museum of Archaeology, which comprised six Roman columns and little else.

On 25 January 1880, Gaudí joined a group of thirty-one that included Domènech and Güell to Santa Maria del Mar; Güell became a member just a week later. Gaudí seemed, even at twenty-eight, content to reacquaint himself with buildings that he already knew intimately. But his presence on these outings could well have been because there was also serious business to carry out. As a result of the Santa Maria del Mar trip, a report was sent off for the attention of the clerk of works with some serious suggestions. How much power the Associació actually exercised is unclear, but in a small city 'influence' often proves more effective than official edicts.

However, these were not the only responsibilities that the ambitious young architect was prepared to accept. In November 1880, Gaudí and the Conde de Bell-lloch joined the committee organising an exhibition celebrating the Fomento del Trabajo Nacional, founded by leading industrialists to promote Spain's industrial needs. The following month Gaudí reviewed the exhibition for the moderate daily *La Renaixença*. His extensive review displayed an assured critical style which leant heavily on Morris and Ruskin. But he was already moving beyond the Arts and Crafts movement in his demands for more attention to the functional and for a greater sensitivity to be shown towards the requirements of industry. The clear impression is of an energetic young man ready to accept almost any responsibility – an enthusiastic participant excited by and willing to join in the city's social and cultural life. The Associació logo was designed by Gaudí and two other members, Torrents and Rusinyol, and he was asked again to take charge of the decorations for the anniversary party.[18]

Gaudí was also an itinerant member of the Associació's rival group, the Associació d'Excurcions Catalana. When this association proposed a trip to Poblet in May 1882 for a select group of more than forty Valencian, Mallorcan and Catalan writers and artists, Gaudí found it impossible to refuse their invitation. The group included Angel Guimerá; the poet, playwright and editor of *La Renaixença*, Jacint Verdaguer; the sculptor Pablo Gargallo and the priest Jaume Collell. On the evening of 17 May the group met up in Tarragona so that the following morning they could attend the cathedral's early mass led by Collell. Spiritually revitalised, they took the train along the same route Gaudí had taken a decade before. For one day at least the cherished dream of an artistic colony might become reality. In L'Espluga, they all took to carriages, donkey and foot for the slow climb up to Poblet. Lodgings had been arranged in three large farmhouses nearby.

While the party dined, Gaudí, the artist Dionisio Baixeras, Verdaguer and the Valencian painter José Brel Giral slipped out to prepare a rapidly improvised *son et lumière* using coloured Bengal lights. Later a phosphorescent light show bounced evocatively off the vaporous night mist, reminding at least one witness of what it must have been like to see the burning monastery in 1835. The overcome party joined Jaume Collell and Verdaguer seated amongst the ruins in a passionate '*Salve Regina*'. Nothing could give a more authentic flavour of the cultural matrix that Gaudí was about to enter: a cocktail of Catholicism, romanticism, fraternity, Catalanism, all mixed up with the romantic love of ruins and lost causes.

Just over the French–Spanish border they visited the Romanesque cloisters of Elne set in the salt flats midway between Collioure and Perpignan. A photograph of the group was taken there which still survives. Hiding shyly behind Angel Guimerà, Gaudí is caught awkwardly in the shadows in profile. This photograph represents a roll call of late-nineteenth-century Catalan cultural life. Others present included, as always, Father Collell, Verdaguer and the Anglophile artist/poet Riquer i Inglada who energetically promoted the Arts and Crafts philosophy of Morris in Spain. Without this group of talented individuals, both the *Renaixença* and the *modernista* movement would have been entirely different.

From Elne the party cut inland to Toulouse. Upon arrival, the group immediately went to admire the simple engineering of the barrel-vaulted nave of the eleventh-century Romanesque church of St Sernin. But Gaudí questioned the supremacy of the native Oc 'eye'. According to Martinell, he compared Saint Sernin unfavourably to the superior Catalan Romanesque. He rounded off the trip dismissively with a self-satisfied 'Let's go home', and from then on, apparently, 'renounced foreign excursions for the rest of his life'.[19] If true, it was in keeping with the increasingly fashionable Catalanocentric worldview. Once Gaudí was asked why he didn't travel more often. He replied brusquely, 'Why should I? It's the foreigners who should come here, especially the north Europeans.'[20]

From summer 1883 on, Gaudí's involvement with the *Excurcionista* movement became far more sporadic. Given his rapidly growing number of commissions by autumn 1883, this is hardly surprising. Gaudí now had the chance to build an architectural masterpiece of his own.

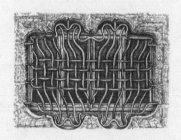

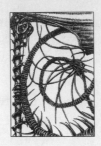

# Views of Heaven and the Harem

Christian stoicism is late brought face to face with Islam,
and from the resulting clash there spring
the most marked tendencies in the religious spirit of Spain –
mysticism and fanaticism.

*R. M. Nadal*

LOOKING OUT AT US from the famous photograph, Gaudí looks
every bit the solid respectable bourgeois. The thick worsted coat,
with its oversize lapels, lends him a certain substantiality defining him as, above all, reliable. Rejecting the costume of the
sophisticated Catalan gentleman – wing collar, white tie with
gold fob – he portrays himself with sobriety, grey highlights in
his beard reinforcing the impression of someone older than their
years.

Here in his late twenties, Gaudí has thickset strong features.
His side-combed hair reveals a high domed forehead, with a
pronounced swelling over his eyebrows. This was the only photography that Gaudí ever consciously posed for. Yet his apparent
phobia of the camera was not a total rejection of photography
itself. Later the camera became an important design tool, a way

of achieving a rapid feel for how a building was progressing. Even more importantly, however, Gaudí used photographic techniques to manipulate, extend and collapse space, and even to play around with perspective.

In Spanish visual culture the depiction of the eye plays a symbolic role that goes beyond vision into the realms of spirituality, magic and faith. This is clear from the other-worldly gaze of Counter-Reformation saints caught in ecstasy by Murillo, Carducho, Alonso Cano, Zurbaran and El Greco: their eyes transmit and transport us into another space. In popular Spanish culture the eye also has magical powers that are more earthbound. It can have a sexual presence. Picasso understood the power of the strong gaze that can stop a woman dead in her tracks. Gaudí, however, was a cerebral Catalan. His ginger hair, fair complexion and piercing blue eyes were already rare enough amongst a predominantly dark people. It was his eyes, in particular, that captured the imagination of almost all who met him. Ràfols, his first biographer and assistant, remembered, 'he seemed to say as much with his eyes as he did in his words, those compelling seer's eyes which in their severity seemed to accuse us of our defections'.[1]

But, if he had seer's eyes, Gaudí understood their limitations. 'We Mediterraneans have eyes unaccustomed to ghosts, only used to images; we are more imaginative than fantastic and therefore better gifted for the visual arts,' he had once told Martinell.

Others, like Josep Pla, also observed Gaudí's extraordinary observation and analysis. He saw in Gaudí a particular nobility coupled with phenomenal concentration.

> Gaudí's eyes! His blue eyes were almost devoid of nervous movement, but their calm showed a singular intensity; it was not a calm tending towards ecstasy and whiteness, but a calm full of force, passion, and life . . . He seemed to transport things and people with his eyes.[2]

The hypnotic appeal of Gaudí's eyes sits right at the heart of perhaps the strangest episode in his life, one that would transform the skyline of Barcelona.

After years of fund-raising the Asociación Espiritual de Devotos de San José, founded in the 1860s by the eccentric bookdealer José María Bocabella Verdaguer, was ready to start building the Sagrada Família on the outskirts of the *eixample* in Sant Martí de Provençals in 1881.[3] During early discussions the diocesan architect Francisco de Paula del Villar y Lozano offered to draw up plans for the Asociación free of charge.

On 19 March 1882, St Joseph's Day, Bishop Urquinaona laid the first stone of Villar's neo-Gothic expiatory temple. By the end of the decade it was hoped (by which point the Catholic Church would be safely shored up against heretic, Protestant, anarchist and atheist attacks) its worthy patrons Pius IX, Queen Christina, the Prince of Asturias – the future Alfonso XIIIth – and the future saint Antoni Maria Claret might celebrate the first mass.

A good start was made. By July 1882 there were fifty masons and general labourers at work, aided by eight horses and carts, but the Sagrada Família quickly ran into problems. Relations between Villar and the temple *Junta* – church council – began to disintegrate. The crisis, which began with a discussion over the appropriate materials for the supporting columns of the crypt (in fact already agreed upon previously by Villar and the *Junta*), soon descended into an ugly quarrel.[4] Juan Martorell, a friend of Bocabella's, was chosen as the *Junta*'s architectural assessor and, perhaps unsurprisingly, he decided in favour of the *Junta*. It was obvious that Villar's continuation as director of works had become untenable. Martorell was an obvious choice as successor. His involvement as assessor, however, debarred him.

Help quickly came to Bocabella in the form of a dream. Local folklore tells us of him dreaming of a young architect whom he would recognise by his piercing blue eyes. The blue-eyed 'seer' would soon come to the Sagrada Família's salvation. When a few days later, in autumn 1883, Bocabella walked into Martorell's office and came face to face with Gaudí he knew immediately that he had found his man. When the time came Gaudí, as the 'chosen one', would be given absolute autonomy over the Sagrada Família.

The real pattern of events was far more prosaic. Villar's replacement was a compromise, acceptable to all parties. Gaudí fitted the bill perfectly. He had been taught by Villar at architectural school and had also worked with him on the *camarín* of the Virgin in the apse of the church at Montserrat. It is likely that Bocabella, a frequent visitor to the mountaintop shrine, had already met Gaudí there. If not, then Bocabella almost definitely met Gaudí while seated at the draughtsman's board in Martorell's busy studio. And Gaudí, at thirty-one, may also have been considerably cheaper than older, more experienced colleagues.[5]

Gaudí started work on the Sagrada Família on 3 November 1883, although it was not until 28 March 1884 that he was officially named director of works. On 3 March 1884, Gaudí put forward a suggestion that he be freed from all the restrictions of Villar's design. It was Rogent – Gaudí's former teacher – who was called in to arbitrate. He decided in his ex-student's favour.

In accepting the commission Gaudí leapfrogged overnight into the rank of Barcelona's top architects. Initially, his ideas were constrained by the way the building's axis was set in a strictly right-angled relationship to the surrounding *eixample*. But no one could have guessed how painfully slow the gestation would actually be, and that in replacing Villar the *Junta* had chosen an architect who would develop his idiosyncratic style over decades rather than months.

Bocabella was an extraordinary man. Sitting in his shop on the carrer Princesa, famous for its obsessively detailed boxwood engravings, he kept all the Associación's funds squirrelled away in a strongbox under the ceramic floor tiles. In Alejo Clapés' portrait he has the concentrated stare of the fanatic, hunched over his desk ready to spring forward into action or rush head-long into debate. His personality, according to Francesc Arenas, was that of an obsessive xenophobic:

> He felt a horror for things of a mixed nature and a foreign origin; he mistrusted all banks, and bought no French products as they reminded him of the French occupation of Barcelona, and even refused to eat any supposedly imported foods.

Despite Bocabella's distaste for things mongrelised, imported liberal ideas and other poison, he remained open to some foreign influences. On his first visit to Rome in 1869 he passed the Holy House of Loreto, which, despite its Italian pedigree, he admired as a model of a pioneering church that, through religious paternalism, was struggling hard to bridge the gap between the employer and the mass of workers.

Bocabella's muscular Catholicism was certainly an accurate reflection of the broader sweep towards faith amongst the establishment and the reactionary elements in society, but his inspiration for founding the Asociación was far more personal. Bocabella was an assiduous visitor to Montserrat and legend has it that he hit upon the idea while contemplating there an image of the Holy Family. Other testimony suggests that Bocabella, frightened by the outbreak of yellow fever in Barcelona, interpreted the epidemic as a visitation on the community for all its sins. An expiation for the materialism of the modern world was required. Either reason will do, for it came at a time that the image of the Holy Family also had political benefits.

The rapid industrialisation of Europe in the second half of the nineteenth century and the stop-start cycle of capitalism had brought in its wake a period of unparalleled and traumatic change. In many cases, and especially so in the city, the traditional structures of society had disintegrated to be replaced by nothing that could act as a convincing or cohesive social glue. The family, marriage, the extended family and other social ties came under attack just as the concept of the village and parish as a stable entity was losing clear definition. Social unrest became endemic to the city, as witnessed once again in Paris with the rise of the Commune, and sought its solace in brotherhood and union. The traditionalists responded by hardening their position on the 'ideal family', and the idealised Christian family was transformed into a Catholic flagship, threatened by many evil forces.

It was against this backdrop that Bocabella started publishing *El Propagador de la Devoción de San José*, which was a direct copy of the French religious tract *Propagateur de la Dévotion à Saint Joseph* edited from Sainte Foix in Dijon by the Marist priest Joseph Huguet.[6] Issue No. 1 of the *Boletin Mensual*, 24 December 1866, the forerunner of *El Propagador*, set out clearly its evangelical stall.

In the text Bocabella likened the present state of the Catholic Church to the apostles' hazardous crossing of the storm-tossed sea of Galilee in Simon's leaking boat. It was their duty as loyal Catholics to fight against the winds of 'immorality' and 'error', and never to doubt, as the apostles briefly had done, the powers of salvation of the sleeping Christ. The 'enemies of the Church

71

will be confounded', Bocabella warned.[7] The enemy was easy to spot. First amongst all the evils was the liberal press.

Bocabella's brand of Catholicism enjoyed popular mass appeal. Gaudí's interest was more refined. Born into a devout Catholic family, he was a passionate admirer of religious architecture. He was also a late-nineteenth-century romantic, and admirer of Wagner, Walter Pater, Pugin and Ruskin.[8] If the Romantic movement had heralded a revolution in style, content and feeling, by loosening the bonds of neoclassicism, the Roman Catholic Church had also enjoyed a parallel awakening of its aesthetic and spiritual potential.

By the late nineteenth century, amongst many intellectuals, the Catholic revival had become a strange hybrid of art for art's sake, symbolism, decadence, dandyism, homosexuality and sadism. For many, the soul-searching and the opening up to novel sensations, one of these Catholicism, had come at a terrible price. Creativity was the result of a prolonged spiritual crisis and Pugin, Ruskin, Holman Hunt and Baudelaire all went mad. But it was the authenticity and danger of the search for creativity and faith that somehow lent it legitimacy.

It may seem strange that the Catholic Church could share ground with those decadents who 'combined intellectualism with a turbid sensuality'. But they shared a common enemy. Materialism had become a brutalising force in society. Aestheticism offered an escape from the unrelenting industrial grind.

The late-nineteenth-century decadent had rapidly become a stock figure, while his overdecorated house with its plumped-up cushions, exotic plants, acres of perfumed satin and silk and its bordello smoking room had become a clearly recognised topos. Don Eusebi Güell, so admired by Gaudí, was the absolute epitome of this blend of religious orthodoxy, wealth and love of 'exquisite things'. The pose of the anticlerical dandy on the point of conversation or of resignation had become an archetype; a fallen angel that through the grace of God had recovered the ability to fly.

The most famous decadent, after Beardsley and Oscar Wilde, was the Duc Jean Floressas des Esseintes, the literary creation of J. K. Huysmans.[9] Des Esseintes, the hero of *À Rebours* (Against Nature) published in May 1884, was based on the eccentric Comte de Montesquiou-Fesenzac whose house on the rue Franklin had been described by Mallarmé as an Ali-Baba's cave.[10]

Huysmans himself was a prime example of the nineteenth-century dandy-convert. After early experiments with realism he was soon persuaded by Edmond de Goncourt to refine his art and study 'exquisite things'. From there it was but a short step to Rome. Gaudí followed a similar path. At the Obrera Mataronesa he had illustrated the walls with fraternal and revolutionary graffiti, and had been briefly tempted to join the left-wing Catalan party Alianza Democratica (while his friend Oliveras was working on a monument to the anarchist Bakunin). But Gaudí 'was only briefly intoxicated by the fresh winds of change'.[11] He quickly moved over to the pattern of religious and aristocratic patronage that would last for the rest of his life.

The scope of Gaudí's religious architecture was impressive. He had provided the furnishings for the Marquès de Comillas' pantheon-chapel, designed a church in Villaricos and had partnered Domènech on a project to complete the façade of Barcelona's Gothic cathedral. He had worked with Martorell on the church for the Jesuit college in the carrer Casp and on the church of the Salesas. And it was through this friendship and collaboration with Martorell that Gaudí established himself as the obvious choice for major religious commissions. Of the younger generation no one had a better pedigree. No one had worked with as many architects of the older generation. And no one had worked on so many of the key religious sites and shrines in Catalonia.

Beneath the deep religious yearnings that fuelled the decadent movement there were barely disguised erotic undertones. The repressed sexuality of the decadents found legitimacy through the renunciation of sex, and the Catholic Church offered them a safe haven. The mechanics of late-nineteenth-century sexual repression have filled libraries of psychoanalytical texts. Dijkstra wrote:

> The apparent increase in homosexuality, which may have been actual or merely the result of a lessening of social circumspection among males inclined to same-sex relationships, quite clearly expressed itself in terms of suspicion, often developing into an outright fear, of the strength of women's sexual appetite and their eagerness to usurp the arena of male privilege. But these same suspicions were a motivating force in the ultimate choice of celibacy which led numerous members of the intelligentsia during this same period to embrace the Church, usually the Roman Catholic Church, with a great deal of intensity.[12]

Some feel that Gaudí's relentless search for perfection, his growing religiosity, and his work's sensuality disguised deep psychological yearnings. The critic Salvador Tarrago wrote:

> Those of us who do not go along with the traditional interpretation of Gaudí cannot help thinking that his Catholicism was no more than an historic method of satisfying his infinite desire for wisdom and his need to love and be loved.[13]

Rejected by Pepeta Moreu, Gaudí had made the 'ultimate choice of celibacy'. There has never been any evidence, however, that Gaudí was homosexual. It was in his work that Gaudí sublimated all his feeling and his passion. Gaudí was clearly, even if subconsciously, using his buildings as metaphors for rather more. Bergos remembered Gaudí's wistful thoughts. In conversation he had let slip the tragedy and the eventual salvation he hoped for as a direct result of the personal sacrifice he had made for his art.

> Those who analyse and then do not achieve synthesis have essentially destroyed all relationships and what they then find has no meaning; this is understandable since out of relationship comes fruitfulness, from separation, sterility.

However, Gaudí's secular architecture was also flourishing. In 1883 he submitted his plans to the Gràcia municipal office for approval to build a villa for the tile manufacturer Don Manuel Vicens Montaner. The Casa Vicens, built using the 15 cm decorative tiles as the defining modular measurement, was Gaudí's most exotic building to date. It says much of Vicens' character that he gave Gaudí such free licence, but it was also a clever piece of marketing.[14] Looking at the Casa Vicens, tiles become the ultimately covetable building material.

Even today, crammed into its space on the narrow carrer Carolinas, the Casa Vicens has an atmosphere of drowsy escapism, with its green and creamy yellow tiles, its blinds permanently down and the iron gates firmly shut. Then and now it is a haven. When Gaudí first inspected the site, he found a giant flowering palm surrounded by a carpet of yellow flowers while birds swooped through its foliage catching insects. All these motifs Gaudí would later include in the design; including a large metal spider's web as an ingenious patio shade cleverly dispersing the sunlight.

In the dining room frieze Gaudí drew attention to the fact

that this private dwelling was placed in an idyllic corner of a very Catalan nature. On the north-west wall, in the shady corner, was inscribed in Catalan the incantation, *Oh, la sombra de l'istiu!* ('Oh, for the summer shade!'). On the opposite wall, facing the south-east and the rising sun, Gaudí chose the motto *Sol, Solet, vina'm a veure* – an abbreviation of the Catalan invitation 'Sun, little sun, come and see me for I'm feeling cold.'

In the garden, Gaudí built a small brick lookout – a *mirador* – overlooking the corner of this mini-estate, two separate fountains, one built into the wall of the tribune balcony, and an elaborate brick cascade that functioned as a gateway and over whose parabolic arch covered steps invite the visitor to enjoy the pleasing view and to feel below the cooling waters of this gentle oasis.[15]

The perimeter wall was made of solid rubble and faced in plaster, with carved end stones. Casa Vicens today is a partly mutilated version of Gaudí's original. In 1883, Gràcia, whose population quadrupled in the second half of the nineteenth century, was still very much a suburb on the outskirts of Barcelona. On the higher edges of the town there were still wide areas of open land. Just down from Casa Vicens, for instance, a medieval farmhouse stood in an open field on the Carrer Gran de Gràcia. Next door the Sisters of St Vincent de Paul had just started work on the chapel of their convent. But today the Casa Vicens is suffocated by surrounding buildings. Its gardens, a key to Gaudí's original design, have been repeatedly eaten into as subsequent owners have sold off portions.[16] Yet the Casa Vicens remains Gaudí's first full-blown essay in the neo-Mudejar or Moorish style.

Gaudí's love affair with Moorish architecture began when he leafed through the pages of Owen Jones' *Grammar of Ornament* (1856), his *Designs for Mosaics and Tesselated Pavements* (1842) and his *Plans, Elevations, Sections and Details of the Alhambra* (1842). Other popular contemporary books were written by the Alhambra's restorer, Rafael Contreras. It was becoming a popular architectural style: there were already a few examples of the neo-Mudejar style in Barcelona that pre-dated the Casa Vicens.[17]

The Casa Vicens has been picked out as one of a few revolutionary works in the growth of the *modernista* aesthetic. It plays games with the distribution, and sometimes vertiginous stacking up, of blocks of geometric forms. The exterior of the Casa Vicens shows a lively multicoloured Orientalism. Its walls interlaced brick coursing with a tiled ribbon banding of the African marigolds that he had earlier found there.

On the balcony was a row of wide-headed sunflowers. There are many fascinating theories on Gaudí's use of sunflowers as a symbol. A wayward, rampant plant, the sunflower is widely recognised as a symbol of the soul. During the 1870s and '80s they were very much in vogue in Britain. Norman Shaw had used them in 1874 at Lowther Lodge, William de Morgan on his Persian tiles. Howell and Evans sold sunflower-faced clocks. In Kensington and Chelsea, Queen Anne-style mansion blocks were fringed with terracotta sunflowers. And one of Chelsea's most famous residents, Oscar Wilde, who had himself described the plants as 'that bright emblem of constancy', was caricatured as one.

Ràfols claimed to have found an English architectural magazine in Gaudí's papers that might well have provided inspiration. A likely source was in the work of Thomas Jeckyll, whose sunflower firedogs were made for Whistler's Peacock Room and whose Japanese Pavilion (designed for the Philadelphia Centennial in 1876) was brought to the Paris Exposition in 1878.[18] It was pictured in one of the first experimental photographs printed in *The British Architect*. This could have been the magazine.

Wrought-iron railings excluded the outside world and these, together with the sunflower motifs on the ceramic tiles, and the iron palmetto-leaf fence, mediated between urban and rural and public and private.[19] But it was on the interior that Gaudí's creative imagination caught fire. He designed a wildly exotic setting in which to entertain family and guests. In the dining

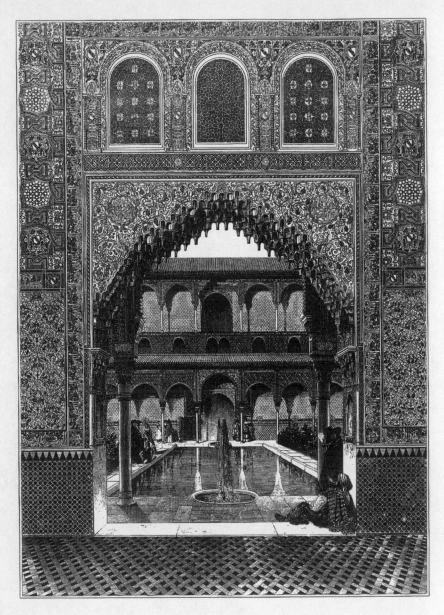

Owen Jones' romanticised view of the Alhambra's Patio
de Comares.

room, the spaces between the ceiling beams are bursting with intricate carvings of bright red cherries and luscious green leaves. Up to the dado rail the walls are either panelled or tiled. But from there on up, every inch not covered in paintings is filled with compressed cardboard reliefs draped in ivy, birds fly through the sky past falling autumn leaves. Beneath, a series of herons and cranes parade. Gaudí had come a long way since he had confided to his diary on 10 August 1878, 'Ornamentation has been, is, and will be polychrome.'[20]

Ornamentation is everywhere in riotous and tasteless profusion; a reclining plaster classical nude sits over the obliquely placed entrance. At the building's corners, he had placed Moorish-style windows that resembled miniature minarets and upon which he had attached totally inappropriate terracotta cherubs.

But the real show-stopper was the Arabian smoking room with its poufs, collapsible coffee table placed on a framework of horseshoe arches and its hookah. This was an essential sign of wealth in fashion-conscious contemporary Spain: even the Royal Family had had one built at the palace of Aranjuez.[21] But where Aranjuez's decor consisted of sections of directly moulded copies from the Alhambra's multicoloured walls and floors, Gaudí's version was a more 'original' pastiche.[22] With its extraordinary stalactite ceiling of *muqarnas* – carved plaster – it showed off perfectly Gaudí's special gift for adapting architectural idioms to new construction processes. The Vicens ceiling was made from moulded cardboard.[23]

The smoking room is a piece of pure escapism for a respectable bourgeois.

His growing success soon made it necessary for Gaudí to employ some assistants. While working on the Casa Vicens he accepted another commission for a house in Comillas known as El Capricho, which Gaudí entrusted to his old friend and classmate Cristóbal Cascante to interpret from Gaudí's own drawings and designs. But the Sagrada Família commission transformed Gaudí's small practice into a business with all the accompanying problems. Craftsmen like the sculptor Lorenzo Matamala, whom Gaudí had poached from Puntí's, were required to carry out the skilled work. Builders needed to be monitored, while in the studio, draughtsmen scaled up and finished the working plans. The plethora of commissions (El Capricho was on the other side of Spain) called for a novel approach to the running of the practice. Local rumour talks of Gaudí's dandified working method. Apparently, without taking off his gloves or descending from his open-top carriage, he would spread out the plans on his lap and imperiously direct work from the street. Furthermore, he took to editing and cropping the building by tearing down walls and whole rooms as he readjusted the broken silhouette as if it were merely a plaster sculpture or a cardboard maquette. It is surely responsible for what David Mackay has described as a 'hesitant symmetrical plan that hides an agile aggregation of domestic rooms'. It was a fantastically expensive way to work even if the spatial brilliance achieved made it all worthwhile. Ganivet has described this improvisation as typically Spanish:

> In Spain, there are no middle terms. The small artists, as well as the great, go on the principle of 'seeing how it will turn out'. When they begin to work they generally have only a vague notion of what they are going to produce and an absolute confidence in their own forces, in their innate genius . . . and are therefore either 'capable of creating a masterpiece or of giving birth to some stupendous monstrosity'.[24]

The construction of the Casa Vicens' distinctive palmetto gate was a sign of a strong and unbroken Catalan tradition of working in iron. Gaudí had an active knowledge of this from his father's forge, but the gate was a collaborative effort with the talented Joan Oños.

There has been considerable dispute as to whether Gaudí's gate should rather be attributed to two different men: Francesc Berenguer and Lorenzo Matamala. It is unlikely although not impossible that the seventeen-year-old Berenguer, a Reus family friend and in his first year at architectural school, was responsible. Records, from an exhibition at the guild of locksmiths and black-smiths in Barcelona held in 1921, show that the gate was pub-lished unequivocally as a design by Gaudí. Matamala, however, remembered collaborating with Gaudí on the gate and casting the palm leaf in clay.[25] This confusion does raise the question whether Gaudí abused his assistants' talents.

After Gaudí's death the daily *La Veu de Catalunya* published a heated debate between Feliu Elías and Josep Camps discussing the real nature of Gaudí's relationship with his assistants. Berenguer, it was argued, never finished his architectural studies and left college to work for Gaudí. Gaudí therefore is cast in the role of seductive demon. According to Elías, Berenguer worked like '*dos negres*' while Gaudí did nothing more than sign his name to his pupil's masterpieces. Pabon i Charneco has researched Berenguer's academic history: it is obvious that exams were not his forte. Gaudí took on Berenguer, putting the Reus connection to one side, precisely because Gaudí admired his talent as a draughtsman and had little respect, as we have seen, for the orthodox architectural education. Berenguer, inciden-tally, while still at college, married Adelina Bellvehí, who gave birth to seven children in as many years.

An accusation thrown at Gaudí was that Berenguer was never permitted to sign his own designs. However, he couldn't because he wasn't a qualified architect. Years later, when Berenguer was employed as an 'architect' by the Gràcia town hall, it was his boss Miguel Pascual Tintorer who signed all of his plans.

Other criticism has focused on Gaudí's wasteful building

methods. Manuel Vicens, some have suggested, was driven to the verge of bankruptcy by Gaudí's extravagance. However, Gaudí was a frequent and welcome house guest at the Vicenses' summerhouse in Alella throughout the 1880s. The Casa Vicens itself is a monument to exoticism. Its use of diverse materials butted up alongside each other like brick, stone, rubble and tile and the play on textures proved massively influential for the growth of the *modernista* style. But it was also the first and the last time that Gaudí produced a building that was not firmly rooted in either the Catholic faith or Catalan myth.

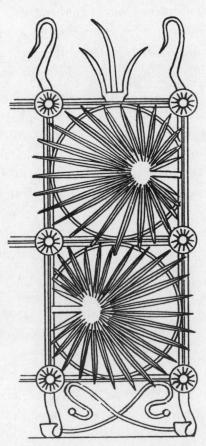

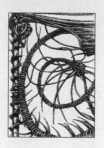

# The Holy Fathers

One must never flatter oneself that one has altogether
escaped the absurd power of Christian morality.
*Michel Leiris*

GAUDÍ'S INVOLVEMENT with the Comillas and Güell clan had
grown increasingly close during the building of El Capricho, the
neo-Mudejar summerhouse. But it was not until September
1883, when Eusebi Güell bought the Can Cuyàs de la Riera
estate, on the edges of the city, that Gaudí finally was established
as the family architect. For the next thirty-five years, until Güell's
death in July 1918, Gaudí attended to almost all the family's
architectural needs; from the small in scope such as designing
laundry facilities for a town house roof, or a stable block and a
modest ornamental fountain, to the more prestigious projects
like a city palace, a private church and a whole garden estate.

Gaudí's respect for Güell was enormous. He explained to Cardinal Casañas the qualities that he felt a man like Güell possessed.

A nobleman is a person of excellent sensitivity, excellent
manners, and excellent position. Excelling in everything,

*83*

he knows no envy and no one bothers him; he is pleased
to see that those around him display their capabilities . . .
Weren't the Medici like that?[1]

Güell also came from Torredembara, close to Tarragona, an
important consideration that Menéndez Pidal drew attention to
in his essay 'Centralization and Regionalism':

> The fact of having been born in the same province creates
> among Spaniards a sense of companionship and an obli-
> gation to help one another which is as great as or even
> greater than that among relatives, and this causes them
> to become rigidly exclusive in dealings with others.[2]

Some saw Don Eusebi Güell as a powerful 'imam',[3] as an over-
bearing, bearded patriarch who protected his womenfolk and
encouraged them to live, in the words of Dolors Monserdà, 'as
a parasitic plant'. But he also proudly described himself (in English) as the son of 'a self-made man'. His father's peasant pru-
dence was echoed in Eusebi Güell's carefully directed generosity.
Gaudí liked Güell's way with money: 'Güell is a gentleman
because the person who has money and does not show off, controls the money, and thus is a *senyor*.'

When Gaudí designed a family shield for Güell it bore the
surprisingly honest motto: *Ahir Pastor Avui Senyor* – 'yesterday
a shepherd and today a gentleman'. This disarming candour
disguised a programme meticulously organised to enhance
Güell's power and reputation.[4]

Güell, a second-generation *indiano*, advanced his position with
far greater subtlety than his forebears. As a 'gentleman', dandy
and dilettante, Don Eusebi could play a much more proactive
role in Barcelona cultural life.[5] In likening Güell to a Renaissance
prince, Gaudí had not been far off the mark. The only real
difference was that the engine of Güell's success was not war or
inherited land but industry.

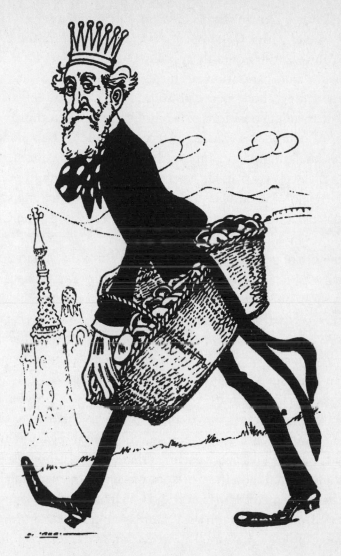

Don Eusebi Güell returns to the Park Güell after a
productive mushroom hunt.

In the previous decade, while Gaudí was doing his military
service, Güell served as a local councillor and in 1878 was elected
senator. These brief excursions into political life, however, seem
to have rather persuaded him that his true vocation lay elsewhere.

Güell was an enthusiastic Catalan patriot, joining a Catalan literary society, Jove Catalunya, in 1870, and in 1882 the Centre Català, and was subsequently appointed its president. The Centre Català was an organisation set up to promote the Catalan cause whilst standing above party politics. This suited Güell's subtle policy of assuming positions of symbolic and moral authority. The reality, of course, was rather different. While in Barcelona the Centre Català might have appeared to serve a broad church, catering to all levels of Catalan society, from the vantage point of the Cortes in Madrid it represented the Catalan federalists and republicans. This was reinforced when in early 1885 the Centre Català presented King Alfonso XII with the *Memorial de Greuges* – both a list of grievances and a wish list for the Catalan people.

Güell was the model of a nineteenth-century Renaissance man. Throughout 1887 and 1888 he actively promoted and helped to finance the 1888 Barcelona Exposition. In 1889 in Paris, he published an academic paper on microbiology entitled '*L'immunité par les leucomaïnes*', and he was also interested in proving the Catalan language's ancient and unique identity.

He was a talented watercolourist and painter. He was also a sponsor of plays, poetry and opera and an active patron to several Catalan painters. But it is Güell's architectural legacy that lasts today. It became clear very early on that Güell was not just going to pay and commission the work but was intent on directing it too.

In the years since 1878, Gaudí and Güell had come to know each other well, not just through the Comillas connection, or the *Excurcionistas*, but through mutual appreciation of the remarkable poet Jacint Verdaguer. For the five years from 1884, this trio of men would forge together a Catalan architectural language and style.

Jacint Verdaguer's relationship with the Comillas-Güell family first began in 1874 when he started working as ship's chaplain on the Compañía Trasatlàntica's *Guipúzcoa*. In 1878, on dry land once again, he published his epic seafaring masterpiece *L'Atlàntida*, which became an anthem of Catalan identity.

*L'Atlàntida* combined Columbus' voyage with the labours of Hercules and the fantasy of a Spain reborn. In *L'Atlàntida* Hercules sets out from Barcelona and slowly circumnavigates Spain. While in Cadiz, he meets the triple-headed oxherder Geryon, who tells him of a magic tree laden with golden oranges and the Queen Hesperis who would marry any man bold enough to cut off the head of the dragon Ladon. For his remarkable feats Hercules was rewarded with deification and was driven up to Olympus on Minerva's chariot. But Verdaguer, Antoni López (the first Marquès de Comillas) and Güell understood these prizes were here for the taking. Supplying tobacco, slaves, molasses and rum, the industries of mining, steel and textiles, and a heavy involvement in the railroads, banking and insurance were the labours of their day. And *L'Atlàntida* served a definite purpose, namely, to authenticate the legitimacy of the new Catalan plutocracy.

It was against the backdrop of *L'Atlàntida* that Gaudí started work on his first major commission for Güell. Güell's father already owned a large estate in Les Corts de Sarrià so his acquisition of Can Cuyàs de la Riera in 1883 extended the Güell presence on the southwest edge of the city. Don Eusebi entrusted these works to Gaudí. It was a large project, with a gatehouse and an indoor stables with exercise yard which still exist today. Other Gaudí additions to the estate, namely a tall polychrome stepped brick lookout and an extensive outdoor exercise area for horses, have sadly long been lost. But it was on the indoor stables, the gatehouse and the famous dragon gate – the Drac de Pedralbes – that Gaudí created a masterpiece.

The stylistic idiom that Gaudí employed at Les Corts was the neo-Mudejar that he had used to such effect at the Casa Vicens and at El Capricho. It was a style that was perfectly suited to the requirements of the commission as it was both appropriately decorative, novel and cheap. A gatehouse and stables were after all working buildings.

The stable block (that today houses the Cátedra Gaudí where

Professor Bassegoda i Nonell spearheads present-day Gaudí research and conservation) incorporates the most interesting innovations. Just inside the door, a tight staircase leads up onto the roof covering the long rectangular hall of the stable block. The stairs are quirky enough, rising step by step, a foot at a time. But the interior stable hall introduces us to Gaudí's first sustained attempt at a new structural ordinance. The exterior walls are low enough to allow a row of transverse parabolic arches to span the space. This had been seen in Catalonia before, most notably at the refectory of the monastery of Santes Creus and the Saló Tinell in the *Barri Gòtic* where Columbus is supposed to have delivered the Americas to the Catholic kings. But Gaudí's stables were fashioned predominantly from brick, plaster and adobe, not stone. Covered by shallow vaults, showing off the Catalan bricklayer's craft at its best, the stables are now populated by researchers, and the horses' feeding pens now house bookshelves for the world's foremost Gaudí archive.

The exterior displays Gaudí's growing decorative ingenuity. The walls' surface is articulated with a delightful interplay of surface, texture and material. Bricks rise up in arches to divide the space clearly. The spaces in between – the infills – rise from the ground up to waist height on a rustic stone base, but use a simple overlaid plaster motif that, repeated again and again, looks like a row of car hubcaps – an effect not unlike early Visigothic decorative designs.[6] The creamy plaster appears subdued in winter but in high summer, sunlight activates it and creates the sensation of colour.[7] Even there, hidden in the mortar, the visitor suddenly notices shards of coloured tile pressed into the running course. At the roof level further games of light are played with perforated brick patterns set diagonally on edge to form balcony railings. It is a beautiful display of artifice.

Antoni López, the first Marquès de Comillas, died in 1883 and Verdaguer was required, like all the seminary students in Comillas who had benefitted from his 500,000-peseta endowment, to read prayers every day for the safety of the Marquès' soul. His liturgical duties over, he and Güell took off together round Europe in 1884.

When they returned, it was to find Barcelona devastated by a cholera epidemic in which 1,300 had died. It was clear that the work at Les Corts should continue apace, but Gaudí, who normally summered at the Vicens house in Alella, had rented his own summerhouse farther away at Sant Feliu de Codines.[8] By the cooler weather of September the epidemic had slowed. Masses of thanks for deliverance were celebrated in Barcelona Cathedral and in Reus, Gaudí's home town, they danced the Devil's Dance to signal the end of the plague.

Now all three men worked together to develop a fitting literary and architectural narrative for the Güell family's summer retreat. A gigantic wrought-iron gate was put in place between the gatehouse and stables. Welded to Gaudí's design at the Vallet and Piqué workshop, the gate depicted a fearsome dragon whose gaping mouth guarded Güell's sanctuary behind. It was clearly Ladon from Verdaguer's *L'Atlàntida*. And if any were left in doubt as to the subject of this allegory a stone sculpture depicted the initial 'G' surrounded by the foliage and fruit of the golden orange tree and the tiny eglantine dog roses – the first prize at the *Jocs Florals* which *L'Atlàntida* had won.

During autumn 1885, Güell and Gaudí started plans for a city palace on the southern side of the Rambles. It was in many ways a strange choice as it was a very unfashionable area. But Güell was following family precedent in choosing the site of the grounds of a former dairy on the calle Conde de Asalto, close to his parents' house on the Rambla de Caputxins.[9] When, in the early 1890s, Güell's palace was finally finished the two family edifices were linked across the rooftops by a long narrow covered passageway that held them together like a winding umbilical cord.

Even if the choice of site made sense in terms of family it was nevertheless a risky piece of property development. Little has changed in the calle Conde de Asalto in the last hundred years. In its cramped alleyways it is as normal today to be propositioned by a platinum blond Colombian transsexual or offered cheap cocaine as it was to be invited indoors by a syphilitic laundress for a poisonous shot of absinthe and even cheaper sex then. In the intervening years, the area came to be known as the *barri Xinès* – Chinatown (not for its Chinese residents but because the journalist Angel Marsá's description of the area in the 1920s has firmly stuck). It has nurtured the dissolute and the decadent like the surrealist pornographer Georges Bataille and Paul Morand (who based his *Ouvert la Nuit* on the *barri Xinès*); and Jean Genet whose *Thief's Journal* records feasts with an everchanging cast of homosexual sailors – Barcelona's equivalent of Oscar Wilde's depraved dockside panthers.

Opposite Güell's relatively small eighteen by twenty-two metre site was the dilapidated Café de la Alegría, soon replaced by the notorious Eden Concert. Upstairs, at no. 12 above the Eden Concert, Carlota Valdivia, the walleyed procuress immortalised in Picasso's blue period painting *La Celestina*, waited patiently for her next client. Next door, at no. 10, the young Picasso shared a studio with Angel de Soto, Josep Rocarol and the increasingly maudlin alcohol and morphine addict Carles Casegemas; and on Sunday afternoons their anarchic salon engaged in childish pranks like throwing water bombs and pulling away coins attached to a long string, downing copious amounts of flaming brandy, while singing *Els Segadors*, the outlawed marching song of the Catalans, and producing with Isidre

Nonell their fried drawings – *dibujos fritos* (sketches prematurely browned by being aged in boiling oil).[10]

Eugeni d'Ors wrote harrowingly of

> the foul slime of city sewers; those wasted by . . . disease, vice and degeneration . . . wanderers without family or homeland, vagrants and tramps and beggars; outlawed races . . . their heads crawling with lice . . . dark spirits at the mercy of animal instincts . . . hooligans, whores, bawds, cretins, madmen, thieves and hired assassins.

This heaving fleshpot, described by the Catalan writer Juan Goytisolo as a kind of 'Hispanic Court of Miracles', was under constant threat of TB, absinthe, syphilis and abject poverty.

But there was a sense of balance. Opposite was Arnau's, Gaudí's favourite hatshop. Farther down the street at no. 32, as late as 1900, Gaudí's friend Dr Santaló employed him to renovate his building. And just twenty metres farther on was the local Raval police station. Continuing down the street the vista opened out to reveal the Romanesque monastery of Sant Pau del Camp, one of Barcelona's earliest Christian monuments.

Even so, Güell's choice was a strange one. Güell's main motivation was to provide himself with a palace to rival the luxurious Palau Moja, the property of his brother-in-law Claudio López i Bru, the second Marquès de Comillas, west up the Ramblas. Güell wanted a building that was in Pugin's term a 'useful, healthy organism' with a 'comely form'.

From the moment Gaudí received the commission he feverishly applied himself, with the assistance of Francisco Berenguer, to the task. Twenty-two different versions of the façade were drawn up, although only three versions still survive. And 12 July 1886 the final project was submitted to the city hall. Gaudí's Palau was a remarkable reinterpretation of a Venetian palazzo squeezed into a hopelessly narrow site.[11] Considering the building's limited scale, Gaudí's ambition was directed at understanding and interpreting its open plan and flowing spaces. Effectively eight storeys tall, its exterior, of grey Garraf marble from Güell's hunting estate south of Barcelona, was entirely unique. At street level two high arches, coach entrance and exit, divided the façade. Each was closed off by gigantic iron gates that were ridiculed in the popular press. The critics mocked Güell and Gaudí's pretensions in a neighbourhood shadowed by poverty and despair.[12] But there between the two gates Gaudí had Joan Oños create an exuberant two-metre-high display of Catalan pride in iron that, shaped as a lantern, depicted the nation's blood-striped heraldic shield crowned by a strange thorn-like helmet bearing an imperial eagle already flapping and making ready for flight. Whether this symbolised nervousness or vigilance is impossible to say. But above this patriotic entrance a main-floor balcony window that crossed the whole elevation imposed a sense of order.

Once inside, Gaudí created an entirely original design. One hundred and twenty-seven limestone columns were used, each designed individually. Many critics have pointed out the similarity between a cross section of the Palau Güell and a drawing of the Alhambra in Owen Jones' study. But, surely, Gaudí's design was a multistorey reinterpretation of Cordoba's great mosque for which marble columns and *spolio* had been imported from all across Europe and the Middle East, raided from cultures spanning more than a thousand years.

Once through the entrance a spiral ramp led the carriage and horses down into the basement, where massive brick piers, shaped like cep mushrooms, supported the flattened vaults. This space, which was used as a torture chamber in the Spanish Civil War, feels ancient. And it has been said that Gaudí's placement of the central stone on the top floor of the façade had been carefully sited in direct relationship to Montserrat.[13]

But Gaudí's promiscuous eclecticism pulled together other ancient cultures – an effect immediately acknowledged by critics.

On 28 December 1889, Rusiñol and Utrillo, two of the *Modernistas* based on the Quatre Gats café, sent in a satirical spoof on the Palau Güell's archaeological pretensions to *La Vanguardia*.

> It seems certain that this construction was Babylonian. If this is true, who can tell the end of all the theories which have up to now been propounded about the origins of our nation? . . . The most probable answer is that this construction dates from the time of Belshazzar or, as Señor Rogent maintains, that of Nebuchadnezzar.[14]

This archaic feeling was something that both architect and patron enjoyed. Güell even hoped to run an aqueduct from his estates in Garraf to benevolently return some of the *Acquae Vergine* and the ancient glories of Imperial Rome to Barcelona. But this was one project too many.

The rear elevation of the Palau Güell faced onto an interior square and featured a canopy of balcony windows elaborately shuttered with a Chinese screen.

Once through the main entrance the guest climbs up a narrow staircase to the mezzanine floor, which provides a waiting room, library and administrative offices. And from there a grand stairway leads to the *piano nobile*, where the sumptuous main salons and its grand central hall attested finally to its regal design. No expense was spared on the Palau's interior decoration. The most intricate ironwork was used. Sconces and candelabras were attached to marble walls and beaten copper sheets. Ebony, tortoiseshell and ivory fragments were inlaid meticulously into wood. One room was eucalyptus, the other was beech; while Islamic-derived decorative sequences of marquetry in pearwood, palisander and padouk referred to the sources of Güell's wealth. In the first two salons, carved wood ceilings, formed from a regular rhythm of polychrome beams, were decorated in applied silver and gold leaf. It was as luxurious and as labour-intensive as anything commissioned by Pedro the Cruel for Seville's

Alcazar, and pushed Puntí's workshop to perform to its best.

Gaudí had been as extravagant as his imagination and knowledge of expensive materials and precious stones had allowed. There was no need to cheat as there was no limit to the budget. Antonio Oliva, an interior decorator, had tried some *faux* marbling on the side columns of a wardrobe which he proudly showed off to Gaudí. The architect rapped it with his knuckles and warned Oliva not to give in to the temptation ever again to cheat. 'Art is a very serious business,' he admonished.

Güell's secretary, accountant and general factotum, the poet Ramón Picó Campamar, was shocked by Gaudí's outrageous freedom. 'I fill Don Eusebi's pockets and Gaudí then empties them,' he complained. On another occasion when Güell returned from one of his many trips abroad, Picó offered Don Eusebi a pile of bills. Misunderstanding the underlying purpose of the Palau Güell's overwhelming conspicuous consumption, Picó received his comeuppance. 'Is that all Gaudí has spent?' Güell asked, annoyed by the interference.

But Picó's rivalry was also professional. He had to play second fiddle to Gaudí and it was only years later that he would enjoy his fifteen minutes of glory with the staging of his poetic drama *Garraf*, an *homage* to Güell and his hunting estate, which was performed before two German princesses and Leo XIII's papal nuncio, Monseñor Cretoni. Although Picó was a poet, the only poem celebrated in the Palau Güell was Verdaguer's *L'Atlàntida*.[15] In the dining room Gaudí called in the eccentric painter Alejo Clapés Puig to play around yet again with Verdaguer's driving theme of a land and people restored to their former glory. Gaudí ordered a large mural of Hercules, sadly long since destroyed.[16]

Throughout the palace Gaudí skilfully drew out royal allusions in order to ennoble the building. If the columns related to Pedro the Cruel, and the carved wooden ceilings to the style of decoration favoured by Isabel and Ferdinand, then the sombre atmosphere created by the cold grey Garraf marble and alabaster was more closely reminiscent of Philip II's forbidding El Escorial. The Hercules painting, however, was a direct reference to Philip IV's Salón de Reinos in Madrid; which, decorated with Velazquez's equestrian portraits of the Hapsburg Royal Family and monumental depictions of Spanish military victories, was rounded off by Zurbarán's series *The Labours of Hercules*. The Salón de Reinos was one of the most carefully orchestrated essays in kingship ever put together.[17] Interestingly, its Castilian flavour never deterred Gaudí from adapting it for the more modest Palau Güell. The Palau Güell was primarily a ceremonial and official residence. Before the Palau was even completed it was visited by the Queen Regent María Cristina, the Infanta María Eulalia de Borbon and Antonio d'Orleans.

If the rationale behind López and Güell's project was to conquer time by absorbing and adapting earlier traditions, then the central zone of the Palau Güell, its three-storey concert room and chapel, represents Gaudí's desire to control and capture space.[18]

Nine metres by nine, almost twenty metres high at the apex of the dome, the central salon was the heart of the whole house. Pushing up through three floors the elongated parabolic dome unified the palace. At its first level, a staggered staircase with open tracery banisters led up to a balcony overlooking the salon itself. On the next, wooden screens shuttered off the musicians' gallery. And above that, the bedrooms and bathrooms were discreetly hidden away. One of the dome's unusual features was that it sat on a bolted square of studded cast-iron girders, brought up from the dockyards. This powerfully demonstrated that even here within unashamed luxury Gaudí was introducing utilitarian and novel designs. Central heating had also been thought of, although as Gaudí discovered later it was only practical in Barcelona's humid climate if coupled with ventilation or air-conditioning. (One morning the entire Güell family woke up horribly congested.)[19] In the main salon the lighting solution was also ingenious: light came through small circular perforations in the dome, and filtered down. Within the Palau the parabolic arch became, in a sense, the leitmotif and unifying form.* Everywhere there was decorative detail, material and texture heaped up like in an Oriental bazaar. But the simplicity and novelty of the parabola held it all together.

Down in the salon, Gaudí placed the family chapel behind two giant marquetry doors like an enormous wardrobe. The shallow oratory was, unfortunately, smashed up in the Civil War as was the organ used by Isabel Güell. But the chapel highlighted the sheer flexibility of the salon created for the pursuit of morally uplifting pleasure and piety. It was a clever trick. Gaudí had inverted the function of the Arab *hammam* where the caliph might peer down unobserved on his harem. In Güell's house, peeping Toms got the Angelus and the early morning mass instead.

For those stifled by funereal opulence there was always the rear balcony. But far more exciting was the roofscape, a cluster of eighteen chimney and ventilator shafts that surrounded a central conical spire that looked like a Christianized minaret. Each chimney was covered in broken tiles, using the flexible *trencadis* technique. Although souvenir hunters have left their bodies in disrepair, they have been restored in the free spirit of their creation, sometimes incorporating fragments of a white Limoges dinner service. (In one of the white towers appears Cobi the dog, Mariscal's mascot for the 1992 Olympic games.) The effect, though, is still pure Gaudí and entirely unique. Both Robert Hughes and Ellsworth Kelly agree 'that no history of fragmentation in modern art could possibly be complete without considering the effects of Gaudí's *trencadís* on the young Picasso', who

---

* The parabolic arch is also known as a catenary arch, based as it is on the inverted shape of the natural drop of a length of chain held at both ends.

during the most formative years of his life enjoyed a rare view of the Palau Güell across the street.

The central spire of the roof, covered in rough greenish Triassic limestone, absorbed rather than reflected the clear Catalan light. It was in complete contrast to the gracious effect of the rest of the house and almost geological in its simplicity – weathered and ancient before its time. And crowning it all there was a weathervane that depicted a bat. The magazine *La Illustración Hispano-Americano* reviewed the Palau Güell:

> From the summit of the cupola emerges the vigilant bat which since the days of Jaume el Conquistador has protected the arms of Catalonia with its wings: there stands the symbol of the powerful soul of this land, giving life to that immense mountain of stone.

Reading the building in a postmodernist light the Palau Güell is nothing if not 'processional'. Spaces and areas open up, one after the other, like acts in a play. From the cellar to the ceiling the viewer's mood and the building's ambience are regulated with careful deliberation. It is almost symphonic, using the central salon as a larger than life protagonist, booming out like a giant hollow-sounding bell. Gaudí is actually depicting the whole Cosmic Order, spiced up with a subtle Catholic twist. The cellar was Hell.[20] The central salon, that joined the whole towering structure together, was both earth and sky, while the roofscape represented Heaven. What the Palau Güell offered then was the language of Redemption and Resurrection. It was a sacred palace for a worldly Prince.

For the first time, in the Palau Güell, Gaudí was able to create a narrative that mixed mythology, allegory and analogy. The general effect of the decor, however, through the muddle of all the historical styles, finally arrived at what Mario Praz perfectly described:

The period of antiquity with which these artists of the *fin de siècle* liked best to compare their own was the long Byzantine twilight, that gloomy apse gleaming with dull gold and gory purple, from which peer enigmatic faces, barbaric yet refined, with dilated neurasthenic pupils.

During the construction of the Palau Güell, Gaudí's architectural studio had grown increasingly busy. On 19 March 1885 the first mass had been celebrated in the chapel of Sant Josep in the crypt of the Sagrada Família. In 1887 he had given advice of an exhibition pavilion for the Exposición Naval at Cadiz, which the following year was brought around the coast to Barcelona for the Exposición Universal of 1888.

The 1888 Exposición Universal represents the moment at which Barcelona realised its image as the least Spanish of all the Spanish cities. Opened on 20 May 1888 by the Queen Maria Cristina and the infant Alfonso XIII, the Expo became the symbol of the rise of Barcelona and the Catalan economy. It became 'the trampoline of the *Modernista* style, and it was the *Modernista* style that would become the new brand and image for Barcelona's industry'.[21]

The Expo was fantastically successful, attracting more than 2 million visitors, 12,000 stands and twenty-five participating countries. But the picture it gave of a unified buoyant economy was a false one – on the contrary, it had just entered a slump. Various architectural wonders helped the illusion, however, like Domènech's Café-Restaurant, for instance (later turned into an arts and crafts workshop, the Castell de Tres Dragons); or his International Hotel, built in just fifty-three days, with its spectacular salons, 400 bedrooms and a further 30 luxury suites. So did street lighting, which had been introduced to most of the central thoroughfares. And the Ciutadella Park had newly provided the city centre with an elegant place to stroll.

Gaudí's contribution to the Expo was not major. But he was not alone. Fontseré, fearing that his Ciutadella Park would be vandalised, resigned in protest, only to be swiftly replaced by Rogent. Gaudí had been approached by Mayor Rius i Taulet, renowned for his long muttonchop whiskers, to revamp the Saló de Cent in the Ajuntament building on the Plaça Sant Jaume, but when his involvement with the council ground to a halt Domènech quickly picked up the work. But in Gaudí's case, other commissions had got in the way. Güell's Palau was too important to put aside, even for a few months, and the Sagrada Família was steadily ongoing. Gaudí's contributions to the city fabric during this period would be far more enduring than the ephemeral creations of most of the Expo.

In early 1887, Gaudí received news of a tempting commission for the Episcopal Palace in Astorga. Bishop Grau's palace had burnt down in December 1886, just two months after he had come into the post. Normally the commission to build a new palace would have gone directly to the diocesan architect, but there wasn't one in Astorga. And after brief attempts to find a local, Bishop Grau suggested Gaudí, whom he knew from Tarragona.

Moon-faced Joan Grau seemed at first the well-fed bishop of anticlerical prints: a gluttonous buffoon. But Grau's exterior disguised an energetic, passionate character. Coupled with his explosive Reus temper it made him a formidable adversary.

In the 1860s, Grau had briefly been president of the Societat Arqueòlogica de Tarragona – a society which followed the latest developments of the sacred archaeology spearheaded in the Vatican by Giovanni Battista de Rossi. But it was quickly clear that Grau's dynamic personality would not be bound by the restrictions of small city life. He was, in the words of one observer, 'a great man who stood out from the crowd of which he never felt himself a part'. His rise through the Catholic hierarchy was never spectacular but he was obviously regarded by his superiors as a safe pair of hands. During the September 1868 revolution, Grau accepted the post of vicar general for Tarragona. The following year, during the First Vatican Council, at which liberal Catholicism was effectively crushed by the declaration of papal infallibility, Grau remained in Tarragona as acting ecclesiastical governor during his archbishop's absence in Rome. In the 1870s it became clear that Grau would play an increasingly active role in the Catholic revival, founding first a missionary organisation, the Asociación de Sacerdotes Misioneros, and then starting up a magazine to promote *La Devoción a los Corazones de Jesús y María*. Grau's reward for years of devoted militant service came in June 1886 when Pope Leo XIII rubber-stamped his appointment to the Astorga bishopric and on 2 August 1886 he received the honour the *Gran Cruz de la Orden de Isabel la Católica*.

Between February and August 1887, Gaudí prepared drawings for Bishop Grau. Their genesis had been rather unusual. Gaudí's normal method, as earlier seen at the Casa Vicens, was to get a real feel for the site and topography first. However, due to other commitments, he was unable to travel to Astorga, so instead Gaudí asked the bishop to send him as many photographs as possible of the local monuments, books on local history, site details and impressions of the vernacular styles. He also studied the proofs of his friend Josep Ixart's *España: Sus monumentos y artes*.[22]

Surrounded by mountain ranges to the west and north, Astorga had been plundered by the Asturians from the north and the Ummayad Arabs from the south, until finally it was established as a key city of the Christian kingdom of León.

More than a thousand years earlier Pliny described Astorga as 'a magnificent city', but all that remained from that era were imposing Roman walls from when it had been a staging post for the Seventh Legion. Astorga's Christian tradition went back at least to A.D. 254. In the fourth century it was established as one of the very first bishoprics in Spain. Astorga's Gothic cathedral was the city's great architectural extravagance. As most Spanish cities, Astorga was full of Baroque. And it was to all aspects of this long tradition that Gaudí looked when designing his Christian palace fort.

On receipt of Gaudí's drawings in the autumn of 1887, Bishop Grau sent his enthusiastic reply by return of post. 'Received magnificent plans. Like very much. Congratulations. Await letter.'

Unlike dealing with the city council, whose directives could often be ignored, as a national monument the Episcopal Palace was directly dependent on the Ministry of Justice, who relied on architectural experts at the Real Academia de Bellas Artes de San Fernando in Madrid, and whose suggestions had to be acted upon before funds were released.

In the late summer of 1888, Gaudí visited Bishop Grau in Astorga. On arrival he was shocked to discover that his initial feelings for the terrain, gleaned from Grau's parcel of photos, had misled him.[23] He rapidly studied the possible modifications.

The Real Academia's architectural commission had already found fault with many aspects of Gaudí's design: the stairs were too narrow, the moat not wide enough, the columns too thin, the vaults too shallow and not enough attention had been paid to fire risks. Gaudí took it in surprisingly good spirit and quickly reworked the plans. Gaudí's second visit to Astorga was in the spring following the Real Academia's final approval. And on 24 June 1889, on the bishop's saint's day, the first stone was laid.

Gaudí visited Astorga eleven times over the next four years to oversee the works on the Palacio Episcopal. He had seen the workings of a church commission – the *Junta* – at first hand at the Sagrada Família and there his bluff, brusque manner had won him artistic freedom. At Astorga, however, the chain of command was far less flexible. A story related in Astorga gives a piquant insight into the working methods of both men. On a morning stroll through the cathedral, when contemplating Gaspar Becerra's marble retable of 1562, with its life-size figures carved in high relief, Gaudí suggested that they remove the canopy that detracted from the work. Grau disagreed. He reminded Gaudí that the canopy was an essential part of Catholic dogma and drew attention to the 'regal dignity of the Holy Sacrament'. But Gaudí insisted that the mantle carved by Becerra, which was supported by angels, already achieved that aim.[24] 'Perhaps you are right in this, at least a little bit right,' said Grau. 'In this and in everything!' Gaudí exclaimed.

Bishop Grau defused the situation by offering to pass on the suggestion to the Sacred Congregation on Ritual, whose reply was unequivocal: under no pretext whatsoever could they allow the suppression of the canopy, a liturgical piece of irreplaceable expressiveness.

Gaudí was well aware of his headstrong, blundering ways. 'All of my life I have made an effort to control my character; I am usually successful, but at times my character is stronger than I am,' he once observed. A photograph of Gaudí taken at exactly this time, for a pass for the Expo, shows a thickset man who had obviously put on some weight. But he looks in rude health, with his head shaved almost completely.

Gaudí spent hours discussing liturgy with Grau. The bishop encouraged the architect to read *l'Année Liturgique* by Dom Guéranger. It became a key text for Gaudí, taking pride of place on his bookshelf with his autographed *L'Atlàntida*. Years later, Gaudí spoke of this being probably the most influential period in his professional life.

By the winter of 1890 the work had progressed enough for Gaudí to assist in the raising of the portico. Respecting local traditions Gaudí had chosen a neo-Gothic design, built around a central hall. Carved from white Bierzo stone, the exterior offered few architectural novelties except for the structure of the triple arches that flared out forwards supporting a balcony like a mediaeval turret. Inventing a wooden cradle to support the stones until firmly in place proved almost impossible. The arches collapsed twice. But then, according to Alonso Luengo, who researched every aspect of Gaudí's sojourn in Astorga, he took to the stage.

> Half the town crowded into the area surrounding the construction site, contemplating the spectacle, and architects all over Spain awaited with ironic smiles the result of that madness, while Gaudí, mounted on a platform and withdrawn from all that surrounded him, throwing up his arms at every movement of the stone, took on the aspect of an impetuous flame.

Gaudí finished his folly at sunset, moments before the snows set in. But, once again, the arches collapsed, and obstinately Gaudí started all over again:

> The architect's hands, the skin blistering, were for a moment one with the stone and his pulse one with the workman who, many years later in recalling that moment with emotion, was to proudly claim that the most valued recognition of his noble craftsmanship had been Gaudí's embrace, once the last stone of the portico was put in place never to move again.[25]

His Herculean struggles, however, had reaped no financial reward over the preceding four years. And so, on 21 November 1892, Gaudí wrote to Bishop Grau thanking him for his hospitality but expressed his profound disgust with the workings of the state.

> Until today, thank God, I have never needed to expend any of my creative faculties on working for the State.

Luckily I have always been in the fortunate position of working for respectable clients who, in complete contrast to the State, understand that an artist has to live by his work and that it is hardly dignified to turn him into a beggar.

It was not until the next year, after nitpicking over Gaudí's receipts, that anything was sorted out. But by then it was almost too late. In September 1893, Bishop Grau hurt his leg while out on a parish visit in the province of Zamora. Instinctively Gaudí knew there was something wrong, reminiscing ten years later in *La Veu de Catalunya*:

Do you know why I knew that the Bishop was dying? I found him so beautifully transformed that I had the idea that he couldn't live. He was beautiful, too beautiful. All of his personal character had disappeared: the lines of his face, his colour, his voice. And perfect beauty cannot live. The abstract face of the Greek divinity could not have lived.[26]

Gangrene had set in and Grau died on 21 September.

The Palacio Episcopal was still roofless but Gaudí resigned, delivering his parting shot to the cathedral canons, 'They are totally incapable of finishing it or of leaving it unfinished.' The canons had put every possible obstacle in Gaudí's way and now he was without his ally and protector. Gaudí's last act in Astorga was to design Bishop Grau's headstone. He had resigned knowing full well that without the bishop's support he could never finish the job. Gaudí wrote of Grau:

His effort to arouse the town was tremendous, but hopeless. He undertook that work in order to set an example and to stimulate the region's activity. He ended up fighting with everyone: with his superiors in León and with the parishioners of Astorga. Everyone, from the mayor, who was contractor for the materials, to the cathedral chapter, set up obstacles. We went there for a large part of each year, and that revived Dr Grau's spirit. Never have I seen a firmer nor more well-intentioned will than his. While he lived we overcame all bitterness.

In his first year as bishop, Grau had managed to push through the rebuilding of the Episcopal Palace with unusual haste; he had also discussed various changes to the liturgy which the canons had rejected outright; had set up a diocesan museum and founded several new schools across the province. His energy or integrity were unquestionable. In 1887 he willed the sale of all his properties to subsidise charitable works. But what Gaudí and Grau had underestimated was the strong resistance to change in Astorga, described by one contemporary traveller as the most 'melancholy city in Spain'.[27]

Years later attempts were made to woo Gaudí back but his treatment had left him embittered. The Palacio Episcopal took decades to finish and never grew to resemble Gaudí's original plans which, in any case, he had burnt in rage.[28]

'I wouldn't even cross Astorga if it was in a hot-air balloon!' he said.

In tandem with the bishop's palace Gaudí was brought in to design a very different religious building – a school for nuns drawn up on the basic lines advocated by Saint Teresa, built by the organiser of the cult of St Teresa, Father Enrique Antoni de Ossó. Ossó had started by using the builder Joaquim Codina Matalí, who as agreed had designed the school and dormitory house in the fashionable Byzantine style. But soon Gaudí was brought in to finish the job. So, as with the Sagrada Família,

Gaudí inherited a predominantly inflexible floor plan once again. The external walls were already two metres high when he was called in.

Exactly contemporary with the grander edifice at Astorga and the luxurious Palau Güell, the Col.legi Teresiano is distinctive for its 'poverty' and 'minimalist' design. Ossó was on a tight budget and frequently interfered. Sometimes this was to Gaudí's obvious displeasure: 'Each to his own, Father Enrique. I'll build houses and you get on with preaching sermons and taking the mass.'

The ground floor (Codina's) was constructed out of brick piers filled with rubble but from there on there is a stunning sensation of verticality and upward thrust to the rectangular four-storey block. At roof level the Gothicising effect was accentuated by narrow gables. Everywhere there were Teresian emblems and invocations to worship the Lord.

Once inside, the building was divided into three bays that ran the building's entire length. This was most effective on the first floor where white corridors of plaster parabolic arches stretched as far as the eye could see. Uncluttered and modern, they were a miracle of restraint. These arched walkways are possibly the most spiritual spaces Gaudí ever created. The corridors are designed for walking but of a very special kind. They are there for a gentle stroll, while meditating on Christ's passion.

Running down the central bay Gaudí divided the space up into seven smaller rectangles alternately open to the sky. In architectural terms it cleverly brought light into the core of the building. But it had a far deeper symbolism. St Teresa's most influential book was *Las Moradas*, also called *El Castillo Interior* (The Interior Castle). This book has obvious appeal to an architect set on lending his buildings both narrative and meaning. St Teresa used the architectural metaphor of seven mansions to describe the seven layers of her spiritual quest. Gaudí's seven spaces, closed off to the corridor but open to the world, are places for just such contemplation.[29] And on my every visit there I have seen the nuns doing exactly that, sitting quietly amongst the potted cacti and the creeping ferns.

Bishop Grau has most often been seen as author of Gaudí's growing involvement with the Catholic revival. But it was also exactly at this time, during November and December 1889, that Gaudí went on retreat to a monastery in Tortosa. Perhaps he was inspired by the Col.legi Teresiano, which he was to finish in record time by the summer of 1890. Slowly but surely he was becoming absorbed into the inner circle of the Catalan Catholic Church.

In the late summer of 1891, Claudio López, second Marquès de Comillas, invited Gaudí to join him on a visit to Tangier to study the possibility of building a Franciscan mission in the city. Travelling through Andalucia and crossing to Africa for the first time from Malaga, Gaudí had the opportunity to extend his knowledge at first hand. From the famous white villages of Andalucia, predominantly cuboid, he moved across to the sculptural curves of the Berber houses.

Of his project, however, there is only a drawing left. The building, if built, would have been almost as ambitious as the Sagrada Família. Wrapped within an oblong turreted wall a cluster of towers rose up like stalagmites coralled within a Benin stockade.

But even without the Tangier project, Gaudí had easily enough to keep his studio busy. In León he had been commissioned to build a palatial headquarters for the Catalan firm Fernández y Andrés, friends and associates of Güell. The Casa de los Botines was one of Gaudí's most restrained buildings. The granite façade with its sculpture of George and the dragon (the Catalan patron saint) disguised an interior commercial space constructed out of cast-iron pillars. Set within view of León's magnificent Gothic cathedral, of all Gaudí's buildings it is the least sensitive to its immediate surroundings. It is a massive block of stone – a hybrid between a palace and a castle (with moat) – whose overall heaviness is only lightened through the clever articulation of the windows and the corner towers. The speed of its construction, however, was quite remarkable – just ten months – and with time it has become accepted as Léon's most important secular building. From León, Gaudí frequently visited Astorga until the death of Bishop Grau. But that project's untimely termination didn't lighten his workload much as by 1894 he had already been commissioned to build a wine bodega for Güell's estate in Garraf. However, the authorship of this bodega has often been attributed to Gaudí's assistant Berenguer.[30]

Midway through all these projects in 1894, Gaudí's increasingly fervent Catholicism was best illustrated by his strict adherence to a complete Lenten fast. Reported on in local newspapers, the haggard architect was sketched laid out under a covering of heavy coats and blankets. Weakening by the day, Gaudí was rapidly bedridden, in his flat at 339 carrer Diputació. Both his father and Santaló failed to persuade him to stop and it was only Torras i Bages, who found exaggerated and fanatical demonstrations of faith and mysticism deeply distasteful, who persuaded Gaudí to finally give up. Witnesses morbidly described Gaudí trapped in his 'profound lethargic sleep' seeing 'nobility and saintlike majesty' in his skeletal features.

Lacking diaries, letters, recorded conversation or access to the confessional, it is impossible now to understand fully Gaudí's need at this time for a profounder faith. What is certain, however, is that by 1894 his observance of Catholic ritual had become so extreme that even Bishop Torras i Bages found it uncomfortable. It is no coincidence that this episode occurred when the Catholic revival in Barcelona was at its most powerful. If to some people Gaudí's increasingly intense relationship with the Catholic Church represented a form of self-indulgent escapism, there was no doubting the authenticity of his struggle.

Two manifestations of this growing religiosity centred on

Gaudí's most intimate circle. It is possible that Gaudí's rather too 'literal', even exaggerated, adherence to the Lenten fast was a reaction to the dismissal of his friend Jacint Verdaguer, whose downfall is one of the most tragic episodes in Catalan cultural life.

Verdaguer returned from sea to take up a position as Palau Moja chaplain. Quite capable of expressing the deepest yearnings in his poems, he prudishly refused to attend the formal banquets because of the women's low-cut dresses. Then relieved from social duties, he was given the exacting post of palace almsgiver.[31] It proved catastrophic.

Verdaguer was wildly profligate with his master's purse; estimates suggest he spent the equivalent of the building works on the Sobrellanos Palace and the vast Catholic seminary. Rumours also surfaced that Verdaguer had tried to persuade the Marquesa to join a convent. Comillas resented Verdaguer's ridiculous behaviour and when reports reached him of demonic possession and violent exorcisms he immediately took action.[32]

After nineteen years under Comillas' roof Verdaguer was finally ejected. It was a terrible humiliation, made doubly so by the intervention of Bishop Morgades, who stripped Verdaguer of his *a divinis*. Verdaguer was tactfully offered exile in the monastery of Gleba in Vic but refused it.

By 1894, on the verge of bankruptcy, Verdaguer pleaded with Comillas for help. But Comillas called in the police. In his short autobiography, *En Defensa Pròpia*, Verdaguer vented his shattered pride. 'A friend for life and he sold me off treacherously for less than thirty pieces of silver!' To Apel.les Mestres he complained bitterly, 'They locked me up in a circle of iron and left me to go round endlessly in circles and circles without ever offering the possibility of escape.'[33]

As the century drew to a close society had become increasingly polarised. At one extreme anarchy, trade unionism and bohemianism flourished, while at the other extreme the Catholic hierarchy, the establishment and an increasingly reactionary government struggled to impose its authority – even, as the Verdaguer incident shows, within its own ranks.

A growing intolerance and fear of decadence was also mirrored in the art world. Disgusted by the drunken, lewd and anticlerical tone of the Círculo de Arte ball, the sculptor Josep Llimona decided it was time to stop the rot. The Cercle Artístic de Sant Lluc, which he founded to promote Catholic art, has as much to do with denial as with creativity. No more female nudes in the life classes was their first edict. As Gaudí lay at home sick, Torras i Bages – the Lluc's spiritual adviser – gave the opening address. Declaring war against liberalism, he announced that art for art's sake was now a bankrupt idea. Gaudí didn't join until 1899 but there is no doubting that his sympathies were fully with his friends.

Much has been written about the Cercle Artístic's 'sanctimonious swarm' and their rivals the bohemians. If the predominant smell associated with Rusiñol's *modernistas* was opium then the Sanc Lluc's smelt, according to the artist Marià Pidelaserra, of 'luxurious funerals and expensive wax'.[34]

The battle lines had been drawn. On 25 October 1900, Picasso wrote to a friend: 'If you see Opisso – tell him to send Gaudí and the Sagrada Família to hell.'

Picasso and the other Quatre Gats were disgusted by the parochial nature of the Cercle de Sant Lluc. Gaudí became a special target for Picasso's acerbic and satirical pen. The disgust was mutual, according to John Richardson; Gaudí 'despised and distrusted the progressive young artists of Barcelona, who would soon include Picasso'.[35]

Easily overlooked in Barcelona's Picasso Museum is a small pen drawing dashed off with characteristic brio, entitled *Hunger*, and dated 1902.[36] In the foreground stand the 'holy' family and behind them the hectoring figure of the artist/architect amongst a debris of classical busts. Bearded, like so many Catalan males of the period, he stands up in his scruffy suit, shoulders sloping forward, berating the crowd.

The family group stares on numbed by hunger. '*Muy importante!*' he says, 'Very important! . . . 'I am going to talk to you about very important issues relating to both God and Art.' 'Yes, talk if you will of God and Art' – the peasant father figure seems to suggest – 'but my children are hungry!'

The figure has never been identified, but it undoubtedly represents a caricature of the ultraconservative Sant Llucs.[37] And in passing bears a resemblance to Gaudí, who was famed for his 'oracular utterances'.[38]

Despite the incessant sniping there were small but symbolic victories for Gaudí's Catholic group. Picasso's bohemian group based at the Quatre Gats had started to split up: Rusiñol spent more time in Sitges and Picasso was on the point of moving to Paris. Pere Romeu, the eccentric owner, whose bookkeeping skills were as bad as his cooking, oversaw the café's closure. On 26 June the Cercle de Sant Lluc finally took over the lease of the legendary but bankrupted Els Quatre Gats.[39] In the short term the revitalised Catholic art establishment – with Gaudí as its figurehead – had clearly won.

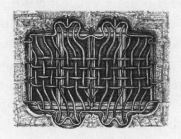

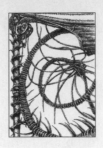

# Towards a New Jerusalem

---

With two rulers and a cord one generates all architecture.

*Antoni Gaudí*

WITHIN SPAIN, these growing divisions were now increasingly marked by violence. By the mid-1890s brutal acts of anarchism, rather than remaining isolated and sporadic, had become a familiar feature of the political landscape. All this was quickly overshadowed, however, by 1898's Cuban catastrophe.

In 1895 a collapse in sugar prices had led to a rebellion in Cuba, then a Spanish colony. The official response was a quick and brutal one. General Weyler, dubbed 'Butcher' by the *New York Journal*, was dispatched to Cuba where his tactics of clearing the land and herding farmers into concentration camps proved effective. Where negotiation might have brought the rebels back into the fold, the cruelty of the camps hardened their resolve to cast off the Spanish yoke.

Cuba's proximity to the United States brought other issues into play.[1] Americans argued that Cuba 'disjoined from its unnatural connection with Spain and incapable of self-support, can gravitate only towards the North American Union.'[2]

The volatile diplomatic relationship between Old and New worlds was stretched to breaking point. Following the sinking of the U.S. battleship *Maine* in Havana harbour, war was declared on 25 April 1898.[3] It lasted just ten weeks. But it was not confined to Cuba. Manila, Hawaii and Guam fell in quick succession. The 'splendid little war' was over and all that was left was to ship the 24,000 demoralised and wounded Spanish troops home. The Treaty of Paris, signed in December 1898, ceded Puerto Rico, Guam and the Philippines directly to the United States, and Cuba was permitted a nominal independence, protected by U.S. naval bases on the island.

For Spain the war had been disastrous and humiliating. This cast a shadow over the disenchanted Generation of '98 – a stunningly talented group that included Ortega y Gasset, Unamuno, the poet Antonio Machado and Angel Ganivet – all of whom shared a brooding pessimism. Economically and artistically the first decade of the twentieth century was fraught with difficulties for many Spaniards. For Gaudí, however, it proved the most creative and successful period of his long career. Secure in Güell's patronage he was liberated from any financial worries. Gaudí reorganised his studio. The increasing workload required greater delegation. Berenguer's contribution was vital as always. A recently qualified architect, Joan Rubió i Bellver (born in Reus) had managed through his mother's intervention to secure a job there.[4] The next commission marked Rubió's rise from assistant to '*colaborador*'.[5] Gaudí was fortunate. Rubió was articulate, a brilliant theoretician, a conscientious practitioner and within the mature *modernista* idiom an architect of huge promise.

In autumn 1897, Gaudí had been commissioned by the widow Doña Juliana Pintó Roldós and the sons of Pere Mártir Calvet to build the headquarters for their textile business, comprising also of a family residence and a set of rental flats.[6]

By 29 March 1898 his plans were ready. The Casa Calvet, sited at 48 carrer Casp, a short walk from Gaudí's fourth-floor flat at 370 Consell de Cent, was built on the lines of a Roman *insula*; the ground floor housed the family business, while the Calvet family lived above. Stuck in the middle of a block the Casa Calvet posed a novel architectural problem. The only opportunity for architects to showcase their talents was in their manipulation of the façade. This was recognised by the enlightened city council who felt that the architecture of façades should be given prestigious awards. But while the beneficial effects of such a policy are obvious, some have criticised what they see as an intrinsically Catalan tendency towards insubstantial design and face-saving elegance. This was satirised by the Basque philosopher Unamuno with his theory of '*fachadismo*', in which Catalonia's obsession with design, at the expense of public health, was mocked. The interior of the Casa Calvet belies any such criticism.

It was awarded the first ever prize for the best building of the year.[7] The jury included the architects Pere Falqués, Bonaventura Bassegoda and Villar. There was just one dissenter, a fellow Sant Lluc, Enrique Sagnier Villavecchia, one of Gaudí's most able competitors, whose support for another building was only won after long debate.[8] The Casa Calvet was a building of obvious quality, but as a 'type' it threw up various problems.

The 1891 Construction Ordinances had undermined Cerdá's much more egalitarian *eixample* plan of 1857, when recognition of the social and economic forces that made it necessary to maximise all available space was implicit. The ordinances pragmatically allowed an increased height limit for buildings of 22 metres; an increase of 2.6 metres. More importantly, it gave freedom to exploit decorative elements: the glazed balconies, corner towers and rooftop sculptures; encouraging an 'eagerness for luxury' and 'a prodigality of ornamentation'.[9]

Despite rapid growth and a steady influx of hard cash the success of the *eixample* was never guaranteed. By the 1890s the hierarchy of housing within the *eixample* had crystallised along clear geographical lines. One property speculator, Sr Gaziel, advised his father to draw a line following the axis of the Passeig de Sant Joan and sell off everything to the right (including the area around the Sagrada Família). Many of the old families still retained an aristocratic disdain for the new. The Marquès de Gelida famously built a palace in the *eixample* but couldn't bear to live there. The 1886 comedy *Un pis a l'Ensanche* centres around the lead character's move from a poky flat in the *eixample* back to the old-world charms of an apartment near the cathedral. The wholesale exodus from the old city only happened after the brutal murder of two prostitutes by their pimps at Don Eusebi's door in 1906.[10]

At the beginning of the twentieth century Europe witnessed an explosion of different styles. Observers were 'astonished to see rising up before their dazzled eyes more minarets than around the Golden Horn, more cupolas than at Odeypour, more gopuras and stone lattice-work than at Kombakoroum or Chillamba-ram'.[11] If the Casa Vicens had reflected Moorish decadence, and the Sagrada Família and Astorga were meditations on the neo-Gothic, then the Casa Calvet was Gaudí's conservative essay on the Baroque and Rococo.

Sitting squarely on massive buttresses the edifice, constructed of Montjüic sandstone, rises up a full five floors. Double banks of pilasters throwing the entrance into shallow relief are a witty reference to the wooden bobbins used in textile manufacture. These in-jokes were a common feature of the *eixample*'s luxury architect-built houses. Each family played with the symbols of their inherited or recently manufactured genealogy. Some features alluded to the source of the owner's wealth and others to their hobbies and interests. But all (if the architect was wise enough) flattered their client and his position.

For the Casa Calvet Gaudí looked as always towards 'the Great Book of Nature'. On the sloping roof of the tribune balcony stone cornucopias of fruit reveal a pair of turtle doves amongst all the apples and pears. The twisted and beaten balcony railings immortalised the late Pedro Calvet's typically Catalan love of mushrooms. They provide a catalogue of edible fungi: *Craterellus cornucopioides* the funereal inky-black horn of plenty, *Clathrus cancellatus* the tasty coxcomb and *Morchella esculenta* – grilled chicken's best ally – the morel.

Some have described the Calvet as 'conventional' and 'almost boring'.[12] Anyone looking for architectural innovation might feel cheated. But the house stands as testament to Gaudí's sensitivity to his client's wishes. There is a restrained Baroque elegance not found elsewhere in his work. The text that accompanied the 'Best Façade' praised Gaudí for observing Beau Brummel's dictum of tasteful discretion in all.

The real delight of the Casa Calvet is in the decorative details of its main door, entrance hall and purpose-built furniture. Much of the imagery and ornament was deliberately pleasant, but underneath lay the presence of politics and pain. Arriving at the house, the visitor took hold of the iron door knocker, in the form of a cross that beat against a wrought-iron beetle. This has been interpreted as faith crushing sin but other readings include a representation of the battle between Catholic Catalonia and parasitic Castile, a favourite topic of the *Renaixença*. Gaudí had little time for what he dismissed as the Spanish culture of flamenco and the clattering castanet. Whenever possible he repeated his theories on the superiority of Catalan creativity. Rafols remembered one famous outburst:

The Catalans have that sense of plasticity which gives the perception of objects as a whole as well as their relative placement. The sea and the light of the Mediterranean give this admirable quality, and it is for this reason that real objects do not deceive the Catalans but instruct them. The Castilians, on the other hand, do not possess this equilibrated perception. They are, with respect to the Catalans, what the Cyclopes were with respect to the Greeks. The Cyclopes had only one eye. As the Castilians take notice of the existence of objects but do not ascertain their exact situation, they do not see the clear image but rather a phantom image.[13]

But there was nothing insubstantial about Gaudí's invention in the Casa Calvet. Once through the grand wooden door the visitor-resident could atone for their sins by repeating the Catholic prayer painted on the wall – *Ave Maria Purisima, sens pecat fou concebuda* (born without sin). Typically Gaudí had rendered this Latin petition into the vernacular Catalan. The tiled hall was also decorated in the colours of Mary – blue and white. For those going out, carefully angled mirrors helped them check their appearance before leaving.

No detail was too insignificant. On entering visitors could clean off the street dust at a fountain supplied with fresh water from a nearby spring. At the end of the hall was a glorious Baroque iron lift. Carried to the first floor, one is at once in the midst of the private space. The intense detailing continues but neo-Baroque is left behind and the theme is something new, something both 'related to vegetation and flowing stone'. Even the door furniture – the spyholes, ventilation grilles and handles are shaped ergonomically.

The Casa Calvet was a success. It married all the different aspects of Gaudí's work well. Even the job's one hiccup was dealt with in a wholly characteristic way. The municipal architect

Falqués spotted that the building's overall height had exceeded the 1891 Ordinances. Gaudí's response was swift and simple. On 24 November 1898, Rubió was dispatched to the council with a drawing of the elevation, where Gaudí had just crossed out the gable with red crayon. A month later permission was granted for the unaltered building to remain as originally designed.

Contemporary photographs of the Passeig de Gràcia and the Plaça de Catalunya are melancholic. In one which shows the Plaça de Catalunya and sweeps up to the Passeig de Gràcia and the slopes of Tibidabo, there are just seven horse-drawn carriages and a single tram along its whole two kilometres. It is autumn. The trees are heavily pollarded. *Flâneurs* with straw boaters idle under the plane trees. A well-dressed gentleman turns round to call to his wife who has stopped to talk to an acquaintance. Strollers walk in the middle of the road. It was set to change.

In contrast to the Baroque Casa Calvet, the tower house of Bellesguard was splendidly archaic. Built up in the Colserrolla foothills on the slopes of Mont Tibidabo, Gaudí looked to the mediaeval Christian fort and the Moorish fortified *hisn* complex of Al-Andalus for his inspiration.[14] The castle was very much in vogue at the time throughout Europe, perhaps because it combined two architectural idioms: a northern romanticism with something very martial.[15] But Gaudí was looking for something altogether more solid.

Bellesguard makes a fascinating cultural narrative. Here, above the ruins of Martí the Humane's royal hunting lodge, Gaudí explored garden design and the relation between a building and nature.

The ruins were testament to the glorious deeds of Catalonia's Catholic warrior caste. On 17 September 1409, King Martí was married there to Margarita de Prades. Sadly within just six months he died, leaving Bellesguard to Margarita who later retired to the Cistercian convent of Valldonzella.

It was a fine foundation stone on which to build. And within months of Gaudí signing the deeds of sale on behalf of the illiterate Doña María Sagués Molins, the earth was cut.

Bellesguard was special for Gaudí. And he discouraged any of his studio from participating in its design. Bellesguard 'beautiful view' – was to become Doña María's country house. The square mass of the building, placed to echo the compass points, was built of ancient rubble much as the Teresianos had been.[16] Diversity was then introduced with thin lancet windows which were stretched out to form expressive breaks in the blocky mass. Just under the cornice of spike-toothed castellations ran a corridor of windows. The roof, with its dangerously narrow walkways, acted as a companion piece to the medieval Mirador del Rei Martí in the *Barri Gòtic* below.

But the deliberately archaic design of Bellesguard was counterbalanced by powerful architectural innovations. In the gardens, amongst the ruins, Gaudí reshaped the sloping terrain with an arcade of inclined columns that formed a viaduct and buttress to hold the soil's enormous weight. Most of the material used was rock and splintered stone, which Gaudí reworked ingeniously. Forming moulds, the hollow shapes were layered with stone fragments and then filled with mortar. This infinitely flexible method – it could be repeated again and again – was a fascinating and cheap exploration of mass-production techniques.

Today's visitor on entering will see the pristine purity of Gaudí's initial design clouded only by the later polychrome additions of his assistant Sugrañes. A variety of simple brick ribs sweeps across the roof. In other areas, metal bands held in tension twist over just above head height, functioning as both tie bars and as metaphors for the perfectly sprung elastic space. Bellesguard is a perfect synthesis of structural science with graceful design.

Gaudí's example was a catalyst: it demanded response from other architects. Farther round the slopes of Mont Tibidabo, looking towards the north, Enric Sagnier designed the Casa Arnús, familiarly known as El Pinar. Sagnier used his signature technique of drawing back the veil of carved stone to reveal the underlying skin of smoothly rendered plaster. In contrast to the deliberately Catalan Bellesguard, Sagnier's citadel is decidedly pan-European, accentuated by its twin towers echoing the steeply pitched roofs of Chambord.

The Casa Calvet and Bellesguard were prestigious commissions. Many other projects undertaken by Gaudí's studio were more modest and mundane, although just as telling about their design philosophy. For the Orfeó Feliuà, a choral society, Gaudí designed a two-metre-high ceremonial banner for religious processions. The huge banner would have been very heavy had Gaudí not ingeniously employed cork. Sant Feliu was one of Catalonia's fourth-century martyrs, ground to death on a miller's stone.[17]

In August 1901, Gaudí started the modernisation of a house for the Marquès and Marquesa de Castelldosrius in the Junta de Comerç. Sadly destroyed in the Civil War, it was yet another lucrative spin-off from the Güell-Comillas connection. The former Doña Isabel Güell had married into the oldest aristocratic Catalan family, the noble Sentmenats: this put the seal on the Güell family's meteoric rise from peasant to aristocrat in just three generations. In many ways Isabel was Gaudí's favourite

Güell. Devoted to her father, she was also a talented musician, who frequently performed at the informal concerts of the Palau Güell. One day, after completing the new house, Gaudí happened to meet the disappointed Doña Isabel. As a present her father had given her an Erard grand piano. But on delivery it was discovered that there was no space to place it in any of the public function rooms. Gaudí's response has entered history: 'Isabel, believe me, take up the violin.'[18]

Gaudí also helped design a new workshop for Josep and Luis Badia, who had been forced to move by the complaints of neighbours. They agreed with Gaudí to repay him in kind as had happened so often with the medieval barter system.

Gaudí's design for the façade of their workshop was simple yet severe, using a shapeliness of form fast becoming recognisably his own. He reused this in the gate, portico and perimeter walls he designed for the Miralles estate in 1902; and again in the unfinished Chalet Graner of 1904.

Gaudí often arrived at the Badia workshop armed with full-scale drawings and plaster models. Oñós, on Gaudí's arrival, would either hide or absorb himself in some other work. This was not due to dislike but rather to the fear of losing valuable time. Oñós was convinced that Gaudí arrived with the intention of teasing him with spatial and technical conundrums. Gaudí would never accept the same solution twice; once discovered it was boring. Luis Badia talked the ideas through with the architect and Oñós only resurfaced after Gaudí's departure to ask what needed to be done. Gaudí preferred a relaxed appearance as if the metal had been formed by the elements rather than man. No other clients were so exacting yet so stimulating. Badia later remarked, 'None of us who've worked with Gaudí can escape his influence. Living next to that swelling sea of ideas they soon become our own.'

Other more basic buildings seem more likely to be the work of Gaudí's studio than of the man himself. In November 1899, Gaudí signed plans for Clapés' house on the carrer Escorial in Gràcia. A simple three-storey building, it was functional rather than a masterpiece. A similar project was the refurbishment of a house at 32 calle del Conde Asalto for Dr Santaló, another close friend. Gaudí's involvement may have been in exchange for Santaló's 'unofficial' medical advice. Silent Santaló was a perfect foil for the architect, who had plenty of opportunity to expound his theories on architecture, religion and life in rambling monologues.[19]

It was at the Ateneu that Gaudí and Santaló became friends. Their close-knit social circle, which included the Café Pelayo and the *Excurcionistas*, meant that they met frequently. On Sundays, after a one-thirty breakfast, Santaló would visit the Gaudís. Independently wealthy, Santaló's life proceeded at a leisurely pace. Twice a week he helped administer the maternity hospital. He turned down the presidency on discovering that the position came attached to an expense allowance. Gaudí and Santaló were linked by more than friendship. There were family links too. Santaló's son Joan returned to ironwork, the family craft, and set up a craft cooperative with Gaudí's cousin Josep Gaudí Pomerol.

Santaló was also a committed Catholic, retreating to Montserrat with his family every summer for a fortnight. Gaudí, his father and niece Rosa visited them there in 1904. Santaló's access to medical records and information later aided Gaudí's anatomical researches for the Sagrada Família's Nativity façade. But no doubt his advice on Gaudí's diet was also requested. As committed vegetarians, Gaudí and his father were obsessed with fresh air, water and the special diet promoted by Dr Kneipp.[20]

In Catalonia there had always been a long tradition of vegetarianism at least as far back as the Romans. In Rome, the Spanish

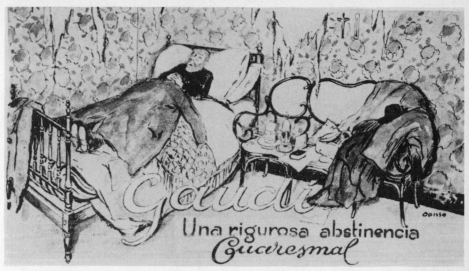

Opisso's drawing of 1894 depicting Gaudí's famous Lenten fast.


Picasso's drawing of 1902 'Very important'
–'I must talk to you of very important things – of God and Art.'
–'Yes, yes. But my children are hungry.'

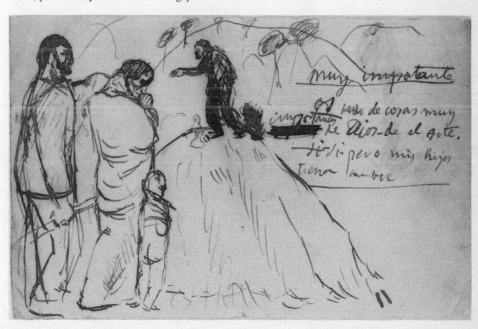

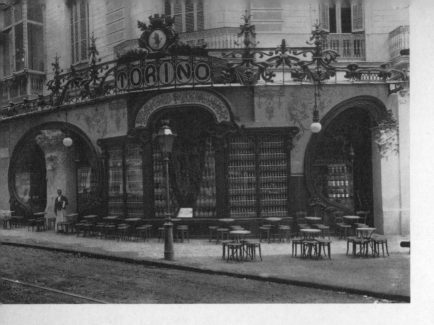

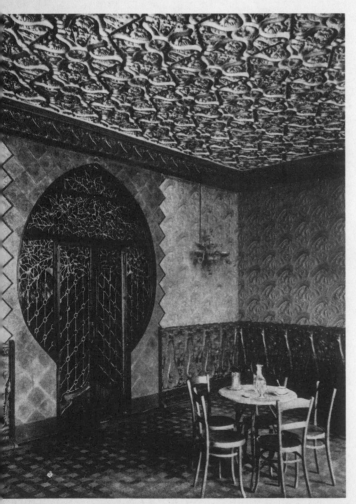

ABOVE Showpiece for the
Modernista style: the Café
Torino in 1902 (since
destroyed).

LEFT Gaudí's Arab salon for the
Café Torino. It was decorated
with compressed cardboard
reliefs.

BELOW Doña Rosa Güell's
Dressing table for the Palau
Güell.

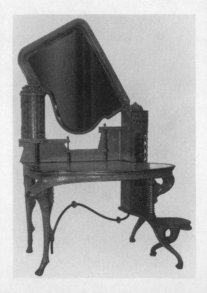

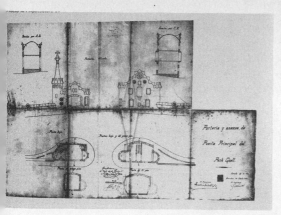

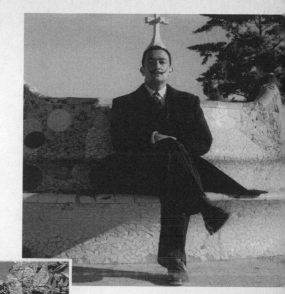

TOP LEFT Signed drawing of the Park Güell entrance pavilion 1904.

ABOVE Salvador Dalí seated on the serpentine bench at the Park Güell.

LEFT A road bridge at the Park Güell.

BELOW The perimeter walls of the Park Güell with goatherd in foreground (c.1906).

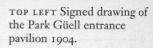

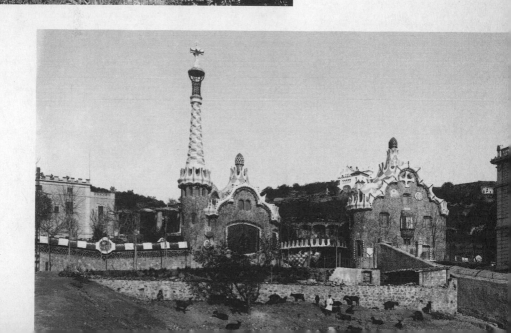

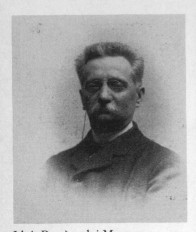

Lluis Domènech i Muntaner.

RIGHT Claudio Lopez, the second
Marquès of Comillas.

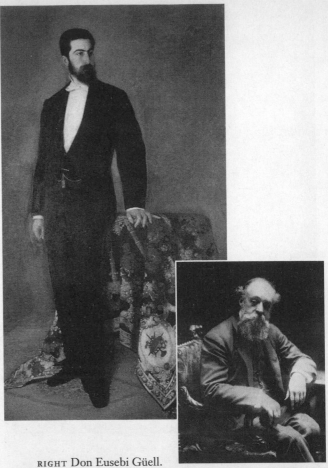

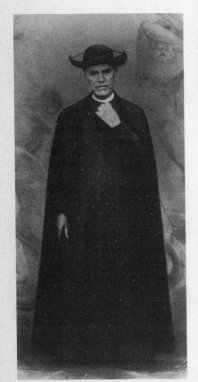

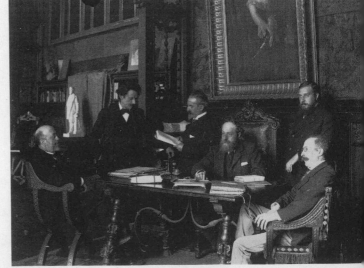

RIGHT Don Eusebi Güell.

The poet-priest Jacint Verdaguer.

RIGHT The Güell Tertulia: Eusebi
Güell (seated)  his secretary Pico
next to him.

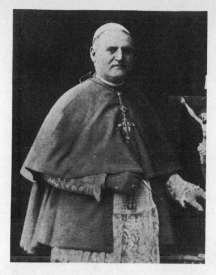

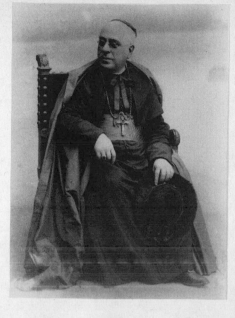

ABOVE Bishop Grau.

ABOVE RIGHT Bishop Torras i Bages.

RIGHT Francesc Berenguer.

FAR RIGHT Josep M. Jujol.

BELOW Joan Maragall.

FAR RIGHT BELOW Joan Rubió i Bellver.

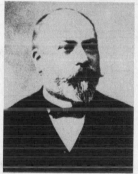

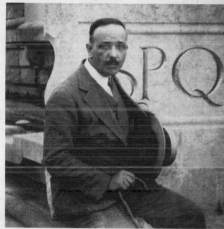

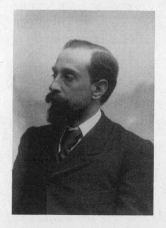

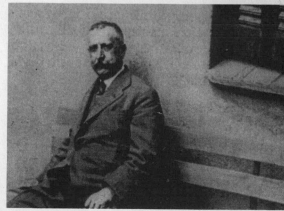

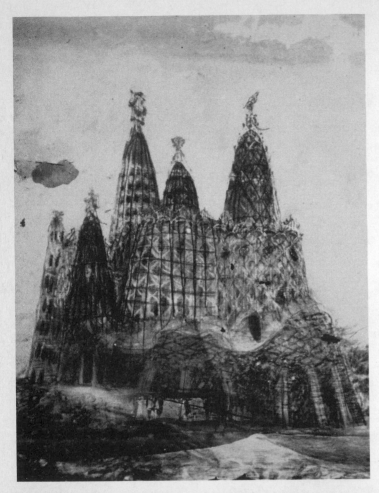

LEFT Colònia Güell drawing.

BELOW Colònia Güell workers prepare themselves to offer skin grafts to the victim of an industrial accident. Much publicised and praised, these donors, nicknamed the Bartolomés, were honoured by both king and pope.

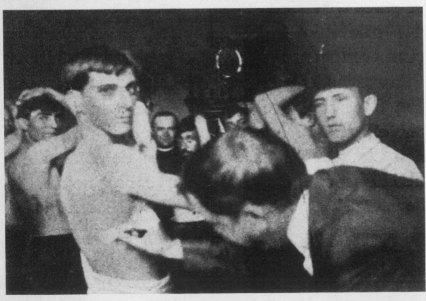

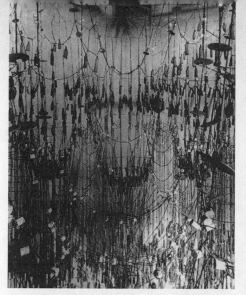

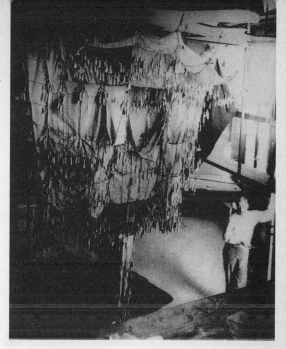

A funicular model for the crypt at the Colònia
Güell 1898-1908

RIGHT The model for the crypt dressed with
material ready to be photographed and
inverted for further work.

The covered porch area of the crypt at the Colònia Güell demonstrated perfectly Gaudí's genius
in controlling materials and space.

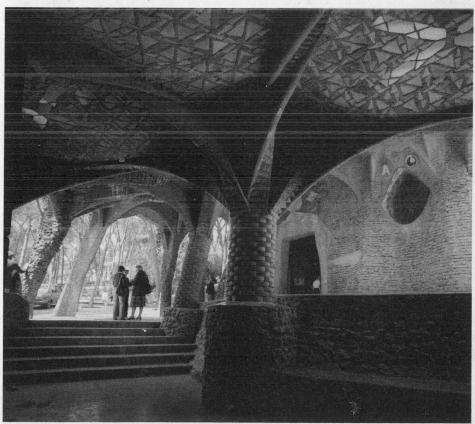

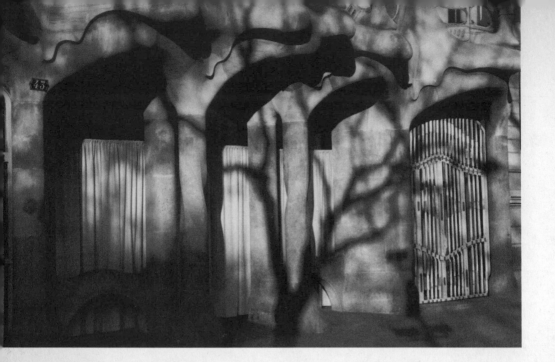

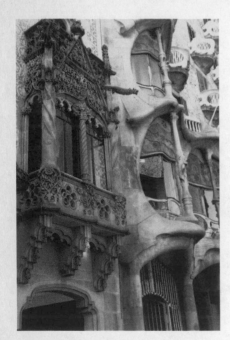

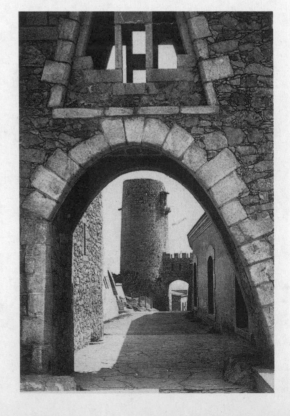

TOP Entrance to the Casa Batlló.

ABOVE The smooth forms of Gaudí's Casa Batlló contrast strongly with neo-medieval detail of Puig i Cadafalch's Casa Amattler in the foreground.

RIGHT Postcard of the Garraf wine bodegas (photograph c.1910).

legionaires were famed for having bodies suited to abstinence and toil. And it has been suggested that what Christ received from the centurion's canteen while up on the cross was gazpacho. Seneca boasted in *Ad Lucilium Epistulae Morales* that all he required was a little bread and some figs to sustain him at mealtimes.[21]

By the Middle Ages, however, great medical men like Arnau de Vilanova, born in 1235, dedicated volumes to the correct diet that a healthy Catalan might eat. In his *Regimen Sanitatis ad Inclinatum Regem Aragonum* Vilanova went through diet, exercise, bathing and even invented an alcohol and herb concoction to help digestion.

In Gaudí's Catalonia, however, there is no doubt that the architect was an exception. Indeed, the smooth running of the *Casa Pairal* depended as much on the successful slaughtering of the pig as almost anything else.

One suspects that Gaudí's diet sprang directly from the Judaic tradition of always leaving the stomach half empty to leave space for the Lord. Gaudí was, after all, a Franciscan at heart. And food was an unnecessary interruption in the efficient working of the body's engine during a day spent at the drawing board. Torres Garcia, his assistant at Palma de Mallorca, said Gaudí worked so hard he doubted if he had a stomach.[22] No more than lettuce, a splash of milk, or a dribble of olive oil, nuts, gently stewed chard stalks, and honey spread on bread was necessary to keep the body in health – along with unlimited water. Or, perhaps, a quick nibble on the dried biscuits, the *Panes de San Antonio* that he carried around with him in little bags to hand out to other people while saving the ones flavoured subtly with toasted cumin for himself.[23] At Christmas, in the same spirit of abstinence, Gaudí would divide the *turrón* he received every year without fail from his client the Torras iron foundry, among family and friends: his cousin Josep Gaudí Pomerol's family, Dr Santaló, the Matamala tribe and the porter at the Park Güell.[24]

The hollow-cheeked artist was, of course, fashionable at the time, among both Catholic and anarchist circles: 'the Prince of Pessimism'. Schopenhauer, wrote in *The World as Will and Idea* that the precepts for the good man were 'poverty, fasting, chastity and self-torture'. The two extreme worlds of Catholicism and anarchism were brought together by Pompeyo Gener, in one of the first issues of Picasso's magazine *Arte Joven* in 1901, in which he wrote, 'If Nietzsche had had the heart of Saint Francis he would have been the greatest prophet the world has ever known.'[25]

Returning to a more pleasure-seeking Barcelona, Italian businessman Flaminio Mezzalana wanted the Café Torino, on the corner of Passeig de Grácia and Gran Via, as his flagship.

The entrance led through a large kidney-shaped opening that was divided down the middle by a carved stone column; fronted by a *modernista* Venus by Eusebi Arnau who pushed her over-flowing cup of vermouth (the building was a showcase for Martini & Rossi) through a vine to be replenished by a woodland nymph. Passing under a glass and iron canopy by Falqués i Urpi, manu-factured by Ballarín, the visitor stepped into a riotous series of rooms created by a catalogue of Venetian and Catalan artists, each acknowledged masters of their own respective craft. Puig y Cadafalch decorated the beams with bright colourful motifs while Gaudí created an evocative Arabian salon in which he experimented again with compressed cardboard mouldings. Gaudí's intervention provided a brief essay on how to mix the austerity of bentwood Thonet chairs with the swirling decor of bordello chic.

Kept busy with ongoing commissions, the façade of the first transept at the Sagrada Família almost complete, Gaudí continued to spread himself thinly over half a dozen Barcelona sites. At the same time, up in the Pyrenees at La Pobla de Lillet on the edge of the Ripollès, he was commissioned by Güell to create a clubhouse-refuge for workers at his nearby Asland factory. It was a strange affair, reminiscent of both the bodega at Garraf and the simple arch of La Poble de Lillet's Romanesque bridge – the Pont Vell – that crossed the foaming River Llobregat nearby. But most unusual of all was Gaudí's contribution to one of Barcelona's earliest cinema-theatres, the Sala Mercé, which was rather bizarrely dedicated to the Virgin.

Cinema was a new and morally dubious – although exciting – field. Gaudí, and he was not alone, wished to integrate an extra moral dimension to it – through architecture. Utrillo and Romeu had already demonstrated a penchant for the moralising *mise en scène*. They had joined up with Léon-Charles Môret to take a shadow theatre laced with heavy symbolism to the Chicago World's Fair. Back home, Romeu explored improving topics like *Jesus of Nazareth* and *The Wreck of the Frigate Aurora* for the younger clientele.

When the artist Luis Graner Arrufí returned from New York full of plans for the Sala Mercé, the status of cinematography was far from clear. Gaudí had just completed a set of unused designs for Graner's house and he was now being asked to come up with ideas for another dubious plan. Eric Rhode, cinema historian, stresses the risky nature of the medium:

> The tricksters, the fast talkers, the cranks, the defeated: all of them took part in the gold rush to invent the cinema. Yet for years the cinema was more likely to lose your fortune than to make it. It hovered in the nether-world of the fairground, the second-class music hall, the beer garden, the penny arcades and the church social.[26]

But Graner had chosen the site well. The new cinema was on the Rambla de los Estudios, close to the buzz of the Plaça de

Catalunya. It was very unlike today's cinemas. Walking down a ramp the audience entered a large rectangular hall with an orchestra pit at one end, served by an ingenious system of air-conditioning. It is still there today as the Cine Atlántico but Gaudí's decoration has long gone.

It was in the space under the ramp that Gaudí built the three-dimensional installations based on Montserrat.[27] A musical (also called *Montserrat*) was written to accompany Gaudí's more permanent piece. Alongside Gaudí's plaster Montserrat, there were a selection of edifying mountain scenes in which various life-size sculptures depicted *The Flight from Egypt*, *The Birth of Our Lord*, *The Annunciation* and a hermit's cave. On special exhibition, for just a few months, they could see an interior of *A Suq in Tehran*, and a topical frieze displaying the deployment of *The Russian Troops in Manchuria* before their terrible defeat by the Japanese. Before taking up their seats for a showing of *George and the Dragon*, or *Scenes from the Passion*, spectators could peer over the rim of a simulated simmering volcano.

For the opening on 29 October 1904, Graner had planned a charitable publicity stunt to advertise the cinema ordering a huge quantity of loaves, and a meaty rice dish, to give to the poor along the Rambles.

But the cinema was not a success: perhaps it was the didactic morality of its decoration and entertainment, perhaps it was Graner's morbid sense of humour. Above the doorway Narbón, a demon automaton, up on a visit from the underworld, shouted, '*Mortales que os reís de mí, todos vendreis a mí*' ('Mere mortals you can laugh at me if you wish but you'll soon be joining me'). This was rounded off by realising, after queuing patiently for one of the two ticket booths, that the usher was a dummy.

Gaudí had no interest in the financial well-being of the Sala Mercé. It didn't matter that the clientele frequently complained to the management that the squeaking of the purpose-built seats made it difficult to hear.[28] What had excited him was the directness and hypnotic power of the cinematic medium, its capacity to use what Walter Benjamin called its 'agile yet penetrating notation'. Above all he welcomed its potential to burn into the collective psyche and highjack the attention of the predominantly illiterate horde. This was something his later architecture explored in greater detail.

Despite the sheer variety of commissions undertaken it was for religious architecture that the Gaudí studio was still justly famous. Gaudí had built up a reputation as one of the great experts on Catalan Gothic.[29]

On 20 November 1899, Gaudí received a visit at the Sagrada Família from the Bishop of Mallorca, who was on a fact-finding mission for the proposed restoration and development of his island see.

Although impressed by Gaudí he delayed inviting him to submit ideas until various internal questions had been answered. In the summer of 1901, after visiting Leo XIII in Rome, Campins returned to Barcelona via the cathedrals and churches of Italy and France. On 19 August, back on Catalan soil, Dr Campins' suggestions were eagerly grabbed at by Gaudí, excited by the plans. Bishop and architect were in agreement. What Palma's cathedral needed was a radical return to its glorious Gothic past. Although Gaudí's instinct warned him 'that it could never become a reality – a project so beautiful would be difficult to execute'.[30] But like Viollet before him, he wanted to work with the stone handled by the medieval master masons, fully confident that with his superior knowledge of structures he would improve on the original. The temptation to take on Mallorca was clearly too strong.

Many opportunities for intervention in Catalonia's national

heritage had passed Gaudí by. Mallorca offered the opportunity to unpick a part of Catalonia's Gothic heritage.

On 27 March 1902, Gaudí arrived in Palma for the first time, staying in the bishop's palace.

Living with his patron might have created unnecessary friction but Gaudí's infrequent visits to the island never lasted more than a couple of months, which gave both sides time to recover from their various heated architectural and liturgical debates. It also provided for the odd comic interlude.

In general a formal lunch was taken at Dr Campins' table. On one side sat Campins, his sister Catalina, brother Don Josep, the sculptor Vilarrubias, and a senior church dignitary. Facing them sat Gaudí, his assistants, and other lowlier clerics such as the bishop's secretary Dr Martí Llovera. Gaudí's pre-lunch ritual was an eccentric one. Having poured water over his hands he dried them and then scrupulously scrubbed them clean with breadcrumbs. He clearly felt at ease.

'From the first day I arrived in Mallorca I was treated so well I found it difficult to turn down anything that Doña Catalina offered me,' Gaudí later told Matamala. 'She once offered me the choicest display of *embutidos* – cured meats. "You can eat it, Don Antoni," she implored me, "I promise. It's home-made and it's *pure* pork!"

'"Thank you, Doña Catalina," I replied. "Unfortunately it's the very *purity* that prevents me from eating it."'[31]

Requesting dietary dispensation, Gaudí continued his usual salt-free diet of vegetables seasoned only with extra virgin olive oil.

Keen to help, Gaudí offered to assist in the kitchen. One day Doña Catalina prepared the simple Mallorquín dish known as *mató* – a lightly set junket, bland but refreshing and delicious with honey. Gaudí watched as Doña Catalina prepared the *mató*, laboriously stirring the warm milk with the twig of a fig tree, cut down its length to release a natural coagulant. Once set, the *mató* was carefully flipped over – a trembling monument to Doña Catalina's housekeeping skills.

Observing closely, Gaudí pondered hard and long then suggested that he could achieve the same consistency with less work and in half the time. With rapid flicks of the wrist a new twig was swirled through the creamy liquid. A short wait, and Gaudí flipped his creation out – a pool of milky slush. Embarrassed at the universal mirth, he quickly retracted: 'Doña Catalina. In future I will hand the preparation of the *mató* straight over to you.'

If the companionship at the bishop's table was appreciated, it was at La Seu that Gaudí felt inspired. Within just three days of arrival Gaudí presented a proposal to the church *Junta* outlining his initial plans. This speed suggests that he had arrived with most of his ideas prepared, to be fine-tuned on site. The *Junta* was rather slower in replying and it was a full year later that Gaudí was invited to come to Palma and begin the works as quickly as possible.

The interim year provided time to work out the logistics and to establish a working team. It also gave Gaudí time for contemplation and to reread some of the writings of Mallorca's thirteenth-century genius, the polyglot philosopher, translator, theologian and Christian martyr Ramón Llull. For at least three centuries Mallorca had been a staging post on the crusader trail to Jerusalem. Before that, Arab and Berber dynasties from Damascus, Baghdad, Cordoba and Fez had fought over it. Llull's mortal remains lay in state in La Seu, returned in 1315 from African Bugia where the octogenarian had been slaughtered by a mob while he was delivering a biblical exegesis.

From the cathedral's sixteenth-century altarpiece a portrait of Llull stares down. Josep Pla, in his *Homenots*, a collection of pen portraits of Catalonia's greats, first drew attention to the relation between Gaudí and Llull. Pla called Gaudí a 'Ramón Llull in another field' who shared that paradoxical quality of 'pure rationality' mixed up with the wayward nature of 'a madman'. There was an explosion of interest in Llull at the turn of the century, kick-started in 1901 with the *Homenatge al Beat Ramón Llull* which pointed to his typically Catalan qualities of intelligence, hard work, faith and tolerance. Llull had played a pivotal role in rescuing the learning of the Arab world and Sephardic Spain after the sacking of Abd al Rahman III's 400,000-volume library at Madinat al Zahra during the collapse of the Caliphate.

Through this, Llull became the vehicle for understanding the cultures of the classical, Jewish and Moorish worlds. This shared heritage was known as *convivencia*. Llull was also important for Gaudí on a far more practical level. 'There is not a manual labour that is not good,' Llull had written, echoing Eiximenes. But Llull went further, discussing the propriety of the concept of the guilds and in *Doctrina Pueril* developing economic ideas that promoted the entrepreneurial merchant classes above that of the landlord. This was a powerful contemporary concern in Catalonia.

Llull and Gaudí shared other characteristics. Llull was a humanist with modernist Enlightenment attitudes to experimentation and powerful empirical skills. Almost nothing was beyond his grasp, and, as with Viollet and Gaudí, Llull's total absorption in his work was born out of early disappointment. In Palma he had fallen madly in love with a woman whom he had obsessively followed from pillar to post and from pulpit to port. Only when he discovered her breast cancer was Llull shocked into passionate Christianity. His belief was encouraged further by seeing multiple apparitions of Our Lord nailed to the cross. Llull consoled himself with a life devoted to religious exposition and missionary work. His tolerant approach was highly unusual.

Llull set about learning Arabic, and translating texts into Latin and vernacular Catalan. Through mutual understanding he hoped the Jew and Moor might be defeated by logic. Although

this was not an entirely new idea this was the first time a nation
– Catalonia – had connected into the history of a much wider
Western culture.

At the heart of most Spanish cathedrals stood the choir – the
*coro* – with its magnificent carved choir stalls, colourful altarpieces and elaborate iron reredos. The *coro* created an impenetrable screen behind which the joint hierarchy of choir,
aristocracy, and cathedral canons formed their own exclusive
parliament. For a church looking to increase its mass appeal,
Campins and Gaudí agreed to remove the *coro* and allow the
communicants a clear view through, returning La Seu to its
Gothic purity.

On 5 April 1903, Gaudí left Barcelona for seven weeks in
Mallorca. This long absence points to a strong confidence in the
ability of his studio. On the voyage to Mallorca Gaudí refined
the ideas behind the removing of the *coro*, clearing the space by
distributing the *coro*'s parts around the cathedral and thus providing further light. A full-blown Baroque altarpiece in the presbytery was removed only to reveal a fourteenth-century Gothic
one behind. This fortuitous decision opened up the Trinity
Chapel and provided easy access to the tombs of the Mallorcan
kings Jaime II and III.

In October Gaudí returned with Rubió to lay their plans for
the stained-glass windows before the cathedral committee. By
now Gaudí had allocated all the separate tasks and planned their
execution for the return trip in early summer the following year.
Rubió would oversee the dismantling of the choir and altarpieces,
and their relocation. Josep M. Jujol i Gibert, still in his early
twenties, was given some of his first practical experience working
on choir stalls. Joan Matamala and Tomás Vila were employed

as sculptors. Torres-Garcia, Iu Pascual and Jaumé Llongueras assisted as painters.

Gaudí elaborated his ideas: 'Let us have architecture without archaeology; our primary consideration is the relationship between the parts as they stand; therefore we do not copy their shapes but produce forms of a predetermined character possessing the spirit of the original.'[32]

With their eyes set on removing the cathedral's historicisms and achieving a radical new Gothicism, Gaudí and Campins managed to offend the sensibilities of the *Junta*. But it was Jujol who upset them most. His vivid palette and technique jarred with the Church commission. It was rumoured that he used the baptismal font to wash out his brushes. Further distress was caused by Jujol's inscription on the back of the choir stalls: *La sang d'Ell sobre nosaltres* (His blood is on our hands) a sentiment not shared by the Church fathers who had been brought up in a profoundly anti-Semitic culture. Some saw 'an aura of inspired prayer' in Jujol's contributions but others baulked at its style.

Despite various misgivings, the initial renovations were completed in record time. Just six months later, on 8 December 1904, Dr Campins presided over a celebratory mass. The local paper, *La Almudaina*, reported on Gaudí's contribution the following day:

> From the main entrance one received, above all, a feeling of grandeur, never before experienced, when looking across the immense central nave where so many thousands of people were kneeling, towards the Royal Chapel, illuminated with great artistry by the arrangement of numerous candles, and towards the Chapel of the Holy Trinity in the background, also brightly lit.

Though a critical triumph it was not appreciated by everyone. Havelock Ellis, happiest when discussing earthbound passions, found it all far too much.

Above all, the Mallorcans are architects and sculptors. Yet the curious latent violence of their temperament – a persistent kernel of Africanism – involves a singular lack of aesthetic sensibility. I have never heard such loud and shrill church organs ... nor seen such loud and shrill church windows of orange and scarlet in ugly tracery, the hideous suggestions, it would seem, of a kaleidoscope ...[33]

The following years saw the completion of the decorative details. As at Comillas, Gaudí had designed special furniture for La Seu: a folding staircase, a giant candelabrum and two splendid wooden pulpits, designed to face each other across the central nave. Gaudí's involvement in Mallorca was littered with anecdotes but none so telling as his brusque response to the criticism that his pulpits looked like nothing but a pair of tramcars parked opposite each other. 'Aren't tramcars beautiful too?'

Montserrat has been central to Catalan faith for centuries. Philip II, Gaudí's favourite Castilian king, built it as a Catalan version of his El Escorial. It is a vital symbol of Catalan identity and independence. Every Catalan artist has respected its singular status— Picasso, Miró, Dalí, Tàpies. Even throughout the dark days of Franco the Catalan priests refused to stop delivering the mass in their native tongue. And the hard work of their publishing house, *Abadia de Montserrat*, helped keep Catalan culture alive.

Gaudí was directly commissioned by Bishop Torras i Bages, on behalf of the Lliga Espiritual de la Mare de Déu de Montserrat

– a collective of right-wing Catholic Catalanists – to work at
Montserrat illustrating some of his fiercely Catalan ideas on art,
religion and popular appeal.[34]

Torras i Bages stood firmly against the prevailing fashionable
pessimism, seeking instead for salvation through obedience to
God. He wished man to become 'integrated with nature' to find
equilibrium, harmony and balance, and rediscover his faith. And
for the artist, his job was clear. He must picture and illustrate
this singular truth.[35]

Gaudí's site was set in the murky shadows of a mountaintop
cave. His brief was an all but impossible one – to celebrate the
Church and Catalonia through the Resurrection. Torras i Bages
had written in his hugely influential cultural history *The Catalan
Tradition* (1892) that Catalonia was 'pre-eminent among all the
Iberic peoples' because of 'her ancient seeds hidden in the earth,
in the Catalan humus'. Pro-Catalan metaphors tripped easily
from the Bishop's tongue but proved far more difficult to transform into great art.

Unsurprisingly the *Primer Misterio de Gloria* was one of the
least interesting of Gaudí's works, due to the nature of the commission and the mendicant mentality of the Lliga's founding
fathers. On 10 June 1899, Don Ricardo Permanyer Ayats and
Bishop Torras i Bages wrote to Abbot Deás Villardegrau for
permission to start. It was a small commission but its subject
matter – Christ's Resurrection and by direct implication also
Catalonia's rebirth – would prove massively significant. To add
further resonance the *Primer Misterio* was close to where the
Black Madonna had been discovered.

A year and a half later Gaudí was awarded the commission
(one of fifteen) and as soon as weather permitted started blasting
the rock and removing soil to enlarge the cave. The noise was
so loud the whole mountain shook. Despite the symbolic importance of the commission, occupied with all his other commitments Gaudí rarely had time to visit the site. The major part of

the work was still rockblasting, earthmoving and excavation. The works were left under the watchful eye of Rubió and the contractor José Bayó Font, who travelled up weekly to pay his workmen and their lodging costs.

The fund-raising programme failed to progress as initially planned. Eventually in 1907 the organising *Junta* added another 250 pesetas, to defray the costs of casting Llimona's *Risen Christ*. It was to be suspended halfway up the bare rock face, as if floating miraculously. At the spring equinox, Christ was illuminated by the sun's first rays. Angry at the work's slow progress Abbot Deás threatened the Lliga that he might pass the commission on to another association and this forced the Lliga's hand. Considering the huge expectations, the Montserrat commission proved a massive anticlimax. Gaudí diplomatically withdrew and a simplified project was completed instead by Jerónimo Martorell Terrats, almost a decade later, in 1916.

The dates for Gaudí's next Güell commission, the crypt at Colònia Güell, are uncertain, but it certainly was the building with the longest gestation period. At some time in 1898, according to Ráfols, Gaudí was requested by Don Eusebi to come up with plans for a church for his rapidly expanding workers' colony at Santa Coloma de Cervelló, south of Barcelona. This textile colony was one of the earliest Catalan attempts to re-create the contemporary European model of workers' colonies set far away from the corrupting city's influence. In France, Le Play had argued for a three-pronged attack: using the weapons of a stable family, effectively administered charity and a devout Catholic faith. Preventing damage to the harmonious balance of a paternalistic society, it was by returning to the medieval feudal model that architects like Pugin fantasised they might create a

New Jerusalem – based on craft. From the start of the industrial revolution architects had sought a new architectural language for the sprouting villages and towns surrounding the factories. On the eve of the French Revolution, Claude-Nicolas Ledoux had provided a neoclassical model at the Royal saltworks of La Saline de Chaux at Arc-et-Senans, but there were many other models from which the interested industrialist might draw: from Bessbrook in Ireland (1846) to Olbrich's 1901 designs for the Opel works at Darmstad.[36]

Güell was not the first in Catalonia to introduce the idea of the industrial village. In 1846, in the town of Esparraguera, upstream along the Llobregat river under the sawtooth Montserrat, Manuel Puig had built the textile village of the Colònia Sedó.[37] Gaudí and Güell would have known about it. At Esparraguera, from the seventeenth century on, the village acted out its famous *Passió d'Esparraguera* – a living version of what had been planned with the mysteries at Montserrat.

The Colònia site had been bought in 1860 by Güell's father, Don Joan. From 1882 onwards it was rapidly transformed by the success of the new steam machinery. Gaudí's assistants, Berenguer and Rubió, were given the responsibility for building the workers' housing, school, clubhouse and the directors' and teachers' houses. Never more than two storeys high, the houses are inventively built. Intricate patterns and textures, based on Moorish models, are developed through the herringbone design of the brickwork: an entire village all neatly of a piece yet fascinatingly different and protected from the violence and disease prevalent just twenty kilometres away in Barcelona.

But it was getting workers away from the curse of alcohol that most exercised magnates. It was also one of Gaudí's obsessions: the struggle to keep his niece Rosa sober was to mark his later years. This was not just a Catalan obsession, although Catalonia's status as the largest brandy-producing area in the world reinforced this view. In Lille the textile tycoon Kolb-Bernard fought fiercely against the temptations of the three A's: Alcoholism, Atheism and Anarchism.[38] None were good for business. In the industrial New Jerusalem the paternalistic society brought true benefits if only the workers obeyed.

Whatever Güell's motives there is no doubt that the Colònia Güell was a comfortable place to live. Even today it has the air of an industrial Eden. For Gaudí the Colònia represented unfinished business; he never had completed his ambitious designs for Mataró. And a fascinating measure of exactly how far Gaudí had come is seen in the deliberate contrast between the respective philosophies and structures that underpinned these two works almost twenty years apart. Cooperative fantasies in Mataró are replaced by strict paternalistic leadership in the Colònia Güell; laminated wood arches by the most unique structure ever produced.

His work at Mataró reveals an optimistic architect of promise and conviction. If we look at the crypt at Colònia Güell, on the

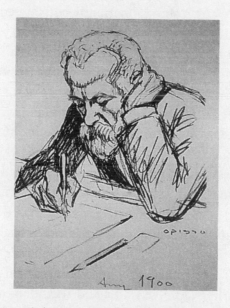

Gaudí at work. Drawing by Opisso, 1900.

other hand, it is clear that Gaudí is unique. Gaudí had said, 'Creation works ceaselessly through man. But man does not create, he discovers. Those who seek out the laws of Nature as support for their new work collaborate with the Creator. Those who copy are not collaborators. For this reason originality consists in returning to the origin.'

This is Gaudí's great paradox. For the farther he travelled away from the idealism of his youth, and the stricter a Catholic he became and the more antiliberal, pessimistic and obsessed with suffering – the more glorious his architecture grew.

In 1898, Don Eusebi had decided that the small chapel of the Sacred Heart would no longer suffice. The Colònia needed something grander.

Although well used to waiting for Gaudí's muse, Güell can hardly have expected it to be a decade before the first stone was laid. For the projected church, for which a whole programme of research was set in place, a catenary model, four and a half metres high, was suspended from the ceiling of a makeshift workshop. Existing photos show it patiently catalogued in its various stages, from elaborate spider's web to dressed-up tent; a complex hanging structure of weights, wires and cords. Unlike other architectural models Gaudí's building hangs upside down like a precarious colony of bats.

The genesis of this model goes back to Gaudí's revelation that the catenary arch used at the Palau Güell, the riding stables at Les Corts, and at the Teresiano, had unique power and grace. In all his previous buildings the catenary arch had functioned as both decoration and structural design. But now Gaudí employed the catenary idea as the defining principle of the whole design. Drilling a cluster of attachment points, in a perfect circle, to the ceiling he was able to start with the building's arches falling gracefully into elegant swags – designing themselves through gravity. If another layer was attached to the apex of these, the original arches were stretched farther still. The problem lay in pulling the building together by gathering the cords up carefully into a bell. So, gradually, the outside circle was pulled together as layer after layer came closer to the floor. And so, the very fragility of the model in its making had transformed itself into a structure of fantastic tensile strength.

This simplistic explanation fails to explain the system of weights attached to the inverted apex of the arches, to compensate for the increased load when reversed; or to outline the complexities of a ground plan – drilled into a peg board – that was not a perfect circle, and which added further to the elaborate puzzle by creating a variety of interior arches and domes. It was a very complex design. Gaudí adjusted it on every visit to Santa Coloma, as did Francesc Berenguer. The engineer Eduardo Goetz Maurer often came there to offer specialist advice. Practical advice also came from Joan Bertran, from the builder Augustín Massip, and Joaquim Tres. Other members of the team, the carpenter Munné, and Matamala, spent thousands of hours painstakingly adding shotgun pellets, one by one, to the tiny canvas bags. The model needed complete rebalancing at least once, after rats gnawed through the tasty string greased unwittingly with pork fat by Bertran after his lunch-time break.

The Colònia Güell had become an architectural laboratory, relying as much on trial and error as any guiding principles. Stuck out there in a makeshift hut amongst the pines it had become arguably the most advanced architectural studio in the world.

It says a great deal about Gaudí's character that he could pursue an apparently madcap venture to its logical end. Behind the scheme stood Güell, the '*aristócrata de espíritu*', disdaining trifling worries over time, and acting as Gaudí's midwife, patiently waiting, as D. H. Kahnweiler would with Picasso and Braque, the birth of a new style.

Once the bare bones of the building's structure were elaborated, the tissue skin of the building was applied. Behind the paper curtain the string tracery hung like the memory of a structure wholly imagined but not yet completely understood. Nothing had been finalised. The interior roofs might well be formed from convex and concave interlocking triangles. The triangle was symbolically rich but was also capable of sustaining immense pressure and strain. As it hung there the upturned parasol read as a structural exposition of Rubió's theory that true art needed the three qualities of integrity, proportion and clarity.[39] Perhaps this was what Gaudí had meant when he said, 'With two rulers and a cord one generates all architecture.'

Gaudí's model, described by Perucho as a 'monstrous, live insect, hidden in the long undergrowth caressed by the wind' responded perfectly to what Ruskin called for in *The Seven Lamps of Architecture* when he asked for a unifying of 'the technical and imaginative elements as essentially as humanity does body and soul'.[40] And Viollet's argument in *Entretiens*:

> Since every part of a building or construction must have its *raison d'être*, we are unconsciously aware of every form which explains its function, just as we respond to the sight of a beautiful tree in which all the parts, from the roots which grip the earth to the very last branches which seem to seek out air and light, indicate so clearly the factors which create and sustain these great organisms.[41]

With the model complete the photographers Vicente Vilarrubias and Adolfo Mas recorded it and inverted the print. From here Gaudí, Berenguer and draughtsmen could sketch over the photographic prints, designing the church's exterior.

Gaudí's crypt is, according to Casanelles,

> the most profound artistic creation executed in the twentieth century in Europe. When the history of contemporary art can be written without national prejudice, it will have to start from this point, for the Crypt is like a great

compass whose guiding influence has been felt by all the creators of this century.

It was

the concrete expression of Gaudí's youthful conception of the feeling of divinity converted into architecture – a conception which throughout his life provoked the difficult human reaction of sacrifice.[42]

This sense of sacrifice was reinforced by an accident at the Colonia. On 23 February 1905 a young worker, Josep Campderrós, fell into a vat of corrosive liquid. It burnt all the skin off his legs. It seemed that amputation might provide the only solution. However, in a remarkable display of community spirit, the parish priest, the Güell brothers Claudio and Santiago and forty-eight fellow workers offered their skin for a skin graft. Six weeks later when Josep Campderrós was well enough to undergo the operation, patches were removed from each man without anaesthetic. This heroism came almost immediately to the notice of the Vatican. Pius X honoured each participant with the Gold Medal '*Benemerenti*'. Even in times of decadence, acts of religious devotion and bravery were still possible.

The 'Bartolomés', as they became known (after St Bartholomew who had been flayed alive), were further honoured by King Alfonso XIII with the Charity Cross, First Class, and Santiago and Claudio Güell were ennobled. In this New Jerusalem these heroic acts of Christian charity might act as a presentiment of future salvation.

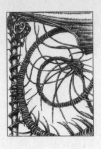

# *In Paradisum*

---

Each race carries within its own primitive soul an ideal of
landscape which it tries to realize within its own borders.

*Ortega y Gasset*

THE LOSS OF CATALONIA's colonial export market, after the
1898 Cuban crisis, had serious economic repercussions. The
slump in industry forced textile magnates like Güell to look for
alternative investments. Property development was one possible
route out of recession.

On 29 July 1899, Güell acquired a farm on the western edge
of the city, at the Muntanya Pelada – the bald mountain – up
above Gràcia. Having also bought adjoining Can Coll i Pujol
farm, the Park Güell covered fifteen hectares. Both patron and
architect's ideas for the site were already well advanced. The
Park Güell was to be a privately financed garden suburb.

The project represented a very different type of social experiment from that at the Colònia Güell. Workers required relatively
little space, but the Park offered garden surroundings, tree-lined
avenues to stroll through, vistas and pavilions to entertain its
wealthy inhabitants.

The site's topography imposed a set of restrictions right from the start. A hundred and fifty metres above sea level at its lowest, 210 metres at its highest, an ingenious solution was required for the layout of the roads, paths and building plots. The meandering design of the plan looked like a compacted spring. Gaudí chose not to cut down the vegetation, so as to leave the site's quirky aesthetic mostly intact. Once again Gaudí chose the triangle as the only shape flexible enough to divide up the sixty projected plots, each between one and two thousand square metres. This would be a small independent community protected by high walls, gates and a porter's lodge.

The Park Güell was designed to provide the dweller with a living essay in Catalan nationhood and Catholic piety.[1] Gaudí now posited that Catalonia's geographical placement and its relationship to the sun was deeply symbolic. He declaimed passionately:

> Virtue lies in the middle; Mediterranean means at the middle of the earth. On its shores with their average light – that of 45° inclination, which best defines bodies and reveals their form – is the place where the great artistic cultures have flourished because of this equilibrium of light: not too much and not too little because the two extremes are blinding, and blind men do not see. At the Mediterranean that concrete vision of things obtains in which true art must repose. Our plastic power lies in the equilibrium between sentiment and logic; the northern races are obsessed with and choked in sentiment, and with the lack of clarity produce fantasies; meanwhile people of the south, because of the excess of light, neglect reason and produce monsters; with the insufficient clarity as with the blinding light people do not see well and their spirit is abstract. The Mediterranean arts will always retain marked superiority over the Nordic because they are

devoted to the observation of nature; the northern people produce at best pretty works but not major ones, and that is why they purchase Mediterranean products; instead they are well endowed for analysis, science and industry.[2]

These ethnocentric theories resonate through his plans. Prospective buyers, as has come to light with the 1902 Martín Trias contract (one of only two plots ever sold), had a whole catalogue of restrictions. The house had to be set back to allow a view across the Mediterranean. But not so far back as to obscure the view from the neighbouring house above. Perimeter walls for each enclosure could not exceed eighty centimetres. Detailed clauses had been drawn up to avoid the proliferation of industry, as had happened in the city centre and in the *eixample*:

> The purchaser or his heirs may not under any pretext make parcels for factories, shops, brick kilns, or bread ovens, blacksmith shops, hospitals, clinics, sanatoriums, hotels, inns, restaurants, hostels, cafés, chocolate shops, lunch rooms, stores, storage depots for drugs or explosives, warehouses, or in any way practice an industry, trade or profession.[3]

To develop a theme for the Park Güell, Gaudí looked at nineteenth-century fairgrounds. New methods of prefabrication and quick assembly were used. And behind an old-fashioned façade lay the very latest in design. The Park, if successful, might function on a whole myriad of levels: the play between private and public space; the binding of religion and nationhood; form and function; the blending of prehistory and the contemporary; and the mixture of archaic techniques and the latest advances. In the search for modernity both architect and patron were at one.

In many ways Güell was the perfect patron. Generous, supportive, passionately interested, and always convinced of Gaudí's genius. But with the Park Güell their relationship subtly changed. Part of the reason was the sheer proximity of the Park to Güell's new palace, a classical eighteenth-century building, set within its grounds. Güell had become increasingly free with advice and ideas, gleaned from his many trips abroad. So free, in fact, that experts described him as co-author of this project.[4]

There was another aspect of their personalities that grew increasingly close. The Park Güell had originally been envisaged as a key element in the diversification of Güell's financial portfolio. Yet during the Park's evolution he and Gaudí increasingly distanced themselves from the claims of money.

The Park Güell had a very English pedigree, that Güell and Gaudí admitted to when they chose the English spelling, over the Catalan *parc* and the Castilian *parque*. A Park, a garden city, an Eden, always intended to provide a haven away from industrialisation. A stake in paradise also demanded a tacit agreement as to one's behaviour when within its walls; Park Güell shared this moral edge with many of the contemporary English forays into utopian community planning.

Güell's business interests had brought him into frequent contact with the urban developments and ideas of his British industrial counterparts in the Midlands. His son Eusebi Güell i López had been sent to study Industrial Engineering at Manchester University. Another son, Joan, later became a founding member of the Catalan Garden City association.[5] Güell's cosmopolitanism broadened Gaudí's more insular approach. Güell often drew on the similarities between Catalonia, England and Germany, at the expense of Castile. Meier-Graefe, a German cultural tourist, describes meeting someone with similar views in Barcelona in 1906.

> We lunched with an industrialist, to whom I had been recommended, in an excellent restaurant. His type was something new to me in Spain. 'You know of course,' he

said in fluent German, 'that we do not wish to be considered Spaniards here. We are Catalonians . . .' He
spoke about Southern and Western Spain like the Mila-
nese speak about the Neapolitans. Quite a different race.
Fat, foolish, lazy and religious, without any needs, without any political instinct and – he assured us he was not
at all hyper-moral – completely degenerate . . . Culture
could only be found in Catalonia although he, of course,
was not subject to any form of local patriotism . . .[6]

Güell admired the North European model because its attitudes
and mores applied perfectly to Catalonia and the Catalan character, sharing an admiration for industry, self-improvement and
hard work.

The nearest Barcelona had recently come to remaking itself
was Cerdà's mathematical *eixample*.[7] But Güell and Gaudí had
gone for the opposite – a partially tamed, individual wilderness.
The Park Güell was an elitist upper-class enclave.

But Güell and Gaudí also found inspiration closer to home.[8]
Just three kilometres' walk from Riudoms lay the Parc de
Samá, the estate of the Marquès de Maríanao. In 1881 the
architect Fontseré, with whom Gaudí had collaborated in the
1870s, set about landscaping the Parc Samá into a miniature
Cuba.[9]

Served by Cuban slaves, Maríanao looked out across his tropical paradise, the lakes, watchtowers, and grottoes, to his private
zoo. The main avenues were planted out with rare trees from
the Americas and the Far East. The tall palms *Phoenix canariensis*
and *Chamaerops excelsa* and the imposing *Washingtonia filifera*
formed the backdrop of the squat *Yucca brasilensis*, a rare *Wichich-
intum* and a cluster of French ornamental vases. To this living
catalogue were added giant oaks, chestnuts, plantains and lin-
dens. And in the centre of all was a pool with an Oriental cascade
and fountains, formed out of the shells of giant clams and snails.

Fontseré and Maríanao shared the vision of an exotic paradise. Its almost savage picturesque quality proved seductive but it was the architectural detail of Samá's follies that inspired Gaudí most.

Above the police station that patrolled the perimeters, at its eastern corner, rose the Torre Angulo, a weird monstrosity formed from rubble and large porous stone chippings. It sat upon a hollow sculpted base that obscured the purpose-built cave beneath, which provided a summerhouse for the Marquès and his guests.

In the Park Güell, Gaudí was looking to invest the 'shallowness' of popular art with 'deep' cultural and religious meaning.[10] His complex narrative programme reflected not only the various historical gardens and follies prevalent in Renaissance Italy but also his two other masterworks, the Nativity façade of the Sagrada Família and the crypt at the Colònia Güell.

Gaudí's architecture has often been seen as too eccentric for the architectural canon but this view ignores the reactive nature of his methodology. If the Palau Güell was a reaction to the neoclassicism of the Comillases' Palau Moja, then the Park Güell was a response to Barcelona's other famous garden retreat, that cultural stage, the Laberint d'Horta.

Michael Jacobs' original voyage through contemporary Spain, *Between Hopes and Memories*, picks up the reader as they are about to enter the Laberint d'Horta's famous maze:

> The maze, with its central statue of Eros, is intended to suggest the 'realization of love', and has an inscription outside encouraging the visitor to penetrate it. 'Enter,' it reads. 'You will emerge without difficulty. The labyrinth is simple. You will have no need of the thread that Ariadne gave to Theseus.' Unfortunately, love is not always so easy to realize, and many visitors have had to force the process by resorting to crawling through hedges.[11]

It was not love's vicissitudes that interested Gaudí in the Laberint d'Horta; in fact, he roundly disapproved of the couples found in the Park Güell undergrowth. What intrigued him was finding a truly authentic Catalan architectural language for the city's public spaces. He wanted garden design that would do for horticulture what Domènech had aspired to do for the city's architectural fabric. The Park Güell provided him with the perfect opportunity to test out his ideas.

It was a 'grand gesture in the spirit of the Restoration Monarchy, with its odd accommodations of ancient principles to modern exigencies'.[12]

Gaudí and Güell's plan for the Park Güell was everything the Laberint wasn't. Where the Laberint favoured the neoclassical, the Park Güell would be built in Gaudí's singular Catalan style. Classical mythology was replaced by the Catalan, with motifs like Wilfred the Hairy's blood-striped shield, fiery dragons and their lairs. Exotic trees from faraway continents were replaced by indigenous scrub. Splintered rock was preferred to marble. Gaudí's deliberate programme mixed classical myth, Catalan history, Catholic liturgy and the memory of martyrdom into something completely unique.

In December 1900 the foreman of the works, Josep Pardo Casanovas, excavating the terrain for roads, found the entrance to a cave. Eusebi Güell immediately alerted the experts Dr Almera and his assistant at the geological museum of the Seminari Conciliar. The news of fossils that included rhinoceros bones, giant tortoiseshells, deer and other bones, delighted the palaeontologists who, for twenty-five years, had been looking for biblical sites in Catalonia that might confirm a literal reading of the Creation story. But now the cave offered enough circumstantial evidence to point to the existence of the Flood and that the Garden of Eden might well be located in Catalonia itself. Dr Almera's lifelong devotion to proving sacred history as a respectable branch of the natural sciences seems laughable today. But the myth of Catalonia as the Ur culture found supporters in Gaudí and Güell.

The roads that wound up to the top of the Park were supported by rows of crude columns that, angled into the hill, carried a system of road bridges. The ground plan, with an abundance of undulating pathways, bore witness to Gaudí's hatred for the sterile straight line.

The Park Güell is very theatrical. The tall perimeter walls are emblazoned with ceramic shields announcing the 'Park Güell' and its delivery from the outside world. And, immediately, the two gatehouses are disturbing and strange. Facing on the carrer d'Olot, these two pavilions seem distorted in scale. They have a hallucinatory Wonderland feel. One roof is even shaped like a magic mushroom. But upturned coffee cups set into the brightly coloured roofs suggest a far more innocent reading.[13] There are echoes of Maragall's contemporary translation of Humperdinck's opera of *Hansel and Gretel* in the coded narrative of Gaudí's entrance scene with its 'fairy-tale salvation'.[14]

Here for the first time was Gaudí's mature style, in which structure, subject, decoration and function were fused together. This is the moment where it becomes possible to talk of Gaudí as one of the twentieth century's great sculptors.

It became clear to Gaudí that by returning to the Catalan craft tradition he could open up a whole new language of forms. The tiled fish-scale skins created by Catalan bricklayers, by laminating layers of thin tile bricks, formed the curves of the arches and vaults which were both sturdy and decorative. Both efficient and cheap, this, coupled with the mass production of certain sections, allowed the ready construction of parabolic arches. Covering the roof structure was a vividly coloured skin of mosaic, fashioned from tiny shards of tile put together in the method known as *trencadís*. *Trencadís* is one of the most distinctive aspects of Gaudí's later architecture. Barcelona myth tells of Gaudí parsimoniously ordering his workmen to scavenge broken tiles from nearby building sites on their walk to work. There were also reports of the workmen taking delivery of carefully transported Valencian tiles and smashing them in front of the horrified delivery man.

The Park was planned like an opera, unfolding in three separate acts. The show would have opened on arrival at the gates flanked by a pair of mechanical gazelles that retreated into their cages as the iron gates creaked slowly open.

Straight ahead, the viewer gazes up a ceremonial staircase towards the covered market. At the bottom of the steps, a small rock pool is fed water through the mouth of a serpent that wears a collar of the Catalan flag. Further up the stairs there is another mythical beast, a dragon straight out of Revelation.

Next was the imposing market hall, which Gaudí described as his Greek theatre. A forest of Doric columns supported a large plaza.[15] But it was below, amongst the columns, that Gaudí envisaged both market and forum.[16] And under its archaic surface was a water-purifying plant. As the rain fell on the plaza above, it was slowly filtered through layers of pebbles and sand until it collected in bowls set directly above each column. From there the water descended through thin pipes inside each column to a cistern below.[17] Gaudí had created a system that simultaneously acted as drainage, filtration plant and reservoir. In 1913, Güell applied for a licence for a mineral water company, called Sarva. Sarva, its logo bearing Alpha and Omega, the first and last letters of the Greek alphabet, was quickly set up but was just as quickly closed down.[18]

Once the visitor had arrived on the plaza, the Park stretched out before them. Meandering paths, signalled by giant stone balls (doubling up as rosary beads) led slowly upwards to the Calvary at the top. The city and the harbour spread out in a wonderful panorama: the Gothic cathedral was clearly visible as was the Sagrada Família.

Joan Maragall recalled a conversation with Gaudí which had left him overwhelmed by the architect's brooding pessimism:

> In his work, in his struggle to make ideas material, he sees the law of punishment, and he revels in it. I can't conceal my repugnance at such a negative sense of life, and we discussed a tiny bit, very little, why I constantly find that we can't grasp one another's ideas. I who think of myself as so basically Catholic![19]

By summer 1906 it must have become obvious to Güell and Gaudí that their project was floundering. The park suffered from poor public transport, unique building restrictions and an uncertain economic climate. Only two houses of the prospective sixty had been sold. It is also likely that the success of the expansion in Sarriá, farther south, on the Avinguda del Tibidabo and the area below Vallvidrera, with their much better transport connections, pulled prospective clients away.[20] The temptation of entering Güell's fiefdom on a permanent basis had not proved strong enough. A change in the character of the Park Güell had become imperative. However, it could still function as a platform for a vibrant Catholic Catalan culture. For a small entry fee, it provided a private paradise.

Slowly over the years the Park Güell insinuated itself into Barcelona life. In 1907 it hosted a charity event to help flood victims. The following year in 1908 the gates opened for the fiftieth anniversary of the *Jocs Florals*; a walking race up to the Calvary; a party to celebrate Catalan education was held, as was the Congress of Pyrenean mountaineers. There were gymnastic competitions, parades of Red Cross volunteers and frequent dances of the Catalan *sardana*.[21] From a failed experiment in urban development the Park Güell rapidly became transformed into what it is today – a pleasure park set above the smog with a panoramic view over the city and the sea.

In June 1906, Julius Meier-Graefe finished off his whirlwind tour of Barcelona with a late-night trip to the Park Güell. It was Midsummer's Eve, or the *Noche de San Juan*, a night celebrated across Spain with almost pagan abandon:

Eventually we reached, somewhere around two o'clock, a kind of grotto or rather a kind of temple or a gigantic roundabout which however did not move. This edifice was supported by pillars which resembled monstrous elephants' tusks. From there we were led along a path by the side of dizzy precipices, which were lined with skulls or what not, to a kind of plateau which on closer examination turned out to be a suspended garden as well as the roof of the temple in which we had been previously. Then we came to a gigantic table of flowers on which we found tightly squashed crowds instead of flowers. Next door there was a similar flower table and so on and so forth, I don't know how many . . . in the twinkling of an eye we were confronted by another building of unintelligible form, half Indian palace, half dog-kennel, made out of pottery or glass or soap, bubbles . . . I decided that I was not in a trance but confronted by modern architecture. How I begged Horta and Guimard, Endell and Obrist and all the other evil-doers to forgive me for all the bitter thoughts I had entertained about them. They struck me as being peaceful classicists beside the invention of this monster in Barcelona.[22]

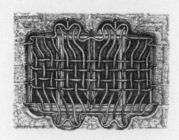

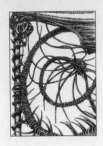

# The House of Bones

This architect has seen the house as a painter and a colourist
who paints for the light of his country.
Why should not a building be conceived entirely as a piece
of pottery or lustreware to respond constantly,
diversely to the reflections of the sun?[1]

*Marius-Ary Leblond*

Colour in architecture must be intense, logical and fertile.

*Antoni Gaudí*, Reus diary, 1876–79

IN EARLY 1901, Josep Batlló Casanovas, a leading member of
one of Barcelona's powerful textile clans, requested permission
from the city council to demolish his house. Built in 1877, the
house looked distinctly jaded alongside its much more fashionable neighbours. Only next door, Josep Puig i Cadafalch, a con-
firmed medievalist, was busy revamping a similarly nondescript
building for the chocolate magnate Antoni Amattler. Batlló
pressed forward with his ambitious plans for a new house. His
various ideas spanned Florentine, Venetian, Catalan Gothic and
Scottish baronial.

In those days family clans stayed with their family architect, as one might with a solicitor. Enric, Pia and Angel Batlló had during the 1890s each in turn commissioned large town houses from the respectable neo-Gothic architect Vilaseca. But José Batlló wanted to make more of an impression.

In May 1904, Batlló reapproached the city council with a more modest plan that stayed within the restrictions set by the building's original shell. In Gaudí, Batlló had found an architect flexible enough to work within limitations yet capable of intense innovation. In November 1904 work started on the Casa Batlló with Gaudí employing the trusted contractor José Bayó Font.[2]

By early 1906 the Casa Batlló was finished and is even today one of Barcelona's most inspired buildings. It is set in a block of the Passeig de Gràcia, known to locals as the *Manzana de la Discordia* (the block of discord) because the five adjoining buildings all explore different aspects of the *modernista* style. To walk along this pavement is to receive a masterclass in Catalan craftsmanship. Everybody who was anybody worked along this stretch. First is Domènech i Muntaner's Casa Lleó Morera, (1902–6), followed by the classically restrained Casa Ramón Mulleras (1910–11) designed by Enric Sagnier, the hiatus of the nondescript Casa Bonet (1915), then Puig i Cadafalch's Casa Amattler (1898–1900) and the Casa Batlló (1904–6). It was a complete vindication of Domènech's attempts in the late 1880s, along with his disciple Antoni Gallissá, to nurture and promote the creative base of Catalan craft in their design school the *Taller del Castell dels Tres Dragons*, housed in Domènech's Café-Restaurant built for the 1888 Exposition.

Along the *Manzana de la Discordia* sculptors worked alongside bronze-casters, cabinet-makers, stained-glass makers, mosaicists and plasterers and ceramicists. At the Casa Lleó Morera, Eusebi Arnau created a remarkable sculpture that projected out into the street.[3] On the first floor, elaborate stained glass pictured the Lleó Morera family at leisure. The Casa Ramón Mulleras was more restrained, but the Casa Amatller was a mock Flemish palace covered in detail from pavement to roof. Again Arnau was called in. Masriera and Campins provided bronzes, Escofet the floors, Joan Coll the exquisite plasterwork, Gaspar Homar the unique furnishings and the ironwork was divided up between the two masters Esteve Andorrá and Manuel Ballarín. The building was full of witty touches. The sculptors Alfons Juyol and Arnau were given free rein and carved a cyclist in contemporary dress as a joking reference to Puig's dashes between the house and another project across town; a fashionably dressed gargoyle leans out from a window jamb to photograph us with his box camera, while a wizened old woman stares enviously at a curvaceous Art Nouveau maiden; while, more traditionally, St George spears the dragon on a pillar by the entrance; and a positive bestiary of animals forms an orchestra: a pig plays the sackbut, a monkey an organ.

With similar commissions, each of the three great architects had quickly arrived at different solutions. As David Mackay writes in *Modern Architecture in Barcelona 1854–1939*, each was entirely distinctive:

> Domènech, rational with eclectic decoration; Gaudí, caught up with a total idea that flows through and gives a Baroque shape to the whole; Puig, patriotic and European, adroitly steering between the mediaeval and the classic.[4]

But what was the original idea for the Casa Batlló? The first sketch showed a seven-storey façade rising up towards a central tower. Kidney-shaped windows punctuated by bony columns accentuated the building's anthropomorphic character. This building has always been known by locals as 'The House of Bones'. Gaudí realised that aligning his building to the neighbouring Casa Amattler would cause an abrupt feeling of fracture. His solution was to reduce the tower by a level, shift it left, creating a small balcony space that reached across to the Casa

Amattler's roof. It has been described as one of the finest examples of 'architectural good manners'. Even so the two houses were still violently at odds with each other. Puig's building is still within a traditional compass. The wit is in the detail. But Gaudí's work pulls away and allows the skin of the building to billow out and form a rhythmic marine swell. Decoration is everywhere. Vivid glistening ceramic shards are in abrupt contrast with the cold stone of the skull-shaped balconies. Lluis Permanyer has suggested an interesting interpretation of the Casa Batlló's subject matter. That it is a homage to Catalonia's patron saint, St George. The skull balconies are the dragon's victims and the bony columns have been picked clean. The thrusting tower on the roof, crowned with a cross, represents St George's lance while the fish-scale roof tiles and curved roofline below suggest a dead dragon. This was a barely disguised reference to the increasingly bitter standoff between Castile and Catalonia.

Although the Casa Batlló is a *modernista* masterpiece, Gaudí and his studio would have hated the label, as it linked them 'with the *modernista* heresy, condemned by ecclesiastical authority as dogmatic progressionism and impossible to reconcile with the official doctrine of the Catholic Church'.[5] However, the Casa Batlló's almost recklessly original display powerfully showed Gaudí's acceptance of a whole set of values and beliefs that linked him closely to his *modernista* peers.

In an amusing anecdote, Apel.les Mestres claimed that it was at this time that Gaudí declared his preference for working exclusively on religious commissions. If any secular work turned up he would first have to pray to the Virgin of Montserrat for guidance and permission. To Batlló's relief, joked Apel.les Mestres, the kind Virgin always capitulated and allowed Gaudí to take on secular work.

It was with the Casa Batlló that Gaudí first became truly himself. And it was also for the first time that Gaudí went far beyond the other *modernista* architects, leaving Puig and Domènech stylist-ically straggling behind.[6] For the first time Gaudí's buildings supply us with a form of architectural autobiography.

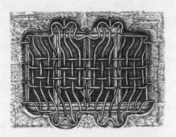

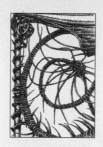

# The Beleaguered Fort

The far-reaching ridges of pastoral mountain
succeed each other, like the long and sighing swell
which moves over quiet water from some far-off stormy sea.

*John Ruskin*

IT WAS THE AUTUMN of 1905 and work was piling up in the studio. Park Güell had reached a critical stage, the Colònia Güell model needed constant alterations, and Palma's cathedral demanded Gaudí's personal supervision. Several smaller jobs added to the pressure: a pennant for the Guild of Locksmiths, a monument to Barcelona's old mayor Dr Robert, a bridge across the Torrente de Pomeret, recommendations on the 'appropriateness' of Sert's murals at Vic Cathedral and designs for ecclesiastical finery juggled with the need to add finishing touches to Bellesguard. There was an interesting commission for a tomb to celebrate the 700th anniversary of Jaume I's death. Puig had approached Gaudí, who immediately saw it as an opportunity for reorganising the whole area around the Plaça del Rei. Nothing was to come of it.[1] It was perhaps fortunate that the haphazard fund-raising for the Sagrada Família had brought work

159

almost to a standstill. But just as it ground to a halt its reputation was raised higher than ever before. During the 1905 municipal elections, *La Veu de Catalunya* embarked on a pro-Sagrada Família panegyric.[2]

Experiments in economic and social engineering were being attempted at the Colònia and the Park Güell. But it was at the Sagrada Família that the Gaudí–Güell philosophy might, it was hoped, achieve a cohesive whole. Here the holy family and the sacred artist might be hitched to 'the chariot of greater national glory.'[3] But despite Gaudí's growing fame the money did not come flowing in.

Most of Gaudí's work came by word of mouth. Pere Milà i Camps had first suggested Gaudí as the right architect for the Casa Batlló. Now, having waited for the right site to appear, it was Milà's turn to commission a building from Gaudí.

Milà was 'a talented dandy', dressed sharply in pearl-grey suits.[4] Politician, property developer and publisher of *El Día Gráfico*, he was also a successful impresario.[5] In 1903 he married a wealthy widow, Doña Rosario Segimón Artells. In June 1905 she bought the prime corner site on the Passeig de Grácia and the carrer Provença. In September Gaudí requested permission to pull down the existing house and clear the site for foundations.[6] The Casa Milà, better known as *La Pedrera* – the quarry – would become one of Gaudí's signature works.

Gaudí's first site visits that autumn were to see how the project might lock into the rigid plan of the *eixample*. The Casa Milà project was Gaudí's fourth along the Passeig de Grácia, after the Farmacia Gibert, the Café Torino interior and the Casa Batlló. It would also be the last full-scale commission he would take on.

The *eixample* was in constant flux. Its open spaces (previously grazing land) were being developed at an astonishing rate.[7] The grid-pattern streets were now being paved. Shanty dwellings were razed. Even palaces, constructed in the 1870s and '80s, were torn down. In the old town a whole swathe of the Ribera district was levelled for the new Via Laietana. Thousands of people were made homeless within a few months.

Changes were occurring even within Gaudí's workshop. Rubió was now getting his own large commissions: the monastery of the Sagrada Família at Manacor, the Casas Rialp, Pomar, Dolcet, Casacuberta and Roviralta '*El Frare Blanca*' on the slopes of Tibidabo.[8] But his loss was more than compensated for with the arrival in his studio of Jujol, during 1906, although the precise date of his entry into the atelier is not clear.

Like Gaudí, Jujol had been forced to work through college, as a student-assistant for Gallissà and Font on the restoration of the Ateneo Barcelonés. It was while working there that Gaudí's friend Dr Santaló forced an introduction between the two.

They made a strange pair. Gaudí, at fifty-four, was revered but also known as abrupt, now slowly losing interest in his personal appearance. Alongside him was the twenty-seven-year-old Jujol, small and dapper, sporting a full black moustache. Their collaboration became one of the great working partnerships of twentieth-century architecture. Jujol's son described Gaudí:

> As an extraordinary genius he was not as others have described him: a solitary person, who wanted to do everything himself and dominate all those around him. Quite the opposite, he was an intelligent man who knew how to delegate, who also knew who would be best suited to which particular job. I am convinced that Gaudí worked with a team in which he was the undisputed master – and even if he had wanted to do it all on his own – he trusted in his collaborators so that the finished building would end up even more perfect at the end of the day.[9]

The rhythm of Gaudí's private life also changed. He was gradually drawing away into himself and into his work. By 1906 he had taken up residence with his father and niece Rosa in one of the two houses built in the Park Güell. Francesc, now in his

nineties, was growing steadily weaker. The doctor Gaudí called
in was Josep Cubero Calvo, living in nearby Gràcia. Sadly,
relations between Gaudí and the doctor were strained as he had
once failed to save the life of one of Gaudí's workmen. But it
was only after a carriage dispatched to pick up Cubero returned
empty that relations were finally broken. Thereafter when Gaudí
saw the doctor he ignored him.

Gaudí spent little time now in the old city; the drawn out
*tertulias* ar the Palau Güell were a thing of the past, as were the
evenings at the Liceu and Ateneu, the poetry readings and public
lectures at the *Excurcionistas*. It was only daily confessional at
St Felip Neri and Sunday mass in the cathedral that kept him
in touch with life in the Gothic quarter.

Gaudí's home life gradually took on the slower rhythms of
village life. The Park's other house was lived in by lawyer Don
Martí Trías Domènech. Gaudí soon became friends with his
neighbour's son, Alfonso. In the evenings after school Alfonso
would walk down to meet Gaudí off the tram. Together they
would stroll up the hill, Gaudí, with a copy of *La Veu de Catalunya*
rolled up under his arm, interrogating Alfonso on how the
builders had got on during his absence. He enquired after visitors
and after Alfonso's studies, family and friends. On Sundays Gaudí
and Alfonso sometimes walked down to the sea together at the
Barceloneta and then back past the Columbus monument to the
Ramblas and across the *Barri Gòtic*. Sometimes, accompanied by
Joan Matamala, his cousin Josep Gaudí Pomerol or Dr Santaló,
Gaudí sat for hours on the sea wall. The happiest day of his life,
he told Matamala, was an afternoon spent listening to Dr Llobera
reading from his translation of Homer into Catalan.[10]

The common perception of Gaudí as a cantankerous hermit
is rather at odds with the ease with which he built a circle of
loyal and admiring friends. He perhaps saw Alfonso as the son
he never had. Again and again, the anecdotal evidence tells us
how he would never forget such and such a daughter's birthday,

Isabel Güell's saint's day, or how he would religiously play the favourite uncle and bring along special pastries and puddings for the children.

With Alfonso he would often stop and chat to acquaintances. Farther up, silhouetted now by the setting sun, he would turn to Alfonso and announce, '*El Català es llaminer*' ('We Catalans have a sweet tooth'). And enter El Caballo Blanco to buy Alfonso a treat and catch up on the local gossip.

Slowly they walked on farther to the Park gates where they would chat with Carlos the porter. Alfonso recalled later that 'the conversation was a monologue by Gaudí who enjoyed commenting on political and artistic events'.[11] Alfonso also remembered Gaudí discussing Wagner at length with two local shepherds – before entering the gates of his private Elysium.

On 2 February 1906, Gaudí submitted the first plans of the Casa Milà to the city council. The initial application was put in early to buy time and clear the site. Gaudí knew from experience that the plan would evolve. It is hardly surprising therefore that the initial elevations look like an extended hybrid of the Casa Batlló; the same façade repeated four times with additional flourishes.

The site itself posed a specific problem. In the *eixample*'s original design the corners of the blocks at crossroads were cut off diagonally to form diamond-shaped squares. The *xamfrà* – the cut-off corner – created new possibilities for these three-sided corner plots. The standard solution had been to ignore the problem; the result was a prosaic architecture for the new bourgeoisie.

By the turn of the century, with the *modernista*'s greater emphasis on craft and decoration, solutions had been found. Balcony tribunes, sometimes five storeys high, making a feature of the decorative ironwork, stone-carving and stained glass,

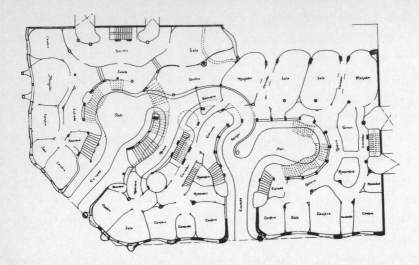

The 1906 floor plan of the Casa Milà with its organic
cluster of honeycomb rooms.

punctuated the two shallow angled corners and personalised the
space. But the decorations most often used came straight from
the pattern books. There were a few notable exceptions. In the
Casa Golferichs (1901–3) on the Gran Via, Rubió created a
stylish villa that turned its back on the street. But the Casa Milà
would become the first building in the *eixample* to fill its corner
site without playing with façades.

For Gaudí, however, the problems of site, structure and style
were always subordinate to the subject. He wanted a building
that displayed character, an edifice based squarely in Catalan
culture while displaying a morality and appropriateness to its
needs. An architecture in which form and function were in harmony, his way in was almost always through visiting the site, to
sense the spirit of place.

The site was full of history. Roman roads surrounded it and
the Casa Milà plot was suggested to be where the eleventh-
century shrine to the Virgin of Gràcia had been.[12]

The scale of the proposed building was in itself impressive,

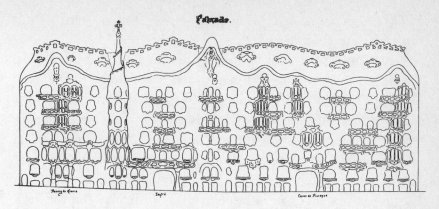

Signed elevation of the Casa Milà dated February 1906.

covering more than 1,600 square metres. But it was the swollen body of the Casa Milà, looming threateningly over the thoroughfare, that drew everyone's attention. This mountain appeared on the Barcelona skyline like a hulk marooned from another era. The building was not Catalan, not Spanish, Iberian or Mudejar. It was neither classical nor Baroque, later than Rococo yet earlier than the Goths. It was a building without precedent.

Early on at architectural school Gaudí developed the practice of looking at every illustration available (like Picasso, he forgot nothing useful and remembered everything practical). He had always walked everywhere; looking, arguing, pointing out errors, banalities and trends, and was always available to the interested student, offering a discourse on the merits of a particular building, the virtues of a particular style. The *eixample*, from the *Manzana de la Discordia* to Gràcia, had become a university of architecture.

While working on the Casa Batlló, Gaudí studied his nearest rivals' work. As a source for the Casa Milà, illustrations of the fountain in the courtyard of Hector Guimard's celebrated Castel Berenger of 1895–98 in Paris – a squashed Art Nouveau mountain of bronze – were in all the international architectural magazines. But even closer to home, within 400 metres of the Casa

Milà, Gaudí witnessed the gradual emergence of what would turn into the Casa Milà style.

Gaudí must have seen Batllevell's nearby Casa Antònia Burés, (Batllevell was also the architect of the other home in the Park Güell). The double arch leading into the shop was divided by a sculpted tree. And not only was this a pine – the sacred Catalan tree – but it was a pun on the builder's name, Enric Pi. Its organic growth sprouted forth images of lignum vitae, the ever-lasting tree of life. Another prime example was Sagnier's Casa Fargas. At first sight it looks deceptively ordinary. But the arch around the door curved outwards, forcing the vegetation carved around it into subtle distortions. The surface of the façade had been pulled along into a gentle sweeping wave. Accurate botanical detail rioted into the fantastical. Falqués with the Casa Bonaventura Ferrer of 1905–6 further developed this theme.[13] But now the floral decoration had taken on its own dynamic. Palm fronds and foliage, blown up and twisted into grotesque shapes, had begun to look distinctly threatening. As the German architect August Endell wrote in his essay 'The Beauty of Form and Decorative Art', 'nature seems to live and we begin to understand that there really are sorrowing trees and wicked treacherous branches, virginal grasses and terrible, gruesome flowers'.[14] Across Europe, architects were anthropomorphising nature.

If Gaudí had, in turn, looked at other buildings in the *eixample*, as he almost certainly had, it was not for the purposes of plagiarism. It was more a confirmation that the new morphology he was busy inventing was not totally divorced from all previous styles.[15]

While the contractor Bayo Font started to pull down the original house, Gaudí's plans for the Casa Milà were undergoing a metamorphosis. Only half of the house was pulled down at first, the remaining half left standing for use as a site office and studio extension. Gaudí kept paring away the unnecessary detail from his earlier plan, trying to understand the volumes of the building. He once explained, 'The intelligence of man can only function on one plane, that is in two dimensions … But the intelligence of the angels is in three dimensions, they can work directly with space. Man can't begin to understand space until he has seen the realised object in front of his eyes.'[16]

The Casa Milà felt both primitive and raw. Its roofscape was a veritable 'wonderland'.[17] Many sources of inspiration have been suggested. These range from the extraordinary churches in Cappadocia carved out of freestanding rocks by the wind; to Petra and to the catacombs of St Peter embedded into Zalsburg hill[18] and the sandstone grain towers in southern Sudan.[19] Togo's clay cone towers have been cited: as have the mosques at Sansannu and Kreis-Següela. The exotic and primitive had become an obsession of contemporary art too. Simultaneously with Gaudí's design for the Casa Milà, the young Picasso was searching for inspiration from African masks and carvings.

But it was not just in the visual arts that primitivism now reigned. The rise of Catalan culture meant a return to basics to find its essence. But across Spain primitive landscapes (as described by Jorge Manrique and the Arcipreste de Hita) that portrayed the 'real' Spain, also enjoyed a new vogue. Underneath the skin of history lay what Unamuno had christened '*intrahistoria*' – the essential.

The first phase of the Milà works was far more prosaic: all energy was focused on clearing rubble and digging the foundations.

A new building type was adapted especially for the Casa Milà – the free plan structure.[20] Using the light industrial structures of railway stations as an example, iron columns were alternated with pillars built out of reclaimed bricks. The house's façade was hinged onto the front elevation of the iron skeleton. The freedom that this gave Gaudí in the design of the exterior is evident.[21] But it was in the floor plans that this became most strikingly obvious. Every house in the *eixample* till then had employed symmetry, straight lines and right angles. In the Casa Milà floor plan rectangularity had been replaced with a very organic design that looked like a loose cluster of bubbles, each signifying a room but attached haphazardly.[22]

Stories abound about Gaudí's eccentric working methods on the Casa Milà. His draughtsman Canaleta complained that he was being asked to scale up floor plans for the builders to such a size that he had to lie across the drawing board, thus smudging his laboriously painstaking work.[23] Might there be a better way of subdividing the plans into manageable sections, or some other solution? Gaudí suggested that Canaleta cut a hole in the centre of his drawing board so that he could presumably crawl underneath, come up in the middle and carrying on drawing.[24]

A pedantic architect asked Gaudí how he could countenance starting work without finished blueprints. Gaudí reached into his pocket and crumpled up a sheet of paper. Patiently, he opened the heavily creased ball and flattened it out carefully. Holding it up against the Casa Milà, he said proudly. 'This is my plan for the Casa Milà, Senyor. *Bon dia i A Deu!*'[25]

This story quickly slipped into Barcelona folklore. By now Gaudí had become a living legend, the most famous architect working in the Iberian peninsula. Eccentric, egocentric and focused, there was no doubting his genius. But there was a gathering backlash. The deep pockets of his select client list, his extreme Catholicism, occasional 'explosions' and the growing feeling that the *modernista* style had run out of steam began to attract negative critical attention.

Gaudí's most productive period, from 1906 to 1909, was also when the critic Eugeni d'Ors began to formulate his anti-Gaudí position.

> It is said that our famous architect, Antoni Gaudí, professes the principle that one cannot make plans and that it is better to commend oneself to the inspiration of each

night. But Gaudí has his particular methods and I have mine.[26]

The Casa Milà continued apace. Gaudí knew how to delegate not only on site and off but also with specialist manufacturers like the Badía brothers and the locksmiths. But he knew when to intervene too. One story describes his reducing a stone-mason to tears as he corrected and recorrected his work. Gaudí then took up the chisel himself, honing the ornamental rose destined for the heights of the façade. The stonemason was carving a specific rose from nature but Gaudí rather wanted the essence of rose. His rose was the one that would symbolise Doña Rosario, his patroness. He blunted back the detail until at last it had become the ideal and nonspecific rose – frozen at the very moment of becoming.

With Jujol, Gaudí was far more trusting. He was given carte blanche to do almost anything he wanted.[27] Considering that he was still only in his twenties Gaudí's respect for him was immense and it is sadly true that Jujol's reputation as one of the century's greatest creative geniuses is still far from recognised.[28]

Gaudí, like an overindulgent father, allowed Jujol free licence. In return, Jujol repaid his master's confidence and shifted Gaudínian taste away from the strictly naturalistic towards an abstract and often surrealist approach. While working at Mallorca, Gaudí was frequently pestered by the cathedral *Junta* and requested to explain Jujol's bizarre, colourful daubings. Gaudí answered, 'I have two cats in the house: one, Sugranyes, does his work where he is supposed to; the other, Jujol, does it exactly where he is not supposed to. You're absolutely right, but what can I do about it?'[29]

Jujol was given the Casa Milà's balconies to complete. Incorporating real, found objects, his insistence on drawing attention to the palpable sense of the artist's touch and his almost hypnotic concentration on detail would later be echoed by Joan

Miró's hallucinatory vision *The Farm*. But his methodology also related very strongly to Gaudí's empirical approach that looked at every new problem as if it were virgin territory, or from '*el origen*'.

Working within one of the strongest of the Catalan craft traditions Jujol set about renewing the language of wrought-iron decoration from the inside out. At the Casa Vicens, the gates and railings, designed by Gaudí during the 1880s, employed palmflowers – stamped out in cast iron – repeated endlessly. One metre could be multiplied without variation to a kilometre in length or onwards towards infinity. But, Jujol, like a rodeo rider, found a new and unique way of breaking in the metal of his formal abstractions in order to contain and restrain their elegant 'ballet of forms'. The jerkiness of the balconies, their energy and jarring dissonance mirrored the subtle and loose arrangements of jazz improvisations.

Jujol's working method was unusual. For each balcony he rolled out lengths of paper exactly to scale 1:1. On these he sketched with charcoal each balcony, unique, but still working within the general theme of washed-up seaweed left hanging on the Casa Milà's rock-like ledges, perhaps even using the balconies as a symbol of nature recapturing a devastated city after the flood, a holocaust or the Second Coming.[30] After Jujol passed over his drawings to the Badia workshop professionals he would encourage them to work *fa presto*, to draw with the metal as if drawing in air and play to the metal's tensile strength, its elasticity and its abstract shapeliness. On receiving the finished item from Badia, Jujol would then set to modifying and relaxing the work and investing its abstract shapes with their appropriate character. Contemporary Spanish architects of the calibre of the Catalans Oriol Bohigas and Rafael Moneo have debated the wilfulness and spontaneity of Jujol's work as opposed to a structured analytical approach.[31] Almost all are agreed on its almost fetishistic quality and Jujol's unique capacity to create a magical world of forms in which 'fantasy seems always to emerge from the kingdom of logic'.[32]

Gaudí was always ready to encourage and urge his collaborators on. Matamala remembered Gaudí returning from the Casa Milà one day. He had been working with his contractor Josep Bayó, the man he called the 'calculating machine'.

> What an amazing thing human intelligence is when it's focused on the area of someone's speciality. Today I worked for hours with Bayó on some calculations and I felt as if I hadn't done a thing. Bayó felt exactly the same even though we were at it non-stop. There's no doubting Bayó's usefulness.[33]

Gaudí loved problem-solving. Late in the planning, Bayó and Gaudí discovered that one of the owners of an apartment in the Casa Milà, the manufacturing magnate Senyor Feliu, had a Rolls-Royce whose turning circle was too wide for the underground garage. The calculations required to resite the offending pillar and compensate for the stresses took Bayó as long as the whole of the building had taken him in the first place.[34] Gaudí insisted on his own correctness. Where other more cautious architects might double up the width of an arch for safety's sake Gaudí would stick to his calculations exactly. In most instances his projections were right. Most impracticalities were ironed out during building. His was an architecture of trial and error. And whilst he was renowned for his professional arrogance, he occasionally admitted a mistake.

Once day walking across the site Gaudí noticed a welder making up T-shaped iron brackets. The Casa Milà was now up to roof level but he definitely hadn't included these anywhere in his plan. Just below the attic spaces Gaudí had planned for a wide rain gutter which Bayó intended to reinforce with these brackets. They wouldn't be necessary, Gaudí said. But while Gaudí was away in Mallorca Bayó fitted the braces all the same. Gaudí was furious: but when a builder working on the roof slipped and was saved by the reinforced gutter he apologised to Bayó.[35]

It was the construction of the façade that raised the most difficulties. While technically the exterior wall wasn't load-bearing, the sheer thickness of the Montjüic stone for the façade demanded that Bayó improvise a system of pulleys and counter-weights to hoist each rock into place. While Bayó had added a generous margin to the estimated cost of the whole building he hadn't anticipated having to lift and lower the same stone up to four times before it found its place. This spatial experimentation, which Gaudí always proudly acknowledged as his most important inheritance from his father the boilermaker, was easy enough to control on the scale of model-making. Manipulating Plasticine façades, cutting out miniature details and twisting card into place all had their own problems. But dealing with rock so heavy that it had to be transported on a special train almost bankrupted Bayó.

Bayó explained his predicament. Gaudí asked Sugrañes if Bayó was exaggerating. When Sugrañes said no Gaudí negotiated an increased budget from Milà. Was he losing money on his devel-opment, someone asked him? 'Not my money,' he spat back, 'I'm losing my patience!'

Both Gaudí and Milà wanted the Casa Milà to be a luxury showpiece. Although a compromise, the drive-in garage was the first of its kind. Gaudí had initially wanted ramps to circle up and round the walls of the inner courtyards so that even residents on the fifth floor could be dropped off at their door. But it proved impractical. The spacious flats were fitted with all the latest modern conveniences however, from central heating to constant hot water.

Although the building of the Casa Milà had been without a major hitch, it was legal complications that slowed the process down. Even before work had begun, it had already been stopped. On 4 October 1905, just one month after Gaudí had been named architect, a council employee protested that the hoardings took in part of the pavement, including a streetlamp. Bassegoda puts it succinctly: 'It was the first of many official complaints that rained down on the intrepid Don Pere Milà.'[36]

Eight days later work was officially suspended. It was the first of many judgments against Milà and initially he fought back in person. Later, exhausted, he didn't even bother answering.

The file of this drawn-out legal epic rests safely in the Archivo Administrativo Municipal.[37] Not a single word has gone astray and while low on literary merit it gives a valuable insight into the workings of the bureaucratic mind.

On 27 February 1906, just one week after Gaudí had submitted his plans, Milà requested permission to pull down the original house. The permit finally came through – twenty months later. It was too late. Work had carried on regardless of legality.

Pere Estany kicked off the next round, with an order demanding that the architect remove a column that stuck out too far into the Passeig de Gràcia. This episode, known as 'The Case of the Elephant's Foot', became part of the Casa Milà folklore.[38] Gaudí ordered Bayó to pass on his message, 'Fine! Tell them that if they want to cut away at my building as if it were a cheese we'll carve a little notice on the smoothed off surface "Mutilated by the order of the Barcelona City Council on such and such a date . . ."'[39]

The council fought back and demanded their order be upheld. The following month, work on the Casa Milà was suspended again. Again Bayó and Gaudí ignored it. On 16 June 1908, ignoring the technicality that work should not have been continuing, Bayó requested that the hoarding be extended. The enormous stones were now being swung into position. Ten days later permission was given.

This legal cat and mouse game continued into the next year. In June 1909, just three years into the project, and with the Casa Milà now completed up to the fourth floor, the council finally accepted Gaudí's plans and a week later reinstated permission. Out of thirty-six months the Casa Milà had been legal for just four weeks.

In late spring 1909 the hoardings finally came down and for the first time the public could see the building that had been talked about for so long. Collins described it as 'a mountain built by the hand of Man'.[40] Like rising dough it filled out towards its perimeters. Perucho described it as 'a kind of stone lung, breathing gently';[41] the bohemian Francis Carco, likened it to 'a fantastic banner of concrete where only the flag-pole is missing'. Each commentator picked up the organic qualities of the Casa Milà and its extravagant reworking of Baroque. What was particularly noticeable about the Milà (especially in spring 1909), before the extraordinary wrought-iron balconies had been added, was how economical the surface decoration was. As Gaudí wrote in his diary while still at architectural school, 'It is patently clear that in a typical building the whole is subjected to a single dominant dimension. The Egyptians developed monumentality, the Middle Ages verticality.'

The Casa Milà was a building that took a single dominant idea: the mountain. But a mountain that shared the sense of movement so central to Art Nouveau. The Casa Milà's gentle forms flowed from the roof like water over cataracts, leading the eye down through a series of whirlpools. As an architectural ensemble it managed to avoid ambiguity while leaving everything open to doubt.

Nicknames followed quickly. The Hornet's Nest and *La Pedrera* – the quarry – were the most common of all. They were playful, childlike and witty. But these descriptions also hid something more melancholy. Carved into gentle folds, the surface of the Casa Milà was 'sparrow pecked'; it had the unfinished quality of Michelangelo's final sculptures of the slaves trapped in stone. Casanelles noted this duality:

Beneath the wrinkled exterior of approaching old age Gaudí preserved elements typical of a child's insight. Or were they perhaps those of a madman? Did he sometimes wonder if he himself was going mad?[42]

The Casa Milà positively exploded onto the Barcelona architectural scene. Its forms reverberated through the art world. The Casa Milà echoed the mountains behind it and, of course, Catalonia's sacred mountain – Montserrat. While working at Montserrat Gaudí had blasted the rock to create a 'natural' space, at the Milà he had gone one stage further and taken the opportunity to imitate and improve on nature itself.

As Ruskin wrote, 'the silent wave of the blue mountain is lifted towards heaven in a stillness of perpetual mercy'.[43]

The forbidding exterior of Casa Milà today is far from Gaudí's original intentions. He planned to tame his artificial landscape by encouraging all the residents to drape their balconies with luxuriant vegetation. Green trailers, hanging baskets and vines would soften the outline while cacti, ferns and palms would relieve the balconies' repetitive horizontality. Gaudí, who was an expert in hydraulics, had even planned a self-irrigation system. But nothing came of it. The Casa Milà's harshness lent it a certain clarity.[44]

Gaudí wanted to petrify the spirit of Catalonia for ever in stone. Natural examples abounded in the weather-eaten rocks of Cap Creus,[45] Fra Guerau, in the centre of the saw-tooth range the Serralada de Prades near to Reus, or the Portals Vells in Andratx;[46] perhaps St Miquel de Fai, which he visited as an *Excursionista*, or the Torrent de Pareis in the north of Mallorca, known locally as 'La Dragonera'. Gaudí had once dragged one of his assistants out of bed at four in the morning to see it

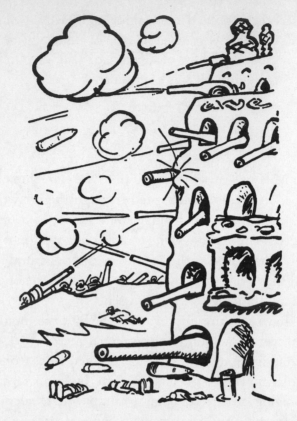

Cartoon of the Casa Milà as war machine.

burn red in the rising Mediterranean sun.[47] Another Balearic possibility was Calescobes in Minorca.[48] Closer to home there was the mountain of San Sadurni near Gallifa in the Vallès.[49] Each mountain has its supporters. But the struggle to find a specific example is far too literal: for Gaudí had no intention of closing down the range of his references.

In Exodus 20:4 the craftsman/artist is warned:

> Thou shalt not make unto thee any graven image, or any likeness of any thing that is in heaven above, or that is in the earth beneath, or that is in the water under the earth.

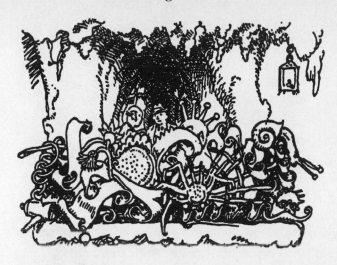

A Casa Milà balcony transformed into a scrap-iron yard
or a twentieth-century modern art assemblage.

In its original sense this prohibition was not just a warning against idolatry but against verisimilitude itself. It didn't seem to bother Bishop Torras i Bages. Or the other Sant Llucs. In Spain there had been a long tradition of super-realist votive objects.[50] The myopic bishop was attracted to the Casa Milà's grandeur, observing that 'This edifice is laughing at all the others in the *eixample*.'

Popular opinion was split. Ramiro de Maeztu had eulogised in *Nuevo Mundo*:

> Every seven or eight centuries, man produces in some corner of the globe an original architecture. Even epics are produced more frequently. In reality one ought not to discuss Gaudí as if he were just any architect. The man's talent is so dazzling that even the blind would recognise Gaudí's work by touching it. Not only has Gaudí attempted something but he has achieved it.[51]

But every cartoonist in Barcelona was using him as a prime target. And as Casanelles wrote:

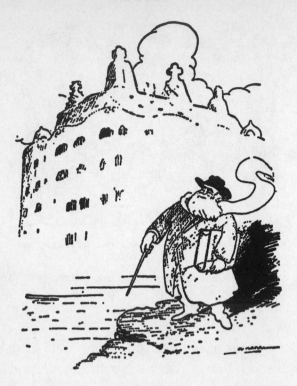

'Wotan Barceloni'. Gaudí's 1910 portrait in *L'Esquella de la Torratxa* as Wagnerian superman.

There was more than simply gossip in the cartoons; there was an intellectual and social undercurrent which was at times purulent and nauseating, at others, irreverent and degrading.[52]

The Casa Milà reminded some of the wreckage of the recent train crash at Riudecanyes. Others thought of Rusiñol's joke about the tenants only able to keep snakes amongst the twisting and curving walls, while others found the cartoon of the little boy asking his mother, 'Mummy, do they have earthquakes here too?' hilarious.[53]

This humour was directed at deflating the deadly seriousness of the Casa Milà. Yet another cartoon depicted it as a garage

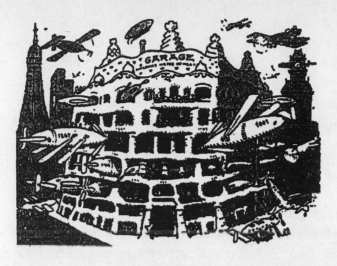

The Casa Milà caricatured in *L'Esquella de la Torratxa* as
a futuristic Zeppelin garage. 1912.

for Zeppelins. Francesc Pujols, a Catalan writer, as eccentric as
Dali, appreciated Gaudí's nerve:

> Gaudí has gambled all, and has gracefully achieved a
> primitive architecture that nevertheless embodies all the
> advances of modern times.

And Pujols was right. The Casa Milà came straight out of the
futurist fantasies of Jules Verne and H. G. Wells. The tenants
that moved into the Casa Milà knew that they were living a
state-of-the-art existence right out on the lonely frontiers of
style. They were also the laughing stock of the city.

A cartoonist in *L'Esquella de Torratxa* called him Wotan Barceloni, picking on the Wagnerian flavour of Gaudí's creation.
Although domestic architecture, its themes were of the grandest.

179

Gaudí's ambitions were growing. In the Casa Milà he had limited himself to a mere microclimate, with its self-irrigation system, but back at the Nativity Portal of the Sagrada Família he wanted to re-create the whole cosmos.

It was a dangerous conceit. Josep Pla recorded Rafael Puget's memories of Gaudí in *Un Senyor de Barcelona*:

> His personality was shot through by a morbid, insoluble pride and vanity. In a country where most things remain to be done and the little that has been done is always in danger of being torn down or left unfinished, our architect was born unique and worked as though architecture itself had begun at the precise moment when he made his appearance on earth.

His work was an

> imitation of cosmic life, inside which people would pass a mystical-troglodytic existence ... He is neither a Roman nor a Catholic in the sense these words normally have in our culture. He is a primitive Christian of the woods ...[54]

There he was, the caped figure of the cartoon, looking up at his work and seeing that it was good. But even more penetrating was the final cartoon of the series. In F. Brunet's caricature the Casa Milà becomes a series of animal-infested caves, a termite mound, or a Noah's Ark. Out of the picture peers an alligator, an owl, a pair of eagles, a snake, pelicans, penguins, a tiger, a seal, monkeys, rats, hedgehogs, moles and a frog. But up on the roof, two piles of human skulls are heaped up in the form of the ventilation shafts that Gaudí was finishing. The Casa Milà has been transformed into a giant sarcophagus, a terrifying monument to nihilism.

In the Casa Milà Gaudí had created an astonishingly powerful building which, open to interpretation, had fished deep into the

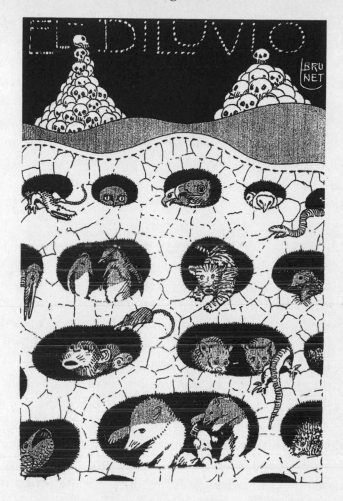

F. Brunet's terrifying *El Diluvio* cartoon of the Casa Milà
as both Noah's Ark and charnel house. 1912.

collective unconscious, sounding out the depths of Catalan racial
identity. But in so doing he had also painted himself into a
corner. The cartoons, quips and stories would forever map out
the boundaries of our future interpretation. From now on the
cultural sport of Gaudí baiting had come out of the small circles
of the Barcelona art world and out into the wider public arena.

Privately for Gaudí, it was a moment of profound crisis.

*181*

Martorell, his early mentor and supporter, had passed away. On 29 October 1906 his father, Francesc, died. They hadn't even lived in their *Casa Pairal* together for a year. Ever since Antoni had designed the Palau Güell twenty years earlier, he had passed his wages directly to his father. He didn't need to soil his hands with money, the mean-minded would observe. But there was far more than that. Francesc had sold his lands, his house and his hold on a handful of *baix camp* soil to put Antoni through architectural school. Now Gaudí lived alone up in the house on the hill. Alone except for his chronically ill niece Rosa Egea and the maid Vicenta.

Rosa, more commonly addressed with the affectionate diminutive Rosita, was sinking fast through alcohol-related illnesses.[55] As in an Ibsen play, in which it was assumed with fatalistic inevitability that 'the sins of the father were revisited on the son', poor Rosita inherited a degenerate inclination towards the bottle's numbing pleasures. Her mother, Rosa, Gaudí's sister, having died when Rosita was just three, had left the toddler with father Josep Egea, a bohemian musician and alcoholic who appeared only too happy to pass on the responsibility for her upkeep to her famous uncle.[56] While Francesc was alive, Rosita accompanied him on his daily therapeutic walks around the Park Güell. He kept an eye on her self-indulgence and provided willing company. On Francesc's death, Rosa's health took a downward slide. Tubercular and prone to palpitations of the heart, the lonely Rosa sought solace in consuming draughts of the potent Agua del Carmen that she kept hidden from her uncle. She claimed that it gave her strength, but the debilitating drink was anathema to Gaudí, whose strict Prussian health regime, promoted by Sebastian Kneipp, favoured the intake of copious quantities of spring water. It was like

> a bitter form of torture for Gaudí. He hated drunkenness
> and had managed to successfully get some of his workers

*182*

off the bottle but had never managed to liberate his beloved niece from her addiction.[57]

Bergós Massó, an early biographer, described this period in Gaudí's life as a '*holocausto*'.

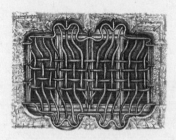

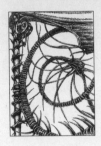

# The Sheltering Cave

You forget that I am Spanish and I love sadness.
*Pablo Picasso*

Originality means going back to our origins.
*Antoni Gaudí*

No archetype can be reduced to a simple formula . . .
It is a vessel which can never empty and never fill . . .
it persists through the ages and requires interpreting ever anew.
*C. G. Jung*, The Science of Mythology

GAUDÍ HAD FOUND in the honey-coloured stone of the Casa Milà a material that was powerfully symbolic. As a symbol, it was infinitely flexible and a passport to the Catalan soil.

Joan Amades i Gelat, protector of Catalan folklore, wrote an essay, 'Stones and the Cult of the Dead', which describes their resonance to the early Catalans.

The primitive mind considered stones to be the containers of spirits, of benevolent geniuses with a will of their own. Whatever use primitive people derived from

184

a stone was not the result of its materiality but the effect
of the empathy and the goodwill of the geniuses within.

In 1910, Francesc Pujols had asked Gaudí how he had found his
unique profile for the Casa Milà. He replied, '*Els Grecs, avui, ho
farien aixi.*' ('The Greeks would do it this way today').[1]

Throughout history, landscape had often been manipulated
for propaganda purposes. Often, though, a lust for giantism and
the lack of a suitable sense of proportion turned these large-scale
experiments into gigantic follies. Gaudí's creation of a mountain
in the centre of the metropolis laid him open to just such an
accusation; and, furthermore, that he was setting himself up as
a godlike figure. This was nothing new. Architectural literature
dating right back to classical times had dealt directly with this
theme. In *De architectura*, Vitruvius warned against excessive
vanity with the tale of Dinocrates, who had tempted Alexander
the Great with a monument at Mount Athos: immortalised as a
giant seated figure with a lake in his left hand and a city in his
right. According to Simon Schama in his brilliantly provocative
*Landscape and Memory*,

> the story of Dinocrates was believed by some later com-
> mentators, not least Goethe, to be historically plausible;
> it functioned principally as a mythical touchstone for
> architectural theorists like Alberti, exercised about the
> relationships between balance and hubris, between con-
> ceptual daring and structural practicality.[2]

There could hardly be a more accurate description of the Casa
Milà, where Gaudí's ambitions were boundless. From Stone Age
to Greek, medieval to Baroque, pagan to Christian, all meditations on the mountain and the cave were studied anew. For
the image of the cave was at the heart of the Christian ideal.

In the medieval world, the mountain-castle sat geographically
and psychologically right at the centre of the landscape where

it functioned as a symbol of authority and control. By the Counter-Reformation mountain scenery had become a very effective tool in the Roman Catholic armoury.

Mountains had traditionally functioned as the judges of human fallibility, and of that ultimate human vanity, the belief in omnipotence, just as man's building the Tower of Babel represented the ultimate example of human pride; while the 'sheltering cave' set within the mountain also sat at the centre of the revelatory mythology of St Teresa of Avila, St John of the Cross and St Ignatius Loyola who had all discovered their faith in these spiritual wombs.[3] Gaudí empathised deeply with their lonely spiritual quests.

It was in the Baroque *memento mori*, however, that Gaudí's linkage to a far more terrifying Spanish tradition is most clearly seen.[4] The most harrowing works were the companion pieces known as the *Hieroglyphs of Death and Salvation* by Juan de Valdés Leal. In *In Ictu Oculi*, Valdés Leal illustrated the choice available to us all between the good mountain and the bad.[5] Commissioned by Miguel de Mañara, on whom Don Juan was allegedly based, it illustrated his own text. In *Discurso de Verdad*, he wrote:

> What does it matter, brother, that you are great in the world if death will make you the equal of the smallest? Go to a bone heap that is full of the bones of the dead: distinguish among them the rich from the poor, the wise from the ignorant, the humble from the mighty. They are all bones, all skulls, they all look alike.[6]

Gaudí's millennial fantasies and his language of forms were outrageously ambitious. This was very much a sign of the times and an accurate indicator of the political scene.[7] As Schama wrote, this kind of megalomaniac

> vision seemed to surface whenever a new generation of architects or sculptors imagine their buildings as a metaphorical vision of the reordering of states and societies.[8]

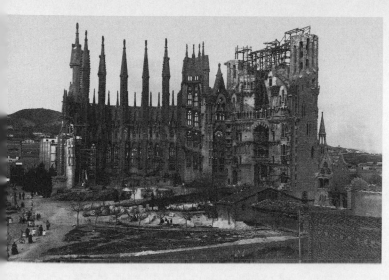

LEFT The Sagrada
Família c.1900.

BELOW The Sagrada
Família: Nativity façade.

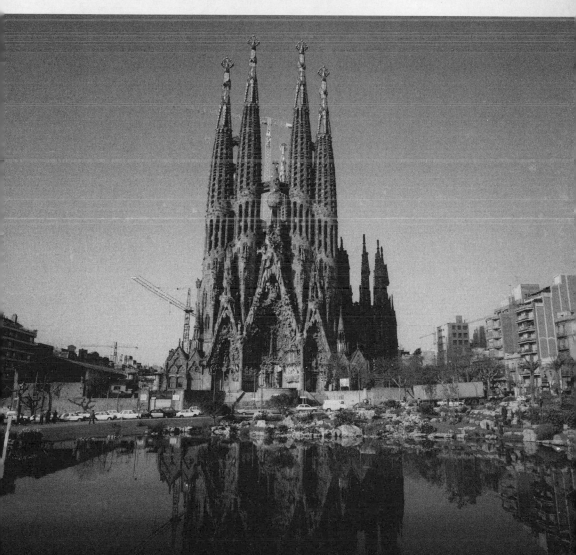

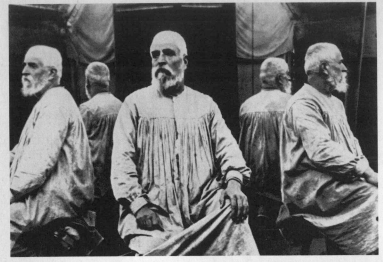

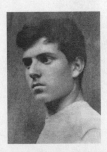

ABOVE Llorenc Matamala: Gaudí's
faithful sculptural assistant.

FAR RIGHT Joan Matamala: sculptor
and author of the unpublished
memoir *Mi Itinerario*.

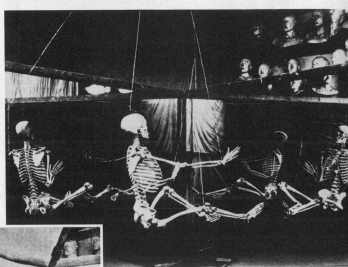

ABOVE Dancing skeletons used to
give Gaudí a profounder
understanding of the body's hidden
structure.

LEFT A crucified model poses in
Gaudí's elaborate system of mirrors.

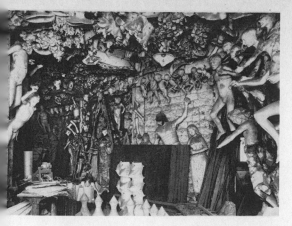

ABOVE Gaudí's studio in the Sagrada Família.

RIGHT The six-toed centurion slaughters the innocents. Nativity Façade. Sagrada Família.

BELOW Life-size sculptural ensemble of the Holy Family on the nativity façade. Sagrada Família.

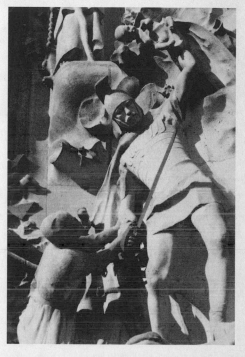

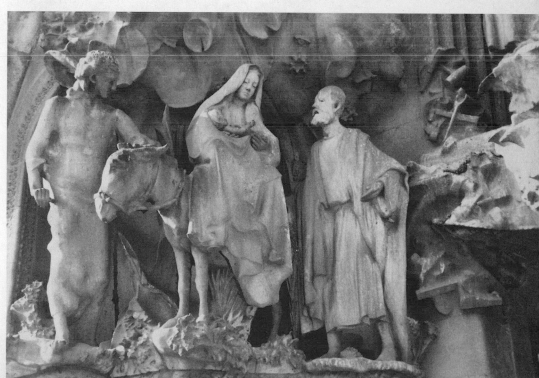

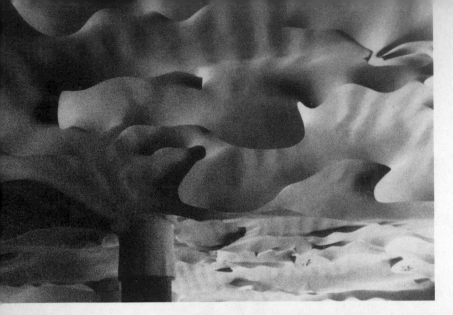

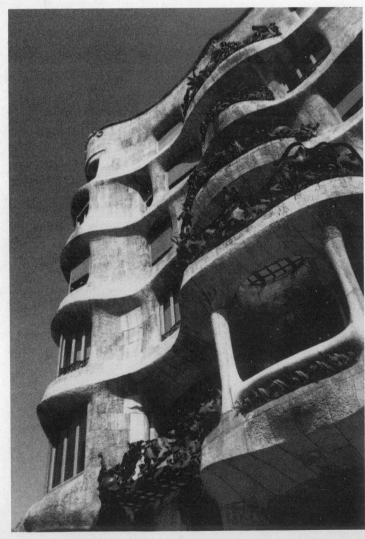

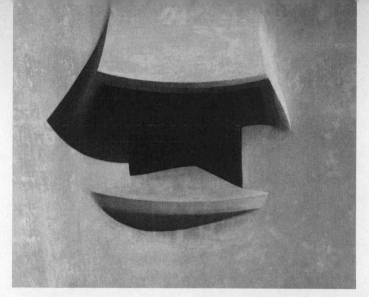

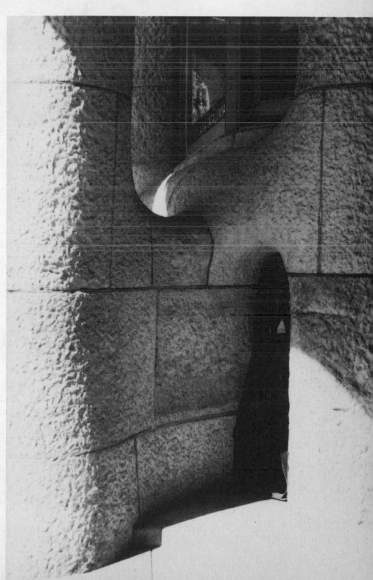

OPPOSITE
ABOVE The pulled and twisted plaster ceiling of the Casa Milà.

BELOW Casa Milà exterior 1906-9.

ABOVE Window with lintel and shade looking onto an interior courtyard at the Casa Milà.

RIGHT Window grille to Casa Milà basement designed by Gaudí.

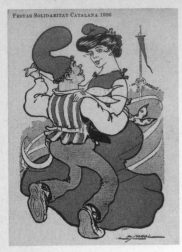

FESTAB SOLIDARITAT CATALANA 1906

Political postcard (1906) celebrating the fragile pact of Solidaritat Catalana.

BELOW Disinterred nuns are stacked up for this macabre record of the anti-clerical riots of 1909.

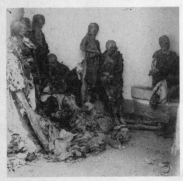

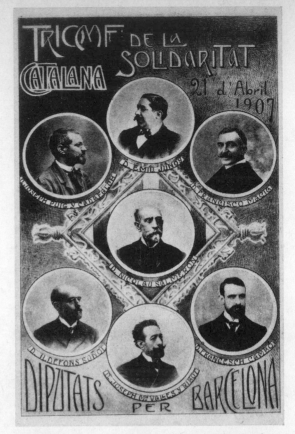

Postcard (1907) celebrating the victory of the Catalan Solidaritat party in the local elections. (Top left) the gifted young architect, politician and future president of the mancomunitat, Josep Puig y Cadafalch.

BELOW View across Barcelona on 28 July 1909 during the Setmana Tràgíca when more than thirty religious institutions were destroyed.

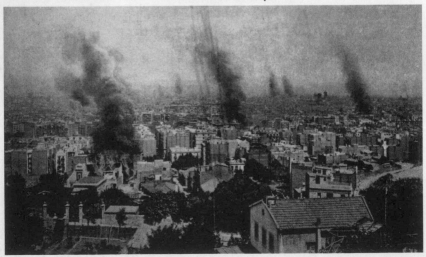

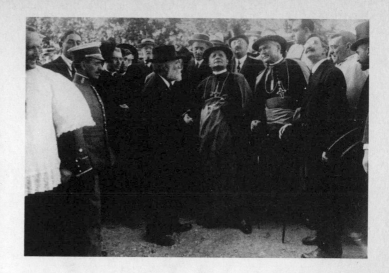

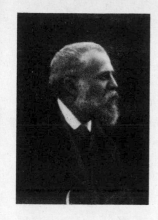

ABOVE Official photograph of Antoni Gaudí for the 1910 Paris exhibition.

ABOVE RIGHT Gaudí explaining the Sagrada Família to Cardinal Ragonesi.

RIGHT Gaudí in Corpus Christi procession (1924).

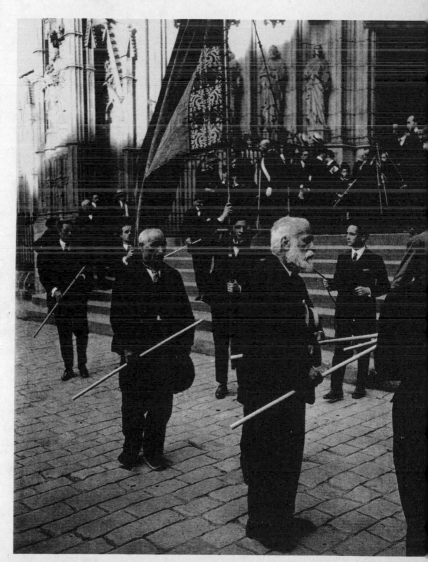

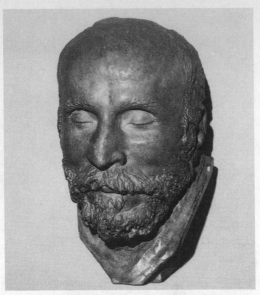

Joan Matamala's death mask of Gaudí (1926).

Gaudí's funeral procession.

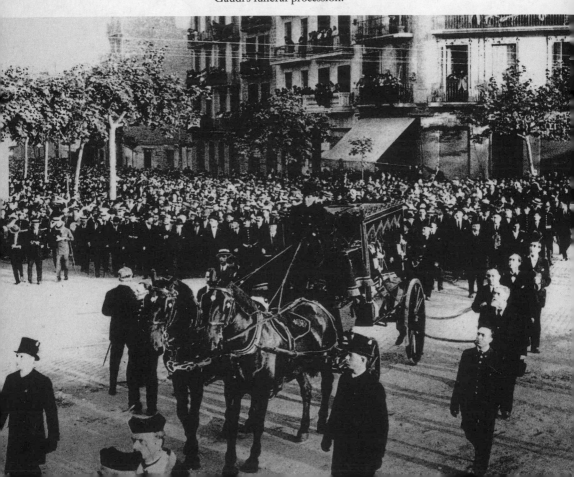

While Gaudí may have abjured politics during the construction of the Casa Milà, he witnessed the complete redefinition of Catalan politics. In 1906, Catalan nationalist tendencies were brought together under Solidaritat Catalana, and in May, Prat de la Riba's hugely influential *La Nacionalitat Catalana* was published. Much the same kind of artistic expression was taking shape in Bismarckian Germany. In Leipzig, in the previous year, architect Wilhelm Kreis and sculptor Franz Metzner had been working on an official monument to commemorate the Battle of Nations. In the crypt the massive columns consist of huge brooding faces of Teutonic knights trapped for ever in a charged Wagnerian space.

That the Casa Milà was overlaid with symbolism is undeniable. But what did the building actually mean? Was it possible for its rich and privileged inhabitants to seek sanctuary there from the corrupting powers of the city? Or were they doomed in their monied ignorance?

'Originality', Gaudí had often repeated to anyone who would listen, 'means going back to our origins.' Behind that impenetrable fortress façade Gaudí had camouflaged his deepest beliefs. In clear contrast to Jung, however, he wasn't in search of explanations. Nor was he conscious of how autobiographical he had really been.

Bishop Ragonesi, on one of his rare visits to the Sagrada Família, had acclaimed Gaudí as 'the Dante of our time'. In the 'Purgatorio' section of the *Divine Comedy*, Virgil goes to a mountainous isle where rocks rise sharply out of the sea. Slowly scaling the terraces and cornices of this Mount Purgatory he arrives at the Earthly Paradise where innocence is finally restored.

On reaching the roof of the Casa Milà we too enter a different world. The chimneys, ventilator and lift shafts, disguised as sculptures, are lined up into well-orchestrated ranks. These eye-less golems appeared to be in hibernation. Even so you could feel their presence even down on the Passeig.

They have the same feeling of inwardness as Henry Moore's sculptures.[9] Wingfield Digby analysed Moore's work. 'It is not so much that the human figure seems to have turned into stone, but rather it seems to have grown into stone; all that was human partakes now of the massive quality of the earth and rock.' Gaudí's figures, like Moore's, were 'antediluvian forms' that were 'the very antithesis of modern man'.[10]

On his Casa Milà roof Gaudí had illustrated the invisible world of the psyche. The function of the statues – to disguise all the usual clutter of a rooftop – was far less important than their appearance. Some, spiralling around the chimneys in barley twists, were shaped that way not to improve the drawing ability of the chimney but to suggest contorted anguish. The roofscape can be read as a three-dimensional diary of Gaudí's desperate struggle in the face of tragedy and isolation; each mute figure is another paragraph in a painful confession.

Unsurprisingly Salvador Dalí empathised deeply. Both he and Gaudí had answered the call of the unconscious with varying success. In Dalí's 1933 essay '*De la beauté terrifiante et comestible de l'architecture modern style*', alongside photos of the wind-eaten rocks of Cap Creus, he doodled over a photograph of the Milà façade and placed large eyes into every window.

Gaudí had always liked playing with the tension between oppo-sites. At first glance, the Casa Milà looked as if it might have mushroomed from the city floor. The architect appeared merely the humble servant of nature while displaying the arrogance of the romantic artist creator. As Walter Benjamin wrote:

The concept of the demonic appears when modernity enters into conjunction with Catholicism.

There was definitely something demonic about the Casa Milà. Arnold Hauser had linked this type of disintegration with romanticism as Goethe had done before.

> The romantic rushes headlong into his 'double', just as he rushes headlong into everything dark and ambiguous, chaotic and ecstatic, demonic and dionysian, and seeks therein merely a refuge from the reality which he is unable to master by rational means . . . He discovers that 'two souls dwell in his breast', that something inside him feels and thinks that is not identical with himself, that he carries his demon and his judge about with him – in brief, he discovers the basic facts of psychoanalysis.[11]

The reality Gaudí was escaping was the dread world of materialism. Yet at the same time he had been working most of his life for Catalonia's leading industrialists. It was a common concern for an artist: as Kandinsky wrote at the time:

> The nightmare of materialism, which has turned the life of the universe into an evil, useless game, is not yet past; it holds the awakening soul still in its grip.[12]

The real subject of the Casa Milà was more than a mountain – it was a volcano. What the loose folds of the building's skin really alluded to was the slow relentless movement of lava.[13] The same 'avenging lava' that had swept over Pompei and buried that city famed for its sexual perversity. Gaudí had set out on his one-man crusade against materialism. The desire to punish bourgeois vanity was the building's unconscious meaning. What kind of architect was it that painted on the side of Doña Rosario's dressing table

> *Memento homo qui pulvis eris et in pulvis reverteris*
> (Man, remember that you were dust and will return to dust)?

On Gaudí's death Doña Rosario completely redecorated her flat, wiping away all traces of his decoration, filling it instead with Louis Quinze reproductions.

For Gaudí, however, the image of the lava and the soft contours of the building mirrored his battle with the seductive qualities of the material itself.[14] The building of the Casa Milà had 'produced a deep wound in Gaudí's mind'.[15] But it would take another year for the disease to manifest itself.

In the early summer of 1909, as the temperature and humidity soared in Barcelona, the Casa Milà was still unfinished. The roof still awaited Carles Mani Roig's sculpture of the Virgin and angels. But in late July one event ended Gaudí's chances of finishing the Casa Milà. It was a trauma that the city of Barcelona would suffer from for decades and eventually led towards the Spanish Civil War. Eternally unfinished, the Casa Milà would remain one of the greatest monuments in the architecture of grief.

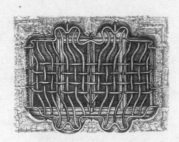

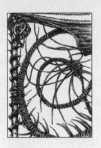

# Storm Clouds

The tradition of all the dead generations
weighs like a nightmare on the brain of the living.

*Karl Marx*

Poor Spaniards do not, in general,
hate the gentlemen (señores),
but they will come to hate them if the gentlemen
do not make themselves loved. And after the day of hate
will come the day of anger.

*Concepción Arenal* (1880), Cartas a un Señor[1]

AGAINST THE BACKDROP of the expanding and increasingly wealthy *eixample* the antediluvian form of the Casa Milà rose quickly. But behind Barcelona's unprecedented building boom lay, in the words of Henry James, 'the rumble of the tremendous human mill'.

During most of the nineteenth century the Catalan textile industry had experienced sporadic bouts of Luddism. The Güells, so prominent in industry, had often been the target. The Bonaplata factory was razed in 1836, followed in 1855 by the assassination of works director Josep Sol i Padrís. In 1885,

Angel Martorell y Montells, brother of Gaudí's mentor, was assassinated while director of Eusebi Güell's Vapor Vell factory.

But the 1890s witnessed an increasingly violent cycle of repression followed by a more widespread, often indiscriminate, anarchy. On 24 September 1893 the captain general of Catalonia, General Martínez Campos, survived an assassination attempt. Within the month, Santiago Salvador launched two Orsini bombs into the auditorium of the Liceu opera house killing twenty people. This was followed three years later by the savage bombing of the Corpus Christi procession as it left Santa Maria del Mar, killing twelve. On 8 August 1897 an Italian anarchist struck at the heart of the political establishment as he gunned down Premier Canovas de Castillo.

In a century Barcelona had been transformed from walled town to seething metropolis.[2] No European city coped with the effects of rapid industrialisation and immigration without growing pains. But Barcelona's appalling living and working conditions placed it second from the bottom in Europe's league table, just behind St Petersburg.

Barcelona's new immigrants – the factory fodder – were, in the words of Catalan historian Vicèns Vivès, millenarian in temper and 'socially irresponsible . . . without associative traditions'.[3] The two value systems, of the medieval village community and the industrial metropolis, were head to head and immigrants from Andalucia, Estremadura and Castile suffered from regional racism. Dismissed as *murcianos* – people from Murcia – they were seen as a danger to Catalan identity.[4]

More dangerously they were also politically impotent. After fifty years of Carlis Wars, 'politics became an exclusive minuet danced out by a small privileged minority'.[5] Palliatives, like the passing of universal suffrage in 1890, meant little in practice as all elections were rigged by the powerful *caciques* – the bosses – whose job it was to return the right result. Soon an inertia set in, which was only exacerbated by the catastrophe of 1898.[6] The

Empire had gone. Ex-colonials came home by the boatload: the evangelising priests, the military, the war-wounded, the bankrupt businessmen and the Catalan regionalists who had moved to the colonies out of frustration.

But the crisis of 1898 was just the latest in a long line of disasters for the Catalan economy. The gold fever of 1888 was over. The vineyards were devastated by phylloxera, shipowners blamed the lack of 'total' protectionism for their falling trade and the influx of cheap unskilled labour gave employers the chance to cut wages.[7] The triumvirate of socialism, communism and anarchism inevitably came to share an almost magnetic religious appeal for the new underclass.[8]

However, the relationship of the Church to industry was to prove one of the most explosive factors. The Catholic Church had clearly left the workers behind. Anticlericalism became increasingly prominent.[9] Contemporary prejudice saw the hypocritical priest abusing every privilege. Nuns, especially those in the closed orders, were dismissed as they had been in the Reformation as the handmaidens of the Whore of Babylon.[10]

Rafael Shaw in *Spain from Within* (1910) pointed out further iniquities, which stretched from simony to financial corruption and abuse of the confessional.[11] According to Shaw, the hated Jesuits were to blame, directed by the Father General, the notorious 'Black Pope', sitting in the Curia in Rome like some Mephistopheles pulling all the strings.

The Vatican's response to liberalism and industrialisation had directed much of Papal policy throughout the nineteenth century. Gregory XVI's (1831–46) *Mirari Vos* of 1832 condemned all forms of liberalism and set the tone for the rest of the century. Pius IX's (1846–78) *Quanta Cura* encyclical of 1864, and the

*Syllabus of Errors*, railed against the 'utter delirium' of freedom of religion, and the 'plague of indifferentism'. Leo XIII (1878–1903), although essentially conservative, promoted a more proactive relationship with modern industrial society. *Rerum Novarum* of 1891, while upholding the ownership of private property, also recognised for the first time the importance of a living wage, workers' rights and the positive role that unions might play. It was an inspirational move towards the working classes but it worked only within Catholic parameters. Gaudí, along with many other employers, interpreted this as a call to restore the supposed idyllic harmony of the medieval craft guilds.

Spain *had* become far less religious.[12] In the face of rapid industrialisation, the patterns of ritual and culture so important to the maintenance of its society had broken down with cata-strophic speed.

However, the Spanish Catholic Church was not entirely reactionary in response to the problems. It too had its reformers.[13] In Asturias, Father Arboleya argued that Catholicism amongst workers should be a voluntary manifestation, rather than a forced expression resulting from bribery, intimidation and the threat of excommunication. Arboleya confronted the Marquès of Comillas, whose Hullera Española mining company was one of the four largest in Asturias. 'He produced in me a sad impression. When I saw the total certainty with which he said that I was completely wrong...'[14] Arboleya recalled. Other voices spoke out against Comillas' narrow view, like the poet Joan Maragall, but the majority of Catholics were less open to change. The Catholic hierarchy was almost unanimous in its distrust of the industrial urban poor: a dispiriting fatalism argued that the worker was at the bottom of the pile because somehow he deserved it.[15]

Mainstream Catalan tradition – from the ultramontane theocrat Jaume Balmes to the neo-Thomist Torras i Bages – remained paternalistic, seeing the church/worker partnership as a one-way relationship. Amongst Spain's intellectual and upper-class circles the Catholic revival, enjoying royal patronage, became increasingly powerful.

Catholic groups were quick to react to *Rerum Novarum*. Catholic workers' circles were set up, that, in principle, differed little from the working conditions favoured at the Colònia Güell. But, like many of those early tests in social engineering, it was only the relative isolation of the workers' colonies from the city that made them viable.

But the most contentious area of the Church's intrusion was in the marketplace where the religious orders conveniently muddled up the distinction between charity and fund-raising. The convents functioned as bakeries and cheap laundries, specialising in needlework, tailoring and alterations. Exempted from taxes, and specialising in the only work, apart from prostitution, that a working-class woman could carry out at home, the convents were bound to be resented. They further benefitted from the *consumo* tax – an excise duty on all essential items – and the sugar, tobacco and matchstick monopolies, owned by a Catholic consortium.[16] But the passing in 1902 of a resolution stating that the religious orders must be 'irreplaceable auxiliaries in the resolution of the social conflict' put the Church on a direct collision course with the workers.

In April 1901, Prat de la Riba formed the united Catalanist party, the Lliga Regionalista, to fight the forthcoming elections, effectively destroying the hegemony that national liberal and conservative parties had held over Catalan politics for the previous twenty-five years. The gamble paid off handsomely with the Lliga winning four of the seven seats in Barcelona – with two of the seats going to Domènech and the popular Dr Robert, whose monument Gaudí would later build.

The Lliga's victory, however, had not diminished the urgency of finding solutions for the pressing economic problems. Strikes and lockouts became the preferred weapons, as workers and employers battled over wages, while industrial reforms were inevitably sidelined.[17]

The Republican party offered the most radical path. Alejandre Lerroux, a skilled rabble-rouser and self-styled Emperor of the Paralelo, inflamed the passions of young militants like the Jóvenes Bárbaros:

> Young barbarians of today, enter and sack the decadent and miserable civilisation of this unfortunate land: destroy its temples; throw over its gods . . . tear off the veils of its novices, and elevate them to the category of mothers in order to invigorate the species.

It was shameless stuff but it caught the popular anticlerical mood.

In November 1905, following another Lliga victory, the satirical magazine *Cu-Cut!* raised once again the chimera of 1898. In a now famous cartoon, a fat bourgeois turned around to a soldier standing guard at a gate.

> 'What's being celebrated here, why are there so many people?'
>   'The victory banquet,' replied the soldier.
>   'Victory? Oh, then they must be civilians.'

Affronted by the slur, army officers broke into the offices of *Cu-Cut!* and *La Veu de Catalunya* and smashed them up. No action was taken against the guilty officers. But on 20 March 1906 a Bill of Jurisdictions, giving military courts authority to try civilians for demonstrations of disloyalty, passed unopposed. It was a clever piece of legislation directed straight at Catalonia's separatist aspirations.

In spring 1906, as Gaudí carefully inspected the curved ridge tiles that were shaping the defeated dragon's back on the Casa

Batlló roof, Solidaritat Catalana was born. From across the whole political spectrum Catalans came together to speak with a single voice. On 20 May 1906, more than 200,000 Solidaritat supporters demonstrated against the pernicious Bill of Jurisdictions. In the same month, Prat de la Riba's seminal *La Nacionalitat Catalana* was brought out, arguing for a Catalan state within an Iberian federation. It proved popular.

In the national elections in April 1907, Solidaritat won a landslide victory of forty-one out of forty-four seats. Prat had tried, in recognition of Gaudí's pre-eminent position in Catalan cultural life, to tempt the architect into the political fray as a Solidaritat candidate. He even requested Puig i Cadafalch to intercede on his behalf. But Gaudí would not be deflected from the Casa Milà. It was Puig, instead, who would travel to Madrid and sit representing Catalan interests in the Cortes.

However, beneath the party politics, anarchism remained active. On 31 May 1906, Mateo Morral attempted to assassinate King Alfonso XIII as he set off on his honeymoon. Morral committed suicide but left behind a trail that led indirectly to Francisco Ferrer – a radical activist – who was imprisoned for almost a year. In June 1907, Joan Rull, a part-time terrorist and police informer, was finally detained. Single-handedly, he had held the city to ransom by planting bombs and then informing on some anarchist patsy. From Scotland Yard, Chief Inspector Charles Arrow was called in to investigate.[18] Prepared by a three-month intensive Berlitz Spanish course, Arrow of the Yard arrived on the coat-tails of the formidable reputation of Sherlock Holmes. Diplomatically, he rapidly concluded that Barcelona was safer than either Paris or London.[19] Throughout the investigations Rull remained silent. One set of rumours, however, surfaced again and again. Inspector León Tressols, investigating the case, suggested that Rull's trail led indirectly to Eusebi Güell. Not surprisingly Tressols was quickly taken off the case and pensioned off. On 8 August 1908, Rull was executed.

The winter of 1908 and the following spring proved cata-
strophic for large sections of the textile industry. In the Ter
valley 40 per cent of men and 30 per cent of women lost their
jobs. All of the ingredients for civil unrest were now in place: a
starving populace, economic recession, high unemployment,
rapid immigration, an anarchist bombing campaign, a repressive
regime and a powerful Church under siege. All that was needed
was a trigger.

The conservative Premier Antonio Maura had never been keen
to implicate his government in expensive colonial adventures.
There were, however, Spanish interests in Morocco to protect
from the French and Riff bandits – particularly harbour facilities
in Tangier and the mines of Beni-bu-Ifrur owned by a consortium led by the Marquès of Comillas, Eusebi Güell and the
Count Romanones. By June the Moroccan crisis reached a head.
On 11 June, just before Maura took off to Santander for the
summer recess, the newspaper *Correspondencia* delivered him an
unequivocal message:

To go to Morocco is to march towards the revolution.

On Thursday 15 July, the radical politician Emiliano Iglesias
stood outside the Casa del Pueblo and harangued the thousand-
strong crowd, arguing that honest workers should never defend
'the interests of Comillas, Güell and Maura, all three of whom
bow down before the Pontiff'.

On Sunday 18 July the latest conscripts marched down the
Ramblas to their ship. 'Barcelona is more like Port Arthur'
announced *El Poble Català*.[20] As the soldiers reached the harbour,
cries went up: 'Send the priests!' ... 'Down with Comillas!' In
disgust the conscripts threw their medals into the water.

On Monday, crowds formed in the covered arcade under the
firmly closed shutters of the Palau Moja's ballroom and screamed
repeatedly, 'Long live Spain ... Death to Comillas!'

Charged with maintaining the peace was the thirty-six-year-

old governor, Angel Ossorio y Gallardo. Ossorio was a potentially brilliant choice. Having worked at the Institute of Social
Reforms he had demonstrated a refreshing openness to socialist
and labour demands.

On 20 July a further forty thousand conscripts were called up
just as the news was wired in of the first fatalities in Morocco.
The seasick troops had been marched directly into battle on
empty stomachs. In neighbouring Tarrassa, the strike committee
prepared their resolutions protesting against 'certain ladies of
the aristocracy who insult the suffering of the reservists' by 'giving them medals and scapularies instead of providing them with
the means of sustenance which is wrenched from them by the
removal of the head of the family'. And, 'sending to war citizens
useful to production and in general indifferent to the triumph
of the Cross over the Crescent Moon, when they could form
regiments of priests and monks who, besides being directly interested in the triumph of the Catholic religion, have no family
nor home nor are they of any service to the nation.'

That night news came from Morocco that Spanish supply lines
in the Rif had been cut, with heavy casualties.

On Saturday morning the press had its last opportunity to
publish an editorial on the growing crisis. *El Poble Català* printed
the prophetic warning, 'The valves have been closed and steam
is accumulating. Who knows if it will explode.'

Sunday 25 July was the anniversary of the 1835 riots. Outside
the bullring, where those riots had begun, police appeared in
overwhelming numbers. Still nothing happened. That evening,
around the Plaça Catalunya, sand was strewn on the cobbled
streets to give surer footing if a cavalry charge was needed. But
nothing happened and the crowds dispersed for dinner.

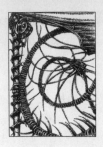

# The Setmana Tragica

---

Eye for eye, tooth for tooth, hand for hand, foot for foot,
Burning for burning, wound for wound, stripe for stripe.

Exodus 21:24–5

For without are dogs, and sorcerers, and whoremongers,
and murderers, and idolators, and whosoever loveth
and maketh a lie.

Revelation 22:15

THE TRAGIC WEEK, remembered by those on the left as the Glorious Week, the Red Week, or the *Semana Viril*, started promptly at 4 A.M. the next day.

It had been a heavy humid night for thousands cramped into their tiny slum flats. Stifled inside, it was more comfortable to be out on the streets. There were still plenty of people out, drinking hot chocolate, brandy or absinthe. But across the working-class barrios of the Raval, Poble Sec and the Ribera, workers were preparing for the day.

Outside the factory gates strike leaders had already started orchestrating the day's events. Employers, frightened of reprisals, were quick to close down the few factories still operative. By 9 the strike was almost complete.

Strike action, however, quickly dissolved into civil disobedience. Along the Paralelo, the prostitute María Llopis Berges, nicknamed '*Cuarenta Céntimos*', set out with a gang to harass and threaten café-owners into joining the strike. In other parts of the city the battle was led by the colourful Josefa Prieto, '*La Bilbaina*', a brothel madam, and her sidekick, the dominatrix Encarnación Avellanada, aptly named '*La Castiza*' – 'The Punishment'. And during the next two days others swept through their barrios like half-crazed valkyries; Enriqueta Sabater, '*La Larga*', sawed down telegraph poles and built barricades; while down in Clot, Carmen Alauch, a fishmonger and leading member of the radical Damas Rojas, rounded up teenagers to join in. The ensuing pandemonium took on the chaotic appearance of a Hieronymus Bosch painting.[1]

Only one group of workers refused to join the strike. Bullied by their boss Mariano de Foronda into staying at work, the tram drivers were seen as the key to the strike's failure.[2] Foronda's trams had an appalling public safety record, causing a series of accidents that were often the result of badly serviced brakes and drivers refusing to slow for crowds. In an attempt to achieve complete compliance with his orders Foronda took to riding shotgun.

Attempts by the authorities to reinstate a semblance of normality collapsed as a personal battle between Minister of the Interior La Cierva and the governor ended in Ossorio's resignation. Reluctant to declare martial law Ossorio packed his bags and, against orders, retired to his summerhouse on Tibidabo. General Santiago, the recently appointed captain general, was called into the breach.

The lack of organisation on the part of the authorities was echoed amongst the strikers. The acting chief of the Republican party was Emiliano Iglesias, who was noted for his procrastination.[3] Other potential leaders included the revolutionary

Miguel Moreno for Solidaridad Obrero, representatives of the Jóvenes Bárbaros, the socialist Fabra Rivas of the strike committee and Francesc Ferrer – who had come into Barcelona on the morning train but was pessimistic about the escalation of the insurrection into full-scale revolution.

As the strike exploded into anticlerical vandalism it became obvious that the leadership had lost control. As Ossorio wrote in his memoir *Declaración de un Testigo*, 'In Barcelona, they don't prepare for revolutions, for the very simple reason that the revolution is always ready.'

On Monday night the Workers' Circle of Sant Josep, run by the Marists, was burnt down by an angry crowd.

Sant Josep was a textbook example of a Church institution resented by the very poor it was supposed to serve: the Marists were linked closely to Comillas; they offered charity and free religious education, competing against a local Ferrer school, and were actively involved in the Catholic workers' circles in opposition to the lay unions.

In the Raval, between the Paralelo and the Ramblas, the narrow streets rapidly took on the aspect of a battle zone. Barricades were thrown up everywhere. Piles of cobblestones, iron bedsteads, wooden doors, kerbstones and sections of iron railing were piled on top of each other to impede the progress of troops. Neither the presence of the Guardia Civil, firing warning shots, nor a detachment of five infantry companies led by General Santiago made any difference at all.

On Tuesday morning, orders were sent out to start a programme of convent burning that would concentrate on destroying Church property. Leaders like Emiliano Iglesias, it was later suggested, accepted this as a way of dissipating the mob's destructive energy on 'soft' targets, rather than all-out revolution. But incendiarism proved even more popular when rumours spread through the city that the priests were about to stage an armed revolt in order to place a Carlist on the throne.

First to burn was the Royal College of San Antoni, belonging to the Piarist fathers, and with it the early Romanesque jewel of Sant Pau del Camp. Close to the Casa del Pueblo two other convents fell to the rioters before dark. Across the *eixample* and down in the Ribera, Romanesque chapels and churches were burnt, religious schools were torched and convents attacked.

At each conflagration the mob discovered evidence that seemed to corroborate their wildest fantasies about the secret cloistered life.[4] At St Anton they found primitive presses 'for the faking of currency'; at Sant Mateo the crowd found and burnt almost a million pesetas' worth of stocks and shares; but, more sinister still, at the Immaculada in Poble Sec they found, displayed in a glass-top coffin, the 'martyred' body of a beautiful nun.[5] Rumours rushed through the city. At the Convent of the Magdalenes the rioters discovered further evidence of the perversity of nuns. Corpses were disinterred, buried with their scourges beside them, and their hands and feet tied. But far more sinister was the discovery of the macabre 'correction' chamber; a room in which the insane Sister Teresa Bonsom was tied to a bed that had been drilled out and piped for gas.

By Tuesday evening the city was in a state of total anarchy. 'The Tragic Night', as it would later be known, produced scenes as terrible as anything in Goya's engravings. And Barcelona wouldn't hear for days that Tuesday had also seen the most costly engagement of the Moroccan campaign. More than two thousand reservists lay dead on the slopes of Mt Gurugú, slaughtered by Berber tribesmen.

On the 'Tragic Night' Gaudí climbed up onto his roof and paced around the parapet. Park residents were relatively safe, protected by the close proximity of the Guardia Civil station at Vallcarça, opened just six weeks before.[6] But he worried about his cousin Josep Gaudí Pomerol who, in Poble Nou, was right in the line of fire.

In one night twenty-three churches and convents had been

gutted in the city centre. A fireball sunset cast its light across the clouds of smoke and the dancing sheets of flame. Gaudí surveyed the city, picking out well-known landmarks as much of Catalonia's unique architectural heritage was destroyed.

Ever since he had drawn up the plans for the restoration of Poblet in his early teens, Gaudí had been sensitive to the damage wrought on the Catalan architectural heritage by civil war, rioting and the selling of Church property. In Barcelona itself a large portion of the Rambles was built over medieval convents, churches and monasteries. In many places enough patches of the old fabric remained to remind the viewer of the glories of Catalonia's past.

To see the wilful destruction of architectural masterpieces, while labouring heroically to save them through restoration and archaeological digs, must have been bitterly disappointing. And what must have dug deepest into his Catholic mind-set was the reaffirmation, in spectacular style, of man's capacity for sin.

Gaudí's immediate circle of church friends, his spiritual counsellor Agustí Mas at St Felipe Neri, his mentor Torras i Bages, the committee at the Sagrada Família and Cardinal Casañas, must have transmitted their anxieties to him. The week prior to the Tragic Week, Gaudí continued, as always, with his evening stroll across the city from the Sagrada Família to confession in St Felipe Neri. While doing so he would have found it impossible to avoid seeing the demonstrations that erupted sporadically up and down the length of the Rambles.

Gaudí's reaction to the unfolding events has become mythical. For liberals Gaudí has become the reactionary coward, hiding in the Park Güell, his silence speaking volumes. He was the stooge of Comillas and Güell. But while he undoubtedly admired Güell, working for much of his life for him, and sharing many of the same religious and political beliefs, Gaudí was first and foremost an architect. Civic duties, like his active membership of the *Excurcionistas*' steering committee, were things of the past.

His energies were focused on architecture and God. He had made this abundantly clear when refusing Prat's invitation to stand for Solidaritat. Gaudí had seen the storm coming. Indeed, his great interest in the workers' status was the result of many ideas shared with the Church's modernisers.

Gaudí was neither a mute nor obedient Christian. Fascinated by the latest liturgical modifications and theosophical conundrums he was often hard on priests. He was tough, too, on what he saw as their capacity to dodge some of their more arduous pastoral responsibilities. In the Plaça Virreina Gaudí stopped to talk to the parish priest Father Brasó. In the words of Martinell,

> Gaudí was advising certain measures to guard against the dominant anticlericalism when the priest replied, 'That is not my business.' Gaudí countered, 'Then wait until they kill you, too, and put someone in your place who *will* tend to business.' Perhaps the Reverend realised the importance of what he was trying to say, but the bad impression left by the rude response stayed with him for the rest of his life.[7]

It was a warning that Father Brasó should have heeded. By Tuesday night two priests had already been murdered and many more were injured. At some time during the day the rioters started on the religious establishments of Gràcia.[8] One witness reported on the demise of Father Brasó's church:

> At Sant Joan, the priest and a few parishioners at first tried to stop the crowd, but soon gave way. Before long altars, chairs and organ were ablaze. The Sacrament Chapel was spared, but the next day at 7 a.m. another group reduced it to ashes. Of the main and flanking altars no trace remained.[9]

The rioting was not a random demonstration of anticlerical hatred. If a religious order, or individual, had successfully mediated between the needs of the worker and the Church they were spared. Not one of the four buildings of the sisters of the Congregation of the Holy Family of Urgel in Barcelona was attacked. Under this scrutiny the fate of the Sagrada Família must have worried Gaudí. It was paid for by a mixture of subscriptions from the wealthy pious and small donations from, amongst others, the parish poor. It was a temple, a religious community, in the middle of a working-class parish close to a much-hated Catholic workers' circle run by the Jesuits, Sant Pere Claver.

Gaudí stayed in the Park. Trapped in its grounds, he must have taken his usual walk up the Via Crucis to the crucifix at the peak of the Mont Pelada behind his house. From the crucifix Gaudí could see south to the Llobregat delta, close to the Colònia Güell. To the right was the Teresiano and hidden just behind the small hill of El Putxet lay Bellesguard. But straight ahead below him festered the city for whose wickedness and corruption the Sagrada Família was being built to atone.

Martinell stated that during the afternoons of the Tragic Week Gaudí paid visits to Alfonso Trias who was sick. Gaudí

> found comfort from his forced reclusion, disclosing his fears that the temple might become a victim of the revolt. The boy soothed him, prophesying that they would not destroy that work which could potentially give jobs to many. Gaudí thanked him with a 'May God hear you!'[10]

But Bassegoda questions this in *El Gran Gaudí*: for according to Bayó, he and the architect were in the city at least once that week, on a site inspection at the Casa Milà.

> From the *ronda* we saw the shooting in the calle Mayor de Grácia . . . and after we looked all over the building, Gaudí said, 'I'm going to the Sagrada Família.' Bayó wanted to accompany him and on reaching the calle de

Aragon they heard the loud report of gunfire. Gaudí asked, 'Those are shots?' And then continued walking calmly on to the Sagrada works.[11]

Bayó's description places Gaudí down in the *eixample* at the height of battle and in breach of General Santiago's order for citizens to stay off the streets. Gaudí's relative isolation at the Park Güell may well have meant that he hadn't heard of Santiago's order. After all, no newspapers had been published. On Tuesday morning people still went out shopping early to try and secure provisions, then rushed home and bolted their doors. If Bayó's recollections are to be trusted, then Gaudí acted quite in character. Obstinate, as always, he was not going to let minor interruptions get in the way of the business in hand. Moreover, Bayó said that they had inspected the whole building, an operation that would have taken considerable time.

Leaving the Park Güell, Bayó said that the first incidents they witnessed were on reaching the *ronda* just above Gràcia. Although it may have been foolhardy to leave the safety of the Park, no one knew the sheer extent of the danger and destruction – two hours later the city teetered dangerously on the verge of total anarchy. While walking to the Casa Milà, Bayó and Gaudí had passed through the eye of the storm. West of them Gràcia was in revolution; to the south, near Universitat, convents were stripped out and burnt; east of the Casa Milà, the barrio Gòtic and Raval were in open rebellion. The only way out was towards the Sagrada Família.

That evening the strike committee, including Moreno and Fabras Rivas, arranged a rendezvous with a large crowd at the Sagrada Família. But it was untouched despite its well-publicised, symbolic status in the city.

On Wednesday morning in Poble, Sec and the Raval attempts to remove barricades by the Treviño cavalry were driven back. In the Plaça del Padró, outside the convent of the *Jerònimes*, a group of fifty women disinterred corpse after corpse of the Hieronymite nuns and carried them on their shoulders to the Plaça San Jaume. Along the carrer Carmen the nightmarish procession threaded its way slowly towards the Rambles. Their final destination was the houses of the worst offenders against workers, the eminent Marquès de Comillas and his brother-in-law Eusebi Güell. The rotting corpses were laid out for all to see under the arches of the Palau Moja and up against the wrought-iron gates at the Palau Güell. Nothing could better illustrate the bitter hatred and contempt felt for these two men.

Comillas and Güell were involved in almost every area of Catalan business. Banking, insurance, textiles, cement, mining, real estate, the Trasatlàntica shipping line, agriculture, the tobacco monopoly and the farming of the hated 'consumo' tax all made up parts of their empire.

Claudio López, second Marquès of Comillas was the great rationaliser of his age. No one understood better the advantages of economies of scale. Despite his sinister reputation (everyone still remembered the Verdaguer case) Claudio López approached the problems of labour with a greater sense of paternalism.[12] With characteristic energy he introduced many reforms: pornographic literature was removed from the Comillas train station bookstall, the liberal press was targeted, atheists in academia were hunted out and his Trasatlàntica ships were transformed into 'floating parishes'. Jesuit training sessions were set up for the miners. Every aspect of the worker's life was watched over and controlled by the Catholic censor – even to the point of forbidding mixed bathing.[13] Comillas' Catholic workers' circles had a tendency to manipulate their members and introduced what Michelet described as the defining characteristic of Jesuit mentality, 'the sneaky habits of the telltale schoolboy transferred from college and convent to the whole of society'.

The Conde Güell remarked, without any exaggeration, that his uncle Claudio López was 'the key to clerical politics' in the Spain of his day.[14] For almost three decades the Comillas clan had been at the forefront of the Catholic revival within the laity. The Seminary they had sponsored in Comillas was just part of a larger picture. Following Leo XIII's edict *Rerum Novarum*, López was quick to respond. Acción Católica was set up, followed by a mass pilgrimage of 15,000 Spanish labourers to meet the Pontiff in Rome.[15] He even entered negotiations to buy Rome as a present for the Pope.[16] Significantly, it was only when Comillas visited the Residencia de los Jesuitas in the calle de la Flor in Madrid that he was treated with normality, everywhere else it was with the utmost respect, often bordering on fear.

In *Conversaciones con Gaudí*, Martinell remembered how, during the Tragic Week, Gaudí had been reading about Emperor Theodosius to 'calm his nerves'. Theodosius, according to Gaudí, had fled from Constantinople in the Middle Ages and watched Santa Sofía burning from the other side of the Bosphorus. This erroneous rewriting of history illustrates strongly Gaudí's pronounced tendency for self-dramatisation and myth-making.[17] It was typical that he should choose nothing less than Santa Sofía, the pre-eminent church of early Christendom – Byzantium's greatest architectural masterpiece.

As always, historical distance placed his trials and tribulations into a clear dramatic context. There had always been suffering and martyrdom. In fact, suffering tempered the steel of the Church Militant; it was cathartic. It was also a necessary evil that purged the body politic of its poison and would by compensation invest the temple of the Sagrada Família with its true expiatory purpose.

By the end of the Tragic Week, Bishop Ricardo of Barcelona recorded in the *Boletín Oficial Eclesiástico* on 9 August 1909 that twelve churches and forty religious establishments had been destroyed. Miraculously, considering the bitter anticlericalism, only three priests had been killed.[18]

The repercussions of Tragic Week ran through Spanish history for years. The 'ministries of hallucination' would continue to stall, obfuscate and dissemble.[19] But Maura's ministry couldn't afford the ambiguity. It had to rapidly sink any possibility that Governor Ossorio's chronic indecision might be perceived as a general party trait.

'Perpetrators' were quickly arrested and charged. In all, five men were executed and the most polemical of all was the 'judicial murder' of Ferrer himself.[20] On 9 October he appeared before the court and with untimely haste the death sentence was pronounced just four days later.[21] His last words, 'Look well, my children! I am innocent. Long live the Escuela Moderna!' rang out poignantly.

In Catalan politics the Tragic Week crystallised opinion. The Lliga that had once repressed Catalan voters across the social spectrum narrowed its remit by backing Maura's repressive policies and became a conservative party of authority. In the December 1909 municipal elections Lerroux's anti-Catalanist Republican party won an overall majority.

It was in the Lliga's handling of the poet Joan Maragall, that the real intellectual crisis of the Tragic Week reached its lowest ebb. Maragall had been out of the city during Tragic Week.[22] At first he could find no way to reply. The official Catholic response came on 18 August with the publication of Torras i Bages' pastoral *Le Glòria del Martiri*. With characteristic humility Maragall felt Torras had said all there was to be said. But Torras, in private correspondence, argued that the people took less and less notice of his 'eternal truth' and what was needed was Maragall's 'human word'. 'We have reached a moment in time when even the stones must speak!'

Days before Ferrer's execution Maragall started to write his most famous article 'La Iglésia Cremada'. It was spiked – as far too sensitive – by the editor of *La Veu de Catalunya*.[23] 'La Iglésia Cremada' – The Burnt-out Church, in which Maragall pleaded for a city of forgiveness – was kept out of the public domain for a full two decades. Maragall's humanity was deeply pragmatic, built on the profoundest of understandings of the Spanish malaise. He had been close to Santiago Salvador's bomb in the Liceu in 1893, sitting in row 7 when twenty people in row 13 were killed. But, he maintained sixteen years later, blame could and should not be apportioned with the apparent ease that manifested itself in most conservative circles. Social responsibility was not the privilege of the few but the duty of society as a whole.

'The true spirit of Christianity', Maragall argued, 'would be better found in the poor and unadorned churches left by the riots than in the comfortable and complacent Catholicism which had preceded them.'

He described a mass in one of these churches:

> I had never heard a Mass like that one. The sacrifice was present there, alive and bleeding, as though Christ had died once again for Man . . . The Bread and Wine seemed newly created: the Host appeared to vibrate, and when, in the sunlight, the wine was poured into the chalice, it was like a stream of blood . . .[24]

Maragall's early judgment of Gaudí had been harsh. In 1903 he wrote:

I come to see that it's he who represents the tradition of
Catholic dogmatism, and that in the orthodox sense he's
in the strong position; that compared to him, I'm a dilettante, riddled with heterodoxies.

But subsequently he had come to admire Gaudí and understand
him better. They had grown close, Gaudí overcoming his reticence and making the occasional social call to take the '*té inglés*'
that Clara Noble (Maragall's English wife) maintained as a ritual
at four every afternoon.

Maragall had long admired Gaudí and through his writing
had displayed an extraordinary empathy with Gaudí's ambition to
create a deeply spiritualised body of work. It had taken Maragall a
while to notice that behind the prickly, pontificating exterior lay
a wounded sensibility. Gaudí's religiosity, his adherence to the
rigid structure of a Catholic day, gave him the stable platform
on which to anchor his passionate nature. But Maragall also
recognised, and the Tragic Week must have re-emphasised this,
that in the face of anarchy and atheism Catholics had to draw
together. Whether in an atmosphere of retribution or forgiveness
only time would tell.

The Gaudí–Maragall circle was highly sensitive to 'the horrific
torment inflicted upon the religious soul'.[25] The Tragic Week
took its first victim with the suicide of Ramón Casellas, an
acquaintance of Gaudí's, whose literary career as both novelist
and critic had charted the development of the *modernista* aesthetic. Maragall wrote immediately, '*Déu meu, Déu meu, teniu-nos
ben fort en la vostra mà!*' – 'My God, My God, give us strength!'[26]

The Tragic Week had damaged far more than Barcelona's
Gothic fabric. A mind-set of extreme caution, fear and retrench-
ment had replaced the optimism of 1888.

Maragall despaired, he had plumbed the depths like 'a rock
falling in a pool'.[27] For Gaudí, the events of the Tragic Week
haunted him for years to come. Everything he produced after-

wards was built in the Catholic spirit of somehow making amends. All his creative ideas had been sucked into the Milà vortex, its meaning magnified through his ongoing struggle with his sacred temple.

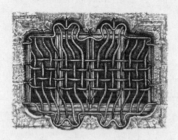

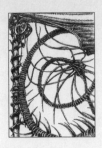

# A Thrown Pebble

Unfinished, a picture remains alive, dangerous.
A finished work is a dead work, killed.

*Pablo Picasso*

Talking about Gaudí's 'taste' is like discussing
the 'taste' of whales.

*Rafael Puget*

THE WEEK-LONG DISTURBANCES in Barcelona had not damaged the Casa Milà. And with the resumption of order Gaudí
found himself once again in breach of the city's planning requirements. In conversation with Martinell he explained that the
Casa Milà was like an icebreaker in the Arctic that smashed and
splintered a passageway through for other, weaker ships to
follow.[1]

On 28 September 1909 the city's chief architect, Planada
ordered that the infringement of Article 118, which established
the roof heights for the *eixample*, could not be tolerated. On 21
October the work was suspended and just three weeks later the
immediate demolition of *all* parts exceeding the legal height limit

was demanded. This meant the destruction of the chimneys, lift shafts and ventilation housing, and thus Gaudí's rooftop sculpture park.

Luckily in December the Casa Milà was saved from the wrecker's ball by its recognition as a national monument, and therefore free of all previous restrictions, but he would have to wait until December 1914 for it to be finally passed.[2] The reprieve had come too late. By spring 1910, Gaudí had washed his hands of the Casa Milà.

The Casa Milà was still missing its final dénouement: Carles Mani's sculptural group of the Virgin Mary flanked by angels.

It was hardly novel. The image of the Virgin had become a late-nineteenth-century cliché. But Mani's Virgin was no shy retiring mother, she was a strapping Colossus.[3] The small plaster maquette, however, suggests that Mani's sculpture was no masterpiece. Gaudí's taste in many areas was magnificent. He had a capacity bordering on genius to extract the best from assistants working in the decorative arts. But when it came to sculpture and painting, the individual contributions were subservient to the completed building itself and to its message.

Gaudí's Virgin for the Milà roof encapsulated the entire meaning of the building. What we see today could be merely the plinth for Mani's monumental monstrosity.

For Gaudí, whose mother had died when he was only a child, the Virgin's idealised image was a surrogate for every woman he had come close to. The Milà Virgin symbolised not so much a step forward as a way back.

Prior to the Tragic Week, the construction of the Casa Milà had stuck closely to Gaudí's plans. Following the riots, however, Milà demanded Mani's sculpture be scrapped. He had witnessed the anarchic energies of the people at first hand when trying to negotiate the rioting's halt on the 'Tragic Night' as president of the Lliga de Defensa Industrial. Milà was worried that the sculpture of the Virgin might give it the appearance of a fortress of the faith.

The Mani model showed the Virgin as the exemplar of enthroned Catholic majesty. But straddling the Barcelona skyline she represented something far more ancient and primeval – Gaia, the earth mother.

Milà, however, was unimpressed. He had already paid a fine of 100,000 pesetas for Gaudí's regulation-breaking. If Gaudí's artistic hauteur provoked city hall into using all the legal weapons at their disposal, there was no better way to provoke their ire than to crown the ensemble with a monstrous Virgin.

Without the Virgin the force of the Casa Milà changed from Catholicism to pantheism. Gaudí travelled down to the coast to see Rosario Segimón to persuade her that the project should not be mutilated at such a late date. For the one hundred and fifty openings that broke through the Milà's wall echoed the beads on a rosary.[4] And, more importantly, the simplified rose sculpted on the façade, and the statue of the Virgin itself, were both in homage to Rosario Segimón. But his exhortations (to her religiosity and vanity) were fruitless and Pere Milà was unimpressed by Gaudí's pushiness.

Gaudí had taken a risk in choosing Mani. He was a singular artist with a highly expressive style.[5] Born in Mora d'Ebre, up in the mountains behind Reus and Falset, Mani had studied in Paris. Hovering on the edges of the Catalan avant-garde enclave that formed around Rusiñol and Picasso, he was seduced by Rodin's expressive mature style.

One day Gaudí and Matamala went down into Mani's workshop to discuss the progress of the Virgin sculpture. The sculptor was furiously rubbing away at the plaster model with a hard bristle brush dipped in watery clay. As they watched, the distracted Mani spattered his visitors with the paste.[6] On another visit, accompanied by Bayó, Gaudí discovered after a few minutes that his legs were being attacked by fleas. So on all future visits he asked Bayó to powder his ankles and fill his turn-ups with a home-made insecticide. He would not have wanted to hurt Mani's feelings.[7]

Despite Gaudí's best efforts, he couldn't change Milà's mind.[8] Indeed, Milà's misgivings about how the project had gone forced him to take action with his only weapon at hand. He held back Gaudí's final settlement fee. This led to a protracted court case that would eventually be decided upon by the Col.legi de Arquitectes – the final adjudicator – when no middle ground between client and architect could be found. The process would take another seven years.

More perhaps than any other building, the Casa Milà represented an essay in autobiography. In the stone façade Gaudí had sublimated all his earthly passions and spiritual yearnings. The three years dedicated to the Casa Milà had left the fifty-seven-year-old architect psychologically and physically exhausted. It was to be his last secular commission.

The details on the Casa Milà still unfinished – the interior decoration, the balconies and the murals for the two large interior courtyards – were completed by other members of his studio.

The 'incomplete' Casa Milà was stunning and infinitely suggestive. It looks much today as it did almost a century ago: a luxury condominium and a Catholic monument to a key moment in Catalan history. Both ancient and modern, it was Gaudí's first and last truly twentieth-century building – a post-modernist masterpiece.

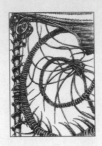

# 'Symbols Dense as Trees'[1]

---

The perfection of architecture is frozen music . . .
*Lord Byron*

Science is a hamper which is being filled with things
and more things that no one can manage until
Art puts handles on the hamper and takes from it
exactly what is necessary to perform the deed.[2]
*Antoni Gaudí*

THE POLITICAL SITUATION in Barcelona during the winter
of 1909 remained explosive. But the fact that amongst so much
iconoclasm the Sagrada Família works had remained undamaged
meant that its sense of purpose and community still remained
very much alive.

On 15 November 1909 the Bishop of Barcelona, Juan José
Laguardo Fenollera, inaugurated and gave his blessing to the
new Sagrada Família schools, the Escuelas Parroquialas de la
Sagrada Família.

This simple school building, thrown up quickly and cheaply
using brick and tile, has since become recognised, primarily
through Le Corbusier's celebration of it in the late 1920s, as a

landmark of twentieth-century architecture.[3] Although the building existing today is not the original (the schools were burnt down twice in the Spanish Civil War) it does follow Gaudí's original plans closely. The simplicity and innovation of the design was as astonishing as it was cheap; the whole structure cost just 4,000 pesetas.[4] In Martinell's words, 'the pavilion constitutes proof of what the master always said: beauty and structural logic transcend all historical styles'.[5] The structural beauty lay in a very simple device. Along the central length of a long rectangle (the school's structure) an H-shaped beam was placed horizontally on three columns that bisected the entire edifice. Across this beam, straight pieces of wood rested at right angles and moved up and down in stages along the length of the H-beam, fanning out like a pack of cards. Where one line was at its lowest on the northern façade it would reach its apex on the opposite side, creating a roof that undulated like a wave and provided perfect drainage. It is best understood in illustration where deceptive simplicity disguises the structural puzzles it has thrown up for future architects, like Luis Candela and Nervi, who have struggled to manufacture it again.

Technical virtuosity was a mere by-product of the Escuelas' real significance in the Sagrada Família's master plan. Adhering closely to the dictates of the Vatican's *Rerum Novarum* the Escuelas constituted just a small part of what was envisaged as an entire, wholly integrated, Christian community. If Gaudí was its architect then Mossén Gil Parés, the parish priest and close friend of Torras i Bages, was its spiritual leader.[6] The Escuelas catered for the local working-class children and their free system of education was designed to bring the children closer to God.[7] Much of the thinking behind the Escuelas rested on Bocabella's firmly held belief, shared by Gaudí and the paternalistic Catholic hierarchy, that to 'reform society' it was necessary to 'reform the individual'.[8] So each pupil was given their own pot plant which was placed under a patio shade in the corner of

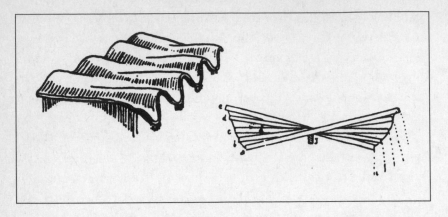

Simplified drawing of the unique roof structure of the
Sagrada Família schools.

the playground. And to further stimulate a sense of belonging, each class had their own flag, designed by Gaudí, which they could march behind during religious processions through the parish.

Even as late as 1909 the Sagrada Família site was at the outer edges of the city. And it therefore became a favoured meeting place and playground for children. Gangs of boys from neighbouring areas chased lizards and hunted for insects whilst goatherds watched their flocks from the shade of the Sagrada Família's perimeter wall. Kite flying quickly caught on and most mornings Gaudí's builders had to climb up the scaffolding to rescue those that had become tangled up in the façade. On warm summer evenings benches were placed out as picnicking families invited the stonecutters to slake their thirst. For high feast days, when the crypt proved inadequate for the number of visitors, it was necessary to hire a marquee. The two major festivities associated with the Sagrada Família fell at the two extremes of the year: the feast of the Holy Family in January and Saint Josep in July. The temple *Junta*, after a few years, began to baulk at the expense of hiring the marquee at least twice a year and suggestions were put forward either to rush through a provisional roof, made from precast concrete, or for Gaudí to design his own marquee. Suspicious that a provisional solution might become permanent, Gaudí opted for the latter. Preparing a model of sailcloth attached to posts all the female members of the Matamala family spent months sewing the pieces together ready to send to a specialised firm for completion. The estimate, however, proved impossibly high and the *Junta* became resigned to the inevitability of hiring the marquee.[9]

The feast of Saint Josep in July offered Gaudí a further chance to improvise on his pyrotechnic skills by organising a fireworks display culminating in a multicoloured homage spelling out *JESÚS, MARÍA* and *JOSEP* in gigantic letters. Care and attention was also offered to the beggars who were 'attracted to the religious institutions like flies to honey'.[10] A polio victim was given prime position at the door to the crypt while another aged beggar was given licence by the church *Junta* to sell postcards of the rising temple and the finished crypt alongside his bookmatches and other smoking paraphernalia officially frowned upon by Gaudí. Both men were protected from bad fortune and the weather, as Gaudí told a fellow artist, 'by the warm overcoat of the Temple, and Christian charity itself'.[11]

The worksite was envisaged then as a perfectly harmonious Christian model community where the nobility of work might be integrated successfully with everyday life. Gaudí was, by all accounts, strict but fair. At a time when social security didn't exist Gaudí allowed elder employees to stay on after sixty-five, permitting the odd sleep and arranging light work like the lighting of candles and the fetching of drinking water.[12] One builder, unbeknown to Gaudí, had used a spare corner of the site as an unofficial allotment to grow produce for his family. The architect, on discovering it, extended permission to all the other workers to follow his Christian example of husbandry skills. Gaudí was rewarded with baskets of produce and in his opinion the siesta time was far better used in gardening than giving in to the temptations of the local bars.

The worksite had also gradually become an unofficial second faculty of the architectural school. From the turn of the century on, the more fervently Catholic students often augmented their morning classes with afternoon visits to sit and listen at Don Antoni's feet. This was the cause of much of the bad blood between Gaudí and Domènech, who had become the school's director in 1900.[13] Gaudí's monologues punctuated by his typical verbal 'hammer blows', argued that Catalonia had been specifically chosen by God to take the long noble tradition of the '*arquitectura cristiana universal*' on into the new century and most likely beyond.[14]

By early spring 1910, however, it had become obvious that the battles of the previous few years had finally taken their toll. The stop-go cycle of work on the Sagrada Família, always dependent on the fluctuating financial resources available to the *Junta*, had proved spiritually draining to Gaudí. And the suicide of Casellas, the aftermath of the Tragic Week and the ongoing Casa Milà saga brought him no relief. One witness described Gaudí's condition as 'an obstinate anaemia contracted through an excess of intellectual work'.[15] This was only added to by his upcoming exhibition at the Société des Beaux Arts in Paris, planned to open in March 1910. It was Gaudí's first architectural venture abroad. Gaudí expressed unwillingness to go (taken by some as false modesty), but Eusebi Güell managed nevertheless to persuade him to agree by offering to pick up all the bills.

'Don't worry about it, it's not an exam,' Gaudí told his student assistant Joan Bordàs, fretting over an exhibition drawing. Gaudí's blasé manner disguised a certain anxiety although the French were in his opinion in absolutely no position, despite his earlier admiration for Viollet-le-Duc, to judge the merit of his work. But almost all the French art papers were complimentary and the critic Marius Ary-Leblond in *L'Art et les Artistes* went so far as to eulogise Gaudí's spatial genius.[16] Diaghilev's set designer Erté, recently arrived from St Petersburg, was so taken by Gaudí's show that he immediately vowed to become an architect.

The 'obstinate anaemia' that Vilaplana had talked of, possibly the result of his radical vegetarian diet, was only part of the complex medical diagnosis of Gaudí's increasing mood swings and low spirits. His friend Dr Santaló had always offered Gaudí advice but he rarely acted upon it. He preferred instead to cure himself with a tough regimen of cold fresh air, exercise and copious quantities of water. He claimed that even failing eyesight could be combatted by continuous exercise and always refused to countenance spectacles.

In May 1910, however, he was stricken by bouts of high fever, rashes, complete loss of appetite and rheumatic and glandular pains. Despite his resistance, he was whisked to bed immediately. Gaudí had picked up a crippling attack of brucellosis, or undulant fever, notoriously difficult to diagnose, even today.[17] Alfonso Trias, his young neighbour at the Park Güell, suggested that Gaudí probably caught the disease from unpasteurised milk.[18] Gaudí's meagre lunches had often consisted of just a bowl of fresh lettuce leaves dipped in milk, finished off later with a handful of nuts or sugared almonds. And, even then, it was typical that he chose to explain this austere choice in architectural rather than nutritional terms, noting that the corrugated surfaces of the lettuce leaves enjoyed a much larger surface area on which to receive the milky unction than other smoother varieties of vegetable.[19]

There was nothing for it but a period of rest and recuperation away from Barcelona as soon as he was fit to travel.[20] The Carmelite sisters from a nearby convent offered to keep a close vigil on Rosa around the clock. In May, Gaudí was sent to Vic where Torras i Bages was bishop and which enjoyed a reputation as Catalonia's spiritual home. Gaudí was removed to the comfort and care of 'the noble and pious Sra Rocafiguera', at the suggestion of his Jesuit friend Ignasi Casanovas, who wrote to the Señora by way of introduction that 'it is of great merit that you console this noble soul who gave such great Christian and aesthetic pleasure to others'.[21]

In Sra Rocafiguera's mansion, Gaudí chose the most humble suite of rooms and breakfasted as was his wont on toast burnt to a crisp.[22] If the city of Vic, shrouded most of the year in cold grey mist, wasn't the most cheerful place, it did provide him with a break from the pressures of the studio. During the day he walked around the wonderful diocesan museum talking to the curator, Father Josep Gudiol. Lunch was sometimes taken with Torras i Bages in his palace and the afternoon set aside for walks around the centre of the town to inspect the architectural fabric with the pharmacist Joacquim Vilaplana and priest Gaspar Puigneró.

Joacquim Vilaplana remembered these afternoons with distaste. The 'diatribes and attacks' that Gaudí rained down on Vilaplana's head as the architect pontificated and droned on endlessly that 'true art had been developed only in Rome and on the shores of the Mediterranean' taxed the pharmacist's patience to its limit. Vilaplana had obviously not learnt, like Santaló, to keep quiet and so maintain the peace. Gaudí's judgment was often outrageous, dismissing the work of the van Eyck brothers, van Dyck and Rembrandt as 'bourgeois living room artists' and 'third-rate decorators', a value judgment that might have suited his favourite painter Clapés rather better. And, on another occasion, he dismissed Michelangelo's understanding of volume as demonstrated in the Sistine Chapel as displaying about as much sensitivity as a butcher squeezing out an endless chain of sausages.[23] Gaudí was, according to Vilaplana, 'a good Christian' but 'as stubborn as a pig'. Clearly infuriated, Vilaplana wrote years later to a friend, 'I, too, have painted and drawn a great deal, and I have read an infinite number of books on art and seen innumerable famous buildings!'[24]

Eusebi Güell's grandson agreed. 'Gaudí was very convinced of the value of his own work. Artists are often like that and I think that contributed to his despotic character. He was very sure of himself, and became very annoyed when people hid things from him or opposed him. Nothing pleased him, and he liked no one.'[25] Another acquaintance, Father Cayetano Soler, was more direct in his criticism of Gaudí's now legendary inflexibility: 'With Gaudí, you've either got to kill him or give in and tell him that he's right.'[26]

Gaudí's reputation as impossibly abrasive and belligerent dates from his stay in Vic and this behaviour became more and more noticeable until his death sixteen years later. Perhaps these explosions were just the outbursts of an increasingly intolerant and arrogant man. But some of the most powerful and distressing psychological symptoms of brucellosis are violent mood swings sometimes leading into suicidal depression. Interspersed with bursts of anger and lapses of concentration, these black moods are accompanied by physical exhaustion, blinding headaches, swollen glands, night sweats and painful arthritis. Shocks could set off further attacks as could physical and mental exhaustion and almost any other common flu or virus that attacked the patient's weakened immune system. There was no cure.

Despite it all Gaudí found time in Vic to prepare designs for a set of monumental lampposts for Vic's elegant Plaça to celebrate the centenary of Jaume Balmes' birth. If his three-week convalescence in Vic had after all been just the result of nervous exhaustion and anaemia, rather than early manifestations of the disease then it was in spring 1911 that Gaudí had a full-blown attack of brucellosis.

Now absolutely sure of his friend's real condition, Dr Santaló was convinced that the main reason for it was Rosa's growing nervous crisis. He immediately accompanied Gaudí to Puigcerdá in the Pyrenees.[27] In the Hotel Europa, a quiet resort hotel, Santaló spent four months nursing Gaudí slowly back to health.

This time there would be no heated arguments and other feverish scenes. Initially Santaló sensibly shielded Gaudí from all visitors, except for Mossèn Gil Parés, the Sagrada Família's parish priest. At one point Gaudí's health became so critical that a local notary was called so that Gaudí might draw up his will. The house in the Park Güell was to be sold off, the proceeds would go to the Sagrada Família, and the other two beneficiaries and executors would be Dr Santaló and Rubió i Bellver.

Slowly Gaudí recovered enough to attend to architectural business assisted by Dr Santaló as unofficial secretary. Friends and clients were now allowed to visit; Lluis Millet, Eusebi Güell, Dalmases i Bocabella, Berenguer and Rubió i Bellver all visited. And the frequent postal service between Barcelona and Puigcerdá permitted Gaudí's gradual reintegration into his studio's work. But along with the plans, drawings, calculations and accounts came Santaló's packets of medicine, which Gaudí refused to take, believing rather in the efficacy of his austere vegetarian diet.[28]

The period of rest also afforded Gaudí the luxury of devoting himself to reading. Verdaguer's *L'Atlàntida* and *Canigou* remained, as ever, close at hand. As did the Missal Romano, the Old Testament, a collection of Ignasi Casanovas' essays, Thomas a Kempis' *Imitation of Christ* and Torras i Bages' *La ciència del sofrir* (The Science of Suffering). All kinds of handiwork were also encouraged by Santaló as a further distraction, particularly sketching, drawing and metalwork to ward off the painful arthritis. By July, Gaudí and Santaló were able to take short walks through the busy resort town. Down in Barcelona it was humid and ovenlike, but in Puigcerdá it still remained pleasantly cool.

But more than ever, the smooth running of the Gaudí architectural practice depended on the talent of his assistants and collaborators. Rubió continued to direct the ongoing and increasingly problematic restoration of Palma de Mallorca's La Seu. Berenguer was in charge of the Sagrada Família works while Jujol finished the serpentine bench at the Park Güell. Almost every member of the design team had continued to oversee the gradual evolution of the crypt at the Colònia Güell.

It was during Gaudí's prolonged illness, however, that in collaboration with Jujol he produced his most exciting and joyous work. Paradoxically, the serpentine bench at the Park Güell appeared to distill and transform all of Gaudí's pain into a sublime uplifting experience. The bench started out in 1909 as a merely functional object: a long bench that bordered the market roof, doubling up as both safety railings and seats; with a large open sand-covered area providing a meeting place for groups whilst also filtering the rainwater. The form of the bench then was designed primarily to channel water while providing a comfortable seat in dry weather. Before, however, any decorative concerns, the bench threw up only structural problems. Constructed out of prefabricated concrete sections, it was one of the first and finest examples in Spain of the material's use.[29] The contractor Pau Gorina remembered that 'Gaudí told a workman to take off all his clothes and make himself perfectly comfortable sitting on a prepared bed of plaster, so as to obtain the perfect form of the seat once the material had hardened.'

It proved effective. But wherever Gaudí had worked with water, from the overblown Neptunes of the Cuitadella some thirty years before to the spouting dragon in the Park Güell entrance below, he had stressed its mythological and symbolic force. And it was with the decoration of the bench that a purely practical object was transformed into something astonishing.

The decoration of this brilliant multicoloured ceramic display at first appears arbitrary. And, as on the roof of the Palau Güell, the serpentine bench's surface has already been heavily restored.[30] The original concept, however, still shines through.[31]

From a distance it delights and teases the spectator's eye. But more than mere decoration, it is sculptural too – an art work that demands participation. Sitting on the bench develops a satisfying feeling of completeness.

Concentrating on the detail, what appeared at first as a decorative, almost Byzantine, chaos slowly blends into coherency. The serpentine bench is a giant puzzle. All along it there are cryptic clues, fragments of messages, incantations, illustrations and deliberate graffiti that remain forever beguiling entrées into its two creators' complex minds.

Along its serpentine length, various types of narrative and visual intervention range from broken-plate pictures, to graffiti and *objets trouvés*.[32] It was a working method that was at once fantastically modern but also ancient. Jujol had introduced into the decorative ensemble a chance encounter with the broken head of a child's china doll.

All over the bench's surface there are separate clusters of strange little clues. First there are small sets of numbers left on fragments of mass-produced cheap porcelain tiles . . . 8-9-10-11. There are bottles and shell forms. Facing the sea, in the fifth bay in, two dismembered arms proudly hold forward the cross of Lorraine that in the Middle Ages was authorised to be transported before any of the five patriarchs but was also a recognised attribute of Gregory the Great. There are stars and butterflies and kitsch little putti sliding off the edge of their plate. And as if nailed to their cream background appear five blood-red fleurs-de-lys. In one passage, primarily of deep blue tiles, a white plate shatters and leaves its separate parts suspended in the ceramic sky, moving rapidly from left to right like a shooting star. The movement, of course, echoes that of the spectator as they progress slowly around the bench.

From left to right the trinity of green, blue and yellow, which represented for Gaudí the chromatic equivalent of the theological virtues Faith, Hope and Charity, worked together throughout to end finally in a blaze of celestial white. This triumvirate of colour underpinned a wealth of detail in bolder contrasting colours associated with the Catholic Church: red for the passion, black for mourning and purple for penitence. Gaudí understood how well colour and symbol work together, conveying their meaning beyond the compass of the rational. Taken as a whole the bench's explosion of colour is like a cinematic version of the famous Rose window at Chartres.

Gaudí's short sojourn in Vic had proved surprisingly important. Whilst strolling through the Diocesan Museum he discussed with Father Josep Gudiol the range of Catalan artistic symbolism. In 1902, Gudiol, who was obsessed with Catalan epigraphy, inscriptions, sacred monograms, hieroglyphs and inscriptions on tombs, had published his *Nocions d'arqueologica sagrada catalana*.[33]

This language of signs and symbols was a personal expression of veneration, but also related closely to the thinking of the contemporary Catalan Catholic revival. Kent and Prindle noted how 'Gaudí and Jujol rather painstakingly evoked signs and formulas that were widely distributed in catechisms, litanies, prayers, and pilgrimage songs to the Virgin of Montserrat then being disseminated in the new studies associated with Catalan sacred archaeology.'

Three-quarters of the way round, on the southern lip, most of the original design remains in place. Jujol had scratched little caricatures or emblematic representations of slippery squid, flowers and the heavenly constellations accompanied by a waxing moon into the curved edging tiles. They are naive and mystical. MARIA appears close by, scratched in upside down, to make it easier to be read from heaven. Farther along the Via Crucis is represented by VIA amongst a scattering of scratched stars – a heavenly crown of thorns. The bench represented in microcosm what Gaudí, Jujol and Güell had hoped to achieve in the Park Güell development, the creation of a sacred public space. And, once again, Gaudí boldly employed popular art. The decorative ensemble of the serpentine bench resembled the abstract arabesques and floral patterns drawn out in the sawdust for religious processions along Riudoms' narrow streets. Other words accompanying the unfolding of colour in the bench are of those vibrant and unadorned expressions of piety shouted by the spectators of the slow procession of images of the Stations of the Cross during Holy Week. But if the bench's programme had been 'to sound the voice of true belief uncontaminated by self-consciousness or contrivance', its total meaning seemed to rest even deeper still.

Casanelles reported the story of two students, Josep Garganté and Santiago Loperena, who were sitting on the bench one fine sunny day.[34] Just as the Angelus struck they saw illuminated faintly under a band of colour '*Angelus Domini nuntiavit Mariae*'. Farther round the lip, Casanelles found '*Ai urbs antiga i atresorada*' and the place name REUS with a date of 1898. What happened in Reus in 1898, Casanelles asked? But the archaic and arcane inscriptions reveal more about Gaudí's attitude to his art than any single autobiographical event. Gaudí and Jujol hoped to invest their serpentine bench with a live religious potential that could prick the sitter's conscience. Without knowing it, they were seated upon a pre-industrial 'Catholiciser' whose catalogue of half-hidden signs and symbols had metamorphosed its surface into a primitive faith machine.

Across the Llobregat valley, the work on the crypt at the Colònia Güell continued but slowly. Throughout 1911 while Gaudí was recuperating up at Puigcerdá the workforce had been cut back to just three. Berenguer and Rubió were constructing other buildings at the Colònia, Rubió's celebrated Mas D'En Perdiu for example, but the crypt awaited the attentions of the master himself.

It soon became clear that Gaudí was heading towards what Ruskin had called 'a science of feeling rather than the rule'. Rubió, the studio's theoretician, tried to analyse their evolving theories and put into words what Gaudí had left suspended in space with the catenary model. In his unpublished manuscript *De la integritat*, Rubió argued that the Christian spirit gave three transcendental qualities to a true work of art: integrity, proportion and clarity.[35] Rubió set no limits on what architecture might achieve. For, he argued, where rationalism ended the search for ideal beauty began. Gaudí, in Rubió's opinion, was the greatest and most misunderstood rationalist of his age. It also became clear that for Gaudí, theory and practice were coming closer together, uniting the attitudes and ideas that had been with him since his student days. This characteristic that Jorge Bonet Armengol has described as *continuidad* is the single most essential element in Gaudí's creative makeup.[36] Gaudí had a tenacious capacity to play with the same idea for decade after decade, constantly refining and perfecting his ideas. In the complex puzzle of his art the Colònia Güell crypt was the final missing piece.

Gaudí's training had taken in Robert Hooke's theories of the catenary arch and Elias Rogent's series of lectures on the history of architecture.[37] Rogent had fallen under the profound influence of the philosopher Immanuel Kant who in *The Critique of Judgement* (1790) and two earlier treatises on practical and pure reason had laid down the fundamental principles of empirical enquiry. Kant was soon taken up by the aestheticians Schiller, Wackenroder and August Schlegel.

By looking back to before the Renaissance and the false path of 'pagan' neoclassicism they produced a body of thought that was essentially nostalgic and that longed for genuine, naive and honest feeling – *einfuhlung*. In one sense it represented a kind of cultural 'primitivism' in which the oversophistication of Renaissance humanism was spurned in favour of earlier simplicity. But, perversely, it was also truly modern. Rogent encouraged his students to analyse architectural styles with the idea of correcting their shortfalls and perfecting them if possible. Architecture was proscribed first by the laws of elementary geometry. Each form, the circle, square, triangle etc. enjoyed a particular expressive potential. A circle was balanced, a cube

invoked quietism etc. . . . And so too the notions of horizontality
and verticality, straight and curved lines used throughout history
expressed other abstract properties, like infinity, balance, change
and durability. If straight lines represented eternity and infinity,
then the use of the curve added a dimension of mutability and
change.[38] Geometry in architecture, Rogent argued, could also
be manipulated to echo specific philosophies and political ideas,
echoing Ruskin's theory of architecture as the ultimate 'political
art'.[39]

Catholic conservatism, not surprisingly, chose the form that
best offered 'integrity', 'proportion' and 'clarity', in the uplifting
verticality of the Gothic style. The structural problem with the
Gothic style Gaudí was keen to remedy was the removal of
the crutchlike protuberance of the flying buttress. Having rid
the Gothic building of its false supports Gaudí could offer the
possibility of a truly transcendental architectural style.[40]

It is certain that Gaudí saw himself within the long tradition
of sacred Spanish architecture where 'geometric proportionality
points to profound Christian verities'.[41] Famous protagonists of
sacred architecture included Juan de Herrera, who wanted to
cement holy relics into the walls of El Escorial in order to spiritually charge the space, and the Jesuit architect, Juan Battista
Villapondo, the designer of Baeza Cathedral in Andalucia, who
as a devout believer in the architectural theory of 'eurythmics'
argued for a 'divine order' that created perfect spiritual harmony.

The Colònia Güell crypt had started with 1898's elaborate
catenary model but its genesis lay thirty years before at architectural school. It was Gaudí's chance to put architecture and the
Christian faith back on the right path again after 500 years.

In 1910, Félix Cardellach Alivés, in his *Filosofía de las Estruc-
turas*, explained that the Colònia Güell crypt was probably the
most perfectly rational building ever planned; using 'rational' to
mean the use of material to support a particular load in the most
effective and economical way.

Through empirical analysis Gaudí used hyperbolic paraboloids to build the exterior façades, hyperboloids to allow in light, and the twisting helicoid, as it had also been used at the Park Güell's serpentine bench, to lend movement. Its effect is breathtaking.

Its structure, perfected over years of experimentation and completely consistent with the laws of geometry, was now almost impossible to change. Gaudí described it thus:

> Creation works ceaselessly through man. But man does not create, he discovers. Those who seek out the laws of Nature as support for their new work collaborate with the Creator.

It was in the choice of material, however, and in the detailing, the decoration and the infinite variety of bricklaying techniques that Gaudí could construct a unique Christian shrine. Set amongst the pines, inside the crypt the columns echoed the surrounding trees.

Gaudí wrote of this interplay:

> The column is like the shaft, the trunk of a tree; the roof is like the mountain with its ridge and slopes; the vault is the cave of parabolic section; the more resistant terraces of the mountain cliff form lintels and corbels over places where the weaker strata have eroded away.[42]

It is hard to argue with the photographer Norman Parkinson who called the crypt 'the most saintly place which I have seen in my life'. But as with so many of Gaudí's works it remains unfinished, in testament to his overreaching ambition. The parish archives of Santa Coloma de Cervelló describe its painfully slow progress. There were never more than a dozen workers on site at any one time. By July 1911, despite Gaudí's absence, the pillars in the presbytery were being constructed. Four years later, on 3 November 1915, the crypt was consecrated for worship. And, three years later still, in 1918, the crypt was left unfinished, as we see it today.

There is never a wrong time of year to experience this magical space but it is best encountered on a hot summer's day with its windows open and with the hot, pine resin–fed wind blowing gently through.[43]

The crypt is an out-and-out masterpiece, but one that would have been impossible without a patron as indulgent and patient as Güell. The exterior walls of rubble and overbaked brick appear to grow out of the soil. Gaudí readjusted the floor plan of the church so as not to disturb a particularly beautiful pine that grew in the grove. As he said: 'I could build a set of steps in three weeks but it takes twenty years to grow such a magnificent tree.'

The ceiling of the portico, directly under the shallow steps that lead up to the imaginary church, plays with inverted hyperbolic paraboloid geometric forms that swell out down towards us seemingly defying gravity and traditional architecture. Juan de Herrera had also used the inverted dome in the entrance to the basilica at El Escorial to announce his supreme control over his craft. Gaudí, confident of his structural analysis, stood directly under the arches as the workmen removed the supporting wooden moulds. He supposedly joked to a visitor that the mason frequently hypnotised the tiles while waiting for the cement to dry.[44] Continuing around outside, the eye has to continually readjust its focus from the columns to the trees to the decorative ceramics and the strange window grilles designed to protect the fragile stained glass. Gaudí constructed a thin metal curtain from old needles from the textile factory. Almost every material used was recycled from a previous industrial use.

Once in through the large wooden doors, the visitor is dazzled by the spatial complexity of the interior. Each column, inclined at exactly the angle necessary to avoid buttressing, is completely unique and produces, in the words of Bassegoda, 'an authentic effect of muscular tension, as if the crypt were a living organism'.[45]

The effect is amplified by four massive basalt columns in the central area. These take the entire weight of the crypt and appear at first shaped by a Neanderthal axe. Gently cushioned from the polished cement floor by a compressed lead pad, the heavy columns seem ready for any seismic vibration. It has become accepted that the finished Colònia Güell church would have offered up yet another meditation on Montserrat, popularly believed to have been formed in a geological explosion at the moment of the crucifixion. The Colònia crypt would thus finish what Montserrat had begun.

Seduced by the sheer power of the crypt's structure, it is hard to take in other decorative details like the giant marine conches lapping with holy water, or the butterfly stained-glass windows with their ingenious system of opening that allows for the flapping of their crystal wings.

Yet again, every structural detail and decoration is charged with the power of 'symbols dense as trees'. Some have painted Gaudí as a Freemason, a high priest of the occult, an amateur astrologist, a drug addict and an alchemist.[46] All these theories are inspired by the sheer richness of the language he used: for there are myriad signs and symbols in the crypt with echoes in other faiths and pagan beliefs that had been subsumed into the Christian fold. At the door is an alpha and omega, but there are also St Andrew's crosses, a mandorla containing Joseph's saw, a multicoloured CHI-RHO monogram; and numerous fishes formed from reflective *trencadis* tiles deepen the symbolic resonance of the building. Gaudí used the hyperbolic paraboloid not just for its structural value but also for its symbolic content. Its twisting geometric form represented the trinity.

Eduardo Rojo Albarrán – self-confessed Marxist, atheist and enemy of secret organisations – sees written in the crypt's masonry a confession of Gaudí's membership of the Rosicrucians or some other secret Masonic-Catholic sect. The building certainly represents a spiritual pilgrimage. Gaudí saw the mechanics of architecture as perfect metaphor for spiritual enquiry and revelation. Furthermore, Rojo Albarrán is almost certainly right in his analysis of the presence of thirteen St Andrew's crosses as symbolic of Christ's life. The thirteen crosses proceed logically from the green of life, through purple and black, to finish finally in a Calvary of crosses coloured in celestial blue. But the language of symbols is an infinitely flexible one – and to limit it is to ignore its potentiality.

There was also a social symbolism latent in the fictional paradise of the Colònia Güell.[47] Because, in return for their ownership of a tiny plot of land and their miniature *casa pairal*, the workers' freedom was absorbed wholesale into the hierarchical Catholic whole. In 1910, when Gaudí had just returned from his rest break in Vic, the Colònia Güell took centre stage as the venue for the annual celebrations of the fifth Semana Social de España, previously actively promoted by the Marquès de Comillas. It was a significant choice considering the proximity, both in time and geographical distance, to the Tragic Week. Torras i Bages's opening address, '*El espíritu en el problema del trabajo*' (The Human Spirit within the Problem of Work) reiterated many of the ideas on the nobility of manual work and on the Christian family at work earlier proposed by Ruskin and the Guild of St George.

Almost a decade before, Prat de la Riba had envisaged a colony that might provide a perfect workers' idyll where capital and labour might co-exist harmoniously. And where, in the words of the 142-page promotional leaflet for the Colònia Güell published in 1910, 'hope and charity, Catalonia's true inheritance' and 'the faith of our grandfathers' might still be maintained behind the colony's protective walls. But Gaudí was not in total agreement with the ideological use of Colònia Güell. He accused one of the organisers, Father Gabriel Palau, of autocratic behaviour. 'You are a tyrant, Father! And God has given me direct dispensation from taking any more orders from you!'

When Gaudí had finally returned from his convalescence at Puigcerdá pressing personal needs demanded immediate attention. Rosa was growing sicker by the day. So Gaudí's first requirement was to look for a childless married couple who might move up to the Park Güell and look after both of them. Failing this, he approached his cousin Josep Gaudí Pomerol who lived nearby but who couldn't help either due to the demands of work. For the meantime they continued with the help of the nuns and a cleaner, but tragedy was rapidly approaching.[48]

For Maragall was also ill. On 1 December 1911 he wound up the *modernista* clock in the corner of the sitting room that he and Clara had wound up for the very first time at the first hour of the new century. It was the same room in which the *té inglés* had been served so many times and where almost everyone in the Catalan art and literary world had left their differences outside in deference to their host and hostess. 'Strife', Maragall had written to his friend Pere Corominas in 1902, 'is repugnant to my nature, which searches for a core of harmony and serenity in all things.'

Maragall wandered into his ground-floor office and, taking one last look out of the window, carefully slipped off his wedding ring, laid it down on the sideboard and walked slowly upstairs to bed. Less than three weeks later he was dead.

Within the next few weeks Rosa was also dead and Gaudí, always difficult to console, ran away, taking the first boat out to Palma de Mallorca.[49] It was time to start work again. And it is an indication of Gaudí's frenetic pace that in December 1912 alone, the carriage from the Colònia Güell was sent out twelve times to collect Gaudí from the nearest station. Early in the same month, Gaudí had also attended the Feast of the Immaculate Conception in Mallorca to see the giant candelabrum fitted precariously in place over the central crossing. After the cables and ropes broke for the third time Gaudí retired to bed defeated, only to be saved at the eleventh hour by the constructor Miquel Sans locating a stronger rope.[50]

Gaudí had changed. Despite his attempts to carry on, he needed much more care. Santaló and Matamala took it in turns to keep Gaudí company, sleeping up at the house. He was fed at work by the Berenguers or the Temple caretaker's accommodating family.

Gaudí's appearance, however, was as much a result of his diet and the ravages of brucellosis as any philosophical or religious faith. He increasingly looked as if he might have walked straight out of a canvas depicting *The Temptation of St Anthony Abbot*. He was, according to Casanelles, 'like a shadow', or like the walking dead, appearing more and more translucent. Following a hernia he had taken to using a walking stick with a rubber end to avoid slipping. He changed from his usual model of shoe (manufactured out of courgette roots), which was proving increasingly painful to his feet, to his own invention of esparto grass soles with leather uppers.[51]

Gaudí's suits now hung off his hollow shoulders, while his trousers flapped around those thin energetic legs that he bandaged every morning to keep out the cold. He took less and less care of his appearance and many remembered the stained suits with their tinge of greeny mould, the collapsed overused pockets, and those shoes held together with elastic.[52] To economise he shaved his head and beard every few months, so his appearance was constantly fluctuating. One day while standing in a feverish state waiting for the Horta tram to arrive at the Plaça Urquinaona, Gaudí was mistaken for a tramp and offered a *limosna* – alms.[53] He did also do the rounds, however, begging for money to swell the coffers of the Sagrada Família.

In a contemporary photograph he appears edgy and passionate, surrounded by a group of religious dignitaries that he is leading around the Sagrada Família. There is a kind of nervous hilarity amongst the group as he explains some of the more arcane references hidden amongst the stones.

When one day a group of doctors visited the Sagrada Família, Gaudí explained to them that by living almost continuously within the patient's circle of pain, as they most certainly did, they were nothing less than the architects of the human edifice.[54] Although the first to reject medical advice Gaudí was always willing to offer others his home cures and advice. One particularly obese sculptor, Ramon, was advised to take more exercise, walk to work and eat less fat.[55]

The Gaudí myth of the hermit and the dejected beggar dates effectively from 1914 on. It was, however, much exaggerated. Gaudí's social circle was certainly hidden away from the public gaze. But within the structure of the Catholic Church and the liturgical renaissance Gaudí still played an active role. In October 1913 he joined the committee of the Primer Congrés d'Art Cristià de Catalunya at which Torras i Bages delivered the inaugural address *Ofici Espiritual de l'Art*, and two papers were read out – Ignasi Casanovas' *L'Art en el Temple* and Josep Tarré's *L'Art i la Litúrgia* – paying homage to their in-house architect Antoni Gaudí.[56] He also remained an active member of the Lliga Espiritual de la Mare de Déu de Montserrat – how could he not – led by Father Lluís Carreras; and in 1915 he attended the Primer Congrés Litúrgic de Montserrat.

Gaudí also continued to go to life drawing classes at the Cercle Sant Lluc and went to see Dr Santaló almost daily. Mass and the evening confessional bound his day together. As did the evening walk around the Park Güell with Alfonso Trias. And, of course, he continued to work in close collaboration with all of his employees at the Sagrada Família.

Gaudí was a perfect example of the laity being closely involved in the mechanics of faith. In 1916, Gaudí became a keen participant in the Curs Superior de Cant Gregorià. With his atonal droning voice he was perhaps unusually suited to the monody of the plainchant. Its subtle variations of rhythm and tone established over the centuries thrilled him. Pius X had written in 1903 of the 'holiness, quality of form' and 'ubiquitous validity' of the Gregorian chant. But behind the haunting beauty of the plainchant Gaudí traced the harmonic structure of a cathedral of sound.

When work on the Colònia Güell effectively ground to a halt in 1914, due to economic downturn, Gaudí was left with only one job – the Sagrada Família. For years almost no new work had come Gaudí's way. In 1912 he had designed a pulpit for the church in Blanes. In 1915 he was asked to look over the proposed restoration ideas for Manresa's cathedral by the architect Alejandro Soler March. It had been built originally by the same master builder who created Santa Maria del Mar and was naturally close to Gaudí's heart.[57] But unlike Santa Maria del Mar, squashed in between other buildings, La Seu de Manresa sits on top of a hill and its stark beauty and use of local material lends it an almost industrial feel. Gaudí took immediate exception to Soler March's plans and became 'violently opposed' and 'very aggressive' with him.[58] Soler March calmed him down and capitulated to his ideas. But it still wasn't new work.

Gaudí's evolution during the first two years of the First World War reveal how he had become trapped in the 'closed iron circle' of the Sagrada Família, and its self-referential Roman Catholic world.

Across Europe and America the Art Nouveau and *modernista* style had become increasingly dated. Frank Lloyd Wright's designs, which had been popularised for the first time in 1910 with the publication of the influential *Wasmuth Volumes*, finally pointed a way out of the Arts and Crafts impasse. In Europe, Frank Lloyd Wright's design principles and his 'grammar of the Protestant' fell on fertile ground. The early Bauhaus and the Dutch movement of De Stijl announced the arrival of a new, cleaner industrial aesthetic.

In Italy the Futurist architect Antonio Sant' Elia drew up his

'*Messaggio*' in which he stated that the modern city should look like 'an immense and tumultuous shipyard, active, mobile and everywhere dynamic, and the modern building like a gigantic machine'. We must 'resolve the problem of modern architecture without cribbing photographs of China, Persia or Japan'. Architecture of subject and narrative was now distinctly unfashionable.

In Catalonia the mood had also changed. Despite the fame of Barcelona's *modernista* architecture, people were tired of what they saw as indulgent excess. This new aesthetic was called *Noucentismo*, its practitioners the New Centurions.

Eugeni d'Ors was convinced that the *modernistas* had skewed their vision towards Paris and northern Europe and that *Noucentismo*'s first job was to refocus the Catalans on their legitimate Mediterranean heritage. What *Noucentismo* called for then was classical harmony, cleanliness and a general stylistic paring down – exactly the opposite of Gaudí's hopes for the Sagrada Família's neo-Gothic Nativity façade. But other more obvious differences lay embedded in their relationship and attitude to notions of the city and the popular arts.

*Modernismo* had been, particularly in the field of private commissions, essentially an aspirational, bourgeois, even aristocratic style.[59] Part of the energy of *Noucentismo*, on the other hand, was directed at trying to establish Barcelona as a 'normal' city; to 'normalise' it so that it might be as modern as and indistinguishable from any other European city.[60] Thus it represented a complete rupture with the outdated and parochial *modernista* style, seeing it perhaps as too deliberately anecdotally Catalan.

By 1917, however, the energies of *Noucentismo* had begun to wane. Exiles from across Europe, benefitting from Spain's neutrality, moved to Barcelona, bringing the latest advances in the avant-garde. The Delaunays briefly visited Barcelona in 1916 with their 'simultaneist' paintings. The following year Picasso also returned to his favourite city for the performance of *Parade*, a collaboration with Cocteau, Satie and Massine, and performed by Diaghilev's Ballet Russes. But undoubtedly the most advanced manifestation of a new aesthetic was the 1917 publication of Francis Picabia's Dada magazine *391*.

For Gaudí, the most significant change was the rapid acceptance of *Noucentismo* as the city's new legitimate style. Just a few years earlier, in 1905 and 1906, the fortunes of the Sagrada Família had benefitted enormously from Maragall, Rubió i Bellver and Cardellach's sustained campaign to bring the Expiatory Temple into the centre of the cultural debate. By 1913, however, it had become obvious that 'official' taste had definitively changed.

A key element of the *noucentista* project had been to 'professionalise' and 'institutionalise' the world of culture through the setting up of institutions like the Institut d'Estudis Catalans, the Biblioteca de Catalunya and the Museu d'Art de Catalunya. The Universitat Industrial, based on the German polytechnics, was also established during this period, as were a whole chain of humanist schools. An essential theme of the 'moral' programme of *Noucentismo* had been the promotion of civilisation and civic pride: the creation of public parks and gardens was central to this. An effective demonstration of *Noucentismo*'s aims was the contrast of Gaudí's exclusive, but fatally flawed, Park Güell with Jean Claude Forestier's successful remodelling and rationalisation of the mountain of Montjüic, which was open to everyone.[61] *Noucentismo* was impregnated with an overwhelming sense of optimism and hope.

It was significant that, just as in 1901, Gaudí had been the only cultural figure of note missing from Picasso's pantheon in his first one-man show at Els Quatre Gats, and the only architect to steer consistently clear of politics, and avoid writing articles and books in the interim years, he had also deliberately avoided any involvement in the great civic projects of the *noucentista* group. By 1918, Gaudí was a completely isolated figure with just one remaining sponsor, the Catholic Church.

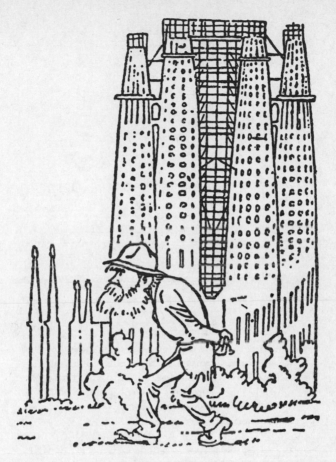

Caricature of a dishevelled Gaudí in front of the Sagrada
Família by Feliu Elies 'Apa'.

People still visited Gaudí at the Sagrada Família to marvel at
his architecture, but others almost certainly came there as urban
anthropologists to see this strange 'romantic', the last of a rapidly
disappearing tribe.

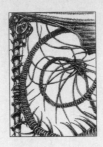

# The Cathedral of the Poor

---

We have reached a moment in time when even
the stones must speak!

*Torras i Bages*

The beautiful has only one type: the ugly has a thousand.
This is because the beautiful, speaking humanly,
is nothing but form considered in its simplest relation,
its most absolute symmetry, its most intimate harmony
with our organism.
Therefore it always offers us an ensemble that is complete
but limited as we are. What we call the ugly, on the contrary,
is a detail of a larger ensemble which escapes us,
and which harmonizes not with man,
but with entire creation. That is why it presents us forever
with new but incomplete aspects.

*Victor Hugo*, preface to 'Cromwell'

FOLLOWING ON FROM the lean war years Gaudí became
increasingly irrelevant to younger architects. He had had to cope
with failing physical health, a profound spiritual crisis and the
deaths of many of his closest friends. In 1910 his old teacher
Josep Vilaseca had died; 1911 saw the death of Joan Maragall,
the eccentric sculptor Carles Mani y Roig and his assistant Joan

Alsina; in 1914, Berenguer, his *brac dret* – his right arm and
principal amanuensis – died; Bishop Campins died the following
year and in 1916, Torras i Bages and Pere i Falques also died.
But with the death of his patron Don Eusebi Güell in June 1918
works at the Park Güell and the Colònia Güell ground to a
complete halt.

There had been a small victory with the final winding up in
1916 of the Casa Milà court case that had dragged on since
autumn 1909. Gaudí was awarded 105,000 pesetas in compensation for fees withheld. An acquaintance, Pau Badia Ripoll,
remembered that Gaudí had proved 'a hard nut to crack', sticking
to his guns and forcing Pere Milà to remortgage the Casa Milà
in order to meet the fine. For Gaudí it had clearly been a matter
of principle and pride as he immediately donated every peseta
to Ignasi Casanovas and the Jesuits. By 1918, therefore, there
was only one project left – the Expiatory Temple of the Sagrada
Família. And having at last arrived at a style that was uniquely
his own, he devoted himself entirely to this building and the
greater glory of God.

The Sagrada Família had been a major part of Gaudí's life
and work for many years. But almost from the beginning the
Sagrada Família had proved a demanding mistress. Not only was
Gaudí responsible for designing the building but at times had to
work as fund-raiser too. The progress of the building over the first
thirty-six years, from 1882 to 1918, had been far from smooth.

The crypt, inherited in its essential neo-Gothic form from
Paula del Villar y Lozano, was finished by 1891. At this early
stage the *Junta* and even Gaudí believed that a mass to celebrate
the completion of the entire temple might be held before the
end of the century. Lack of money, however, and Gaudí's unpre-
dictable genius coupled with the catalogue of untimely deaths,
got in the way. On 22 April 1892, Bocabella, president of the
*Junta* of the Sagrada Família, died. His son-in-law Manuel de
Dalmases y de Riba took over, only to die just months later in

1893; the position was then passed over to his widow Doña Francisca de P. Bocabella y Puig, who also died before the end of the year. From 1895 on the post of president was conferred unanimously upon the incumbent Bishop of Barcelona.

By 1900 the first transept façade, the Nativity, and a portion of the exterior wall of the cloister and the Rosario Chapel had been completed. Eighteen years later Gaudí's team, working with extraordinary attention to detail, had still proceeded no further than the endless refining of ideas and models for the central nave and crossing, and drawings for the opposite transept façade of the Passion. Above the Nativity façade, however, four circular campanile towers were slowly rising up. The first of these towers, completed in 1918, had an outer masonry shell that was perforated like a honeycomb with asymmetrical window settings spiralling slowly up to the tower's full height. Seen from a distance it looked exactly like a blown-up reworking of the fragile staircase seashells found along the Catalan coastline. The St Barnabas tower, covered in a brash mosaic of Murano glass, was the only one completed by the time of Gaudí's death.

Gaudí's ambition far outstripped anything achievable within his own lifetime. But his labour-intensive methods were not entirely to blame for the interminable delays. In the period 1903 to 1905, Leon Jaussely had started to work up his competition-winning designs for rethinking the Barcelona city plan.

Jaussely, careful to consult leading architects, almost immediately recognised the appropriateness of Gaudí's suggestions for the Sagrada Família and the surrounding urban landscape. The temple would increase its monumental presence in the city by leaving the triangular areas of all the adjoining *eixample* squares undeveloped, therefore allowing for clear sightlines through to the temple from hundreds of metres away. Although the resulting form, a star shape, was never adhered to, it fitted in perfectly with the rationale of Domènech's nearby Hospital de Sant Pau, set at an exact diagonal of 45 degrees to look down a long avenue at the Sagrada's Nativity façade. Reflection and change had always been the two absolutes of Gaudí's design process as he continually rethought, readjusted, rescaled and remodelled aspects of the building – sometimes almost daily. 'The bigger the better' had always been one of the main design concepts behind the temple.[1] But it was not just megalomania as five hundred years before at Seville Cathedral where the Chapter had boasted of building an 'edifice so great and of such a kind that those who see it finished shall think we are mad'. There was also political expediency at work. If the Sagrada Família were too small it might lose its autonomy and fall under the jurisdiction of its parish, Sant Martí de Provençals, its property therefore transferring to the control of the Bishop who might easily have entirely different plans. The Gothic cathedral, the Bishop's mother church, despite attracting sponsorship from the fabulously wealthy Manuel Girona, still remained unfinished seven hundred and twenty years after its beginning.

In 1907, Cardinal Casañas delicately edged his foot through the door by addressing the *Junta* in the most diplomatic of terms:

> The growth of Sant Martí has led the Most Excellent Cardinal Casañas, bishop of Barcelona, to request the *Asociación*'s authorisation – while we wait for the establishment of a new parish – to set a parish branch in the temple, with the understanding that if such provision would hurt the temple in the very least they should say so freely for he will find another solution.

Capitulating gracefully and allowing the crypt to serve the local parish, there was always the potential that the Sagrada Família might benefit in its direct access to the parish's 'thirty thousand souls'. By 1912, however, under the new bishop, Dr Laguarda, rumours surfaced suggesting that a decree transforming the

Sagrada Família to a mere parish church was awaiting immediate ratification. Coinciding with the rumours of Gaudí's failing health, it gave real cause for concern. Gaudí immediately sought out Prat de la Riba who quickly interceded on his behalf. On 21 December 1912, *La Veu de Catalunya* published an article by Prat de la Riba which made public the result of his negotiations. Under the banner headline 'Is Gaudí leaving the works of the Sagrada Família?' he explained:

> There have been hot debates in one of the spots fre- quented by our country's artists over the news that Gaudí would abandon direction of his genial work, the Expia- tory Temple of the Sacred Family, before witnessing the mortal blow that the conversion of the temple into one of the many parish churches of the city would signify.

Prat then continued to explain that he had received verbal assur- ances from Dr Laguarda that this would never happen. Conclud- ing respectfully, Prat firmly bolted the door shut on the bishop:

> Since we cannot question the honesty of the most respectable words from our prelate, we think we may safely state that, for the time being, there is no reason for alarm.

In 1898, Joaquim Mir, a leading member of the Col de Zafra group more commonly associated with the production of lumi- nous chromatic landscapes, took the Sagrada Família as the sub- ject for one of his great masterpieces, entitled *The Cathedral of the Poor*.[2] In the foreground a starving family sits amongst the walls of the temple begging. It is quite possible that Mir's paint- ing is in fact an ironic critique of this vast money-draining pro- ject.[3] But the usual interpretation is that *The Cathedral of the Poor*

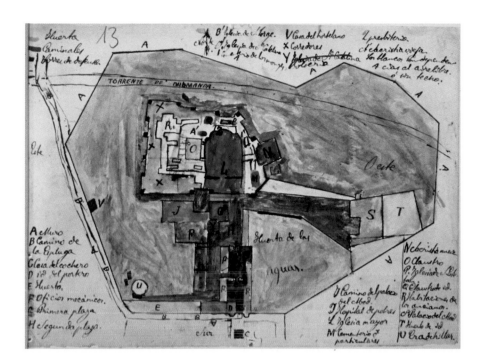

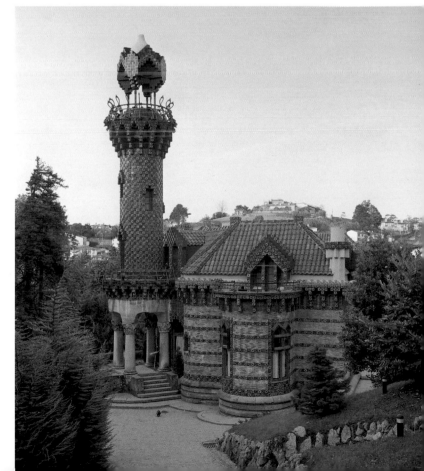

ABOVE A plan of
Poblet copied from
a guidebook by
Gaudí and Eduardo
Toda (1870).

RIGHT El Capricho.

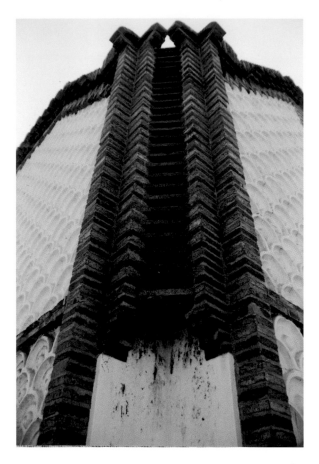

LEFT A corner detail with the open rhythm of brickwork set against plaster relief. Gatekeeper's house at the Finca Güell, Pedralbes.

BELOW Shards of tile set into the mortar enliven the surface at the Finca Güell pavilions.

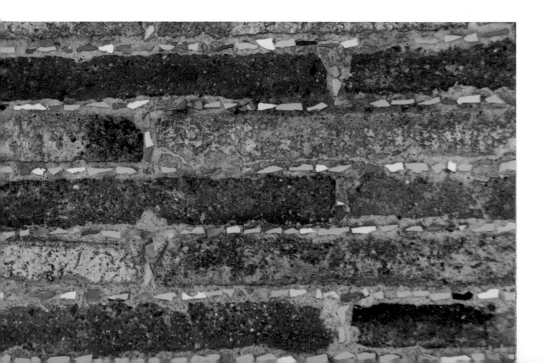

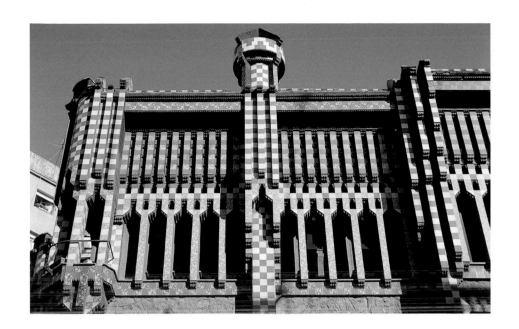

ABOVE Exterior of the
Casa Vicens 1883-5.

RIGHT Interior of the Casa
Calvet.

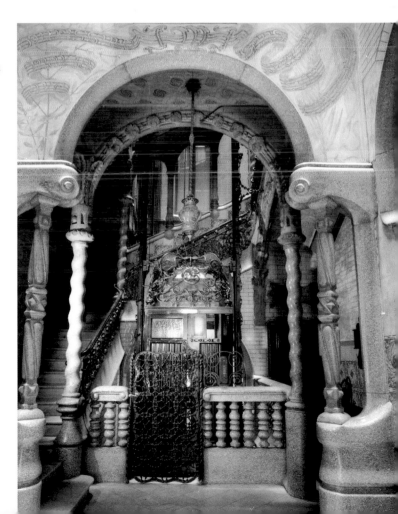

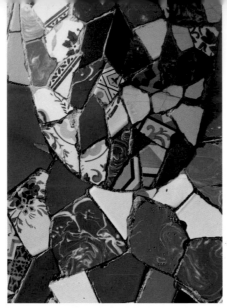

LEFT The flexibility of the broken tile – *trencadís* – technique is perfectly illustrated in this detail of a chimney from the Palau Güell.

BELOW The Apostles' Towers at the Sagrada Família flank the polychrome cypress tree.

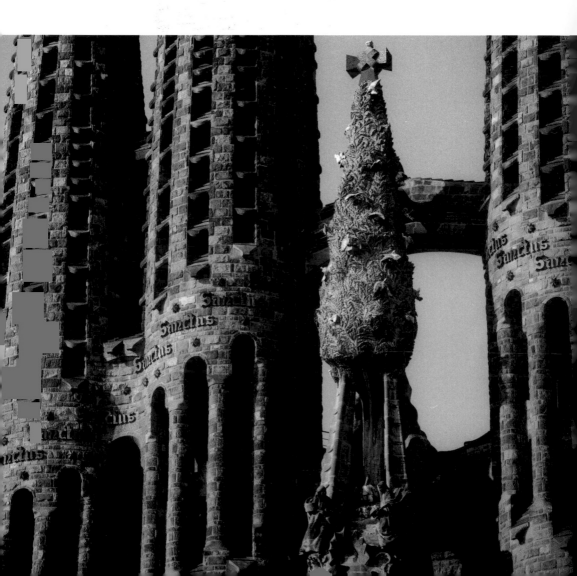

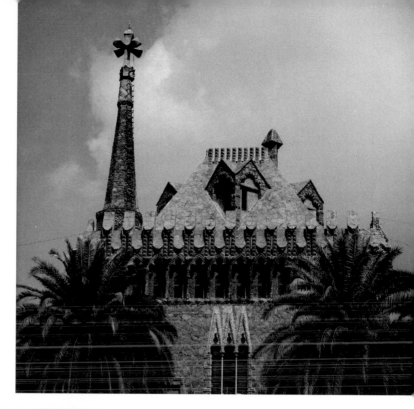

ABOVE Bellesguard.

LEFT Windows over entrance door to Bellesguard.

BELOW Decorated tile benches at Bellesguard are on either side of its entrance.

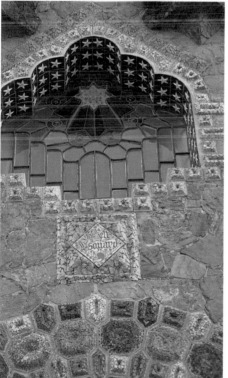

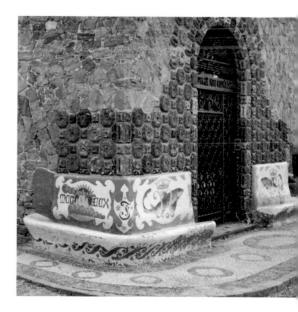

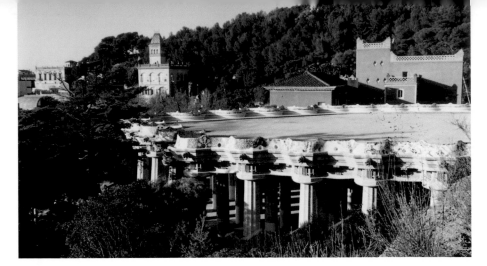

ABOVE The marketplace, Park Güell – (background right) the residence of Eusebi Güell.

LEFT An upside-down inscription to the Virgin along the back support of the serpentine bench at the Park Güell.

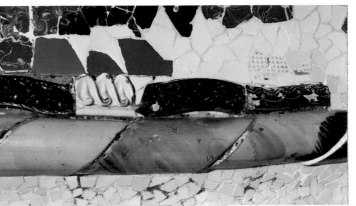

RIGHT Shattered plate and shell set into the *trencadís* tile decoration of the serpentine bench.

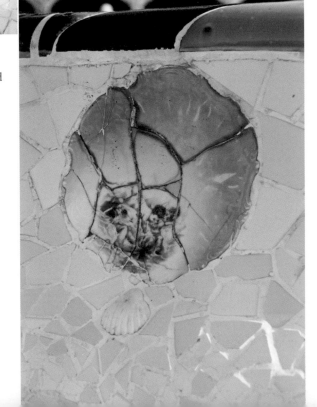

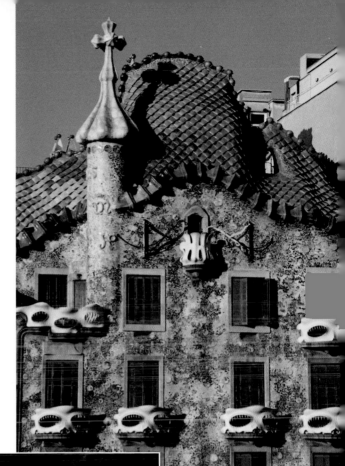

RIGHT Casa Batlló (1904-6).

BELOW A network of thin brick arches lead the eye towards the butterfly windows at the crypt in the Colònia Guell.

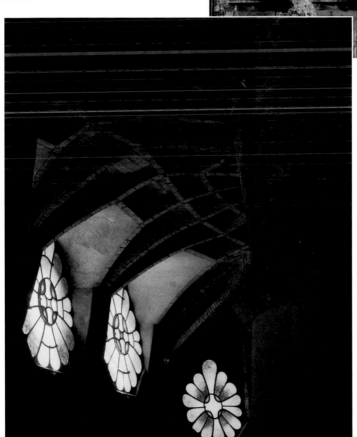

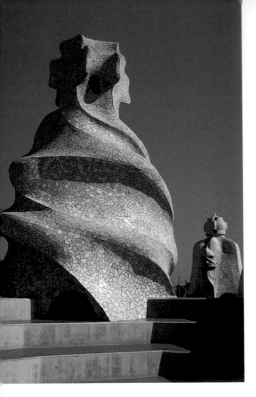

LEFT Rooftop figure on the Casa Milà.

BELOW Postcard (1913) of the recently finished Casa Milà. Note the horse-drawn carriages and the trams.

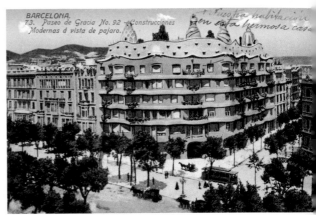

BELOW Roofscape of the Casa Milà.

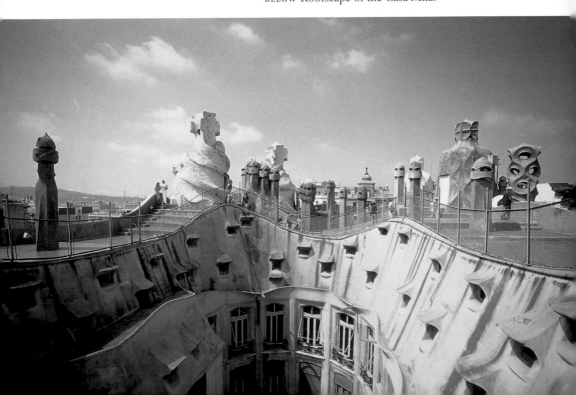

was an accurate portrayal of an egalitarian religious structure which was open to all.

Gaudí was extremely proud of the one peseta he brought most mornings to the Sagrada Família, a donation from a local shop. As Bocabella wrote in 1884: 'we need stones of all sizes'. Suffering and denial were an essential element in the chemistry of this church. 'Can't the smoker give up just one cigarette a day? Or the shopkeeper deny himself the pleasure of just one cup of coffee in a single week?' Bocabella continued. But the giving of alms was also a policy that enjoyed full papal support where donors were rewarded with 100 days of indulgences and a papal blessing.

Over the years, even during Gaudí's lifetime, the Sagrada Família had become a place of pilgrimage. King Alfonso visited the site, although Gaudí almost certainly caused displeasure by refusing to speak in anything but Catalan.[4] Doña Luz de Bourbon also visited as did the Infanta Isabella. Cardinal Ragonesi, the papal nuncio in Spain, came to see the works as did Albert Schweitzer. Schweitzer fared no better than King Alfonso with Gaudí explaining to the 'White Doctor' in Catalan that there were certain things that could only be understood in this marginalised Mediterranean tongue.

But most tragicomic of all was the well-documented visit by the philosopher Miguel de Unamuno in 1906. Considering that Unamuno had come to Barcelona to attend the First Congress of the Catalan Language, it was not entirely unreasonable that Gaudí expected him to have basic Catalan. Slowly Unamuno, a respected ally and friend of Joan Maragall, stalked around the building site, spluttering '*No me gusta! No me gusta!*' – 'I don't like it!' in Castilian. A few steps behind him Gaudí imitated his every move. '*No li agrada! No li agrada!*' – 'He doesn't like it!' he repeated in Catalan. Gaudí had never gone an inch out of his way to promote himself. With Unamuno's support his fame and acceptance in Spain might have come rather sooner.[5]

The day ended rather quaintly, however, with the two men having at last buried their differences, sitting face to face across Gaudí's work desk in the studio, as the distinguished rector of Salamanca showed off his origami skills and made the architect some perfect paper doves. Although Gaudí treasured them for the rest of his life, at the sound of the Angelus bells he cut Unamuno's visit curtly and abruptly short.

For decades Gaudí had orchestrated and perfected the precise liturgical arrangement of the Sagrada Família's symbolic content and space. Thanks to the experiments at the Colònia Güell, which had already demonstrated the efficacy of the parabolic arch, the structure was almost completely resolved. But in the workshop alongside the temple he struggled daily to create a 'total' vision.

At each corner of the Sagrada Família site an obelisk was placed, at the cardinal points, to symbolise the four periods of fasting during a Catholic year. They would also 'sing in advance' – in Gaudí's words – 'the praises of the Holy Family and proclaim the virtues of penitence'. To accompany the obelisks there would also be a giant fountain and a monstrous lantern which symbolised the purification by water and fire.

Inside the Sagrada Família, Gaudí planned seating for thirteen thousand worshippers, and the main columns were assigned to the major apostolic missions around Spain, which included cities like Valencia, Granada, Santiago de Compostela, Burgos, Seville, Toledo, Segovia and even smaller sees like Burgo de Osma with a population of only five thousand souls.

Gaudí's architecture was, despite its superficially fantastical appearance, profoundly literal in a way that had not been seen in Europe for hundreds of years. Gaudí did what Goya and El Greco had done before him – illustrated precisely the plastic reality of the spiritual world. Gaudí once said that 'Hearing is the sense of Faith and seeing is the sense of Glory, because Glory is the vision of God. Seeing is the sense of light, of space, of plasticity, vision is the immensity of space; it sees what there is and what there is not.'[6] The Sagrada Família illustrated this ambition perfectly. The temple was planned not just as an intermediary between heaven and earth but also as a battlefield of the senses. Gaudí understood perfectly the psychological effect and importance of sound, particularly in religious buildings.

For years Gaudí had experimented with new forms for the Sagrada's elongated tubular bells. But the entire fabric of the building was also designed to function like a massive organ. Wind, it was hoped, would blow through the perforated towers and sing a natural chorus. 'The murmuring stone is trying to say Noël,' Maragall had written in 1900.

Colour would also play its part. It is one of the ironies of Gaudí's work that while for many he has come to symbolise all the values we associate with 'Black Spain' – inquisitorial, suspicious and intolerant, he had planned something far more attention-grabbing than the glittering mosaic HOSANNAs that swept up the tower. He envisaged the entire exterior of the Sagrada Família as a bright multicoloured anthem to the glory of the Lord.

Gaudí's Nativity façade was literally awe-inspiring. Not in its subject matter, which was neatly divided into the three gates of Hope, Charity and Faith, but certainly in its overall effect. Standing under the gigantic sculptural frieze the whole building still feels as if it's about to collapse on the viewer's head. The precipitous overhang, that Gaudí also used at Astorga and the Colònia Güell, seems to defy gravity and belittle the viewer.[7]

Crossing over to the north-facing Nativity façade we come face to face with a bizarre mountainous growth. The central doorway, divided by a central column, is capped by a life-size sculptural group of the Holy Family. At our feet the two palm-tree columns that divide the whole space sit upon the backs of two tortoises, an *impresa* and symbol also chosen by Cosimo de Medici – its motto *Festina lente* ('Make haste slowly') a perfectly appropriate symbol for Gaudí's temple. Moving up to eye-level the façade seems to rise up in a pinnacle to dwarf its smaller neighbours and, flanked by the apostles Barnabas, Simon, Thaddeus and Matthew, the coronation of the Virgin takes place thirty metres above the ground in the shade of a giant Christmas tree.

Hope depicts life-size groups: the marriage of Joseph and Mary, the Flight to Egypt, the Massacre of the Innocents and Jesus in his father's workshop. Faith shows the presentation of Jesus in the Temple, Christ amongst the Doctors, and the mature Jesus practising his father's trade. Everywhere there are cameos: birds in flight, a sardine boat turning into harbour at Cambrils, the star of Bethlehem, the Holy Spirit and the Milky Way. The heavenly twins Castor and Pollux and other signs of the Zodiac hover above our heads as if trapped in aspic. Here's a bull's head; there a selection of shellfish and reptiles, sea urchins, sea anemones, salamanders and snails crawling over the seaweed. Olives, oranges, pomegranates, almond trees and roses burst into flower.[8] 'I believe like Da Vinci that decadence sets in as soon as man forgets to look at nature,' Gaudí had lectured to Juan Matamala.[9] At the edges of each scene the stone was carved as if in gradual lava-like movement.

With its contemporary references to the importance of the nuclear family and its healthy reverence for honest labour the Sagrada Família's external decoration was a perfect illustration of Vatican policy. But it was also an Expiatory Temple, and around the corner at the Rosario door Gaudí placed two capitals, one of a woman tempted by the devil with a bag of money, and the other a contorted demon handing a workman an Orsini bomb, of the same type that had almost killed Maragall at the Liceu. It had an alarming contemporary ring, just like the in-jokes directed at the clergy, hidden high in the masonry of the medieval Gothic church. It also reflected a dreadful pessimism and almost nihilistic loss of faith in everyday man.

The whole Nativity façade had a distinctly operatic feel to

it; sweeping and grandiose. It was, as Ortega had said of the Escorial, 'a credo made visible'. It was nothing more, carped the critics, than 'a treatise on pure effort'. But Gaudí's unfinished magnum opus employed a wild stylistic kleptomania that pulled together the language of the waxworks, the diorama, the carnival, the landscape, the grotto, the fairground and the religious shrine into an elaborate whole. It was, Pevsner dismissed, a 'frantic concoction possible only in the country of Churriguera'.

Oscar Tusquets, architect and restorer of Domènech's Palau, explains how Gaudí 'works in dialogue with God ... the type of dialogue with God that a Japanese potter could have'. And, in one sense, it is absolutely true. For Gaudí worked also like a miniaturist, modelling tiny details into clay. He was an acclaimed constructor of enchanting miniature nativity scenes but blown up on a giant scale.[10] But there are other references to popular entertainment. The towers relate also to the *Xiquets de Valls*, the elaborate human towers that are built up during fiestas, as at the circus, in any number of different configurations reaching sometimes a dizzying nine levels high.[11] These human towers have often been discussed as a plastic representation of the Catalan capacity for communal work. The Nativity façade also meditated on the effect of the dioramas and the cinema on the public consciousness with their control over reality, movement and space.

Gaudí and his patrons, the Sagrada Família *Junta*, had struggled hard in a 'godless time' to reinvest the religious building with moral purpose and religious authority. But, typically, Gaudí tried to solve the problem by reaching for the moral high ground through a programme of orchestrated vulgarity.

The scale of it all is sheer madness, a folly. But, as Seneca wrote, 'there is no genius without madness'. Picasso too had made a joke of it.

For Picasso, Gaudí's famous church, the Sagrada Família, was something of a joke – more to Salvador Dalí's taste, he once commented, than his. In the living room in La Californie there used to be an enormous panettone that mice had reduced to a ruin: 'Gaudí's model,' he would say.[12]

Standing in front of the Sagrada Família amongst half-carved lumps of stone, left abandoned since Gaudí's death, it is hard not to dwell on all the expense and waste of such a monstrous project and to feel a certain Protestant distaste.

> Karlstad, Zwingli, and Calvin were not only preaching the destruction of works of art – they were attempting to re-landscape totally the visual experience of the Christian ... for to destroy images is to destroy the past.[13]

Just as at the Colònia Güell, Gaudí built a workshop to cater for the new techniques the façade required.[14] Up some wooden steps, over Mossèn Gil Parés' house, a large drawing studio joined onto a photographic studio with a mobile roof to allow for the manipulation of natural light, reminiscent of La Sibèria, the freezing cold drawing hall at the architectural school of fifty years before. There was another room tall enough to house the model of the Temple's nave on a scale of 1 to 10, and a room for maquettes. When not in use for either scaling up or copying, the plaster models were hung up from the ceiling, giving it the appearance of 'a reptiles' cave', according to Matamala.[15] At the end was a small room, packed full of plans and rolls of paper, in which stood a narrow iron bedstead, where Gaudí slept for the last six months of his life.

When preparing the decoration of the façade, what Gaudí wanted was an exact copy of nature, so he roamed the parish for years looking for the right models. To copy God's handiwork was the highest form of praise and showed the artist's humility. 'It is mad to try to represent a fictional object,' Gaudí had written in his Reus diary many years before. And still true to this philo-

sophy he hunted out people who might pose for Christ, for
Joseph, the Virgin Mary and all the saints and angels. The alcoholic caretaker Josep, who later died of delirium tremens, was
Judas. Gutiérrez, a potbellied goatherd, was Pontius Pilate. A
six-toed giant, found in a bar, posed for the centurion slaughtering the Innocents. The 666 reference delighted Gaudí who
saw all the diabolical energies of the holocaust pictured in him.
But the search was not restricted to humans. There was the right
Christmas tree to find, the correct chicken and the kind of
donkey that looked like a beast of burden after days of walking.
The local scrap dealer lent his animal. When models were hard
to locate Gaudí found the requisite nobility expressed in the face
and bodies of his staff. A sculptor became Simon, a transporter of
stone the apostle Thaddeus and a strikingly handsome plasterer
became David.

The next stage was even more eccentric. Chickens and turkeys
were chloroformed, greased and quickly cast in plaster before
coming round again. The donkey was trussed up and lifted in a
harness, where it could be more easily modelled. A dead owl
found one morning was quickly used by Gaudí as a perfect
emblem for Night. It was only when Gaudí decided to take a
full life cast of Ricardo Opisso, who fainted in the process, that
he realised the limitations of this technique.

Gaudí looked towards other ways of verifying nature's truth.
In the photographic studio he and Opisso set up a carefully
angled bank of mirrors so that each subject might be inspected
and recorded in the round. Standing in the right place the model
might be seen at five different angles, but Gaudí was still not
satisfied. What he really wanted was an X-ray to locate the
hidden bone structure. So he was provided with skeletons from
the hospital which were photographed suspended in different
positions. To go one step further still in his investigations he
patiently rebuilt the skeleton's armature out of twisted wire.

But Gaudí needed to know more still. With special permission he was allowed to observe autopsies at the Hospital de Santa Cruz.[16] We are all God's puppets, Gaudí had once intimated to Matamala.[17] In 1919, when Alfonso Trias was halfway through his medical degree, he got permission from the University rector and the professor of anatomy to dissect an entire corpse and demonstrate its ligature to Gaudí. Once finished the skeleton was taken to the workshop where it was wired together and made more rigid with metal tubing and dressed in clothes for further examination.[18]

On another day Gaudí entered the Hospital to request whether anyone had recently died. The nursing sister announced that with God's grace no one had died that night but if he and Matamala wished to see someone actually expiring they could follow her and witness the patient receiving extreme unction. They looked on, Gaudí was convinced that he had seen the exact moment when the soul had been greeted by the Holy Family.[19] Stranger still was Gaudí's use of plaster casts of stillborn babies to represent the hundreds of children slaughtered by Herod. They made a chilling spectacle of the drawing hall ceiling, hung in row upon row.

After all the research there were still numerous further stages before the final sculpture was finally in position on the Nativity façade. Firstly, the plaster cast was hauled up and put in position. Satisfied, Gaudí had the piece lowered and taken back to Opisso's photographic studio, where it was immediately photographed. The finished print was pinned to a board at exactly the angle necessary to compensate for the perspective distortion arising from the sculpture's height from the ground. The resulting photograph looked like a saint by El Greco – who was the contemporary height of fashion.[20] From there Gaudí's final 'distorted' photograph was used, along with other research such as photographs of bodies in movement or chickens in flight, squared up on paper for easier transposition into 3D, for the eventual plaster version. Hoisted up once again, Gaudí then permitted the sculptors to transform the plaster into stone.

It was a time-consuming process and one that some sculptors found difficult to adapt to. Torres García, Llonguers, Pascual, Sala and Ramón Bonet y Save, who later went to work on Rodin's *Gates of Hell*, all left the Gaudí workshop.

From the opulence of the New York's Hotel St Regis Salvador Dalí listed what he saw as 'the five principal perfidies':

1. Those who have not seen his militant vision are traitors.

2. Those who have not touched the bony structures and the living flesh of his delirious ornamentation are traitors.

3. Those who have not heard the chromatic, glowing stridence of his colour, the striking polyphony of his organ-pipe towers, and the clash of his mutating decorative naturalism are traitors.

4. Those who have not tasted his superbly creative bad taste are traitors.

5. Those who have not smelled the odour of sanctity are traitors.

But under the histrionics there is a subtle critic at work. In Gaudí's workshop, passions and obsessions were being carefully distilled into stone.

By the beginning of the 1920s the pattern of Gaudí's day was fixed into an unchangeable routine – morning mass, work at the Sagrada Família, confession and home to bed.

The Tragic Week ten years before was believed by some to have relieved civil unrest but the next few years would show this to be naive. In 1916, in spite of two years of wartime privations, Spain's policy of neutrality enormously benefitted Catalonia's economy. This boom, however, led to further tensions in industrial relations. The CNT, the Confederació Nacional del Treball, a Catalan workers' union linking up with the Spanish UGT in 1916, was quickly countered by the formation in December of a Catholic union, the Confederació de Sindicats Catòlics. The year 1917 brought the crisis to a head. Shadowing events in Russia it became clear to many on the left that a general strike might force the issue. With increased calls for Catalan autonomy during the summer, and with the Cortes in Madrid refusing to entertain any such concept, the stage was set again for the complete collapse of law and order. During August the military was called into Barcelona to break the strike, resulting in thousands of arrests and more than thirty dead. As before, bloodletting and repression only resulted in pushing rebellion momentarily underground.

Catalan autonomy remained a central issue in the crisis which was to grow in strength when, in 1919, the Catalan politician Francesc Macià demanded that Catalan autonomy and workers' rights were essentially inseparable. In February the workers at Catalonia's largest hydroelectric plant went out on strike. In an almost exact replay of the events leading up to the catastrophe of 1909, political murders on both sides destabilised Barcelona. Unions swapped their allegiances by the week, murdering each other's members and leaders, and in turn suffering state persecution. And once again in Morocco during the summer of 1921 the Spanish army suffered a massive defeat in the Rif with the loss of 15,000 lives.

Gaudí walked peacefully every day through the growing political tempest; distancing himself from a world that might still at the eleventh hour find salvation at his church. People crossed to the other side of the road when they saw him coming, fearing his claims on their pocket. Just a few pesetas more might pay the next week's wage bill.

Despite all his attempts to remain outside the political fray Gaudí was finally drawn in. Primo de Rivera's successful coup d'état in September 1923, although bringing anarchy to a swift end, had brought in its wake a set of laws that would have direct repercussions on Gaudí's enclosed Catalan world. The use of

Catalan in public was immediately banned, as was the 'inflammatory' flying of the blood-striped Catalan flag. One of the first
acts of cultural vandalism was the removal of Gaudí's ornamental
lampposts, celebrating the centenary of Jaume Balmes, from
Vic's main square. In March 1924, however, Primo de Rivera's
dictatorship was faced with a strong demonstration of solidarity
from Spain's intelligentsia, with many of the Madrid generation
of '98 signing a manifesto in favour of the continued use of
Catalan. But it was denied. Demonstrations of regional identity
needed to be crushed.

Under just this provocation Gaudí's Catalan character and
stubbornness came to the fore. Just a few years before, at the
end of the celebration of the 1920 *Jocs Florals*, the day had disintegrated into a minor riot. Gaudí, finding himself beaten back by
police batons, shouted insults at the 'miserable' and 'bloodthirsty
swine'. Pulled away by two priests he was saved from a further
beating.[21]

But on 11 September 1924, at the mass celebrated to commemorate the bravery of the Catalan martyrs of 1714 at the
church of Sant Justo, Gaudí was finally provoked into making
his own display of Catalan solidarity. The events of the day
were recorded in Cesar Martinell's conversation with Gaudí the
following day.[22]

Gaudí, according to Martinell, had been arrested, after remon-
strating with the Guardia Civil on finding his path blocked while
attempting to enter Sant Justo and attend the mass.

'There is so much aggressiveness that goes against Catalonia,'
he told Martinell, 'her language which is mine, and for that
reason in those moments of persecution I didn't want to abandon
it. The aggressiveness that they felt against me was because I
spoke to them in Catalan.'

Taken to the cells, Gaudí was thrown behind bars with a
criminal in transit from the Modelo jail and a street hawker.
The rumours of Gaudí's arrest quickly spread around the city

and an assistant immediately came to pay his fifty peseta fine. The brief incarceration, however, left him with a lasting resentment of the Guardia Civil. 'The whole thing affected me like a miniature Hell: skinny guards with the sort of appearance that people call that of a "poor devil", the chiefs, better paid, with massive bellies, are the Lucifers who give the orders.'

And then he continued prophetically:

'When I think about what has happened it bothers me to think that we are going up a dead-end alley and that a radical change must definitely come.'

He wouldn't live to see it but just twelve years later, in 1936, Mossen Gil Parés and Ignasi Casanovas would become two of the first victims of the Civil War and the Sagrada Família would be burnt out as the marauding gangs desecrated Gaudí's grave in the crypt. The collapsing Republic would soon be replaced by Franco's Catholic dictatorship that couched its messianic ambitions in terms of another holy war. But El Caudillo Francisco Franco was no more favourable to Catalonia's claims for autonomy and the use of its own tongue than Primo de Rivera had ever been. Gaudí died before he had to make the difficult choice between religious orthodoxy and his beloved Catalunya.

After years of facial cancer, Llorenc Matamala, who for years had shared the night vigil with Santaló up at the Park Güell, was finally invalided off work. It had been the longest creative partnership in Gaudí's working life, dating right back to November 1883 when Gaudí had invited Matamala to join his team. 'Come and work with me at the temple, Senyor Llorenc, and you will have work for life.' Forty-three years later their collaboration had finally come to an end.

In autumn 1925, Gaudí finally made the decision to move down to the studio in the Sagrada Família. Looking more and more like the proverbial 'poor devil', he continued to cross the city in the early evening to St Felipe Neri to see his spiritual counsellor Agustí Mas and then afterwards to visit Dr Santaló, who was making a slow recovery after a prostate operation. One of his last forays out into the art world was to the exhibition of Liturgical Art held at the Sala Parés, which displayed some of Gaudí's ecclesiastical furniture.[23] But otherwise day-to-day life continued as normal.

On Monday 7 June 1926, at precisely 5.30 P.M., Gaudí set off from the Sagrada Família to walk the three kilometres across to Sant Felipe Neri. On leaving he gave his last order of the day: 'Come early tomorrow, Vicente, so we can make some more beautiful things.'

Following his habitual route Gaudí walked down carrer Bailén to where it crossed the much wider avenue of the Corts Catalanes. Joan Matamala had bumped into him a few days earlier on his usual route and noted that Gaudí, failing at first to reply, had been unusually distracted.[24] At just after six, according to the tram company report, the Number 30, unable to slow down, hit what the driver described as a drunken tramp. Stopping briefly, the tramp was pushed to one side and the tram continued on its way.

It is impossible now to accurately reconstruct the accident. There are many contemporary records of tram drivers pushing impatiently through the crowds, and of their failing brakes. There is one story, however, recalled by Martinell in conversation with the architect, that sheds some possible light. Gaudí always felt that pedestrians should have priority over trams and cars. While crossing the junction of Trafalgar and Bruch one day, Gaudí was given warning of an oncoming tram by frequent blasts of the horn. He refused to break his measured pace and forced the tram to brake immediately. The irate driver took a handful of sand (used to assist slipping wheels on steep inclines) and threw it forcefully into the architect's face.[25]

In the evening of 7 June 1926, the driver of No. 30 claimed, as well he might, that Gaudí wasn't looking where he was going and tripped over the tram tracks smashing his head against a lamppost. (It fails to excuse the callousness of his subsequent behaviour.)

Two pedestrians went over to help the victim who was bleeding from the ear but neither recognised him as the famous architect of the Sagrada Família. There were no papers on him and just a handful of raisins and nuts in his pockets. His hat had also gone missing.[26] Four times they tried to flag down taxis to take Gaudí to the nearest hospital but each time they were refused. (Three of the taxi drivers were later fined under the Good Samaritan Law for failing to help a person in obvious distress.) Finally with the help of a Guardia Civil, a taxi was ordered to take the victim to the dispensary on the Ronda de Sant Pere. Both strangers, wishing to remain anonymous, went on their way. But recently the family of the late Angel Tomás Mohino, the owner of a textile shop, have come forward to relate how the twenty-three-year-old Angel, upset by the callousness of other witnesses, accompanied Gaudí to the dispensary.[27]

While at the dispensary Gaudí was quickly diagnosed with fractured ribs, cerebral contusions and a haemorrhaging ear, and it was decided to send the victim to the Hospital Clínico. The tragic farce continued. The ambulancemen, who were about to go on their break, decided it would be quicker to drop him off at the nearby medieval Hospital de Santa Cruz. It was a hospital that Gaudí knew well from his anatomical research. Again he was not recognised and his name was entered in the list of admissions as Antonio Sandí. Placed in bed 19 in a public ward, he slipped in and out of consciousness during the night, one more patient amongst many.

For Gaudí's friend Mossèn Gil Parés the alarm bells had started to ring at around eight when Gaudí failed to return for his frugal dinner. Parés called the architect Sugranyes and they waited impatiently till nightfall before finally deciding to set out on a systematic search of police stations, hospitals and first-aid posts around the city. Arriving at the dispensary in the Ronda de Sant Pere, Parés was told of a tramp roughly fitting the priest's description of Gaudí who had suffered a tram accident and was found with a Gospel in his pocket and his underpants held together by safety pins.[28] His dishevelled, half-starved appearance, compounded by heavily bandaged knees as prevention against arthritic swelling, bedroom slippers and his baggy worn-out suit, go a long way towards explaining the reluctance of the taxi drivers to take a passenger incapable of paying the fare and likely to damage their brand-new upholstery.[29] Parés and Sugranyes followed on Gaudí's trail. First to the Hospital Clínico where it seems he had never arrived, until finally late into the night they located him in the public ward at the Hospital de Santa Cruz.

By the next morning, 'the patient regained consciousness after a night's prostration and requested the Last Rites which he fervently received'. Soon news of Gaudí's plight was all around the city. By Tuesday evening he had been moved to a private room, and clung precariously to life, after the resetting of his ribs. Dignitaries, friends and admirers lined the hospital corridors: the Bishop Miralles, Puig i Cadafalch, Cambó, Rubió i Bellver, the locksmith Mañach, Sugranyes, the poet Melchor Font, and an envoy from the mayor, Baron de Vivar, whose offer to move Gaudí to a more luxurious private clinic was politely declined. Gaudí wanted to die amongst the people. He was almost completely silent, his heavy breathing now punctuated only by deep sighs: '*Jesus, Déu meu!*' and his immobile right hand, placed gently on a white handkerchief, gripped a crucifix.

By Wednesday morning in a demonstration of public grief all the newspapers reported the tragic news, in collective contrition and shame, as they tried to piece together the hopeless muddle of the previous two days' events.

On Thursday 10 June 1926 at 5 P.M. Antoni Gaudí finally died.[30] His death underscored the passing away of a heroic age in

Catalonia's long battle to re-establish its true independent identity. Gaudí's epic ambition to construct a three-dimensional record of the history and credo of the Catholic faith, placing Catalonia at the centre of Christendom, had been an impossible one.

Nevertheless, Gaudí's peculiar Christian humility understood that we should all try, each within the bounds of our own gifts or limitations, to play a part in God's greater design; however large or small that might be. Each time we push our way through the Sagrada Família's turnstiles we pay for another stone to be laid and expiate another sin. We should never try to finish the Sagrada Família, otherwise we undo the web of power that is elaborately woven into this mysterious religious spell. It is a monstrous vanity to attempt to complete the temple too soon. The timing is all. 'A finished work is a dead work, killed,' Picasso warned.

If Gaudí's Sagrada Família is for some reason finished before Judgment Day then somewhere someone will have to start all over again. It is a measure of our capacity for faith whether anyone will ever rise to Gaudí's challenge.

In recognition of his Herculean labours the great Catalan architect was to be honoured with the funeral he deserved and as an epitaph receive the attention so recently denied. Bishop Miralles telegraphed the Pope for permission to bury Gaudí in the Sagrada Família crypt. Late on Thursday night Joan Matamala worked into the night making a death mask, while pencil studies were made of his perfect repose. Watching over the scene stood a select group of his assistants, friends and earliest biographers: Alfonso Trias, Ràfols, Puig Boada and César Martinell. Just three streets away, in his sick bed, still waiting for his friend to visit, Dr Santaló was kept deliberately in the dark.

On Friday Gaudí's body was embalmed and laid out in a monk's black habit with his left hand gripping a string of rosary beads.[31] On Saturday afternoon, 12 June 1926, the horse-drawn cortège pulled slowly out through the Hospital gates towards the Rambles. Behind the coffin every official group that had ever enjoyed Gaudí's membership and support sent delegates: professional bodies like the Asosiació de Arquitectos de Catalunya; cultural groups like the Orfeó Català, the *Excurcionistas*, the *Ateneu* and the Cercle Artístic de Sant Lluc; religious bodies from the Sagrada *Junta* to Barcelona's bishop, churchmen from Reus, Montserrat and Tarragona, and representatives from those associations that had sprung up to drive through liturgical reform, like the Lliga Espiritual de la Mare de Déu de Montserrat and the Amics de l'Art Litúrgic; politicians from Reus, Riudoms, Barcelona's city council and the recently abolished Mancomunitat; and, of course, members from all the workers' guilds whose handicrafts Gaudí's architecture had helped to popularise and sustain against relentless mechanisation. It was the nearest approximation to a Catalan state funeral. There was a popular element to the tributes that spoke eloquently of Gaudí's universal appeal. As the cortège entered the carrer Carmen hundreds of singers from the Orfeó Català sang psalms. As the procession wound its way through the *Barri Gotic* into the Plaça Sant Jaume and past the cathedral, hundreds of thousands of mourners lined the streets. As the cortège entered the Plaça de Catalunya the broad sweep of the Portal del Àngel was filled with a sea of faces, fifty deep in places, and as far as the eye could see. On reaching the Sagrada Família, and as the coffin was taken slowly down into the crypt, the Orfeó accompanied the journey's last leg with the moving responsory '*Libera Me*', from Tomas Luis de Victoria's *Mass for the Dead* – Philip II's favourite composer. It was a perfect ending to an extraordinarily creative and religiously charged life.

The response of the Catalan press was immediate. Alongside the eulogies, obituaries and poems came reminiscences from old colleagues and friends. News of his death filled all the front pages and old rivalries and architectural battles slipped discreetly into the past. There was no more talk of social divisiveness or of the decadence of the *modernista* style. Gaudí's favourite newspaper *La Veu de Catalunya* set the tone: 'In Barcelona a genius has died! In Barcelona a saint has passed away! Even the stones cry for him.'[32] Lauded not just for his architectural brilliance but also for his saintly virtues, within a few days his reputation had passed into myth. Many eulogies concluded that Gaudí's life of suffering had been further purified in the crucible of death.[33]

The full symbolic meaning of the manner of his death was deliberated over. Obituaries pointed out the irony that tramline 30 was known by the people as 'the Red Cross'. Attention was drawn to the fact that it was God's will to deliver Gaudí – due to the laziness of the stretcher-bearers – to the architect's favourite hospital Santa Creus – the church of the Holy Cross.[34] Divine providence had obviously played its hand. He had died on the anniversary of the death of that other great Catalan figure Jacint Verdaguer. How fortunate, some argued, that the Catalan homeland be nurtured by the deaths on the very same day of such an illustrious pair.

For Ràfols, Gaudí's first biographer, a deep abyss divided Gaudí from the common man. Most agreed with him that Gaudí represented the 'exemplary Christian' – living in poverty and enduring the cathartic properties of suffering and pain.[35] But without faith Gaudí's work would have remained meaningless for Ràfols. Others went further: seeing him as nothing less than 'God's intermediary' creating a gigantic poem in stone in our world.[36] A Catholic broadsheet, *La Paraula Cristiana*, likened him to St Thomas Aquinas and St Francis of Assisi, recognising his enduring inspiration to the Catalan Catholic Revival.

Beneath Gaudí's dishevelled (but Franciscan) appearance lay the peerless architect-creator. Suddenly there was complete unanimity about Gaudí's originality and his genius for discovering new forms. He was, according to Andrea Escuder (predating Josep Pla), to architecture what Ramón Llull had been to the written word. Llorenç Riber, who had met Gaudí frequently while he was working on La Seu in Mallorca, described him as a Titan and Charlemagne. Riber particularly emphasised Gaudí's piercing blue eyes that 'gave the impression of a deep and mysterious sea'.[37] Very few of the obituaries concentrated on the quality of Gaudí's work, his engineering genius or structural analysis. Instead they focussed almost exclusively on his spirituality. If buildings were mentioned, it was almost always the Sagrada Família that held centre stage. The expiatory temple had, as Maragall predicted, embedded itself firmly and forever into the Catalan collective psyche. Within days of Gaudí's death the foundations had been laid for all future interpretation of him as an exemplary architect-saint.

Gaudí's epitaph is written in brick and stone. David Mackay, the architectural historian, has concluded that

> His abundant imagination, private wit and public self-confidence finally became mortgaged to a consuming and reactionary religiosity that grew up around him through his work on the Sagrada Familia temple. He misread his brief, and it destroyed him. His architecture became subjected to a religion of symbols.[38]

Led up an artistic cul-de-sac by Torras i Bages he becomes the victim of overambition and a fatal incapacity ultimately to understand the human scale.

The sheer number of mourners that lined the streets from the Hospital de Santa Cruz to the Sagrada Família suggests otherwise. And the millions who still make the pilgrimage to Barcelona would certainly disagree. But the decorative delights that lie on the surface of Gaudí's work may be deliberately misleading. Juan José Lahuerta stresses emphatically the overwhelming pessimism that paradoxically he sees just under the seductive surface of his buildings.

> The Sagrada Família is more than a church, more than a shrine: it is a mountain that grows and grows by alluvion, accumulating mire kneaded with blood that, in the words of Maragall, have made the streets of Barcelona. But it is not only the Sagrada Família: the entire work of Gaudí is raised upon an evil spirit, on Hell![39]

This is too harsh. Gaudí's ambition may well have been Olympian, his attempt to rebuild a more perfect imitation of Catalan nature, as in the Casa Milà, a further example of boundless vanity. But the sheer depth and resonance of his work makes it the architectural equivalent of Wagner's highly charged *Ring Cycle*.

Some have seen Gaudí's work as prophetic. Josep Subirachs, the sculptor, who has worked over the last few decades on the decoration of the Sagrada Família's Passion façade, thinks so. Concerned that we are once again slipping back into another Dark Age, Subirachs has written:

> If that is true, and the signs appear to bear it out – the resurgence of Islam; the great plagues: AIDS and cancer; the simultaneous devolution to local authorities and the great ideological blocks; the new form of piracy that is terrorism and the re-emergence of esoterical practices – Gaudí will have been, as he was in so many fields, a prophet when he said: 'The Sagrada Família is not the last of the cathedrals, but the first in a new age.'[40]

To counter Subirachs' millennial tone, a major aspect of Gaudí's genius – whether planned or not – was his work's sheer open-ended exuberance and generosity. Complex structures and meanings lay hidden behind an explosion of textures and colours and

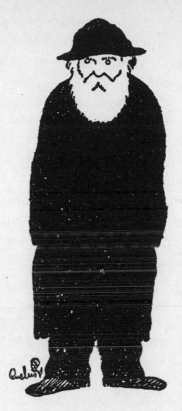

Quelus' portrait of Gaudí in his final years.

seductive design. Yet no other architect in history has given us
so much pleasure and joy.

The most fitting tribute to Gaudí's architectural and sculptural
genius comes from the architect many see as the heir to Gaudí's
unique gift for the finding of significant form, the Valencian
architect Santiago Calatrava.

> People have tried to understand Gaudí in terms of pagan-
> ism, Freemasonry, Buddhism or atheism. I think that he
> was indeed a man who served a religious idea. But that
> the God, or rather, the Goddess that Gaudí venerated
> was architecture herself.

269

But Gaudí's legacy in terms of the strict canon of architecture is still far from clear. He had some followers but created no global new style. If Gaudí's ambition was to rethink the whole language of architecture, it was an impossible one. From the early graffiti on Mataro's walls, Gaudí progressed relentlessly through the history of styles; from Moorish pastiche, through Rococo and the Baroque; through Victorian engineering to the sophisticated simplicity of a peasant's mud hut. What Gaudí strove for – in vain – was universality.

Looking at Gehry's Guggenheim – heavily influenced by Gaudí's fluid use of space – we see just how far ahead of his time Gaudí was. It is only now that we are discovering his genius' full potential at work. As the Sagrada Família rises we are forced to recognise that his popularity and reputation still grows. Our focus, however, on this most polemical work deflects our attention from the sheer extent of his achievement.

For he produced with the Casa Milà and the Colonia Güell two of the greatest buildings ever built; buildings which could be enjoyed by Christian and atheist alike.

Gaudí's own preferred epitaph was far more modest: the simple repetition of the words of the Magi on seeing the star: '*Fa Goig!*' – It gives me joy!

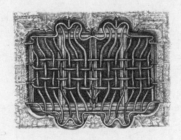

I am an old man, poor and ridiculed,
No man that is born will help me
and I have taken on too great a task.
I have sought a vast project in this world
and given many a good example:
I am unloved and unknown.

*Ramón Llull,* Cant de Roman

# NOTES

## Introduction

1. Menéndez Pidal, R. & Starkie, W., *The Spaniards in Their History*, Hollis & Carter, London 1950. Essay 'Material and Moral Austerity', p. 135.
2. Roger Fry wrote: 'I only saw its megatherian skeleton from the train, looking by now rather dirty and disconsolate, rather more of a ruin, and rather less of a building, than before.' Fry, R., *A Sampler of Castile*, 1923.
3. Translation from Sobrer, Josep Miguel, *Catalonia, a Self-Portrait*, Indiana University Press, Bloomington and Indianapolis, USA 1992.
4. Orwell, G., *Homage to Catalonia*, London 1938.
5. Gropius, W., quoted in *El Propogador de la Devoción a San José* vol. LXVI, Barcelona, 1 June 1932.
6. Louis Sullivan quoted T. E. Tallmadge in *Western Architect* vol. XXI, March 1922.
7. Finsterlin, H., *Gaudí und ich*, a monologue for the 'Amigos de Gaudí', Barcelona 1967.
8. Schapiro, M., *Romanesque Art*, Chatto & Windus, London 1977, p. 3.
9. Guerrand, Roger-Henri, in Russell, *Art Nouveau Architecture*, Academy Editions, London 1979, p. 10.
10. Benton, T. in *Art Nouveau Architecture*, p. 51.

11. Ortega y Gasset, J., *Invertebrate Spain*, George Allen & Unwin, London 1937, p. 72.
12. Ibid., p. 156.
13. See *Joan Rubió i Bellver y la Fortuna del gaudinismo*, Ignasi Solà-Morales Publ., Colegio Oficial de Arquitectos de Cataluña, Barcelona 1975.
14. The real extent has only recently come to light with the 1990 publication of *El Gran Gaudí* by Professor Juan Bassegoda i Nonell that covers fifty years of painstaking detective work.
15. Molema, J., essay collection.

## 'People of Space and Circumstance'

1. Antoni Gaudí, 13 December 1924 from Martinell, C., *Gaudí: His Life, His Theories, His Work*, Editorial Blume, Barcelona 1951, p. 134.
2. Ortega y Gasset, J., *Invertebrate Spain*, p. 111.
3. The plaque was placed on the façade of the Mas de la Calderera on 23 June 1952 by the Ayuntamiento de Riudoms to celebrate the centenary of Gaudí's birth. A mass was celebrated to pray for the safe and speedy passage of Gaudí's soul on its journey through purgatory.
4. An extensive genealogical tree for Antoni Gaudí, researched and drawn up by José María Armengol

Viver, was first published in an article entitled *'La gènesi de Gaudí'*, on the eve of the Spanish Civil War, on 21 June 1936, in the Sunday supplement of the *El Matí* newspaper in Barcelona. It is reproduced in Bergós Massó, J., *Gaudí, el hombre y la obra*, p. 19.

5. Antoni Gaudí on 13 December 1924, quoted in Martinell 1951, p. 134.

6. Bassegoda i Nonell, J., *El Gran Gaudí*, Editorial Ausa, Barcelona 1992, p. 17.

7. It is almost possible to speak of a Reus-led renaissance in the arts at the end of the nineteenth century.

8. Matamala, J., *Mi Itinerario con Gaudí*, Unedited manuscript, Catedra Gaudí.

9. Eduardo Toda, bibliophile, diplomat and Gaudí's lifelong friend, bought Escornalbou, a one-time home of the Franciscans, but disbanded in 1835, which he restored between 1910 and 1925. He will be discussed in greater detail further on in this chapter.

10. The two villas known as Planes and Timba.

11. This is repeated so often by biographers that it is assumed that Gaudí himself would not miss the opportunity to reiterate this 'truism'. However, the MOMA New York curator James Johnson Sweeney, in Sweeney, J. J. & Sert, J. L., *Antoni Gaudí*, The Architectural Press, London 1960, p. 55, claims that it was Lluís Bonet i Garí, one of Gaudí's assistants, who suggested that it was the example of Gaudí's father which lay behind the architect's preference for working from models rather than plans and elevations. Regardless of these academic arguments, it is very easy to imagine Gaudí introducing his aged father to strangers, as much out of courtesy as respect, as the person who taught him most about thinking in three dimensions. It has the same ring to it as when Ben Nicholson, the English abstract painter, allegedly claimed that he learnt more about the placement of colours from playing billiards than he did from the whole history of art.

12. Bassegoda i Nonell, J., *L'Estudi de Gaudí*, seleccío d'articles publicats a la revista Temple. entre 1971–1994 Ed. Temple Expiatori de la Sagrada Família, Barcelona, 1996, p. 14.

13. Toda Güell, E., *Records d'Antoni Gaudí a Reus abans de 1870*, *El Matí* supplement, 21 June 1936.

14. Matamala, p. 12.

15. In 1992 I visited the privately owned *modernista* palace, the Casa Navas, built by Domènech i Muntaner, in the centre of Reus. Up in the attic, alongside Domènech's bomb-damaged lantern from the Spanish Civil War, I was shocked to find a collection of original Art Nouveau furniture in a poor state of repair littering the space: Mackintosh, Thonet etc. The gracious owner, on discovering that I was Dutch, opened up a desk which contained original bills of sale dating back to the eighteenth century that testified to a considerable trade directly with the legendary Amsterdam merchants of the Herengracht.

16. Reus had witnessed some of the worst confrontations in the Carlist wars. Remembered in local folklore was the assassination on 22 July 1834 of twenty-two priests in revenge for the killing of seven of the Reus militia by Carlist guerrillas.

17. Fortuny was the favourite subject of the small magazines *Foment* and *Avui*, and endlessly discussed in the debates, lectures and *tertulias* at

the cultural club based at the Centre de Lectura.

18. Collins, G. & Bassegoda i Nonell, J., *The Designs and Drawings of Antoni Gaudí*, Princeton University Press 1983, pp. 25–6.
19. Between Reus and Tarragona the small village of Constanti also boasted a Roman mausoleum and a villa whose mosaic complex, hidden at the time behind the workings of a *masia*, was discovered in 1877 while Gaudí was finishing off his architectural studies in Barcelona.
20. From Maragall, *Proses y Reculls*.
21. Casanelles, E., *Nueva visión de Gaudí*, La Poligrafa, Barcelona 1965. English edition 1967, p. 16.
22. Bassegoda i Nonell, J., *El Gran Gaudí*, p. 31.

## Voices in the Desert

1. 'Voices in the desert' was the title of an early article describing Gaudí and Toda's work at Poblet by Jorge Miranda, the pseudonym of the priest Mossèn Barrera. *El Correo Catalán*, 1 October 1926.
2. Martinell, p. 23.
3. Gaudí memorandum 17 July 1878 from '*Candelabro: apuntes descriptivos del proyecto de candelabro de grupo para plazas y paseos de la cuidad de Barcelona.*'
4. Martinell, p. 29.
5. In an 1870 letter to Toda, Gaudí admonished his younger friend, 'Don't do as you did with the paintings of Goya where you neither described them nor gave me your opinion.'
6. In *La Razón*.
7. Translated by author from Bassegoda i Nonell, J., *El Gran Gaudí*, p. 39.

## City of Marvels

1. Vicèns Vivès, J., '*Los Catalanes en el siglo XIX*' translation from Fernández-Armesto, F., *Barcelona – A Thousand Years of the City's Past*, OUP 1992, p. 151.
2. In his first year at the Escalopians in 1863 he had failed practical arithmetic and its principles outright. By 1867, as we have seen, his Mathematics was *notable* – excellent.
3. Hare, Augustus, *Wanderings in Spain*, London 1873.
4. Kahn, Albert E., *Joys and Sorrows – Reflections by Pablo Casals*, Macdonald, London 1970.
5. The papers for October 1869 cite Patricio Barnusell, living at the same address, and possibly the landlord, as Gaudí's sponsor. His brother, Francisco, had just passed his eighteenth year. At the next three lodgings, spread out over four years, his brother acted as sponsor. And, if we accept Toda and Matamala's assertion that Gaudí had to wait a year for lack of money, we can safely assume that for reasons of economy and fraternal affection they lived together.
6. Designed and executed by Fontsère it is suggested by Bassegoda that the student Gaudí may have had a hand in some of the detailing.
7. Milá, E., *El Misterio Gaudí*, Editorial Martínez Roca, Enigmas de la Historia, Barcelona 1994, pp. 28–36.
8. Martinell, p. 31.
9. Commentators have reported this incident in reference to Gaudí's admiration for the writings of Viollet-le-Duc – the 'lighthouse' of the nineteenth century. But it is sure to have come down to posterity as a result of Emilio's irritation at having had one of his

GAUDÍ

own books scribbled over by a
friend and fellow student.

10. In 1879 he also designed an
*Ad Honorem* float for the
Excurcionistas to celebrate the
250th anniversary of the death of
the famous seventeenth-century
baroque poet Mossèn Francesc
García – who was rector of the spa
town Vallfogona de Riucorb, just
five kilometres from Gaudí's own
ancestral village of Santa Coloma
de Queralt – who had been
responsible in 1617 for the
building of the Capella de Santa
Bàrbara. Fitting into the tradition
of the mobile pilgrimage shrines,
still in use in Spain today, Gaudí
pulled together the decorative
ensemble with an overabundant
cornucopia of harvest produce
hanging in swags off the structure
of a modest gypsy cart.

11. Matamala, pp. 36–7.

12. McDonogh, G., *Good Families*.

13. See Elias, J. for discussions of
Domènech. When Gaudí qualified
as architect there was only one
vote cast against him out of Villar,
Serralach, Fontserè, Vilaseca, Font,
Rogent and Domènech. The
voting is not known. Gaudí had
worked with all but Domènech.
Did Domènech see Gaudí as a
potential rival? Gaudí, while still a
student, had entered a competition
for the Clavé monument against
Domènech.

14. Martinell, p. 39.

15. Casanelles, p. 28.

16. These included the Bassegoda
brothers, and the dynasty of
Domènech i Muntaner and his
cousins Domènech Estapà,
Domènech Mansana and his son
Domènech Roura. There were
other masters like Pere Falqués,
Font, Fontserè, Jujol, Muncunill,
Puig i Cadafalch, Rogent, Rubió,
Sagnier, Vilaseca and Gaudí
himself, amongst twenty more.

17. Pabon i Charneco 'el valor de
l'ensenyança es purament de
disciplina, de modo que'l criteri
dels profesors es de major ó menor
dels dexeibles, pero no de llur
capacitat.' pp. 2–3.

18. According to Gaudí himself.

19. Ràfols, *Antoni Gaudí*. Ed. Conosa,
Barcelona 1929, p. 24.

20. Viollet-le-Duc admired Cost who
had alerted him to the beauty of
Islamic architecture; indeed, he
contributed introductory essays to
Jules Bourgoin's *Arts Arabes*, Paris
1873 and Léon Parvilées
*Architecture et Décoration Turques au
XVe Siècle*, Paris 1874.

21. By the time of the 1889 Paris
Exhibition Charles Garnier was
inspired by Viollet-le-Duc's
encyclopaedic *Histoire de Habitation
Humaine* of 1875, to create a
model for every building type
known to man. Down the length
of the Champ de Mars conflicting
styles from Tibet, Egypt and
Timbuktu sat cheek by jowl with
Mexican, Maori and Moroccan.

22. Gaudí attended lectures by Rubió i
Ors and Milá i Fontanals on
aesthetics and he followed a series
on history and philosophy by the
eminent critic Xavier Llorens y
Barba.

23. First in lecture series delivered to
the Ecole des Beaux Arts after his
appointment in November 1863,
against fierce opposition, as
professor of art and aesthetics.
Translation by Michael Keyte in
*Eugène Emmanuel Viollet-Le-Duc
1814–1879*, Architectural Design
Profile, Academy Editions, London
1980, pp. 20–25.

24. It is ironic that Viollet-le-Duc's
*Dictionnaire raisonné* and his
lecture series *Entretiens sur
l'architecture* were later used as
pattern books, and some of his
illustrations, in particular, have
been directly related to specific

works of Gaudí.

25. G. E. Street, a 'hard', whose Law Courts 1874–82 were the last great public buildings in the Gothic style, perhaps instinctively grasped this national tendency in his book, an architectural homage entitled *Gothic Architecture in Spain*.

26. Jaume Fabré buildings at Mallorca and Barcelona, or Guillerm Bofill's work at Gerona in the fifteenth century placed the Catalan builders amongst the most innovative and daring in Europe. Unlike other regions in Spain, Catalonia had kept up with north Europe and taken readily to the Pre-Raphaelite style. It was telling that Verdaguer, Catalonia's most famous poet, had used an illustration by Dante Gabriel Rossetti to illustrate his *Cants Mistics*.

27. For a detailed study of Rogent and the Architectural School see Pere Hereu, *'La Idea d'Arquitectura a l'Escola que Gaudí Conegué'*, in *Gaudí i el seu temps*, Barcanova, Barcelona 1990, pp. 13–42.

28. Ràfols, J., p. 22.

29. Martinell, p. 49.

30. Translated by author from Calaverada–Maragall collected works.

31. Matamala, p. 50. Carcasonne is added in pen, over another previous destination now blanked out. Matamala agreed with Maragall and stated that the Carcassonne trip was Gaudí's opportunity to finally catch up with his lost love.

32. Bergós Massó, J., *Gaudí, el hombre y la obra*, Universidad Politécnica de Barcelona 1974 edition, p. 23.

33. Pabon i Charneco, A., 'The Architectural Collaborators of Antoni Gaudí', unpublished Ph.D. Thesis Northwestern University, USA 1983, p. 3.

34. Bassegoda i Nonell, J., *El Gran Gaudí*, p. 59.

## The Architectural Apprentice

1. Martinell, p. 36.

2. Projects included a sixty volume *Biblioteca Arte y Letras*, including Horace's *Odes* and a collection of one-act *sainetes* by the eighteenth-century dramatist Ramón de la Cruz; while also designing mastheads for the newspapers *La Renaixença*, *La Veu de Catalunya* and *El Poble Català* and writing in his spare time three of the eight volumes of the epic *Historia General de Arte*. Later, faithful to his deep belief that the architect's role and responsibility was to construct society as a whole, he became one of Catalonia's leading politicians. Domènech played a central role in drawing up the celebrated *Bases de Manresa*, one of Catalonia's first attempts to codify its nationalist ambition; was one of four parliamentary members of the Cortes representing Barcelona; served as president of the political parties the Lliga de Catalunya and the Unió Catalanista; in addition to acting as president of the *Jocs Florals* and the Ateneu Barcelonès, which he served as president an unprecedented four times.

3. In the 28 February 1878 issue of *La Renaiçensa*.

4. Translated from Fernández-Armesto, F., *Barcelona*, p. 147.

5. The entry in Gaudí's diary for 4 January 1877 recorded his attendance at a celebration dinner in honour of the recently qualified architects, among them Joan Martorell i Montells, who had received his licence at the relatively late age of forty-four. Although this is the first record of their meeting they must have known each other almost from Gaudí's first day at the school. Gaudí would later join Martorell's

studio where he would work alongside Cascante and Oliveras.

6. Kent, C., and Prindle, D., *Park Güell*, Princeton Architectural Press 1993, p. 72.

7. Pagès was a self-made man who had made a fortune in New York before returning to Mataro. *Gaudí La Vida d'un Visionari*, Castellar-Gassol, J., Edicions de 1984, Barcelona 1999, p. 53. Gaudí may also have come across Pagès via the 1876 Philadelphia Centennial where Pagès had a display. *L'Estudi de Gaudí*, Joan Bassegoda in Nonell seleccío d'articles publicats a la revista Temple entre 1971–1994 Ed. Temple Expiatori de la Sagrada Família, Barcelona 1996, p. 39.

8. It predated Behren's work at AEG and the work of the Bauhaus by two decades.

9. Martinell, p. 48.

10. Castellar-Gassol, p. 67.

11. He would often read the writings of Luis de León, Luis de Granada, Saint Teresa and St John of the Cross.

12. *La Pedrera: Gaudí and his work*, Fundació Caixa Catalunya, p. 23.

13. The best record of the *Excurcionistas* is in the *Butletti* – the club magazine. Of great interest is *Associació d'Excursions Catalana 1878–1891* by Maria de l'Assumpció Saurí i Pujol, Tesi de Llicenciatura: Univ. Barcelona September 85.

14. On 1 February 1880, Don Eusebi Güell i Bacigalupi was first welcomed as a member – just one of many new recruits. Other members of the *gent de bé*, the Golferichs, Batllo's, Calvet's, the Marquès de Dou and the Comte de Bell-lloch, and other sponsors of the new architecture, were prepared to join other commoners in the Asociació Catalanista d'Excursions Cientiíficas.

15. Iglesias, J., *Presencia de L'Excursionisme en la Cultura Catalana*, Ed. Fundació Carulla i Font.

16. In 1879, Valentí Almirall founded the Catalan daily *El Diari Català*, which lasted just two years, and the next year organised the first Catalanist Congress in an attempt to safeguard Catalan civic law through collaboration.

17. Bassegoda i Nonell, J., *L'Estudi de Gaudí*, p. 60.

18. On 20–21 November 1880, Gaudí joined another fifteen *Excurcionistas* on a two-day trip to Vilafranca in the Alt Penedès and Olesa de Bonesvalls in the neighbouring *comarca* of Garraf.

19. Martinell, p. 49.

20. Bassegoda i Nonell, J., *L'Estudi de Gaudí*, p. 294.

## Views of Heaven and the Harem

1. Casanelles, p. 109.

2. Pla, translated Sobrer.

3. Within three years of its foundation the Asociación Espiritual received official Vatican support when Pius IX permitted it to collect funds, half of which in return for this *imprimatur* found their way back to fill the coffers in Rome. It attracted widespread support: 572,000 medallions were disseminated, 392,000 certificates sold, and at Father Rodríquez's urging Bocabella's 15,000 print run of the pamphlet *Los siete domingos de san José* – the Devotion of the Seven Sundays, was quickly sold out.

4. Bassegoda i Nonell, J., *El Gran Gaudí*, pp. 210–12.

5. With the problem resolved to the *Junta* and Gaudí's satisfaction Villar soon changed his tactics. Despite ample written evidence to

the contrary, including sworn affidavits witnessed by a notary and an article in *El Propogador*, thanking him for his generous offer which he himself insisted should be published, Villar denied that he had ever offered his services for free. On the afternoon of 23 April 1884 while Bocabella was walking down the carrer Santa Anna he was subjected to threats and insults from an irate Villar who was still claiming the back pay of all his honoraria.

6. Considering its specialist subject matter and dubious editorial merits, it has shown extraordinary resilience and is still published today under the Catalan title *Temple*. Josep Pla has suggested a brief acquaintance might suffice. 'Take a look – I would not dare ask for more – at the volumes of *El Propagador de la Devoción de San José*. You will find, taking the inevitable tone of the times into consideration, one of the vastest and most important concentrations of inanities, of clichés, and apologetic trash this country has ever produced!'

7. Bocabella and his allies, the Fathers José María Rodríguez, his spiritual counsellor, and José Mañanet Vives must have been highly persuasive. Within a decade subscriptions had risen from an initial two hundred to many thousands. See Quintana, A., *Tres Grandes para un gran templo: Manyanet, Bocabella, Gaudí*, Ed. Hijos de la Sagrada Familia, Barcelona 1985.

8. Ruskin's writings were popularised through the translations of Cebrià de Montoliu in his magazine *Civitas* and the journal *Catalunya*.

9. Between 1902 and 1905 the gaunt bearded wizard of the Generation of '98, Ramón María del Valle-Inclán introduced to his reading public the inimitable Marquès de Bradomín, an aesthete, versed in the erotic arts, who like Huysmans was sufficiently religious to derive a perverse joy from profanity. For a further discussion see Herrera, J., *Picasso, Madrid y El 98: La Revista 'Arte Joven'*, Ed. Cátedra, Madrid 1997, pp. 64–5.

10. A Spanish version, the fashionably anticlerical Antonio Bustamente, the Marquès de Soler, togged up in white gloves and dressed *à la* Duc de Morny, was a neighbour of the Marquès de Comillas and a welcome guest at the Güells'. Renowned for his *'picara imaginación'* and his appearance of a stretched-out Don Quixote he was like so many decadents 'lascivious in word but pure in life'.

11. Pabon i Charneco, A., 'The Architectural Collaborators of Antoni Gaudí' unpublished Ph.D. Thesis, Northwestern University, USA 1983, p. 62.

12. Dijkstra, p. 206.

13. Tarrago, S.,

14. Gaudí, as so many of his generation, had a great interest in decorative tiles. It is recorded, although the exact date is unknown, that Gaudí made a visit to the tile centre of Manises, near Valencia, in order to research this craft. It is possible that these researches coincided with the Casa Vicens. See further Bassegoda i Nonell, J., p. 108.

15. It is very reminiscent of the walled garden complex of a 'Carmen' in Granada and makes one think of the Baroque poet Pedro Soto de Rojas' couplet *'Paraiso cerrado para muchos jardines abiertos para pocos'* – Paradise closed to many, gardens open to a few.

16. The house itself was twice altered since its original design, once in Gaudí's lifetime, in 1925 by Juan

Bautista Serra de Martínez, a reworking which Gaudí grudgingly approved, and once again in 1964 when the tribune windows were altered. There is, however, enough of the original left to get an authentic feel for Gaudí's decorative concept.

17. In the 1850s the folly-park of the Laberint de Horta had the main house completely revamped in the neo-Mudejar style. Along the Passeig de Gràcia, the master builder Domenec Bale i Nadal had completed the five-storey Casa Pere Llibre in 1872 in a neo-Mudejar style. In Madrid, too, the legendary Las Ventas bullring, designed by Rodriguez Ayuso and Alvarez Capra, was finished in 1874. Ángel Isac in *Gaudí i el seu temps*, Ed. Institut d'Humanitats Barcanova, Barcelona 1990, p. 51, draws attention to a lecture by José Amador de los Ríos as early as 1859 entitled '*El estilo mudéjar en arquitectura*', given in San Fernando de Bellas Artes in Madrid.

18. Built by the Norfolk-based fine art wrought-iron company of Barnard, Bishop and Barnard, it can't help but have caught Gaudí's eye.

19. The 1857 lecture to Architectural Association at the Lyon's Inn Hall.

20. Martinell, p. 475.

21. Designed by Rafael Contreras, the restorer of the Alhambra, the work was completed by 1850. Casa Vicens represents Gaudí's first response to a royal model.

22. Similar moulds were sent in 1876 to the Philadelphia Centennial as the Escuela de Arquitectura's contribution to the Spanish pavilion.

23. It was supplied by the manufacturer Hermenegildo Miralles Anglés.

24. Ganivet, A., *Idearium*, p. 70.

25. Bassegoda i Nonell, J., *El Gran Gaudí*, p. 247.

## The Holy Fathers

1. Martinell, pp. 53–4.
2. Menéndez Pidal, p. 178.
3. Matamala, p. 89.
4. Lahuerta, J. J., *Antoni Gaudí 1852–1926 Arquitectura, ideologia y politica*, Ediciones Electa, Spain 1993. In this groundbreaking study Lahuerta carefully analyses Güell's orchestrated rise to pre-eminence. Often citing the findings of the French sociologist Pierre Bourdieu, Lahuerta tracks the way in which art and culture was appropriated by the Comillas and the Güells to create for themselves an ideal genealogy.
5. *El Palau Güell*, coll. essays ed. Jaume de Puig, Publ. Diputacío de Barcelona, Barcelona 1990, p. 14.
6. To be seen at Toledo's Puerta del Cambron and in many other fragments housed in the Visigothic Museum of San Roman in Toledo.
7. This is reminiscent of the Mudejar '*esgrafiado*' technique seen in Castilian buildings like Segovia's Torre d'Avila, a photo of which Gaudí studied.
8. Les Corts' exclusive tranquillity was best indicated by Verdaguer who had nicknamed it the Torre Satalia, after a famously luxuriant citrus grove in Asia Minor that was like a paradise on earth.
9. Bassegoda i Nonell, J., *L'Estudi de Gaudí*, p. 105. The Palau Güell was built on a site that consisted of a dairy and the cramped, insanitary dwellings of no less than seventeen families.
10. Richardson, J., *Picasso*, p. 67.
11. Some have seen it therefore as a direct homage to Eusebi Güell's Italian inheritance through his

mother, a Bacigalupi from Genoa.

12. In *El Palau Güell*, Ed. Jaume de Puig, Publ. Diputacío de Barcelona, Barcelona 1990 p. 19 he talks of the Palau Güell as an '*edificio belligerant*'.

13. Pabon i Charneco, p. 386.

14. Trans. Casanelles.

15. Other literary allusions were to be found in the stained-glass windows by Alexandre de Riquer who depicted King Lear and Bertram from *All's Well that Ends Well*.

16. Gaudí and Clapés were both anachronisms. Clapés' style, in particular, had more in common with the dark spiritual canvases of the sixteenth-century painter Luis de Morales, 'El Divino', and that of the seventeenth-century artist Fray Juan Rizi, a Benedictine monk at Montserrat, than it shared with the artists of his own day. Rizi was, like Gaudí, a vegetarian who favoured sleeping with his windows open all year round.

17. Brown, J., and Elliott, J. H., *A Palace for a King: The Buen Retiro and the Court of Philip IV*, Yale University Press 1980.

18. See Lahuerta.

19. Ràfols, p. 62.

20. The design of the basement in the Palau Güell has been linked to the crypt in the monastery church at Sant Cugat, deriving much of its underworld symbolic content from this analogy.

21. Mendoza, Cristina and Eduardo, *Barcelona Modernista*, Planeta, Barcelona 1991, p. 74.

22. Ràfols, p. 62.

23. *Gaudí en Astorga*, Maria Jesus Alonso Gavela Publ., Instituto Fray Bernardino de Sahagún, Leon 1971, p. 35.

24. Martinell, p. 60.

25. Luego, A., *A Gaudí en Astorga*, 1954, pp. 17–18, trans. Martinell.

26. Pijoan, J., *La Veu de Catalunya*, 20 January 1906, trans. Martinell, C., p. 62.

27. It is also highly likely that Gaudí's insistence on using Catalan builders upset the locals.

28. *Gaudí en Astorga*, p. 49.

29. Born to *converso* parents, St Teresa was perhaps unusually receptive to concepts derived from other faiths. In Islam, paradise is also organised in seven different levels. The number seven also had profound symbolic significance in Golden Age garden design. The poet Pedro Soto de Rojas had created his seventeenth-century paradise, a Carmen, in Granada's Albaicin which consisted of seven open-air rooms – mansions, clearly quoting St Teresa's inspirational book. See Andrés Soria Olmedo, *Paraíso cerrado para muchos, jardines abiertos para pocos* in *Jardines y Paisajes en el Arte y en la Historia*, Cursos de Verano de El Escorial 1993–4 Ed. Complutense, Madrid 1995, p. 251 for a more in depth discussion.

30. Garraf was given to Berenguer by David Mackay. It is interesting that Mackay, in his passionate resurrection of Berenguer's reputation, also gives two works in the Colònia Güell to Berenguer: the director's house and the Cooperativa. In *Joan Rubió i Bellver y la fortuna del gaudinismo*, Ignasi Solà-Morales Rubió, Publ. Colegio de Arquitectos de Cataluña, Barcelona 1975, p. 40 the author attributes these works almost entirely to Rubió.

31. Carner, A., *La Verdad sobre la Vida y la Tragedia de Verdaguer*, Editorial Gea, Barcelona 1971.

32. In the mid-1890s Dr Charcot had been working in Paris on the psychological confusion between hysteria and demon possession. In Vienna Sigmund Freud's surgery couch was kept warm with a train of hysterical and sexually repressed

middle-class women.

33. Verdaguer's 'breakdown' and consequent illness has been well covered, in Delfí Abelle, *Mossen Cinto vist pel Psiquiatre 1958* and R. Nolle Panades, *La Tuberculosis Pulmonar de Mossen Jacinto Verdaguer.*

34. *1893–1993 Cercle Artístic de Sant Lluc*, Exhibition catalogue, Departement de Cultura Generalitat de Catalunya, Barcelona 1993. Another invaluable source is: Jardi, Enric, *Cercle artistic de Sant Lluc.*

35. Richardson, p. 62.

36. The drawing in the Museu Picasso is catalogued MPB 110.472.

37. In Picasso's first ever one-man show at the Quatre Gats, in direct competition with the graphic brilliance of Ramón Casas, he set about caricaturing all of the most important members of Barcelona's artistic community. All that is, except for Gaudí, and some other less important members of the pious Sant Llucs.

38. Collins, G. R., *Antonio Gaudí*, Masters of World Architecture, George Braziller, New York 1960, p. 8.

39. See *Picasso and Els Quatre Gats: The key to modernity* ed. Maria Teresa Ocaña, Exhibition catalogue Museu Picasso, Editores Lunwerg, Barcelona 1995.

## Towards a New Jerusalem

1. In 1845 the New York newspaperman John O'Sullivan had written that it was 'the fulfilment of our manifest destiny to overspread the continent alloted by Providence for the free development of our yearly expanding millions'. By mid-century the West had been won.

2. Wood, M., 'Don't tell nobody', *London Review of Books* Vol. 20, No. 17, 3 September 1998, p. 16.

3. Latest scholarship suggests that the Spanish did not sink the *Maine* but that there was an explosion in the engine room.

4. Pabón i Charneco, A., p. 82.

5. Ibid.

6. One of the sons, Eduardo Calvet, economist and politician, in his position as president of the Fomento del Trabajo Nacional would later introduce Gaudí to possible future clients.

7. Martinell, p. 309.

8. Bassegoda i Nonell, J., *El Gran Gaudí*, p. 357.

9. Rogent Pedrosa, F., *Arquitectura moderna de Barcelona*, Parera y Cia, Barcelona, p. 10.

10. Marfany, J. L., '*Gaudí i el Modernismo*' in essay collection *Gaudí i el seu temps*, ed. Juan José Lahuerta, Ed. Barcanova and Institut d'Humanitats, Barcelona 1990, pp. 86–7.

11. Henri-Guerrand, R., *Art Nouveau Archiecture*

12. Zerbst, R., *Antoni Gaudí*, Taschen Verlag, Köln 1993, p. 98.

13. Ràfols, p. 141, trans. from Collins, *The Drawings*, p. 42.

14. Glick, T. F., *From Muslim Fortress to Christian Castle*, Manchester University Press 1995.

15. Guimard's Castell Henriette 1899–1900 at Sèvres mixed a half-timbered romanticised northern vernacular with military motifs.

16. It comes as no surprise to discover that Gaudí's placement of Bellesguard's deliberate geographical layout has direct reference to the polar axis and that the stairwell windows and their stained glass depicting the stars and the heavens hint at further Christian and esoteric meanings.

17. In the same year Gaudí designed

for his fellow Rueseños, resident in Barcelona, a standard dedicated to the Virgin of the Misericordia, with additions by Clapés who executed the relevant biblical scenes.

18. The story has been wrongly attributed to two other houses built by Gaudí for other clients completed during the same decade: the Casa Batlló and the Casa Milà. None of these houses, designed by Gaudí, enjoyed the luxury of a functional straight wall. Taking into account floor plans, door widths and piano sizes Bassegoda has finally made a firm attribution of the piano story to the Casa de la Marquesa de Castelldosrius. Bassegoda i Nonell, J., *El Gran Gaudí*, p. 435.

19. Ibid., p. 378.

20. Kneipp was the parish priest of Wörishofen in Germany who promoted the value of hydrotherapy and fresh air. Patients received hot and cold water shock treatment and were encouraged to sleep with their windows open all year round.

21. Edwards, J., *The Roman Cookery of Apicius*, Publ. Rider, London 1984.

22. Bassegoda i Nonell, J., *L'Estudi*, p. 297.

23. Cardoner Blanch, F., '*Gaudí en la intimidad*', essay in *Jornadas Internacionales de Estudios Gaudinistas*, p. 89.

24. Matamala, p. 617.

25. Herrera, p. 100.

26. Rhode, E., *The History of Cinema*, Allen Lane, London 1976.

27. When Gaudí worked in the Ciutadella Park as an architectural student, a large model of Montserrat was created for the Expo.

28. Torii, T., *El Mundo enigmático de Gaudí*, Instituto de España, Madrid 1983, Vol. 1, p. 254.

29. In 1900, Gaudí's hometown, Reus, suggested reforms to the Sanctuary of the Misericordia. After producing initial sketches and a model, work ground to a halt in 1906. Whether Gaudí's plans had just been too ambitious, or it was just an outburst of small-town pique, remains another puzzle in Gaudí's career left permanently unsolved after the loss of documentation due to the ravages of the Spanish Civil War.

30. Martinell, p. 411.

31. Matamala, p. 358.

32. Bergós Massó,

33. Ellis, H., *The Soul of Spain*, Constable, London 1908, p. 202.

34. The Lliga had come directly out of the religious propaganda arm of the political party Unió Catalanista, a small department under the control of Torras i Bages, set up in 1892 at the Bases de Manresa and further refined in 1893 at the Assemblea de Reus.

35. In *Llei de l'art* Torras i Bages followed Leo XIII's lead in reviving Thomism and forging a 'rapprochement between Catholicism and contemporary culture'.

36. Other examples include Pullman City in Illinois (1867), Saltaire in the Midlands (1852) and a string of villages built by Krupp, roughly contemporary to Güell's planned colony, Alfredshof (1894), Altenhof (1900) and Margaretenhof (1906), and Richard Riemerschmid's competition-winning designs for low-cost housing for the Dresdner Werkstätten für Handwerkskunst.

37. In Catalonia there were many other industrial colonies that pre-dated the Colònia Güell. Other examples: Can Bros (1854), Colonia Rosal (1858), L'Atmella de Merola (1864), Viladomiu Nou (1880) and founded in the same year as the Colonia Güell, Els Anglesos. For a further discussion

see *Arquitectura Industrial en España 1830–1990*, Sobrino, J., Ed. Cátedra, Madrid 1996.

38. In Quaker Bournville it was also advisable to take the pledge.

39. In Rubió i Bellver's unedited manuscript '*De la Integritat*', he elaborated a trio of closely-connected concepts: 'For a work of art to be a true work of art it needs three qualities. These are the three transcendental qualities that the Christian spirit has given art – and without them beauty is impossible: namely, integrity, proportion and clarity.'

40. Perucho, J., *Una Arquitectura de Anticipación*, Editorial Poligrafa S.A., Barcelona 1967, p. 66.

41. Viollet-le-Duc, E., *Entretiens*, 1863, p. 332.

42. Casanelles, pp. 102–3.

## In Paradisum

1. It showed a nodding acquaintance with Olmsted's organic layout in the 1870s for New York's Central Park. Even closer were Olmsted's designs for Mountain View Cemetery, Oakland California (1865), and Prospect Park in Brooklyn (1871). See *A Clearing in the Distance* by Witold Rybczynski publ. New York (1999).

2. Collins, *Drawings* trans. p. 42.

3. Ibid., p. 69.

4. See Conrad Kent and Dennis Pringle's wonderful monograph *Park Güell*.

5. Armando de Fluvia y Escorsa, *Una Familia Catalana de Industriales y Mecenas Ennoblecidos: Los Güell*, Instituto Salazar y Castro Hidalguia, Madrid 1970.

6. Meier Graefe, p. 294.

7. In England Dr Benjamin Ward Richardson, a sanitary reformer, had called for the establishment of a town in Britain called Hygeia, and so too in Barcelona, with an eye to the future, Catalans had shown some sympathy for the radical Frenchman Étienne Cabet's socialist paradise Icaria.

8. In *El Park Güell – Historia y simbología*, Eduardo Rojo Albarrán Los Libros de la Frontera, 1997, the author argues that the Park was designed almost as an act of nostalgia, relating directly to the Parque de la Fontaine in Nîmes, where Eusebi Güell studied at university, and to the layout of some of Paris' monuments, the Madeleine, the Obelisk, the National Assembly and the mercantile centre of Les Halles.

9. Vidal i Mas, Josep., '*El Llàrg camí d'un Poble Cròniques Cambrilenques*', Ed. de l'Adjunctament de Cambrils, in Sala de Lectura, Reus.

10. See Geertz, C., *The Interpretation of Cultures*, Basic Books, New York 1973 for an anthropologist's account of the cultural significance of popular art.

11. Jacobs, M., *Between Hopes and Memories – A Spanish Journey*, Picador, London 1994, pp. 215–16.

12. Kent & Prindle, p. 41.

13. Although Eduardo Rojo Albarrán in *El Park Güell*, p. 101 draws our attention to Gaudí's dislike of the intoxicant coffee and relates this building to the witch's lair in Hansel and Gretel.

14. Kent & Prindle. Maragall was the cosmopolitan conduit through which much of extra-Catalan culture had flowed: Nietzsche, Goethe, Wagner and Novalis all had works translated and championed by Maragall.

15. It is significant that Schinkel regarded the Doric order, of all the classical orders, as the most primordial of all. For a comparative study of Gaudí's use of the Doric and possible sources

see Bassegoda i Nonell, J.,
*L'Estudi*, pp. 148–9.

16. A reworking, perhaps, of the
3,500-year-old Egyptian site at
Karnak or the partially submerged
third-century B.C. Temple of Isis at
Philae.

17. It was not entirely novel, both
Paxton at Crystal Palace and
Fontserè at the Mercat del Born
had employed the system before.

18. At the very same time, Jujol, who
worked on the Park's decorative
ensemble, was working on another
house for the physician Salvador
Sansalvador who also owned the
Aguas Radial mineral water
company and bottling plant on the
hill just behind.

19. Trans. Hughes, R., p 499.

20. The formation of the Sociedad
Anónimo del Tibidabo proved very
effective and pulled in sponsorship
from *gent de bé* like the Arnus,
Macaya, Roviralta, Fornells,
Casacuberta, Alsina and Fabra i
Puig dynasties.

21. Bassegoda i Nonell, J., *L'Estudi*,
p. 145. The visit was on 30
October 1911.

22. Meier-Graefe, J. It is possible that
this is a description of the
serpentine bench. In which case,
this puts the date of the bench
much earlier than previously
thought.

## The House of Bones

1. Leblond, M. A., '*Gaudí et
l'architecture méditerranéen*', *L'Art et
les artistes*, vol. 11, Paris 1910,
p. 70.

2. Bayó Font's detailed memories of
the works in progress were
recorded in an interview with
Professor Bassegoda just before the
contractor's death in 1970.

3. Since destroyed by the building's
present tenants, the luxury retailers

Loewe.

4. Mackay, D., *Modern Architecture in
Barcelona 1854–1939*, BSP
Professional Books, Oxford 1989,
p. 55.

5. Solà-Morales, I., Exhibition
catalogue essay 'Modernista
Architecture', *Barcelona*, Hayward
Gallery, p. 123.

6. For an illuminating discussion see
Joan-Lluís Marfany, '*Gaudí el
Modernisme*' in *Gaudí i el seu temps*,
Barcanova, Barcelona 1990,
pp. 71–99.

## The Beleaguered Fort

1. Rubió i Bellver would later take it
up again after Gaudí's death.

2. Many architects entered politics:
Domènech i Muntaner, Puig i
Cadafalch, Joan Martorell, Félix
Cardellach and Gallissà.

3. Solà-Morales Rubió, I., *Eclecticismo
y vanguardia*, Gustavo Gili S.A.,
Barcelona 1980, p. 43.

4. Casanelles, p. 68.

5. Projects included Barcelona's main
bullring the Plaza de Toros
Monumental and a dance hall, La
Paloma. Alvarez Izquierdo, R.,
*Gaudí*, Ediciones Palabras,
Barcelona 1992, p. 134.

6. Bassegoda i Nonell, J., *El Gran
Gaudí*, p. 512.

7. Between the years 1901 and 1920
the construction industry averaged
5,000 new dwellings per year in
Catalonia, the vast majority in
Barcelona. Carlos Sudrià, '*La
Modernidad de la capital industrial de
España*, p. 54 in *Barcelona 1888–
1929* ed. Sánchez, A., Alianza Ed.,
Madrid 1994.

8. *Joan Rubió i Bellver y la fortuna del
gaudinismo*, Ignasi Solà-Morales
Rubió, Publ. Colegio de
Arquitectos de Cataluña, Barcelona
1975, p. 25. Solà-Morales discusses
the likelihood that the transition to

the Batlló and Casa Milà style was also an important element in the cooling off between Gaudí and Rubió, although there was never a real falling out. In 1906, Rubió also accepted a part-time job as architect for the Diputación.

9. Julol's son in '*Se cumple hoy Primer Centenario de Jujol*', *Diario Español*, 16 September 1979.
10. Matamala, p. 564.
11. These anecdotes were recorded in an interview with Dr Alfonso Trias Maxenchs on 2 and 20 June 1964 by César Martinell in *Gaudí: His Life, His Theories, His Work*, ed. Blume, Barcelona. English Translation 1975, p. 90.
12. Ràfols, J., p. 122, and also discussed in Pabon i Charneco, A., *The Architectural Collaborators of Antoni Gaudí*, unpublished Ph.D. thesis, Northwestern University, USA 1983.
13. Pere Falqués i Urpi's buildings would, like that of Gaudí's, become the butt of the jokes of the satirical cartoonists, particularly in the weekly *L'Esquella de la Torratxa*. But attention was specially accorded to these famous lampposts that still line the Passeig de Gràcia today.
14. Endell, A., '*The Beauty of Form and Decorative Art*' in *Dekorative Kunst I, 1897–8*, München – translation from T. & C. Benton and D. Sharp, *Form and Function*, London 1975.
15. Bayó remembered Puig sneaking in one day, while Gaudí was away, to have a good look at the catenary arches Gaudí was using in the attic of the Casa Milà. In 1913, Puig would use a similar system at the champagne bodegas of Codorniu. Bassegoda i Nonell, J., *El Gran Gaudí*, p. 515.
16. Bergós Massó, p. 30. '*La inteligencia del hombre sólo puede actuar en un plano, es de dos dimensiones: resuelve ecuaciones de una incognita, de un grado. La inteligencia angélica es de tres dimensiones, actúa directamente en el espacio. El hombre no puede actuar hasta ha visto el hecho, la realización.*'
17. A description attributed to George Collins, the late, great American Gaudí scholar and president of the American Friends of Gaudí.
18. Zerbst, p. 29.
19. Cirlot, Juan-Eduardo in *Antoni Gaudí*, essays, Estudios Criticos Editorial del Serbal, Barcelona 1991, pp. 93–4, edited by S. Tarragó.
20. In Chicago, Louis Sullivan had completed the Carson, Pirie, Scott department store, that relied on a metal frame structure, just as Gaudí started work on the Battló in 1904.
21. In Germany, in 1909, in the city of Berlin, Peter Behrens was arriving at a similar form of flexibility in the AEG Turbine Factory that also, at first glance, appeared massively solid. A modern pyramid!
22. The section of the *eixample* between carrer Aribau and the Passeig Sant Joan in which most of the notable *modernista* houses were built.
23. Bassegoda i Nonell, J., *El Gran Gaudí*, p. 513.
24. This story originated from Bayó and has since been accepted by experts Professor Bassegoda i Nonell and Dr Arleen Pabón-Charneco-de Rocafort, as an example of Gaudí's peerless capacity for problem solving and lateral thinking.
25. Translated literally as 'Good day and go with God!'
26. Eugeni d'Ors, *Complete Works in Catalan, Glosari 1906–10*, Editorial Selecta S.A., Barcelona, p. 1233.
27. Flores, C., *Gaudí, Jujol y el*

*modernismo Catalán*, pp. 246–7.

28. This is partly due to the strange notion amongst Gaudí scholars and fans that to celebrate Jujol is to denigrate Gaudí. In fact, exactly the opposite is true. Gaudí's genius is not self-contained, it lies also in his capacity for bringing the best out in others.

29. Ligtelijn, V. and Saariste, R., *Josep M. Jujol*, p. 14.

30. At the millennium it is salutory to note that some of the finest works of art being produced today, by the German artist Anselm Kiefer focus on the notion of looking back from the future towards our present industrialised world but disintegrated into an archaeological artefact: skyscrapers, industrial plants, swallowed up and covered in weeds and grass.

31. Bohigas, O., 'Josep M. Jujol' in *Arquitectura Bis*, March 1976. Moneo, R., '*Arquitectura en los márgenes*' in *Arquitectura Bis*, March '76.

32. In his own work in the Barcelona suburb of St Joan Despi and especially in the Torre de la Creu, 1913, affectionately known as the Torre dels Ous, – 'the egg tower' – and the Casa Negre, built from 1915–26, and a handful of half-finished and abandoned churches and shrines in the *Baix Camp* Jujol would lay a belated claim to his position as the Godfather of twentieth-century abstract sculpture, particularly the school of 'assemblage'.

33. '*¡Que gran cosa es la inteligencia, en la especialidad de cada uno! Hoy, con Bayó, nos hemos pasado muchas horas inmersos en el cálculo y me siento como si no hubiese hecho nada. Lo mismo le occurrió a Bayó, y eso que las operaciones han sido constantes. Sin duda, Bayó es un caso de admirable rapidez, de suma utilidad en semejantes circunstancias.*' Matamala

Flotats, J., unpublished manuscript in the Cátedra Gaudí '*Antonio Gaudí, mi itinerario con el arquitecto*' 1960 Chapter XXIII Vol 2: p. 445.

34. Bassegoda i Nonell, J., *El Gran Gaudí*, p. 514.

35. Martinell, p. 84.

36. Bassegoda i Nonell, J., *El Gran Gaudí*, p. 523.

37. Order number 10.526 of the Comisión de Ensanche de Barcelona.

38. Gaudí's previous work, the Casa Battló, has been described as a masterpiece of 'prefigured' architecture where the building either shares a narrative or has a recognisable personality—i.e., the theme of St George and the dragon. It may well be coincidence but the most famous project in this genre, and illustrated, was C. F. Ribart's Triumphal Elephant of 1758, titled, 'Grand Kiosque à la Gloire du Roi', planned to stand on the Champs Elysées. It was a two up, two down, house in the shape of an elephant with the animal's trunk doubling up as both fountain and waste pipe, evacuating the overflow from the 'powder room' set in its brain.

39. Bassegoda i Nonell, J., *El Gran Gaudí*, p. 523.

40. Collins, G. R.

41. Perucho, p. 154.

42. Casanelles, *A Reappraisal*, p. 78.

43. Ruskin, J., *Modern Painters 4*, pp. 133–4.

44. Behind the Milà there is also an Oriental aesthetic seen in the popular prints by Hokusai. Vilaseca's Bruno Cuadras house of 1883 was clearly inspired by the Orient as was Domènech's Hotel España. In eighteenth-century engravings by J. B. Fischer von Erlach tiny figures look up at stylised Chinese mountains. Perhaps Gaudí had seen George le Rouge's engravings in his *Jardins*

*Anglo-Chinois* of 1767–87.

45. Dalí, S., illustrates examples of these rocks in his *Minotaure* article.
46. Hughes, R., *Barcelona*, p. 516.
47. Torii, p. 265.
48. Bassegoda i Nonell, J., *Antoni Gaudí*, Caixa de Catalunya, Barcelona Ediciones 62, Catalan edition 1992, p. 107.
49. Permanyer, p. 114.
50. It is also worth noting here that super-realism was the term that André Breton had first used rather than surrealism. Hyper-realism would do just as well but wouldn't explain the Casa Milà's appeal to Salvador Dalí·and many of the other surrealists.
51. Ramiro de Maeztu, 'El Arquitecto del Naturalismo', in *Nuevo Mundo* No. 897, 16th March 1911.
52. Casanelles.
53. Published in *Cu-Cut!* 21 January 1909.
54. Trans. Hughes, R. p. 499.
55. Bergós Massó, J., *Gaudí, el hombre y la obra*, Cátedra Gaudí, Barcelona 1974, p. 49.
56. Bassegoda i Nonell, J., *El Gran Gaudí*, p. 17 gives Rosita's dates as 1876–1912. Her mother Rosa did not therefore die in childbirth as suggested by so many authors, including Bergós Massó.
57. Bergós Massó, p. 49 '. . . *un amargo suplicio para Gaudí, que odiaba la embriaguez y la había corregido en algunos de sus obreros, pero no logró librar de esta inclinación a su querida sobrina.*'

## The Sheltering Cave

1. In Salvador Dalí's article in *Minotaure* he further draws our attention to the Apollonian classicism of the Casa Milà when he transforms the drapery of the mutilated Parcae of the Parthenon into this *modernista* masterpiece. With a few artful scribbles and the introduction of tiny admiring figures the surrealist takes the building back into the classical age.
2. Schama, S., *Landscape and Memory*, HarperCollins, London 1995, p. 404. The Dinocratic model for Mount Athos was, coincidentally, also illustrated by Johann Bernard Fischer von Erlach in his *Sketch of Historical Architecture* in 1721.
3. In *La Pedrera: Cosmos de Gaudí*, Josep M. Carandell, Fundacío Caixa de Catalunya, Barcelona 1992, the author points out the similarities between one of the Milà's entrance doors and the form of the human foetus.
4. In *Visionary Experiences in the Golden Age of Spanish Art* by Victor I. Stoichita, Reaktion Books, London 1995, the author discusses the problems of 'portraying the unrepresentable'. On p. 7 he writes: 'The word "vision", according to Thomas Aquinas, has two meanings: the first is what the organ of sight perceives; the second, what the imagination or intellect perceives internally. On the mystical plane, the visionary experience is not necessarily an optical one, though it remains the perception of an image.' In this sense it would be true to describe the Casa Milà as a 'visionary' masterpiece of architecture.
5. Ibid.
6. Brown, J., *Images and Ideas in Seventeenth-Century Spanish Painting*, Princeton University Press, 1978, p. 136.
7. One of the most radical of the French romantic sculptors, Auguste Préault, much admired by Baudelaire, failed to achieve his lifetime ambition of sculpting the whole mountain of Le Puy.
8. Schama, S., p. 404.
9. This analogy is also pointed out by the sculptor Josep M. Subirachs in

*Gaudí: El Jardí dels Guerrers*, Pere Gimferrer, Ed. Lunweg, Barcelona 1987, p. 150. It is Subirachs who has been charged with the completion of the Sagrada Familia.

10. Ibid., p. 63.

11. Hauser, A., *The Social History of Art*, Routledge & Kegan Paul, London 1962, p. 170.

12. Kandinsky, W., *Concerning the Spiritual in Art*, Dover Publ., New York 1977, p. 1. First published in 1910.

13. In *La Pedrera*, Carandell cites Verdaguer's Fourth Canto in *L'Atlántida* with its geological cataclysms as a possible source.

14. 'Putrid matter as punishment for the sins that continue their temptation: the paroxysm of love that can only be sin is answered by the most exemplary death, the one with which he can deal directly, decomposition.' Lahuerta, J. J., in Dalí Architecture exhibition catalogue at *La Pedrera* 1996 in essay '*Gaudí, Dalí: The Elective Affinities*, p. 54. For further discussion on Gaudí and the architecture of ruin, see Robert Harbison's *The Built, the Unbuilt and the Unbuildable*. Cambridge, Mass. (1991).

15. Casanelles

## Storm Clouds

1. Translation from Shubert, A., *A Social History of Modern Spain*, Unwin Hyman, London 1990.

2. 85,000 in 1800 to 533,000 in 1900. Life expectancy in Barcelona in 1900 was just twenty-six.

3. Vicèns Vivès, J., *Els Catalans*, p. 165.

4. In fact, according to the *Enciclopedia Catala*, Murcians in the period 1900–1930 made up no more than 1.5% of the Catalan population. And just 17.4% of

total immigration. In Spain's other industrial centre, the Basque country, *Euskadi*, outsiders were collectively dismissed as *maketos*.

5. Preston, Paul, *The Spanish Civil War*, Weidenfeld & Nicolson, London 1986, p. 12.

6. *Abulia*, a loss of will, was a central concept in the Generation of '98's analysis of Spain's decline. It was most frequently used by the philosopher and cultural critic Ortega y Gasset.

7. Lack of capital investment (Comillas was the exception) in changing from sail to steam was in part responsible for the dramatic fall off in the number of shipowners. See Raymond Carr, *Spain 1808–1939*, p. 435.

8. Like so many revolutionary ideas anarchism had been imported from north of the Pyrenees. In 1854, the same year as the general strike, the Catalan federalist politician Pi y Margall had published *Reaccion y Revolucion* in which he gave voice to the ideas of Proudhon. 'Every man who has power over another is a tyrant.' The real presence behind the growing anarchist movement in Spain was Michael Bakunin and his disciple Giuseppi Fanelli who visited Spain in 1868.

9. As much as 40% of the republican programme consisted of a pure anticlerical diatribe. Supposed links between the monarchist Carlist cause and the ultramontane church had further popularised the anticlerical cause.

10. Cohn, N., *The Pursuit of the Millennium*, Temple Smith, London 1970, p. 81.

11. Part-time journalist and insurance salesman, Rafael Shaw has been dismissed by Raymond Carr as always biased, thus providing a perfect catalogue of all contemporary *prejudices* against the Catholic Church.

12. In Logroño observance of Easter had dropped from 70 per cent in 1870 to below 40 per cent at the turn of the century. In Barcelona and Vic, an even more useful indicator was the noticeable fall-off in those availing themselves of the last rites. Shubert, p. 162.

13. Vicèns Vivès, J., *Approaches to the History of Spain*, University of California Press, 2nd ed. 1970, p. 145.

14. Shubert.

15. Father Vicent, a Valencian Jusuit, in his *Anarquismo y Socialismo* (1895), equated poverty with original sin.

16. Ullman, J. C., *The Tragic Week*, Harvard University Press, Cambridge, Mass. 1968, p. 49.

17. It had increased its membership to 73,000.

18. Recently pensioned, after twenty-six years of loyal and distinguished service in the CID, Arrow had become famous as the scourge of D Division; notorious and universally feared in the gaming houses of Soho and Leicester Square. Arrow's most famous cases were successfully breaking up a gang of West End blackmailers of young upper-class gentlemen and solving the famous Case of Admiral Nelson's Missing Watch, by the application of the novel fingerprinting technique.

19. From *The Police Review and Parade Gossip* ed. London – the Metropolitan Police in-house gazette, editions 26 July 1907, p. 357, and 2 August 1907, p. 363.

20. 22 July 1909.

## The Semana Tragica

1. The best discussion of the Tragic Week still remains Ullmann, J. C., *The Tragic Week*.

2. An old style *cacique*, Foronda had brought many of the workers up from his village, Castorza in Andalucia. Divorced from local politics and without union representation the workers found their livelihood was within Foronda's personal gift.

3. Nicknamed the 'Laxative Hero' – he had swallowed a heavy dose of laxatives to ensure non-attendance at difficult negotiations.

4. In 1886, Jaume Piquet's play *The Nun That Was Buried Alive*, set in the Hieronymite convent, enjoyed much success at the Teatro Odeón.

5. That, in the course of time, these particular 'bizarre' discoveries found perfectly reasonable explanations, was of little use during the height of the storm. The 'illegal' printing press was for the production of indulgences, certificates and devotional '*estampas*' – religious postcards; the Hieronymite nuns had inherited the government bonds; and the beautiful nun was Leonor, Princess of Aragon.

6. It was common practice amongst aristocrats to secure their own safety by 'encouraging' the Guardia Civil to co-occupy their estates. The Marquès de Marianao had such an arrangement at the Parc Samó as did Comillas in Asturias. His head office at Ujo was next door to the station.

7. Martinell, p. 91. The original text comes from an interview by Martinell with the sculptor J. M. Camps Arnau on 27 April 1955.

8. St Felipe Neri on the calle Sol was set on fire, so too the convent of the Barefoot Carmelites on the calle Angel.

9. Amalang, *12 Walks*, p. 145. Maragall would write his most famous article, the highly polemical '*L'Esglesia Cremada*' in late 1909 about the burning of

Sant Joan.
10. Martinell, p. 90.
11. Bassegoda i Nonell, J., *El Gran Gaudí*, p. 517.
12. Years later it still remained highly topical. The *Cu-Cut!* issue (no. 25) of 19 June 1902 was dedicated entirely to Verdaguer. In 1904, En Patufet dedicated both their June and August issues to this remarkable man.
13. Shubert, p. 162.
14. In 1948 a petition was sent to the Vatican to promote Claudio López's beatification.
15. In France Lucien Harmel, a Catholic industrialist, had arranged pilgrimages during the 1880s. The 1889 'exodus' to see Leo XIII was supported by 10,000 workers. *Saints and Sinners – A History of the Popes*, Eamon Duffy, Yale University Press, 1997 p. 239.
16. Kent & Prindle, p. 47.
17. The disturbances Gaudí must have been thinking of were either the construction of the second basilica by Theodosius II in 415 A.D. in the face of attack from the Goth and Hunnish hordes, or the great Nika riots of 532 A.D. after which Emperor Justinian vowed to rebuild the great church for the third time.
18. Amongst the security police, Guardia Civil and military, there were eight deaths and 124 wounded. The rioters body-count was 104, a figure that many historians accept as a gross underestimate due to the need for rioters and their families in the subsequent weeks to distance themselves as far as possible from the insurrection.
19. Rafael Shaw.
20. Bookchin, M.
21. Originally, it was thought Ferrer had successfully escaped across into France. In fact, like the

Christian martyrs before him, he had hidden away in caves behind the Mas Germinal. Ferrer's error was to be tempted out of hiding by the necessity of completing on some urgent stock transactions that alerted the authorities he was still in Spain.
22. Benet, Josep, *Maragall y La Semana Trágica*, Ediciones Peninsula, Madrid 1966.
23. Prat de la Riba was the editor and the censors Father Clascar and Ignasi Casanovas had earlier made heavy excisions. If published it might have saved Ferrer's life. It is typical of Maragall's generosity of spirit that he never held this against Prat de la Riba. Indeed, one month later he read out a eulogy to Prat at an official banquet.
24. Barcelona 1985 Arts Council catalogue. trans. Arthur Terry.
25. Benet.
26. Margarida Casa Cuberta in *Els noms de Rusiñol* describes the effect of Casella's suicide under a train on Barcelona's intelligentsia. Barcelona (1999).
27. Benet.

## A Thrown Pebble

1. Martinell, p. 84. The Casa Milà opened up the way for others. Notably, according to Martinell, the Vicente Ferrer building on the corner of the Ronda San Pedro and the Plaça de Catalunya.
2. Martinell gives the date as 28 December 1910 whereas Bassegoda i Nonell states categorically 28 December 1909. Which makes sense when the final permission for the building is passed without prejudice on 5 July 1910.
3. Mani shared with Gaudí a penchant for enormous megalomaniac scale. When asked

how big he wanted his sculpture *Els Degenerats*, he replied, 'I would like to see it in the desert as large as the Egyptian Sphinx.' Bassegoda i Nonell, J., *L'Estudi*, p. 307.

4. Torii, p. 270. Originally quoted from '*El Santo Rosario en Cataluña*' in *Templo*, Año 103, Barcelona, October 1969, pp. 6–7.

5. Bassegoda i Nonell, J., *El Gran Gaudí*, p. 517.

6. Ibid., pp. 516–17.

7. On another occasion he deliberately made a point of washing his face in the same sink as Matamala senior who had skin cancer.

8. Buenaventura Bassegoda i Amigo in his role as President of the Col.legi d'Arquitectes settled the Casa Milà case in 1916 in Gaudí's favour.

## 'Symbols Dense as Trees'

1. *Correspondences*, Charles Baudelaire.
2. Bergos Massó 1969 no. 52 trans. Collins, *Drawings*.
3. *Manuales de Arquitectura* 7, Jornades Internacionales de Estudios Gaudinistas Publicaciones de Colegio Oficial de Arquitectos de Cataluña Baleares Ed. Blume, Barcelona 1970, p. 76.
4. This is Martinell's figure although Bassegoda i Nonell in *El Gran Gaudí*, p. 548, gives it at double that, namely, 8,000 pesetas, although this calculation might include furniture.
5. Martinell, p. 332.
6. Mossèn Gil Parés and Ignasi Casanovas were both executed in 1936.
7. Bassegoda i Nonell, J., *L'Estudi de Gaudí, Selecció d'articles publicats a la revista Temple entre 1971–1994* Ed. Temple Expiatori de la Sagrada Família, Barcelona 1996, p. 220.
8. Matamala, p. 117.

9. Ibid., p. 501.
10. Joaquin Mir, the author of the painting '*Catedral de los Pobres*'.
11. Matamala, p. 268.
12. Ibid., p. 605.
13. Years before at an official Architectural Association dinner Gaudí had humiliated Domènech i Muntaner, mocking his use of historicist pastiche, to the delight of the assembled throng.
14. Rohrer, J. C., '*Una Visió Apropriada*' in essay collection *Gaudí i el seu temps*, ed. Juan José Lahuerta, Barcanova 1990.
15. Joaquin Vilaplana, a pharmacist in Vic, where Gaudí had gone to recuperate.
16. Many books on Gaudí stress the fact that the Paris show was an out-and-out failure.
17. There is no absolutely convincing explanation as to whether Gaudí suffered from anaemia in 1910 before his removal to Vic and brucellosis the following year, 1911, when he was taken higher into the Pyrenees to Puigcerdá, or whether both 'nervous' collapses were one and the same thing.
18. Trias, Alfonso, '*Gaudí visto por un amigo*', *Jornadas Internacionales de Estudios Gaudinistas*, p. 94. Within a generation of Louis Pasteur it was common knowledge that *brucella malitensis* came directly from goat's milk, probably an innocent gift from one of the Sagrada Família goatherds.
19. Martinell also relates a story of how Gaudí often carried a raw egg around in his pocket, as an instant snack, boasting its shell was the strongest form nature had to offer. He gave up the practice when Mayor Alberto Bastardas slapped him jovially after celebrating Mass, leaving the egg's contents to dribble down his leg. Martinell, p. 114.
20. Bassegoda i Nonell, J., *L'Estudi*,

p. 180.

21. Castellanos, J., essay 'Torras i Bages i Gaudí' in *Gaudí i el seu temps*, p. 176.
22. Elias, J., *Gaudí*, p. 168.
23. Martinell, p. 113.
24. Ibid, p. 92.
25. *Gaudí and Modernisme Catala – Human Love and Design* Exhib. Catalogue World Design Exposition, Japan 1989.
26. Matamala, p. 529.
27. Ibid., p. 473.
28. Ibid., p. 475.
29. In France one of Viollet's pupils, Anatole de Baudot, and his assistant Cottancin developed a system of working with concrete. But in 1897 their radical structure the church of St Jean de Montmartre was closed down for three years as unsafe.
30. *Trencadís* carefully controls the processes of disintegration and reintegration as objects we previously recognised are shattered and splintered to form new decorative patterns and motifs. It is therefore a perfect metaphor for the creative process and Gaudí's fragile state of health at the time.
31. Many critics have noted its kinship with the collage techniques of Picasso and Braque. But it also feeds off the symbolist and cloissonist style of Gauguin with its blocks of intense colour, whilst leapfrogging forwards towards the Dada collage of Kurt Schwitters' *Merzbau* from between the two great wars. It is revolutionary; a seminal work of twentieth-century modernist art.
32. Perucho, p. 140.
33. Kent & Prindle, p. 179.
34. Casanelles, p. 87.
35. Rubió i Bellver, *'De la integritat'* unpublished manuscript, p. 14: *'Tres grans qualitats ha de tenir l'obra perque sigui verament una obra d'art. Tres són las transcendentals*

*participacions que l'esperit cristia ha comunicat als estils artistics – son aqueles qualitats sense les quals no pot existir res que es pugui der bell: són la integritat, la proporció i la claritat.'*
36. Bonet Armengol, J., *'La plástica de Gaudí'*, essay in *Manuales de Arquitectura 7 – Jornadas Internacionales de Estudios Gaudinistas*, Ed. Blume, Barcelona 1970, p. 36.
37. While at the Escuela de Arquitectura the young Gaudí had studied the theories of the natural philosopher Robert Hooke, a close friend of Sir Christopher Wren's, who as curator of experiments at the newly founded Royal Society had elaborated his ideas on the catenary arch. Gaudí had either studied Hooke in the original or a more up-to-date and clearer exposition supplied by the Professor of Mechanics at the Royal Institution, John Millington, whose *Elementary Principles of Natural Philosophy*, published in 1830 while serving as chief engineer to the Guanaxuato silver mine in Mexico, had been translated into Spanish in 1848. Jean-Baptiste Rondelet's *L'Art de Bâtir* of 1817 and Humbert de Superville's *Essai sur les signes inconditionnels dans l'art* of 1827 and the writings of Quatremère de Quincy had also interested Gaudí. The catenary or parabolic arch and its associated dynamics had exercised the minds of Galileo, Descartes, Bernouilli, Huyghens, Leibnitz, the Scotsman David Gregory and Isaac Newton.
   In Collins, G. R., *The Design Procedures and Working Methods of the Architect Antonio Gaudí*, International Congress of Art History, Granada 1973, Collins draws attention to other funicular models: in the eighteenth century

Giovanni Poleni's analysis of the dome of St Peter's in Rome and Heinrich Hübsch's theoretical speculations in the 1830s but doubts that Gaudí was directly influenced by them.

38. This idea went right back to St Thomas Aquinas' *Summa Theologiae*. This text proved so influential that Torras i Bages, once described as 'the conscience of Catalonia', took it over almost unaltered.

39. Ruskin, J., *Seven Lamps of Architecture*, p. 2.

40. Bessagoda i Nonell, J., *El Gran Gaudí*, p. 371.

41. John F. Moffitt, *The Arts in Spain*, Thames & Hudson, London 1999, p. 142.

42. Bergós, J., 1954, p. 96.

43. *The Idea of the Holy*, Rudolf Otto

44. Martinell, p. 113.

45. Bassegoda i Nonell, J., *El Gran Gaudí*, p. 371.

46. Most notably Eduardo Rojo Albarrán in *Antonio Gaudí: ese incomprendido*, Ernesto Milá in *El Misterio Gaudí*, Joan Llarch in *Biografia Magica*. Josep Carandell's *Park Güell: Gautí's Utopia* and the fascinating story by Juan Antonio Ramírez 'The Beehive Metaphor' from *Gaudí to Le Corbusier*.

47. Lahuerta, pp. 193–201 & Castellanos, J., 'Torras i Bages i Gaudí', essay in *Gaudí i el seu temps*, pp. 182–5.

48. Matamala, p. 479.

49. Abella, D., 'Retrat caracterològic' in *Antoni Gaudí*, Criterion, ed. Franciscana, Barcelona 1964, p. 15.

50. Martinell, p. 114.

51. Matamala, p. 625.

52. Trias, Alfonso, 'Gaudí visto por un amigo', Jornadas Internacionales, p. 95.

53. Ibid.

54. Cardoner Blanch, F., p. 87.

55. Matamala, p. 275.

56. Castellanos, p. 186.

57. Berenguer de Montagut.

58. Bassegoda i Nonell, J., *El Gran Gaudí*, p. 557.

59. This despite the fact that many of its practitioners, like Gaudí, came from the Catalan *menestralia* – the sons of shopkeepers, small-time entrepreneurs, skilled workers and artisans.

60. Molas, Isidre, 'Barcelona, a European City', Arts Council Exhibition, p. 89.

61. Within a decade the Park Güell, just like Montjuic, would come into the public domain.

## The Cathedral of the Poor

1. Matamala, p. 140.

2. Acquired in 1999 for the Carmen Thyssen-Bornemisza collection.

3. Rohrer, p. 195.

4. Gaudí felt Alfonso was 'llarg de cames i curt de cos' – long in the shirt but short in substance.

5. Gaudí and Unamuno were on opposite sides of the debate on Catalan autonomy. Unamuno was proud to be born a Basque, but was prouder still of Spain as a nation which he felt could only be maintained by allegiance to Castile.

6. Collins & Bassegoda, *The Drawings*, p. 43.

7. In architectural terms its restless energy looks back to Churriguera, or Narcis Tomé's chapel of El Transparente in Toledo Cathedral of 1732. Tomé's Transparente inverts perspective using the Baroque technique of anamorphosis where everything comes into balance as if seen by God, Revelation 4, through 'a door opened in heaven'. See Moffitt, pp. 125–6. This kind of symbolic use of perspective was employed by Gaudí on the serpentine bench at the Park

Güell.

8. Is this Gaudí's illustration of the ideas on rebirth and regeneration current at the time as put forward by the Spanish writer Azorin, or does it relate perhaps to Nietzsche's concept of the *ewige Wiederkunft* – the eternal recurrence? Perhaps the building is trapped in a state of Bergsonian flux?

9. Matamala, p. 667.

10. For visitors to Barcelona who don't arrive at the right time of year to see the *belens*, or the delightful market of miniature figures in the shadow of the Sagrada Família, there is a year-round display at the Monestir de Pedralbes which now holds the Thyssen collection and is not to be missed.

11. *Xiquets* are built in many Catalan cities, Valls is just the most famous. Bookshops stock many books on *Xiquets – Castells i Castellers* by Xavier Brutons is well illustrated, as is *La Colls Xiquets de Tarragona* by Josep Bargalló Valls, but they are as pigmies to the towering two-volume, 2000-page magnum opus entitled *Món Casteller* published by Rafael Dalmau, 1981.

12. Richardson, p. 62.

13. Camille, *The Gothic Idol*, p. 347.

14. Gómez Serrano, J., *L'Obrador de Gaudí*, Editorial UPC, Barcelona 1996.

15. Matamala, p. 162.

16. The tradition of anatomical study, often seen as one of the great legacies of the Renaissance and humanism, had actually started in the School of Medicine in the Monastery of Gaudalupe soon after 1322 with the full knowledge and support of the Catholic Church. Calvo Serraller, F., *Paisajes de Luz y Muerte*, Tusquets 1998, p. 125, cites the book *La*

*Muerte y la pintura española* by Manuel Sánchez Camargo, published in 1954.

17. Matamala, p. 219. Also Martinell, p. 159. In Gijon's sculpture 'El Cachorro' the dying Christ was allegedly sculpted/cast from a murder victim – thus lending Gaudí's technique pedigree.

18. Trias, p. 95.

19. Matamala, p. 256.

20. For an excellent explanation as to the importance of El Greco to artists at the beginning of the twentieth century see: the MNAC Exhibition catalogue '*El Greco: La seva revaloració del Modernisme català*, Barcelona 1996.

21. Martinell, p. 105.

22. Ibid., pp. 106–7.

23. Ràfols, p. 212.

24. Matamala, p. 681.

25. Martinell, C., *Conversaciones con Gaudí*, Ediciones Punto Fijo, Barcelona 1969, p. 108.

26. Trias, p. 96.

27. In January 2000 through a chance meeting with Joan Bolton, a Spanish teacher in Dorset, who knew the Tomás family well, I was told of this story that had been common knowledge within their family. Angel Tomás had always wished to make light of his intervention, particularly during the period of hysteria surrounding Gaudí's death.

28. Martinell, p. 116.

29. Alvarez Izquierdo, p. 291.

30. At exactly this moment the bedridden Lorenzo Matamala, according to his wife and daughter Teresa, lifted his head and said, 'Look. It's Don Antoní . . . Won't you come in?' and a few seconds later, 'I'm glad you came . . . what a lot of light there is!' Matamala, p. 690.

31. Martinell, C., *Conversaciones con Gaudí*, p. 121.

32. CHIRON, the pen-name of Joan

Llongueras in *La Veu de Catalunya*.
33. A. Martí Monteys in *La Veu de Catalunya*.
34. R. Rucabado, *La Veu de Catalunya*.
35. Josep F. Ràfols, *La Veu de Catalunya*. 'Un abıs dificilment franquejable separa el comú de la gent d'avui dia d'un home com l'arquitecte Gaudí, perquè el comú de la gent d'avui dia no tolera l'esperit de pobresa i sobretot de pobresa voluntària.'
36. Manuel Trens, *La Publicatat* 'una humilitat tot mediaeval que ell únicament era un intermediari, sense el qual l'obra aniria també descabdellant-se, un participant de la joia secreta i inefable de la Mare de Déu'.
37. Llorenç Riber, *La Veu de Catalunya* 'donaven la impressió d'una mar desconeguda i fonda'.
38. Mackay, p. 48.
39. Lahuerta, J. J., *Dalí Architecture*, exhibition catalogue in the Casa Milà, Fundació Caixa de Catalunya 1996, p. 54.
40. Gimferrer, essay by Subirachs, '*Nocturnal Gaudí*' p. 150.

# BIBLIOGRAPHY

Alvarez Izquierdo, R *Gaudí* Palabra, Madrid 1992

Bassegoda I Nonell, J *Gaudí: La Arquitectura del Futuro* Barcelona 1984

————*Gaudí* Barcelona 1985

————*El Gran Gaudí* Sabadell, Barcelona 1989

Bassegoda I Nonell, J & Collins, G R *The Designs and Drawings of Antoni Gaudí* Princeton 1983

Bergos Masso, Juan *Antoni Gaudí – l'home i l'obra* Ariel, Barcelona 1954

————*Gaudí* 2nd rev edition anotada por Juan Bassegoda Nonell ed: Dirreción General del Patrimonio Artítico y Cultural Ministrio de Educación y Ciencia, ISBN: 84–369–0032–4 1976

Canela, M *La fantasía inacabable de Gaudí* Barcelona 1980

Carandell, J *La Pedrera, cosmos de Gaudí* Barcelona 1992

————*Park Güell: Gaudí's Utopia* Menorca 1998

Casanelles, E *Nueva visión de Gaudí* La Poligrafa, Barcelona 1965 English ed. 1967

Castellar-Gassol, J *Gaudí: La Vida d'un Visionari* Barcelona 1999

Cirlot, J *El arte de Gaudí* Barcelona 1950

Collins, G R *Antonio Gaudí* Bruguera, Barcelona 1961

————*A bibliography of Antonio Gaudí and the Catalan Movement 1870–1930* W. B. O'Neal, Charlottesville 1973

Descharnes, R L *Vision artistique et religieuse de Gaudí* Lausanne 1969

Elias, J *Gaudí, assaig biogràfic* Circo, Barcelona 1961

Flores, C *Gaudí, Jujol y el Modernismo catalán* Madrid 1982

Fundació Caixa de Catalunya *La Pedrera – Gaudí and his work* Barcelona

Gaudí, Constructor *Informes de la Construcción* Vol. 42 No. 408

Julio-Agosto 1990, Instituto Eduardo Torroja, Consejo Superior de Investigaciones Científicas, Madrid

Gimferrer, P *Gaudí: El Jardí dels guerrers* Barcelona 1987

Güell, X *Antoni Gaudí* Barcelona 1990

Kent, C & Prindle, D *Park Güell* Princeton Architectural Press, USA 1993

Lahuerta, J J *Antoni Gaudí 1852–1926: Arquitectura, ideologí y política* Electa, Madrid 1993

———ed. Lahuerta, J J *Gaudí i el seu temps* Barcanova Istitut d'Humanitats, Barcelona 1990

Llarch, J *Biografía mágica de Gaudí* Barcelona 1982

Martinell, C *Gaudí, Su vida, su teoría, su obra* Barcelona 1967

Matamala, J *Antonio Gaudí: Mi itinerario con el arquitecto* unpublished, held in *Catedra Gaudí* 1960

Milá, E *El Misterio Gaudí* Barcelona 1994

Molema, J *Antonio Gaudí* Torrelavega 1992

Mower, D *Gaudí* Oresko Books, London 1977

Pabon-Charneco, A *The Architectural Collaborators of Antoni Gaudí* (unpubl Phd Thesis), Northwestern Univ. USA 1983

Pane, R *Antonio Gaudí* Ed. di Communità, Milan 1964

Perucho, J. *Una Arquitectura de Anticipacion* Ediciones Poligrafa, SA, Barcelona 1967

Pla, J *Homenots* Barcelona 1969

Poblet, J M *Gaudí, l'home I el geni* Barcelona 1973

Puig Boada, I *El Temple de la Sagrada Familia* Barcelona 1929, 1952

———*El Pensament de Gaudí* Barcelona 1981

Ráfols, J *Gaudí* Canosa, Barcelona 1929

Rojo, E *Antoni Gaudí, aquest desconegut: El park Güell* Barcelona 1986

———*Antoni Gaudí, ese incomprendido: La Cripta Güell* Barcelona 1988

Sola-Morales, I *Gaudí* Barcelona 1983

Sweeney, J J & Sert, J L *Antoni Gaudí* The Architectural Press, London 1960

Tapié, M *La Pedrera* Barcelona 1971

Tarragó, Salvador, Prologue: George R Collins *Gaudí* (1st English edition) Escudo de Oro, Barcelona ISBN: 84–378–0020–X 1974

————(ed). *Antoni Gaudí* Estudios Criticos, Ediciones del Serbal, Barcelona 1991

Tarragona, J M *Gaudí: Biografia de l'artista* Barcelona 1999

Tomlow, J *Gaudí* Delft 1979

Torii, T *El mundo enigmático de Gaudí* Madrid 1983

Vinca Masini, Lara *Gaudí* Hamlyn, London 1970

Zerbst, R *Antoni Gaudí* Taschen Verlag, Köln 1993


GENERAL BIBLIOGRAPHY

Allison Peers, E *Catalonia Infelix* Methuen & Co., London 1937

Andrews, C *Catalan Cuisine* Headline, London 1989

Ashton, D *Picasso on Art* Thames & Hudson, London 1972

Aslin, E *The Aesthetic Movement – Prelude to Art Nouveau* Ferndale Editions, London 1981

Balcells, A *Catalan Nationalism* Macmillan Press, London 1996

Bohigas, O *Reseña y catálogo de la arquitectura modernista* Barcelona 1983

Bookchin, M *The Spanish Anarchists: The Heroic Years 1868–1936* Free Life Editions, New York 1977

Brett, D C R *Mackintosh The Poetics of Workmanship* Reaktion Books, London 1992

Camille, M *The Gothic Idol – Ideology and Image-making in Medieval Art* Cambridge University Press 1989

Carandell, J M *Salons de Barcelona* dibuixos Aurora Altisent, Editorial Lumen, Barcelona 1984

Carr, R *Spain: 1808–1939* Oxford at the Clarendon Press 1966

Cohn, N *The Pursuit of the Millennium* Temple Smith, London 1970

Collins, P *Papal Power* Fount, HarperCollins, London 1997

Conrads, U & Sperlich H G *Fantastic Architecture* (trans G Collins and C Collins) The Architectural Press, London 1963

Crow, J *Spain: The Root and the Flower* University of California Press USA, 1985 ed.

Crow, T *Modern Art in the Common Culture* Yale University Press, 1996

*Dalí Architecture* Exhib Catalogue: 1996 La Pedrera, Fundació Caixa de Catalunya. essay J J Lahuerta 'Gaudí, Dalí: The Elective Affinities'

Digby G W *Meaning and Symbol* Faber & Faber, London 1955

Dijkstra, B *Idols of Perversity: Fantasies of Feminine Evil in Fin-de-Siecle Culture* Oxford University Press 1988

Dixon, R & Muthesius, S *Victorian Architecture* Thames & Hudson, London 1978

Ellis, H *The Soul of Spain* Constable & Co, London 1st publ. 1908, New ed. 1937

Fernández-Armesto, F *Barcelona* Oxford University Press 1992

Ganivet, A *Idearium Español – Spain: An Interpretation* Eyre & Spottiswoode, London 1946

Goldwater, R *Symbolism* Harper & Row, New York 1979

Gray, P *Honey from a Weed* Prospect Books, London 1986; Papermac 1987

Hansen, E C *Rural Catalonia under the Franco Regime* Cambridge University Press 1977

Hauser, A *The Social History of Art* Routledge & Kegan Paul, London 1962

Howard, Ebenezer (ed.) *Garden Cities of Tomorrow* essay: Lewis Mumford 1st publ as 'Tomorrow: a Peaceful Path to Real Reform 1898' Faber & Faber, London 1955

Hughes, R *Barcelona* Harvill 1992

Jardí, E *Torres García* Polígrafa, SA, Barcelona

Kamen, H *The Phoenix and the Flame: Catalonia and the Counter Reformation* Yale University Press, New Haven & London 1993

Kandinsky, W *Concerning the Spiritual in Art* Dover Publications, New York 1977

Mackay, D *Modern Architecture in Barcelona 1854–1939* Oxford 1989

McDonogh, G W *Good Families in Barcelona* Princeton 1986

McKim-Smith, Gridley *Spanish Polychrome Sculpture 1500–1800* Exhib. cat: Spanish Institute New York, 1994

Meaker, G H *The Revolutionary Left in Spain, 1914–23* Stanford University Press 1974

Meier-Graefe, J *The Spanish Journey* (trans. J Holroyd-Reece) 1st publ 1906 ed. Jonathan Cape, London 1926

Mendoza, C and E *Barcelona Modernista* Barcelona 1989

———Eduardo *City of Marvels* London 1988

Ortega y Gasset *Velazquez, Goya and The Dehumanization of Art* (trans. Alexis Brown) Studio Vista, London 1972

Permanyer, L *Barcelona: A Modernista Landscape* Polígrafa SA, Barcelona 1993

Pevsner, N & Richards, J M *The Anti Rationalists* The Architectural Press, London 1973

Praz, M *The Romantic Agony* 2nd ed. Oxford University Press, Oxford 1970

Purdom, C D *The Garden City* J M Dent & Sons Ltd, London 1913
———*The Letchworth Achievement* J M Dent & Sons Ltd, London 1963

Ramirez, J A *The Beehive Metaphor: From Gaudí to Le Corbusier* Reaktion Books, London 2000

Richardson, J *A Life of Picasso Vol 1: 1881–1906* Jonathan Cape, London 1991

Rosen, C & Zerner, H *Romanticism & Realism: The Mythology of Nineteenth Century Art* Faber & Faber, London 1984

Ruskin, J *The Seven Lamps of Architecture* Smith, Elder & Co., London 1849

Russell, F (ed.) *Art Nouveau Architecture* Academy Editions, London 1979

Sánchez, A (ed.) essays *Barcelona 1888–1929: Modernidad, ambición y conflictos*... Alianza Editorial 1994

Schama, S *Landscape & Memory* HarperCollins, London 1995

Schapiro, M *Romanesque Art* Chatto & Windus, London 1977

Sembach, Klaus-Jürgen *Art Nouveau: Utopia: Reconciling the Irreconcilable* Benedikt Taschen Verlag, Germany 1991

Shaw, R *Spain from Within* T Fisher Unwin, London 1910

Shimomura, J *Art Nouveau Architecture* Academy Editions, London 1992 ISBN 1 85490 155 9

Sobrer, Josep Miquel *Catalonia, a Self-Portrait* Indiana University Press, Bloomington & Indianapolis USA 1992

Solà Morales Rubió, I *Eclecticismo y vanguaria* Gustavo Gili, Barcelona 1980
———*Joan Rubió I Bellver y la fortuna del gaudinismo* Barcelona 1975

Stoichita, V I *Visionary Experience in the Golden Age of Spanish Art* Reaktion Books, London 1995

Stokes, A. (ed. Lawrence Gowing) *The Critical Writings of Adrian Stokes Vol 1, 2, 3* Thames & Hudson, London 1978

Sutherland, Halliday *Spanish Journey* Hollis & Carter, London 1948

Tóibín, C *Homage to Barcelona* London 1990

Trueta, J *The Spirit of Catalonia* Oxford University Press, London 1946

Ullmann, J C *The Tragic Week* Harvard University Press, Cambridge, Mass 1968

Unamuno, Miguel de *Poemas de los Pueblos de España* Ediciones Catedra, Madrid 1982

Ussher, A *Spanish Mercy* Victor Gollancz, London 1959

Vicens Vives, J *Cataluña en el siglo XIX* Rialp, SA, Madrid 1961

———*Approaches to the History of Spain* (trans. Joan Connelly Ullman), University California Press 1967

———*An Economic History of Spain* Princeton University Press 1969 in collaboration with Jorge Nadal Oller

Warnke, M *Political Landscape: The Art History of Nature* Reaktion Books, London 1994

# CHRONOLOGY

**1298–1900s** Barcelona cathedral is built.

**1329––84** Santa Maria del Mar is completed with unusual haste.

**1833–76** Spain racked by a series of civil wars known as the Carlist wars.

**1833** Publication of Aribau's *Oda a la Patria*, which becomes the anthem for the growing Catalan revival, the Renaixença.

**1835–37** Prime Minister Juan Alvarez Mendizábal introduces a series of laws expropriating church property.

**1836–40** Porxes d'en Xifré designed by Josep Buixareu and Francesc Vila.

**1849** John Ruskin's *The Seven Lamps of Architecture* published.

**1851** John Ruskin's *The Stones of Venice* published.

**1852** 25 June, Antoni Gaudí I Cornet is born.

**1853** The *Jocs Florals*, a medieval poetry competition in Catalan, reinstalled.

**1854** Eugène Viollet-le-Duc's *Dictionnaire Raisonné de l'Architecture* published.

**1863** Gaudí starts his studies at the Escalopians in Reus, in the convent of St Francis.
Eugène Viollet-le-Duc's *Entretiens sur l'architecture* (first series) published.

**1868** Abdication of Queen Isabella.

**1869** Gaudí starts his university education in Barcelona with a preparatory course in the Science faculty.

| 1872 | Eugène Viollet-le-Duc's *Entretiens sur l'architecture* (second series) published. |
|---|---|
| 1873 | Gaudí enters the recently opened Architectural School. [Over the next few years he works on the fountains in the Ciutadella park, the Born market, Montserrat and various industrial projects.] |
| 1873–74 | The First Republic lasts just one year (ends in January 1874). |
| 1874 | Gaudí fails to win competition to design a monument for the Catalan musicologist Ansem Clavé. |
| 1875 | February, Gaudí's acceptance into the infantry reserves |
| 1876 | September, death of Gaudí's brother Francesc. November, death of his mother Antonia. |
| 1877 | Gaudí fails to win an open competition for the Applied Arts at the Ateneo Barcelonés. Jacint Verdaguer wins the *Jocs Florals* with his epic poem *L'Atlàntida*. |
| 1878 | 15 March, Gaudí officially qualified as an architect. [His first projects are his work desk, visitor's card, lampposts for the town council and a flower kiosk/ urinal for Enric Girossi (never constructed), a display stand for the 1878 Paris Expo for the glove manufacturer Comella and furniture for the Comillas pantheon-chapel in Comillas]. Domènech I Muntaner publishes his seminal essay 'In Search of a National Architecture'. |
| 1879 | Gaudí designs a refit for the Farmacia Gibert on the Passeig de Gràcia. Gaudí joins the *Excurcionistas* society. The Pasatje del Credit, an entire street built on cast-iron columns, off the Carrer Ferran in the Barri Gotic, is completed – demonstrating the flexibility of this industrial material. Death of Gaudí's elder sister Rosa. |
| 1879–82 | Gaudí completes two projects for an altar at the convent of Jesús-María in San Andrés del Palomar and |

a chapel for the convent school Jesús-María in Tarragona.

| | |
|---|---|
| **1880** | The First Catalanist Congress. |
| **1881** | Gaudí plans the workers cooperative La Obrera Mataronense. |
| **1881–86** | Domènech i Muntaner builds the Editorial Muntaner I Simon edifice, one of the first signature works of the *modernista* style. |
| **1882** | 19 March, Bishop Urquinaona laid the first stone of the Sagrada Família.<br>Gaudí designs a hunting pavilion for the Güells in Garraf (never built). |
| **1883** | Gaudí starts work on the Casa Vicens in Gràcia.<br>Gaudí works on plans for a chapel in San Félix de Alella (never completed).<br>Gaudí designs El Capricho in the village of Comillas, the work is supervised by Cristóbal Cascante Colom.<br>3 November, Gaudí takes over the Sagrada Família from the architect Francisco de Paula del Villar. |
| **1884** | 28 March, Gaudí appears in documents as the official architect for the Sagrada Família. Gaudí starts work on the Güell estate at Pedralbes, known as Las Corts de Sarrià. |
| **1885** | January, a cross section of Catalan nationalists present Alfonso XII with the Memorial de Greùges – a list of Catalan aspirations and complaints.<br>Gaudí designs a private altar for the Bocabella family, the founder of the Holy Family association and promoter of the Sagrada Família works.<br>Yellow fever epidemic in Barcelona.<br>November, Alfonso XII dies and the monarchy passes into the regency of Maria Cristina. |
| **1886** | Gaudí starts work on the Palau Güell. |
| **1888** | 20 May, inauguration of the Exposició Universal in Barcelona.<br>Gaudí displays his pavilion for the Marqués de |

Comillas' Compania Trasatlàntica at the exhibition.
The Arc del Trionf built by Josep Vilaseca, a gigantic
brick construction, becomes focus of the exhibition.
Domènech i Muntaner builds the Grand Hotel and the
Castell del Tres Dragons for the Expo.
Gaudí starts work on the Teresianas convent.

**1888–91**   Gaudí's projects for the Casa de los Botines in León
and the bishop's palace in Astorga under way.

**1891**   Gaudí's probable visit to Tangier with the Marquès
de Comillas to develop plans for a Franciscan mission
(never completed).

**1892**   Bases de Manresa passed by Catalan politicians led by
Domènech i Muntaner arguing for a growing separ-
ation of legislative and judicial powers to the regions.
First Festa Modernista in Sitges organised by Santiago
Rusinyol and the other 'decadent' Quatre Gats.

**1893**   Gaudí leaves the works at Astorga following the death
of Bishop Grau.
24 September, attempted assassination of captain general of Catalonia Martínez Campos
7 November, Maragall witnesses the bombing of the
Liceu opera house in which twenty die.
Formation of the Catholic art society, the Cercle
Artístic de Sant Lluc.

**1894**   Expulsion of Jacint Verdaguer from the Comillas
household.
Gaudí's Lenten fast brings him close to death.
Anatole de Baudot creates first cast-concrete church,
St Jean de Montmartre, Paris.

**1895**   Gaudí and Berenguer start work on the Güell wine
cellars in Garraf, south of Barcelona.
An insurrection starts in the Spanish colony of Cuba.
Joan Maragall publishes his first book *Poesies*.

**1896**   Casa Marti – Els Quatre Gats (centre of the bohemian
Modernistas) opens, designed by Puig i Cadafalch.
The bombing of the Corpus Cristi procession, in which
eleven die, escalates anarchism. Harsh repression and

torture, centred on Montjuic prison, fuels an international call for a retrial.

1897    8 August, Premier Canovas del Castillo is assassinated.

1898    Gaudí starts work on his award winning Casa Calvet. He also begins the catenary model for the crypt at the Colonia Güell.
Gaudí joins the Catholic Cercle de Sant Lluc
The Spanish-American war ends in an humiliating Spanish defeat and the loss of many of its colonies from Cuba to the Philipines.
Victor Horta constructs the Maison de Peuple in Brussels.

1900    Gaudí starts to plan the Park Güell development and starts work on Bellesguard. Restoration of Dr Santaló, Gaudí's friend's house at 32 Conde del Asalto.
Work on the standard of the Orfeó Feliuà of Sant Feliu de Codines.
Gaudí prepares a Salon Arabe for the Cafe Torino on the Passeig de Gràcia and, in counterpoint, begins work on the Primer Misterio shrine at Montserrat.

1901    Gaudí takes on the refurbishment of Isabel Güell's house and works on entrance gates of the Miralles estate.
The formation of the Lliga Regionalista, the first truly Catalanist party, wins four of seven seats in local elections.
The May week General Strike highlights growing dissatisfaction with harsh working conditions.

1902    Alfonso XIII assumes power.
10 June, death of Jacint Verdaguer.
Ebenezer Howard's *Garden Cities of Tomorrow*. published.

1902–12    Domènech i Muntaner's project for the Hospital de San Pau.

1903    Gaudí begins the ten-year restoration of Mallorca cathedral.
July, the Catholic Cercle de Sant Lluc take over the Els

Quatre Gats building triumphing over their bohemian rivals (Rusinyol, Casas, Utrillo, Picasso etc.)

**1904**    Gaudí designs part of the Sala Mercè cinema complex on Barcelona's Rambles.
Starts plans for the Casa Batlló 'The House of Bones'.
(Gaudí also worked on projects for a railway station, a chalet for Lluis Graner, a workshop for the Badia brothers and a worker's refuge at La Pobla de Lillet.)

**1904–14**    Rubio I Bellver works on 'El Frare Blanc'.

**1905**    Gaudí, his father and niece Rosa Egea move to the Park Güell.
November, the *Cu-Cut!* incident in which its caricature of army incompetence leads to military attack on the *Cu-Cut!* and *La Veu de Catalunya* offices.

**1905–8**    Domènech i Muntaner's Palau de la Musica Catalana completed.
Hans Hoffman builds his temple to the arts in Brussels, the Palais Stoclet.

**1906**    Gaudí suggests reforms for the Misericordia sanctuary in Reus (his first work there) but fails to win support. His plans for a viaduct over the Torrente de Pomeret are also rejected.
Designs a banner for the guild of locksmiths.
A 'Bill of Jurisdictions' passed, effectively introducing state of military law under certain conditions.
In response, the formation of Solidaritat Catalana, a cross-party Catalan alliance, presages a growing friction between Barcelona and Madrid.

**1906**    May, Prat de la Riba's *La Nacionalitat Catalana* is published.
Gaudí turns down offer to enter politics.
October Gaudí's father, Francesco, dies.

**1906–9**    Gaudí starts work on the Casa Milà – *La Pedrera*.

**1907**    Uncompleted Gaudí project for a monument to Jaume I.

**1908**    Gaudí is rumoured to have won commission for a giant hotel-exhibition complex in New York.

Work starts on opening the Via Laietana through the Ribera district, under architect Enric Sagnier.

**1909**    In mid-July the Spanish government reacting to growing insurrection in Morocco move to protect their mining interests, owned by Count Romanones, Güell and Comillas. Soldiers drafted predominantly from Barcelona are shipped across. In Barcelona, demonstrations, beginning with a general strike on 26 July lead to the anticlerical rioting known as the Setmana Tragica – the Tragic Week. There are more than a hundred dead as dozens of convents, churches and religious schools are razed. Harsh repression follows.

**1910**    Gaudí's first exhibition abroad at Paris' Grand Palais.

Eusebi Güell enobled as a Count.

First publication in Europe of Frank Lloyd Wright's work by German publishers Wasmuth.

**1911**    Gaudí contracts brucellosis and retires to Puigcerda in the Pyrenees accompanied by Dr Santaló.

**1912**    11 January, Gaudí's niece Rosita Egea I Gaudí dies.

Gaudí designs pulpits for church of Santa Maria in Blanes.

The publication of Eugeni d'Ors' *La Ben Plantada* heralds the rise of the Noucentista movement.

**1914**    8 February, Francesc Berenguer dies.

The outbreak of the First World War, Spain remains neutral.

Sant'Elia proposes a futuristic city.

**1915**    Jujol starts work on his masterpiece, the Casa Negre in Sant Joan Despi.

Bishop Campins of Mallorca dies.

**1916**    7 February, death of Bishop Torras i Bages.

**1917**    Barcelona becomes increasingly open to the international avant-garde: Picabia publishes his magazine *391* and Picasso revists the city with the Ballet Russes production of *Parade*.

The foundation of De Stijl in the Netherlands.
2 August, Prat de la Riba dies. He is succeeded as president of the Mancomunitat (a limited Catalan parliament) by Puig i Cadafalch.

**1918**  8 July, death of Eusebi Güell. Now Gaudí's only remaining work is for the Sagrada Família.

**1919–21**  Anarchy in Barcelona leads to a catalogue of strikes and murders.

**1921**  8 March, Premier Eduardo Dato is assassinated.

**1920**  Publication of Ozenfant and Le Corbusier's *L'Esprit Nouveau*.
Le Corbusier visits Barcelona and declares Gaudí's Sagrada Família schools a masterpiece.

**1923**  September, a coup d'état by José Primo de Rivera, captain general of Catalonia, is followed by an introduction of anti-Catalan legislation and press-censorship.

**1925**  In January Gaudí witnesses the completion of the first of the apostles towers of St Barnabas at the nativity façade of the Sagrada Família.
The abolition of the Mancomunitat.

**1926**  Walter Gropius completes the new Bauhaus in Dessau.
7 June, Gaudí knocked down by a tram.
10 June, Gaudí dies.

**1936**  20 July, the Sagrada Família crypt is desecrated and Gaudí's archives and models destroyed.

# INDEX

Page numbers in *italics* refer to illustrations

# Index

Canina, Luigi 35
Canovas de Castillo, Antonio 192
*Cants Mistics* (Verdaguer) 277n
Capra, Alvarez 280n
Carandell, Luis 219
Carcassonne 42, 277n
Carco, Francis 174
Cardellach Alivés, Félix 232, 242, 285n
Carlist Wars 16, 47, 62, 192, 274n
Carlos VII 47
Carreras, Father Lluís 239
Casa Amattler 154, 155–7
Casa Antónia Burés 166
Casa Arnús (El Pinar) 120
Casa Batlló 155–7 160, 163, 165, 196–7, 283n, 287n
Casa Bonaventura Ferrer 166
Casa Calvet 114, 115–18
Casa de los Botines, León 107–8
Casa Fargas 166
Casa Golferichs 164
Casa Milá 163–80, 184–91, 222, 268, 270, 283n, 288n
  balconies 169–70, 175, 177
  commissioning of 160
  completion of 217
  elevation 163, 165, 172, 217
  free plan structure 167
  ground plan 164, 167–8
  influences 165–6, 167, 175–6
  legal problems 172–4, 214, 216, 217, 245, 292n
  as national monument 215
  ornamentation 166
  plans 163, 166–7
  roofscape 187–8, 190, 214–15
  satirised 176–9, 177–9, 181
  scale of 165
  site 163–4
  symbolism of 184–90, 217
  underground garage 171, 172
  Virgin and angels sculpture 190, 215–16
Casa Navas, Reus 274n
'*Casa Pairal*' (Gaudí) 49, 50
Casa Vicens 75–80, 82, 89, 100, 115, 170, 279–80n
Casals, Pablo 25
Casañas, Cardinal 83, 204, 247
Casanelles, E. 13, 34, 140, 174–5, 177–8, 230, 238
Casanovas, Ignasi 224, 226, 239, 245, 260, 292n

Casas, Ramon 282n
Cascante i Colom, Cristóbal 48, 56, 80, 278n
Casegemas, Carles 90
Castel Berenger, Paris 165
Castell de Cambrer, Reus 9–10
Casellas, Ramón 212, 222
Castelldosrius, Marquès and Marquèsa de 120
Catalan Garden City Association 145
Catalan language 4, 52–4, 86, 249, 259
*Catalan Tradition, The* (Torras) 134
Catalanist Congress 278n
Catalonia:
  anarchy 191–3, 197, 257–8, 289n
  architecture 41, 204, 241, 276n, 277n
  *baix camp* xxvi–xxvii, 4–6, 9
  Church in 5, 15–16, 53, 133
  foreign links 4, 9, 131, 274n
  Gaudí on 116–17, 143–4
  mountains 175–6
  national identity 53, 146
  nationalism 52, 86, 187, 197, 258–60, 277n
  political movements 60, 187, 195–7, 210
  relations with Spain xvi, xix, 52, 146, 157
  *Renaixança* 24, 52–3, 61
  textile industry 191, 198
Cátedra Gaudí 87
Catholicism of 208–9, 291n
  house of 91
  as industrialist 194, 198, 208
  and Tragic Week 202, 204, 208
caves 186
'Centralization and Regionalism' (Pidal) 84
Centre Catalá 86
Cercle Artistic de Sant Lluc 110–11, 177, 239, 265
Cerdá (architect) 114, 146
Cézanne, Paul 11, 24
Chalet Graner 121
Charcot, Dr Jean 282n
Cheval, Ferdinand xxii
Chicago World Fair 125
Christina, Queen 68
Churriguera (architect) 253, 294n
*Cièncá del sofrir, La* (Torras) 226
Ciné Atlántico, Barcelona 126
cinema 125–7, 253
*City of Marvels, The* (Mendoza) 26

313

# Index

Tarrago, Salvador 74
Tarragona 4, 9, 12–13, 16, 28, 62, 63,
    84, 99–100
Tarrassa 199
Tarré, Josep 239
Teresa of Avila, St 105, 106, 186, 281n
Theodosius, Emperor 209, 291n
*Thief's Journal* (Genet) 90
Tibidabo, Mount 62, 118, 120, 161
Tintorer, Miguel Pascual 81
Toda Güell, Eduardo 5, 8–11, 17–22,
    61, 274n, 275n
Toledo 280n, 294n
Tomás Mohino, Angel 262, 295n
Tomé, Narcis 294n
Topete, Admiral 10
Torras Guardiola, Juan 47
Torras i Bages, Bishop Josep 53, 108,
    177, 194, 204, 244, 267, 283n, 294n
    addresses 110, 236, 239
    death 245
    Montserrat commission 133–4
    in Vic 223, 224
    writings of 134, 210–11, 226
Torras iron foundry 123
Torrente de Pomeret bridge 159
Torrents (Associació member) 63
Torres Garcia (Gaudí's assistant) 123,
    132, 257
Tortosa 6, 107
Toulouse 64–5
Tragic Week (1909) xvi, 200–13, 236,
    257, 291n
Tres, Joacquín 138
Tressols, Inspector León 197
Trías Maxenchs, Alfonso 162–3, 206,
    223, 239, 256, 264
Trías Domènech, Martín 144, 162
Tusquets, Oscar 253

Unamuno, Miguel de xxii, 113–14, 167,
    249–50, 294n
Unió Catalanista 277n, 283n
United States 112–13
Universitat Industrial 242
Urquinaona, Bishop 68
Utrillo (*Modernista*) 93, 125

Valdés Leal, Juan de 186
Valdivia, Carlota 90
Valle-Inclán, Ramón María del 279n
Vallet and Piqué workshop 89

Van Gogh, Vincent 24
*Vanguardia, La* 93
Vapor Vell factory 192
Velazquez, Diego 95
Verdaguer, Jacint 54, 226, 277n, 280n,
    289n, 291n
    death 266
    dismissal of 109, 208
    and *Excurcionistas* 63–4
    and Güell 86–7, 89
    Palau Güell mural based on 94
*Veu de Catalunya, La* 81, 104, 160, 196,
    211, 248, 266
Vicar, Baron de 263
Vicens Montaner, Manuel 75, 82
Vicente Ferrer building, Barcelona 291n
Vic 159, 223–4, 229, 236, 259
Vila, Tomás 131
Vilanova, Arnau de 123
Vilaplana, Joacquin 223, 224, 292n
Vilarrubias, Vicente 140
Vilaseca, Josep 60, 61, 155, 244, 276n,
    287n
Villapondo, Juan Battista 232
Villar y Lozano, Francisco de Paula del
    48, 49, 51, 114, 276n
    and Sagrada Familia 68–70, 245,
    279n
Villaricos 73
Villavecchia, Enrique Sagnier 114
Viollet-le-Duc, Eugène 33, 38–42, *40*, 52,
    60, 127, 139–40, 275n, 276–7n
Vitruvius 185
Vives, Vicens 192

War of Succession 26
Waugh, Evelyn xx
Weyler, Gen. 112
Whistler, James McNeill 77
Wilde, Oscar 73, 77, 90
Workers' Circle of San José 202
Workers' Solidarity 202
*World as Will and Idea, The*
    (Schopenhauer) 124
Wright, Frank Lloyd 240

Xifré i Cases, Josep 30
*Xiquets de Valls* 253, 295n

Zola, mile 11
Zorrilla y Moral, José 10
Zurbarán, Francisco 95